DATE DUE

MAR 1 9 1997	
APR 0 8 1997	

Equivocal feminists takes a new look at the relationship between socialism and feminism in the years before the First World War. The book presents a detailed examination of a neglected organisation – the Social Democratic Federation (SDF), Britain's first Marxist party. It reassesses the history of the SDF, exploring for the first time SDF ideas and practice on issues such as marriage and 'free love', women and work, and the suffrage. It goes on to look at the party's attitudes to women as potential socialists, its understanding of women's politicisation, and the roles women took within the party. Dr Hunt shows how the SDF came to equivocate officially on the woman question and how this shaped what it meant to be a socialist woman in the following years.

Through this fascinating examination of the links and antagonisms between the feminist and socialist movements, Dr Hunt not only reclaims the history of a forgotten group of socialist women, but also sheds new light on the perennial debate about the comparative significance of sex and class in defining political identity.

Equivocal feminists

Equivocal feminists

The Social Democratic Federation and the woman question 1884–1911

Karen Hunt

CAMBRIDGE
UNIVERSITY PRESS

Published by the Press Syndicate of the University of Cambridge
The Pitt Building, Trumpington Street, Cambridge CB2 1RP
40 West 20th Street, New York, NY 10011–4211, USA
10 Stamford Road, Oakleigh, Melbourne 3166, Australia

First published 1996

Printed in Great Britain at the University Press, Cambridge

A catalogue record for this book is available from the British Library

Library of Congress cataloguing in publication data

Hunt, Karen.
    Equivocal feminists: the Social Democratic Federation and the
    woman question, 1884–1911 / Karen Hunt.
        p.   cm.
    Includes bibliographical references.
    ISBN 0 521 55451 9 (hardcover)
    1. Women and socialism – Great Britain – History.   2. Women
socialists – Great Britain – History.   3. Feminism – Great Britain –
History.   4. Women in politics – Great Britain – History.   5. Social
Democratic Federation – History. I. Title.
    HQ1597.H85 1996
    305.42′0941 – dc20   95–22984   CIP

ISBN 0 521 55451 9 hardback

CE

To Sonja and Holman Hunt

Contents

Contents

Acknowledgements

This book has been a long time in the making. I therefore want to thank those who have helped and encouraged me to complete this project.

I hope it is no longer too obvious that *Equivocal Feminists* is based on a PhD thesis. David Howell was its supervisor and has over the years provided support and encouragement. His wealth of information on the labour movement, past and present, and his own enthusiasm have been a spur to the development of my ideas. Jane Rendall was a very positive external examiner and has been both helpful and kind in the journey to publication. In 1990, my PhD won the Sir Ernest Barker Prize, awarded by the Political Studies Association, and this boosted my confidence when I was working outside higher education. I should like to thank all those involved.

Many friends and colleagues have played their part in bringing this book to fruition – even the scepticism of some has proved a challenge! In particular, I should like to thank Pat Ayers, Andy Davies, Alan Fowler, June Hannam, David Howell, Nev Kirk, Laura Mitchell, Jane Rendall and Mike Rose. Pat deserves especial thanks for sharing a room with me at Manchester Metropolitan University and much else besides.

I cannot imagine *Equivocal Feminists* existing without the women's movement. Over the lengthy gestation of this book the Manchester women's movement has taken different forms as has my involvement in it. Despite many ups and downs I know that without the women's movement I would have had no context and, just as importantly, little of the necessary challenge and support to develop this work. I should like to thank all my friends who have been part of the Manchester Women's History Group over the years; the women I worked with to promote women's education in Manchester during the 1980s; those at the WEA who supported me and my work when I was women's education tutor organiser; the team who fought successfully to put Women's Studies on the map at Manchester Metropolitan University; and, finally, all those women who make the Women's History Network a stimulating and important forum. Without the interminable meetings, the arguments and the laughs I might have finished this book some years ago but it would not have been the same.

Finally, I should like to thank the Hunt family for all their support over the years. Indeed, I dedicate *Equivocal Feminists* to my parents, Sonja and Holman Hunt, who have not only continued to be interested in their wayward daughter's opus but are already asking after the next book.

As all connoisseurs of feminist books will know it has become essential to acknowledge the role of the cat in one's life, so thanks to Mega and TC for all the distractions they provided. But most of all, there are two people without whom I would not have been able to complete this work. Their support has been fundamental. They have both read and discussed *Equivocal Feminists* in all its stages and have given me a great gift – their time. Ann Hughes has been, and is, a generous friend. Colin Divall's love and confidence in me has been crucial. I would especially like to thank them both.

Introduction

The woman question has always haunted socialist politics. Today, the policy of women-only shortlists unsettles many Labour Party members. At the same time, many women are concerned by the apparently unbridgeable gap between socialist rhetoric on sexual equality and the priority given to women's issues in practice. It was ever thus. Certainly the woman question was a contentious issue in the nineteenth and early twentieth centuries.

What was 'the woman question'? It embraced all aspects of the relations between the sexes in the public sphere – including work and politics – and those in the private sphere – including the family, marriage and sexuality. The woman question was also where the concepts of 'the public' and 'the private' were analysed. But as a contentious issue which concerned the nature of women's oppression, the woman question encompassed a range of perspectives. This book is concerned with the ways in which a particular group of socialists – the Social Democratic Federation – understood 'woman' in its theory and through its practice.

For socialists the woman question was often reduced to the phrase 'sex versus class'. Their purpose was to identify what constituted the defining feature of an individual woman's identity and hence her collective loyalty. The crucial question was where should working-class women put their hopes and commitment – with their class and therefore to socialism, or with their sex and therefore to feminism. Or was some kind of socialist feminism or feminist socialism possible? I explore these issues in a specific historical context, namely the socialism of the Second International (1889–1914) – the internationalist umbrella organisation which brought together representatives of national socialist parties and labour organisations from across the world, particularly Europe and the United States. The focus of this study is Britain's first marxist party, the Social Democratic Federation (SDF), described by Eric Hobsbawm as 'the first modern socialist organisation of national

1

importance in Britain'.[1] Formed in 1884, the SDF lasted, with a minor change of name, until 1911 after which it became the most significant component of the British Socialist Party (BSP).[2]

Originally I was drawn to this project by a desire to explore the relationship between socialism and feminism. Some might see this as an old-fashioned issue, embedded in a 'modernist' feminism untouched by the claims of post-structuralism or the critiques of black and lesbian feminists.[3] The focus and, indeed, the language of feminism may have changed: but the way in which socialism understands 'woman' continues to have implications for the politics of many women.

Michèle Barrett and Anne Phillips recently contrasted the feminism of the 1970s with that of today. They argue that the former took the notion of 'women's oppression' to be unproblematic and searched for causes and answers at the level of social structure. Consequently the late 1970s and early 1980s saw attempts to 'dissolve the hyphen' in socialist-feminism in the search for a plausible means of cementing the two analyses of class society and of patriarchy.[4] For example, Heidi Hartmann's 'The Unhappy Marriage of Marxism and Feminism' prompted much discussion which focused particularly on the inadequacies of Marxism.[5] This theoretical debate was never successfully resolved and it could be argued that feminist debate moved on 'from grand theory to local studies'.[6] But does this mean that in the 1990s there is no longer a need to consider the relationship between socialism and feminism, that the sex versus class debate is over – somehow dissolved or simply irrelevant?

I would argue that this debate remains relevant precisely because it is unresolved. And we can return to it with the lessons learnt from the 1980s,[7]

[1]   E. J. Hobsbawm, 'Hyndman and the SDF', in *Labouring Men*, Weidenfeld and Nicolson, 1964, p. 231.

[2]   The SDF was renamed the Social Democratic Party (SDP) in 1907 but as this did not indicate any change in the party's politics or practice I will use SDF as the general term to describe the party up to 1911, except when there is a specific reference to the SDP.

[3]   Introduction to M. Barrett and A. Phillips (eds.), *Destabilizing Theory: Contemporary Feminist Debates*, Polity, Cambridge, 1992, pp. 1–9. See also L. C. Johnson, 'Socialist Feminisms', in S. Gunew (ed.), *Feminist Knowledge: Critique and Construct*, Routledge, 1990, pp. 304–31.

[4]   Z. R. Eisenstein (ed.), *Capitalist Patriarchy and the Case for Socialist Feminism*, Monthly Review Press, New York, 1979, including R. Petchesky, 'Dissolving the Hyphen', pp. 373–89.

[5]   L. Sargent (ed.), *Women and Revolution: A Discussion of the Unhappy Marriage of Marxism and Feminism*, Pluto, 1981.

[6]   Introduction to M. Barrett and A. Phillips (eds.), *Destabilizing Theory*, p. 6.

[7]   The debate on sex and class did not disappear in the 1980s: examples are J. L. Newton, M. P. Ryan and J. R. Walkowitz (eds.), *Sex and Class in Women's History*, Routledge and Kegan Paul, 1983; A. Phillips, *Divided Loyalties: Dilemmas of Sex and Class*, Virago, 1987. But a significant challenge was posed by acknowledging and

as much from women's politics as from disputes within the academy. There are still socialists who argue for the pre-eminence of class,[8] but there are fewer feminists who would argue for such a crude dichotomy. Class, we now habitually agree, is clearly one of the differences between women – but so are, for example, race, sexuality and age. Class itself has little meaning unless the process whereby it is gendered is continually explored. For feminists, at least, it is no longer 'sex versus class', as the ways in which we understand one term are framed by our understanding of the other. Yet historically the polarity of 'sex versus class' has structured so much of the relationship between socialism and feminism. These political movements have constructed historically specific meanings for the categories crucial to their ideologies and patterned them in relation to each other. These meanings inform our present understanding of 'socialism', 'feminism' and the relationship between them.

Although it may seem that the earlier debates on the nature of the relationship between capitalism and patriarchy were intensely theoretical, they were prompted by very real concerns about the practical relationship between the politics of feminism and of socialism. In Britain these concerns included not only the conduct of Women's Liberation Conferences, specific campaigns and local women's groups but also the choices and compromises that individual women made on where to put their political energies. Emblematic of that debate and the tensions between socialism and feminism – including the ramifications for practical politics – was *Beyond the Fragments: Feminism and the Making of Socialism*,[9] particularly Sheila Rowbotham's contribution. This drew as much on the exploration of historical antecedents as on contemporary anxieties about the 'macho' tendencies of the Left. Rowbotham's approach is part of a tradition within the Left of exploring contemporary questions and dilemmas with reference to the past which the British women's movement has also shared. My study has grown out of this tradition.

My subject matter – the SDF – is traditionally seen as the province of labour history but my approach is derived from feminist history. This is because British labour historians have been reluctant to integrate gender

dealing with differences between women, especially race and sexuality. See, for example, K. K. Bhavnani and M. Coulson, 'Transforming Socialist-Feminism: The Challenge of Racism', *Feminist Review*, 23, 1986, pp. 81–92. For one account of the interaction of these debates with practical politics, see K. Harriss, 'New Alliances: Socialist Feminism in the Eighties', *Feminist Review*, 31, 1989, pp. 34–54.

8 See, for example, L. German, *Sex, Class and Socialism*, Bookmarks, 1994.
9 S. Rowbotham, L. Segal and H. Wainwright, *Beyond the Fragments: Feminism and the Making of Socialism*, Newcastle Socialist Centre and Islington Community Press, 1979.

into their practices and concerns in any systematic fashion.[10] Women scholars are doing some of this work but their concerns, insights and questions remain marginal to much of what passes for labour history today.[11] It is not just a question of placing women, in all their diversity, back into the accounts of working-class life and politics. A new labour history has to analyse the ways in which the questions and concepts used within labour history are themselves structured by assumptions about gender. What I sought to understand in this work was the ways in which socialists had come to understand the category 'woman' at that moment when there was for the first time an organised women's movement and a socialist movement. Did it have to be sex *versus* class, and what was meant by these terms? Were women socialists always perceived as different from socialists? These questions form part of a feminist re-evaluation of socialism. Socialism and feminism have affected one another's evolution, in both a pro-active and a re-active manner, and their conceptual developments are tangled together. It is only by tracing the complex conceptual and historical roots of socialism that we can begin to examine the way that this ideology has understood women's experience.

Such a feminist re-evaluation of socialism can learn from the equivalent reconsideration of organised feminism. Despite the growth of women's history, there has only recently been a considered exploration of 'first wave' feminism. This has sought to untangle the meaning of 'feminism' or 'feminisms' from the diversity of campaigns, politics and personalities which made up the women's movement. This project is

---

[10]   In comparison, see recent discussions of American and German labour history: A. Baron, 'Gender and Labor History: Learning from the Past, Looking to the Future', in A. Baron (ed.), *Work Engendered: Toward a New History of American Labor*, Cornell University Press, Ithaca, NY, 1991, pp. 1–46; A. Baron, 'On Looking at Men: Masculinity and the Making of a Gendered Working Class History', in A. L. Shapiro (ed.), *Feminists Revision History*, Rutgers University Press, New Brunswick, NJ, 1994, pp. 146–71; *Labor History*, 34, 2–3, 1993, essays by L. Fink (pp. 178–89) and A. Kessler-Harris (pp. 190–204); K. Canning, 'Gender and the Politics of Class Formation: Rethinking German Labor History', *American Historical Review*, 97, 3, 1992, pp. 736–68.

[11]   See, for example, the marginality of gender in the debate about 'class' and the linguistic turn prompted by P. Joyce, *Visions of the People: Industrial England and the Question of Class, 1848–1914*, Cambridge University Press, Cambridge, 1991. See in addition to Joyce, J. Belchem, 'A Language of Classlessness', *Labour History Review*, 57, 2, 1992, pp. 43–5. Also see the debate in *Social History* with contributions from D. Mayfield and S. Thorne (17, 1992, pp. 165–88), J. Lawrence and M. Taylor (18, 1993, pp. 1–5), P. Joyce (18, 1993, pp. 81–5), J. Vernon (19, 1994, pp. 221–40), and N. Kirk (19, 1994, pp. 221–40). Although feminist texts are cited in contributions to this debate, particularly Joan Scott's, the issues raised by her and others in seeking to engender 'class' are, if recognised at all, thrown to the margins – peripheral to the central noisy combat.

influenced by sensitivities derived from the varied experience of the current women's movement. The focus is less on labelling past women as 'socialist feminist' or 'liberal feminist' – as earlier accounts of the development of the women's movement did[12] – and more on exploring the diversity, conflicts and shared assumptions between and within individual feminists. Susan Kingsley Kent has drawn a picture of a late Victorian and Edwardian feminism which, while centring on the suffrage, contextualised that demand within a much broader feminist critique.[13] Barbara Caine and Phillipa Levine have shown the complexity of Victorian feminism in its relationship to party politics, the inter-weaving of single issue campaigns into a women's movement and how this was played out in the lives of individual women.[14]

British socialist women have been relatively neglected in this revisio-nist history, a welcome exception being June Hannam's work on the Independent Labour Party (ILP) and on Isabella Ford.[15] There is a range of biographical studies of individual British socialist women from Eleanor Marx to Selina Cooper by way of Margaret McMillan.[16] All are more than narrowly focused biographies and in their different ways address aspects of the political context encountered by their subjects, as well as what it meant for these individuals to be both women and socialists. Organisationally, there have also been some studies of the Women's Labour League. These include the descriptive account given by Christine Collette as well as more specific articles by Caroline Rowan and by Pat Thane which consider the links between Labour women and welfare issues into the interwar period.[17] This work enables some

[12] For example, O. Banks, *Faces of Feminism*, Blackwell, Oxford, 1981.

[13] S. K. Kent, *Sex and Suffrage in Britain, 1860–1914*, Routledge, 1990.

[14] B. Caine, *Victorian Feminists*, Oxford University Press, Oxford, 1992; P. Levine, *Victorian Feminism, 1850–1900*, Hutchinson, 1987; P. Levine, *Feminist Lives in Victorian England: Private Roles and Public Commitment*, Blackwell, Oxford, 1990.

[15] J. Hannam, '"In the Comradeship of the Sexes Lies the Hope of Progress and Social Regeneration": Women in the West Riding ILP, *c.* 1890–1914', in J. Rendall (ed.), *Equal or Different: Women's Politics, 1800–1914*, Blackwell, Oxford, 1987; J. Hannam, *Isabella Ford*, Blackwell, Oxford, 1989; J. Hannam, 'Women and the ILP, 1890–1914' in D. James, T. Jowitt and K. Laybourn (eds.), *The Centennial History of the Independent Labour Party*, Ryburn, Halifax, 1992.

[16] Y. Kapp, *Eleanor Marx*, 2 vols, Lawrence and Wishart, 1972 & 1976; J. Liddington, *The Life and Times of a Respectable Rebel: Selina Cooper*, Virago, 1984; C. Steedman, *Childhood, Culture and Class in Britain: Margaret McMillan 1860–1931*, Virago, 1990.

[17] C. Collette, *For Labour and for Women: The Women's Labour League, 1906–18*, Manchester University Press, Manchester, 1989; C. Rowan, '"Mothers Vote Labour!" The State, the Labour Movement and Working-Class Mothers, 1900–18', in R. Brunt and C. Rowan (eds.), *Feminism, Culture and Politics*, Lawrence and Wishart, 1982; P. Thane, 'The Women of the British Labour Party and Feminism, 1906–45' in H. L. Smith (ed.), *British Feminism in the Twentieth Century*, Edward Elgar, Aldershot, 1990; P. Thane, 'Visions of Gender in the Making of the British Welfare State: The Case of Women in the British Labour Party and Social Policy, 1906–45', in G. Bock

comparisons to be drawn with the practice of women in the SDF but more directly useful to the broader questions I want to raise is Eleanor Gordon's work on women and the labour movement in Scotland which includes a chapter on women and working-class politics.[18] Together these works contribute pieces of an incomplete jigsaw but there is nothing that explores women's relationship to British socialism in its entirety in the way that Barbara Taylor's *Eve and the New Jerusalem* did for the earlier Owenite version of socialism.[19] *Equivocal Feminists* lays the ground for such a study by considering one organisation and, more importantly, the particular construction of the woman question which underlay the practice of Second International socialism in Britain.

My discussion is premised on the need to relate theory to practice, and practice to theory. It is the inter-relationship of these traditionally separate areas which constituted the socialist understanding of the woman question. I therefore analyse the theoretical underpinning of the woman question and its place within the SDF's understanding of socialism. I do this not only through an assessment of the party's, and particularly, individual members' perception of the question as a whole, but also through a closer study of the theory and practice concerning particular aspects, such as marriage and 'free love'. To understand the impact of the party's construction of the woman question on the lives of existing and potential female SDFers,[20] I explore the ways in which the question affected the party's assessment of women's potential for politicisation, and their actual organisation within the party. In this way the interplay between socialism and feminism is explored in a specific historical context and in relation to practical outcomes.

I am interested in establishing a history for women within the SDF. But this is not just an archaeology of SDF women – who they were and what they did. It is also important to consider whether one can generalise about 'SDF women', or whether theirs were such diverse experiences that little generalisation is possible. I am equally concerned to understand the strategies and choices women adopted individually and

and P. Thane (eds.), *Maternity and Gender Policies: Women and the Rise of European Welfare States 1880s–1950s*, Routledge, 1991; P. Thane, 'Women in the British Labour Party and the Construction of State Welfare, 1906–39', in S. Koven and S. Michel (eds.), *Mothers of a New World: Maternalist Policies and the Origins of Welfare States*, Routledge, 1993.

[18] E. Gordon, *Women and the Labour Movement in Scotland 1850–1914*, Clarendon Press, Oxford, 1991, esp. ch. 7.

[19] B. Taylor, *Eve and the New Jerusalem: Socialism and Feminism in the Nineteenth Century*, Virago, 1983.

[20] It has become a convention among historians to call members of the SDF, 'SDFers', although they themselves tended to use the term 'Social Democrat' for the same purpose.

collectively in a mixed-sex political party. This is a feminist history of a political organisation which, unlike traditional histories of the British labour movement, self-consciously foregrounds gender.

To do this requires us to move beyond the stereotype of the SDF which has shaped its representation by many historians. Secondary sources are often unreliable. In order to understand my argument regarding the SDF's theory and practice, we must consider the origin and nature of this stereotype.

The stereotype of the SDF

In 1967 Paul Thompson argued that 'a misleading picture has been painted of the Social Democrats as a bitter, dogmatic and impractical sect inherently unsuitable to English politics'.[21] Yet this stereotype of the SDF has been remarkably tenacious. Two groups have contributed to this, contemporaries and historians. Contemporaries of the SDF – particularly members of the ILP – made judgements coloured by political rivalry. These have been used as 'objective' evidence by historians. This can be illustrated by one of the most cited judgements of the SDF made by an ILPer, who said:

there is no disguising that the ways of the SDF are not our ways. If I may say so, the ways of the SDF are more doctrinaire, more Calvinistic, more aggressively sectarian than the ILP. The SDF has failed to touch the heart of the people. Its strange disregard of the religious, moral and aesthetic sentiments of the people is an overwhelming defect.[22]

The context of this remark is rarely given, yet it is crucial: this was not a considered judgement by an observer but part of an inter-party polemic. John Bruce Glasier,[23] the author, was a leading opponent of the SDF and was on this occasion attempting to persuade his own party's rank and file from fusing with the SDF to form a united socialist party. His purpose was therefore to emphasise difference, even at the expense of truth.[24] A stereotype of the SDF as sectarian and alien to British political

---

[21]   P. Thompson, *Socialists, Liberals and Labour: The Struggle for London, 1885–1914*, Routledge and Kegan Paul, 1967, p. 297. See also D. Howell, *British Workers and the Independent Labour Party, 1888–1906*, Manchester University Press, Manchester, 1983, who describes the stereotype of the SDF as 'tendentious, partial and misleading' (p. 389).

[22]   *Labour Leader*, 14 April 1898.

[23]   For Glasier, see L. Thompson, *The Enthusiasts*, Gollancz, 1971.

[24]   For the implications of, and context to, the socialist unity debate of 1896–7, particularly the ways in which the ILP leadership 'managed' the debate by emphasising differences with the SDF, see D. Howell, *British Workers and the Independent Labour Party*, pp. 314–6, 393–4.

culture was of value to the SDF's opponents. Yet this image has too often been taken up uncritically by historians.

Before examining the degree to which this stereotype was anchored in the reality of the SDF, we must pause to consider what exactly is understood by the term 'SDF'. The answer might appear obvious – the party, consisting of the entire membership. Yet in many accounts, the organisation is reduced to its leadership and particularly to H. M. Hyndman, its leader. This tendency has been exacerbated by the only major work dealing solely with the SDF, Tsuzuki's *H. M. Hyndman and British Socialism*,[25] written over thirty years ago. It is essentially Hyndman's biography and not an analytical history of the party. Tsuzuki's verdict was that 'the SDF always bore the imprint of Hyndman's personality, and its weekly organ, *Justice*, spoke constantly with his voice – bitter, tactless and narrow minded in its support of "the Cause", but also (as H. G. Wells said of Hyndman) possessed of a "magnificent obstinacy"'.[26] Yet the SDF *was* much more than one man. Nevertheless, his idiosyncracies – which included anti-semitism and jingoism – have been substituted, in many cases, for a more considered study of a party which was more diverse than any stereotype will allow. The personal views of one top-hatted, frock-coated stock-broker are taken to represent a party where he was the exception, not the rule.[27]

The SDF's membership was largely working class, organised in branches scattered across the country. Its strongholds were Lancashire, particularly Burnley, and Northampton, as well as London. Obviously the geographical problems of organising a tightly disciplined party would have been enormous, but then that was never the SDF's intention. The SDF was never a mass party, although it aspired in the long term to widespread popular support. It was in effect a vanguard, a trustee for socialist theory in a hostile environment. As the official history of the party noted, the SDF 'has been the Socialist conscience of the Labour Movement, the Movement's mentor, the guardian of the sacred fire'.[28] The SDF saw itself as a vanguard and on that basis distinguished itself from the ILP. As one SDFer asked:

Should we mix in with this slow moving crowd, trudging along, abating our pace, in order to keep company with the rest, stopping and halting wherever they

---

[25]   C. Tsuzuki, *H. M. Hyndman and British Socialism*, Oxford University Press, Oxford, 1961.

[26]   Ibid., p. 273.

[27]   See, for example, G. Foote, *The Labour Party's Political Thought: A History*, Croom Helm, 1985, p. 21; R. Moore, *The Emergence of the Labour Party, 1880–1924*, Hodder and Stoughton, 1978, p. 35.

[28]   H. W. Lee and E. Archbold, *Social Democracy in Britain*, SDF, 1935, p. 13.

choose? Or should we rather dash forward, place ourselves in front and explain to the crowd the meaning and significance of the road, the aim of the journey. and in general act as guides. The first means being led by elemental forces, the second means leading and guiding them. The ILP adopted the first, we of the SDF the second.[29]

But, vanguard or not, the party gave considerable autonomy to its branches, and their practices also belie the stereotype.[30] The SDF was at least the sum of its parts: not merely the London-dominated Executive, the London-based leadership or even Hyndman himself.

The major element in the stereotype of the SDF is the accusation of sectarianism. This was made by contemporaries[31] and has been amplified by subsequent historians. It is usually associated with other pejoratives such as bitterness, aridity, rigidity and dogmatism.[32] But was the SDF a 'sect'? The party was certainly not large, numbering 2–3,000 at any one time, with quite a high turnover of membership.[33] Indeed the German Social Democrat Eduard Bernstein estimated that the SDF had had over 100,000 temporary recruits. Walter Kendall believes even this to be an underestimate while Hyndman suggested in 1896 that a million men (sic) had already been members of the party.[34] What is clear is that the numbers of people who had for a time been SDFers ensured that the party had a much more significant influence in the labour movement than its actual membership at any one time might indicate. Keith Burgess asserts that the SDF 'influenced the thinking of an entire generation of working-class leaders', while Laurence Thompson wrote

---

29 Social Democrat, October 1907, pp. 607–8.
30 C. Tsuzuki, H. M. Hyndman, p. 274; E. J. Hobsbawm, 'Hyndman and the SDF', p. 235. This is born out in the few local studies of the SDF which have been conducted, for example, on London by P. Thompson, Socialists, Liberals and Labour; on Reading in S. Yeo, Religion and Voluntary Organisations in Crisis, Croom Helm, 1976; and on Burnley in K. Hunt, 'An Examination of the Burnley Social Democratic Federation, 1891–1914', MA dissertation, Manchester University, 1979.
31 For example, G. B. Shaw, The Fabian Society: Its Early History, Fabian Tract, 41, 1892, p. 21.
32 For example, K. Burgess, The Challenge of Labour, Croom Helm, 1980, p. 102; S. Rowbotham, Hidden from History, Pluto, 1974, p. 77; S. Pierson, Marxism and the Origins of British Socialism: The Struggle for a New Consciousness, Cornell University Press, Ithaca, 1973, p. 273; E. J. Hobsbawm, 'Hyndman and the SDF', p. 232; H. Pelling, Origins of the Labour Party, 1880–1900, Oxford University Press, Oxford, 1965, p. 173; G. Foote, The Labour Party's Political Thought, p. 27. Even Tony Cliff of the Socialist Workers Party describes the SDF as 'sectarian'! (Class Struggle and Women's Liberation, Bookmarks, 1984, p. 110)
33 For membership figures of the SDF, see P. A. Watmough, 'The Membership of the Social Democratic Federation, 1885–1902', Society for the Study of Labour History Bulletin, 34, 1977, pp. 35–40.
34 W. Kendall, The Revolutionary Movement in Britain, 1900–21: The Origins of British Communism, Weidenfeld and Nicolson, 1969, pp. 322–3.

of the SDF that there was 'scarcely a pioneer of British Socialism who did not pass through it or owe some debt to it'.[35]

The party defined itself in terms of socialist orthodoxy and was opposed to labourism. As Hyndman wrote, 'It was the principles that counted, not the numbers that embraced them'.[36] This is certainly the basis of a sect, but that does not necessarily imply sectarianism. Indeed SDFers, such as Theodore Rothstein writing in 1900, were concerned that the SDF might be a sect and sought to explain this and explore means to overcome it. He felt that the SDF had been 'more of a sect than a party' because it had been born before its time. Rothstein argued against self-conscious isolation and for the kind of political practice which could put a mass socialist party on the agenda. He wrote:

The very principle of class war which formerly served as a cloud that hid our august personality from the eyes of the world and kept us high above it, ought to become the unbreakable chain that keeps us in constant touch with all parts of society. Only it must be understood as applicable to *all* social phenomena, to *every* movement, however inaccessible to a strictly economic interpretation.[37]

Clearly for Rothstein the party's practice was crucial. Local activity by SDFers in organising the unemployed, fighting for school meals and working in trade unions meant, as Henry Collins has observed, 'that the party never became just another sect'. Collins continues, 'But if the SDF was not *just* a sect it was *partly* a sect and the reason for that is linked closely with its disbelief in the possibility of effective industrial action'.[38] The SDF's attitude to trade unionism has been seen as emblematic of the SDF's sectarianism.

To understand the party's position on trade unionism, its whole political strategy needs to be elaborated. For the SDF political action centred on its programme of 'stepping stones to a happier period'. These included public provision of low cost housing, free compulsory education with free school meals, the eight-hour day, progressive income tax, and nationalisation of the railways, the banks and the land.[39] The party chose to use the parliamentary and local government electoral system as a platform for its programme and more general socialist propaganda. Its belief that more capital could be gained from organising campaigns around demands on the state, such as the Right to Work campaign and that for Free Maintenance, was reinforced by early

[35]   K. Burgess, *The Challenge of Labour*, p. 61; L. Thompson, *The Enthusiasts*, p. 34.

[36]   H. M. Hyndman, *Further Reminiscences*, Macmillan, 1912, p. 2.

[37]   *Social Democrat*, June 1900, p. 169.

[38]   H. Collins, 'The Marxism of the Social Democratic Federation', in A. Briggs and J. Saville (eds.), *Essays in Labour History, 1886–1923*, Macmillan, 1971, p. 68.

[39]   Ibid., p. 57.

scepticism of the organised labour movement of the 1880s and, in particular, of its leadership.[40] The SDF viewed the unions of this period as representative of only a fraction of the working class. More importantly, in its early years the party felt that 'trade unions as they now are' could not hope to participate in the victorious outcome of the class struggle.[41] This initial suspicion of the trade unions led to some contemporaries and many historians assuming that the SDF was completely antipathetic to industrial action; the later rejection of Syndicalism seemed to confirm this.[42]

Yet the SDF was not insensitive to the value of trade unions. During the Socialist Unity debate of the late 1890s, the ILP explicitly criticised the SDF: 'We have differed from the SDF almost solely because we have refused to adopt certain rigid propagandist phrases and to cut ourselves off from other sections of the Labour movement, particularly trade-unionism and co-operation, and the advanced elements in the humanitarian movements'. In reply, it was argued for the SDF, 'If one comes to the actual facts I think it will be found that the SDF has as large a proportion of active trade unionists in its ranks as any organisation in the kingdom, and I do not think we should suffer at all by comparison with the ILP in this respect'.[43] Certainly the SDF increasingly felt that it was being misrepresented as anti-trade union. At the SDF's Annual Conference in 1897, party members were urged to join trade unions.[44] Why then do historians continue to present the SDF as anti-union?[45] The kind of political practice in which SDF members engaged and through which they sought to win recruits to the party was admittedly diverse. Yet it certainly included participation in unions and in strikes. In 1898 *Justice* cited a long list of party members who were active in their trade unions – this included many of the party's leading figures. Local studies of the SDF show the extent of unionisation and militancy amongst rank and file SDFers.[46] But what the party could not accept was that industrial activity had primacy: that it alone formed the basis of socialist strategy. For the SDF, the unions formed but one arena for socialist propaganda. This did not amount to a thorough hostility to the

---

40 For the SDF's attitude to trade unions, see ibid., pp. 53–6; C. Tsuzuki, *H. M. Hyndman*, pp. 87–106. In contrast, M. Bevir has recently suggested that the SDF objected to the apolitical nature of British trade unions ('The British Social Democratic Federation: From O'Brienism to Marxism', *International Review of Social History*, 37, 1992, p. 228).

41 'The SDF Manifesto to Trade Unions', in *Justice*, 6 September 1884.

42 B. Holton, *British Syndicalism, 1900–14*, Pluto, 1976, pp. 179–80.

43 *Labour Leader*, 14 April 1898; *Justice*, 23 April 1898.

44 *Justice*, 7 August 1897; *SDF Conference Report*, 1897, pp. 21–2.

45 K. Burgess, *The Challenge of Labour*, p. 61.

46 *Justice*, 23 April 1898; K. Hunt, 'Burnley Social Democratic Federation', pp. 83–104.

ethos of the British labour movement. Nor was it evidence of either dogmatism or sectarianism.

Some historians see the SDF's position on trade unionism as a function of a dogmatic Marxism.[47] Even Engels criticised the early SDF – which he had sought to influence – because it 'managed to transform our theory into the rigid dogma of an orthodox sect'.[48] Yet the SDF's Marxism was not very different from that of its sister organisations in the Second International – theirs was also an orthodox, economistic Marxism. If criticism of the SDF was particularly sharp, perhaps this was because more was expected from the British version of Marxism. The presence of Marx and Engels in Britain contributed to this perception, but so too did the advanced development of the British labour movement, specifically the trade unions. The SDF's alternative socialist strategy, which focused on the unemployed, rather than on pre-existing labour organisations and radical Liberal sympathies, fitted awkwardly with such expectations. Not surprisingly, those historians sympathetic to the socialist project see a real failure of imagination in the SDF. Eric Hobsbawm wrote that the SDF's 'tradition was not so much revolutionary as intransigent: militant, firmly based on the class struggle, but quite unable to envisage ... the problems of revolt or the taking of power, for which there was no precedent within living memory in Britain'. Sheila Rowbotham concluded her assessment of the SDF equally disappointed, 'Tragically, revolutionary ideas and politics were poisoned at source in Britain'.[49] Certainly the SDF's was a 'narrow and unimaginative interpretation of Marxism'[50] – but then so was that of most of its contemporaries. Historians who see in the SDF a 'complete lack of political wisdom' and an ability 'on almost every issue ... to hit upon a consistent but unpractical stand'[51] must produce more evidence of the party's alleged dogmatism. The contrast with the

[47] W. Kendall, *The Revolutionary Movement in Britain*, p. 11; R. Challinor, *The Origins of British Bolshevism*, Croom Helm, 1978, p. 12; H. Pelling, *Origins of the Labour Party*, p. 217; G. D. H. Cole, *History of Socialist Thought, vol.2: Marxism and Anarchism, 1850–1890*, Macmillan, 1954, p. 410.

[48] H. Pelling, *Origins of the Labour Party*, p. 20; C. Tsuzuki, *H. M. Hyndman*, pp. 59–62; Engels to Sorge, 10 November 1894 quoted in H. Collins 'The Marxism of the SDF', p. 48. See also Engels to Sorge, 12 May 1894, quoted in W. Kendall, *The Revolutionary Movement in Britain*, pp. 11–12.

[49] E. J. Hobsbawm, 'Hyndman and the SDF', p. 236; S. Rowbotham, *Hidden from History*, p. 95. See also J. Hinton, *Labour and Socialism: A History of the British Labour Movement, 1867–1974*, Wheatsheaf, Brighton, 1983, pp. 51–2.

[50] H. Collins, 'The Marxism of the SDF', p. 48. See also S. Pierson, *British Socialists: The Journey from Fantasy to Politics*, Harvard University Press, Cambridge, Mass., 1979, pp. 26–30.

[51] J. H. S. Reid, *The Origins of the British Labour Party*, University of Minnesota Press, Minneapolis, 1955, p. 51.

'pragmatism' of the ILP is perhaps not as sharp as we have been led to believe.

This point can be linked to another more general one about the 'unsuitability' of Marxism to British political culture. The SDF has been described as an exponent of a 'foreign gospel', and its lack of success has been ascribed to the 'failure of the Marxist form of socialism to find points of growth in British life'.[52] For many commentators, past and present, the SDF's ideology was at root alien and inappropriate to Britain. '[T]he incurable exoticism' of the SDF was contrasted with the 'thoroughly English lines' of the ILP.[53] Halévy commented on the SDF's 'sour creed, imported from abroad, which refused to set before its adherents an ideal which made appeal to the heart'.[54] The ideology of Marxism and its dogmatic adherents in the SDF were defined from the first, as 'un-English' and hence marginal to the development of the labour movement.

Not all historians are so sure. Paul Thompson identifies 'inept leadership and their rejection of the labour alliance' as the cause of the SDF's lack of success. He concludes that the SDF's 'lack of confidence in the labour alliance, a feeling which they shared with the Fabians, was due rather to their failure to appreciate Marxist doctrine than to their excessive insistence upon it. There is no evidence that their Marxist theory impeded the spread of Socialism in Britain.' Indeed he believes that 'their characteristics, their inconsistencies, were thoroughly English'.[55]

Nevertheless, the 'foreign' ideology of the SDF, with its implications of unsuitability and untoward outside influence, is part of a wider stereotype in British labour history which assumes that the SDF and the ILP were dichotomous organisations. For example, K. D. Brown writes of the marked differences of emphases and tactics between the ILP and the SDF which was 'well symbolised when the ILP ended its founding conference to the strains of *Auld Lang Syne*, rather than the *Marseillaise* favoured by the Social Democrats'.[56] The received view of the two

---

52 G. D. H. Cole, *Marxism and Anarchism*, p. 410; S. Pierson, *British Socialists*, p. 348.
    See also R. McKibbin, 'Why was there no Marxism in Great Britain?', *English
    Historical Review*, 1984, pp. 297–331, where he argues that specific structural and
    ideological conditions in Britain precluded Marxism mobilising any significant
    following unlike continental Europe. His discussion focuses on the Labour Party
    rather than the SDF.
53 R. C. K. Ensor, *England, 1870–1914*, Clarendon Press, Oxford, 1936, p. 222.
54 E. Halévy, *History of the English People, vol. 5: Imperialism and the Rise of Labour, 1895–
    1905*, Ernest Benn, 1961, p. 221.
55 P. Thompson, *Socialists, Liberals and Labour*, p. 297.
56 K. D. Brown, *The English Labour Movement, 1750–1951*, Gill and Macmillan, Dublin,
    1982, p. 182. See also W. Kendall, *The Revolutionary Movement in Britain*, p. 8.

groups is that the ILP was based on strong working-class traditions of non-conformism, teetotalism and Liberalism, whilst the SDF was alien because it was atheist, anti-Liberal, drunk and immoral! ILPers who fitted their party's stereotype fostered this image of the SDF. Keir Hardie was particularly prone to this. He said of the SDF: 'Born and reared as I had been in the country, the whole environment of the clubs, in which beer seemed to be the most dominant influence, and the tone of the speeches, which were full of denunciation of everything, including trade unionism, and containing little constructive thought, repelled me'.[57] R. C. K Ensor, a Fabian, reinforced Hardie's view when he noted the qualities of the SDF: 'their impressive contempt for compromises, the easy laxity of their moral standards, their habitual discouragement of all thinking outside an imposingly narrow range'.[58]

Yet historians have found no evidence that the SDF as a whole was drunken or immoral.[59] Indeed some contemporaries had more positive memories than Keir Hardie. Annie Besant said that 'none save those who worked with them know how much of real nobility, of heroic self-sacrifice, of constant self-denial, of brotherly affection, there is among the Social Democrats'.[60] Certainly, some SDFers were atheists, but by no means all, and, moreover, religion was recognised as a matter of conscience for the individual party member. Similarly within the ILP there was a diversity of opinions which the stereotype does not acknowledge. Indeed, branch life within the two organisations seems to have been remarkably similar, particularly in the 1890s.[61] At the local level there was little of the aggressive differentiation between the parties which characterised the national leaderships. Yet after the turn of the century – particularly when the SDF left the Labour Representation Committee (LRC) to the ILP and the trade unions – the choice between the ILP and the SDF did become more stark. Even then, some local branches continued to cooperate in local LRCs, such as those in Burnley, Bow and Bromley and Hammersmith.

It certainly seems that the received view of the British socialist movement has been used at the expense of the SDF, whilst the ILP has

---

57   Keir Hardie quoted in H. Pelling, *Origins of the Labour Party*, p. 64. See also F. Bealey and H. Pelling, *Labour and Politics, 1900–06*, Oxford University Press, 1958, p. 104.
58   R. C. K. Ensor, memorandum, September 1907 quoted in P. Thompson, *Socialists, Liberals and Labour*, p. 124.
59   Ibid., p. 125.
60   A. Besant, *An Autobiography*, Fisher Unwin, 1893, p. 302.
61   P. Thompson, *Socialists, Liberals and Labour*, p. 234; S. Yeo, 'A New Life: The Religion of Socialism in Britain, 1883–1896', *History Workshop Journal*, 4, 1977, pp. 35–6.

emerged virtually unscathed. Fred Reid has re-evaluated this dichotomy and concluded that:

The history of the relations between the two British socialist parties is too often written as if the issues were simple: the sectarianism of the SDF is singled out for condemnation; the ILP is praised for its consistent efforts to relate to the trade union movement. Yet the issues cannot be thus limited, time and again it was the SDF which generated the socialist policies which proved to have longest relevance to the problems of working class poverty. Time and again it was the ILP which compromised with non-socialist collectivists to lead the labour movement into blind alleys. The sectarianism of the SDF should be seen as a reflex to the willingness of socialist labourism to compromise the interests of the poor. The result was a tragic confusion of effort ... For this confusion, Hardie and the Christian Socialist tradition are just as responsible as the worst anti-trade unionism to be found among the Social Democrats.[62]

Nevertheless, the party continues to be generally dismissed as narrow, dogmatic and sectarian with an unlikely leader whose personal views undermined the whole party's espousal of socialism.

The stereotype of the SDF has a particular bearing on the woman question. The SDF is generally represented as being much more hostile to feminism and to women than the ILP. Yet such judgements are rarely substantiated. For example, Olive Banks merely asserts that the ILP was 'feminist from its inception' and the SDF was 'anti-feminist'. In a similar vein, Carolyn Steedman contrasts the ILP with 'the blatantly misogynist SDF'.[63] Joseph Clayton, looking back in 1926, noted the important influence of women in the ILP while he maintained that in the SDF they had been of no importance. This point has been reiterated more recently by James Hinton, although again he provides no real evidence.[64] Historians who do offer evidence do so selectively. As with other aspects of the SDF's stereotype, individuals tend to be cited as representative of the party as a whole. Thus Jill Liddington and Jill Norris maintain that the SDF's 'general attitude to feminism was unsympathetic', citing Hyndman and Harry Quelch.[65] Jeffrey Weeks has discussed Hyndman and the misogynist Ernest Belfort Bax's views on women as though they represented the SDF as a whole.[66] This is not an

---

[62] F. Reid, *Keir Hardie: The Making of a Socialist*, Croom Helm, 1978, p. 153.

[63] O. Banks, *Faces of Feminism*, p. 123; C. Steedman, *Childhood, Culture and Class*, p. 132.

[64] J. Clayton, *The Rise and Decline of Socialism in Great Britain, 1884–1924*, Faber, 1926, pp. 83–4; J. Hinton, *Labour and Socialism*, p. 78.

[65] J. Liddington and J. Norris, *One Hand Tied Behind Us*, Virago, 1978, p. 44.

[66] J. Weeks, *Sex, Politics and Society: The Regulation of Sexuality since 1800*, Longmans, 1981, pp. 169–70. Also see S. Rowbotham and J. Weeks, *Socialism and the New Life: The Personal and Sexual Politics of Edward Carpenter and Havelock Ellis*, Pluto, 1977, p. 16.

approach confined to historians, for contemporaries also generalised from the views of a few idiosyncratic SDFers. Sylvia Pankhurst described the SDF solely in terms of Hyndman and Bax and their opposition to women's enfranchisement.[67] Part of my purpose is to re-examine the stereotype of the SDF in relation to the woman question, and to challenge the assumption that the party as a whole can be characterised by the views of its male leadership.

The stereotype of the SDF also shaped the sources available to me. Contemporary and secondary sources were obviously affected by it. Moreover, the stereotype and its attendant assumptions have, over the years, shaped the perception of the historian and the archivist as to what is of 'interest' which has compounded the loss of relevant material. As a consequence much has been discarded – such as branch records – which might have provided a more balanced picture of the party. Indeed, my interest in women and in a socialist party marginal to the concerns of labour – and other – historians means that I was doubly disadvantaged in the search for sources. The main source for the SDF is its own press – the weekly *Justice*, the monthly *Social Democrat*, and pamphlets. The rest of the socialist press – particularly *Clarion* and *Labour Leader* – provide a context for the party's own press and another view of the SDF. Unfortunately, the records of individual SDF branches have not survived, with a very few partial exceptions, and neither have those of the branches' women's organisations, the Women's Socialist Circles.

Using the press as a principal primary source raises some methodological problems, particularly in interpreting the significance of the voices heard through this medium. It is important, in assessing the material available, to be aware not only of the patterns of the evidence but also the ambiguities and absences within it. Editorship implies selection: but the shoe-string operation of *Justice* seems to have meant that the vast majority of letters submitted were printed. No protests at censorship ever seem to have surfaced within the pages of *Justice*, within the wider party, or in criticism of it. Yet we still cannot assume that women's contributions to the SDF's press reflected their standing in the party as a whole. Few had the time and self-confidence to write to the socialist press, let alone write for it. It is not easy to reach the views of rank and file women. The picture has to remain impressionistic. Certainly, I do not assume that one can knit together views of individuals – even if they were members of the rank and file – and call it the SDF's. I therefore distinguish between 'the SDF', which represents a decision or position taken as an organisation, and 'SDFers', that is members of the

[67] S. Pankhurst, *The Suffragette Movement*, Virago, 1977, p. 111.

organisation who are expressing their own views and versions of arguments. Similarly I do not assume that a single woman SDFer constitutes 'SDF women'. I am interested in exploring where there is homogeneity of views and where not; where the factions within a debate are positioned by gender; and where the concepts used in these debates have been or are in the process of being engendered. Altogether, these have consequences for the woman question. Handled with this sensitivity, an analysis of the SDF press does indicate the development and shape of ideas within the party as well as their impact on the party's practice.

Finally, I want to say something about the way in which the book is organised. Despite Joan Scott's strictures,[68] I have found it useful to employ a number of dichotomies, in particular those of 'theory and practice', and 'public and private'. What becomes apparent is how fluid these concepts are, each defined in opposition to the other, yet, at the same time with highly permeable and moving boundaries. I not only explore how 'theory' was marked by the needs of a pragmatic 'practice' but also the extent to which the SDF's and SDFers' practice was framed by an understanding of theory. The structure of the book reflects this. The first section focuses on theory and the last on practice: a bridging section explores the theory *and* practice of the SDF around a number of key elements of the woman question. These are the family, marriage and 'free love'; work; and the suffrage. The topics are deliberately drawn from across the spectrum of the public and the private spheres, a notion particularly familiar from studies of the nineteenth century.

Feminists have criticised and sought to subvert this dichotomy,[69] so why have I used it here? Because this was a framework used not only by contemporaries but also more specifically within Marxism. One of the reasons why the woman question sat awkwardly within Marxist socialism was because it questioned the accepted meanings of these concepts. The SDF as a Marxist party simply assumed that there was a public and a private realm: it was the woman question which exposed how contingent these realms were, their boundaries shifting and reforming. Analysing the changing notion of 'the public' and 'the private' contributes to an understanding of how the SDF constructed the woman question, and

---

[68] J. W. Scott, *Gender and the Politics of History*, Columbia University Press, New York, 1988, pp. 168–77.

[69] For feminist discussions of the public/private dichotomy, see J. B. Elshstain, *Public Man, Private Woman*, Martin Robertson, Oxford, 1981; A. Phillips, *Engendering Democracy*, Polity, Cambridge, 1991, ch. 4. For a discussion of the historiography of separate spheres, see A. Vickery, 'Golden Age to Separate Spheres? A Review of the Categories and Chronology of English Women's History', *The Historical Journal*, 36, 2, 1993, pp. 383–414.

how that was affected over time by the broader historical context as well as the specific politics of the organisation.

Part 1 of the book therefore deals with the SDF's theoretical construction of the woman question. I argue that the SDF's understanding of the issue was anchored in contemporary socialist orthodoxy, and was not – as some historians would have it – an aberration. The ambiguities inherent in the works of Engels and Bebel are crucial to this argument, as their work formed the basis of the Second International's orthodoxy on the woman question. The reception of these ideas in Britain influenced the SDF's understanding of the woman question. The party's position is then explored in a number of short case-studies. These consider the misogynism of Belfort Bax; the influence of Clara Zetkin and internationalism; and compare the SDF's treatment of 'race' with that of 'sex'.

Part 2 provides a bridge between the exploration of the SDF's theoretical construction of the woman question and its practice in relation to women, which forms part 3. This section examines a number of elements which constitute a significant part of the woman question, in order to understand that question as it was perceived and lived within the SDF. The case-studies which form part 2 are drawn from across the spectrum spanning the private and public spheres. The family, marriage and 'free love', work and the suffrage are explored in terms of the SDF's theory and practice and the inter-relationship between the two, as is the extent to which the meanings of these issues changed over the SDF's lifetime. These case-studies give shape to the woman question as a dynamic whole and allow an exploration of whether all aspects of the question were treated consistently by the party.

Part 3 is concerned with the practical implications for women of the SDF's understanding of the woman question. The attitudes expressed by SDFers towards women as potential socialists were affected by the party's theorising of the woman question. They reveal a gender-specific model of politicisation which in turn affected the particular approaches taken to recruit women and the limited success of those measures. The differing theoretical positions taken and practical solutions offered by male and female SDFers to the involvement of women within the party also shaped women's perception of the SDF. It is only by understanding SDFers' attitudes to women's politicisation that the actual roles of women within the party can be placed in context. Similarly the whole question of women's organisation within the party, its perceived function and degree of success, can best be measured in relation to SDF attitudes towards women.

What is apparent in part 3 is the ambiguous message that the SDF gave women. For their understanding of the woman question allowed some SDFers to stereotype and even malign women whilst the party earnestly declared that they wanted and needed women's support. This clearly had ramifications for women's perception of the SDF, and indeed socialism, and affected the extent and nature of women's involvement in the party.

Part 1

The woman question: the theory

1   The contribution of the founding fathers

The SDF's theoretical construction of the woman question was shaped by contemporary socialist arguments. Yet the Second International did not have a large body of theory on the woman question. Marx himself had never studied women's oppression in any detail. The scattered and rather general references to the family in *The German Ideology*, *The Communist Manifesto* and elsewhere hardly provided a coherent socialist conception of the woman question,[1] and in any case much of Marx's work was either out of print or otherwise unavailable.[2] British socialists were particularly hampered by the fact that much of what was available remained in the original German. Hence the contribution of Marx's thought to the Second International orthodoxy on the woman question lay with his class analysis rather than with any direct examination of the issue itself.[3]

Instead, the texts which set the framework for the socialist under-standing of the woman question were Engels' *The Origin of the Family, Private Property, and the State* (1884) and Bebel's *Woman Under Socialism* (1879). The authors were two of the most influential men in the Second International. Engels was, after Marx's death in 1883 until his own death in 1895, the *de facto* leader of the international socialist movement and attempted to influence domestic and international politics accord-ingly. Bebel was the leader of the largest and most influential party of the Second International, the German Social Democratic Party (SPD).

[1]   Some commentators have tried to piece together Marx's disparate remarks on women in order to present an apparently coherent picture. See for example, L. Vogel, *Marxism and the Oppression of Women*, Pluto, 1983, pp. 41–72. For another perspective see M. Barrett, 'Marxist-Feminism and the work of Karl Marx', in A. Phillips (ed.), *Feminism and Equality*, Blackwell, Oxford, 1987.

[2]   For the availability of Marx's work during this period see D. Torr, *Tom Mann and his Times*, vol.1, Lawrence and Wishart, 1956, p. 326; W. Kendall, *The Revolutionary Movement in Britain*, p. 69; S. Macintyre, *A Proletarian Science: Marxism in Britain, 1917–33*, Cambridge University Press, Cambridge, 1980, pp. 91–2.

[3]   Marx's class analysis was available to SDFers through *Capital*, which some SDFers read, and more generally through popularisers such as Hyndman in his *England for All*, Harvester, Brighton, 1973 (first published 1881).

Bebel's book, originally titled *Women in the Past, Present and Future*, was later substantially revised in 1883 and 1891 to incorporate Engels' work as well as new empirical material, and its influence may be gauged by the fact it reached its fiftieth German edition in 1910 and was translated widely.[4] Perhaps it was the very authority of Engels and Bebel as 'founding fathers' of socialism that made these key works the last words on the subject for this and many subsequent generations of socialists. It certainly gave particular significance to the ambiguities, absences and limitations of these two texts.

In *Origin*, Engels focuses primarily on the family as the unit of society rather than on women's oppression. Nevertheless, he argues that class society and women's oppression have the same origin. This became the central orthodoxy of socialist feminist analysis. It is the way in which this argument is made which is crucial to the later construction of the woman question.

According to Engels, the growth of private property resulted in the patriarchal family which was the first form of the family to be based 'not on natural but on economic conditions'.[5] Women's oppression had an economic cause. This in itself was an important development in feminist theory.[6] Engels argued that the earliest form of society had a sexual division of labour but accorded equal respect to both sexes and was therefore egalitarian. Primitive society was also matrilineal. All this was threatened with the domestication of animals and the growth of agriculture, for with them came productive capacity, the possibility of surplus and thus private property. Engels maintained that private property necessarily belonged to the male. It was in order that this private property, as distinct from the previous communal property, could be inherited by other males, sons, that the matrilineal form of descent or 'mother right' had to end. Hence 'the overthrow of mother right was the world historical defeat of the female sex. The man took command in the home ... the woman was degraded and reduced to servitude; she became the slave of his lust and a mere instrument for the production of children'.[7]

Engels supplemented this economic explanation for women's

---

[4]   R. J. Evans, *The Feminists*, Croom Helm, 1977, p. 157; L. Vogel, *Marxism and the Oppression of Women*, p. 96; L. A. Coser's Introduction to A. Bebel (trans. D. De Leon), *Woman Under Socialism*, Schocken Books, New York, 1971, p. vii.

[5]   F. Engels, *The Origin of the Family, Private Property and the State*, Lawrence and Wishart, 1973, p. 128.

[6]   For accounts of earlier forms of feminism, see J. Rendall, *The Origins of Modern Feminism: Women in Britain, France and United States, 1780–1860*, Macmillan, 1985; B. Taylor, *Eve and the New Jerusalem*.

[7]   Engels, *Origin*, pp. 120–1.

oppression with one in terms of 'sex antagonism'. In considering the relationship between men and women within the family, he said, 'The first class opposition that appears in history coincides with the development of the antagonism between man and woman in mono-gamous marriage, and the first class oppression coincides with that of the female sex by the male'.[8] This comparison is of primary importance for Engels. Yet the nature of the original sex antagonism is not made clear; it merely slides into one of class antagonism. This is essentially what became known as the sex/class analogy. For so central a concept it remains remarkably muddy. The economic definitions of class in the wider society were used to describe relations within the family, as with Engels' statement that 'within the family he is the bourgeois, and the wife represents the proletariat'.[9] It is simply assumed that both forms of oppression are at base economic, and that both will cease only with the end of class society.

The wider significance of Engels' approach is illustrated by its uncritical acceptance by Bebel. He wrote, for example, that 'Woman was the first human being to come into bondage: she was a slave before the male slave existed. All social dependence and oppression has its roots in the economic dependence of the oppressed upon the oppressor.'[10] Thus Bebel, like Engels, thought that 'the Woman Question is only one of the aspects of the Social Question';[11] the woman question would only be resolved under a socialist society, and therefore it was in women's interests to join with the proletariat in the fight to overthrow capitalism.

It cannot be too strongly stated that although the sex/class analogy was the linchpin of Engels and Bebel's argument, neither fully explored its ambiguities. Was women's oppression to be understood in theoretical terms as a qualitatively distinct kind of oppression from that of class? Upon this shaky foundation was built the edifice of the Second International's understanding of the woman question. Women were to be integrated into the heart of socialism, its class analysis, through the sex/class analogy; yet that analogy precluded the emergence within socialist thinking of any developed understanding of women's oppres-sion. All too often, the woman question found a socialist 'answer' by disappearing into the class, or 'social', question. There was no clear theoretical space to develop an understanding of patriarchy, as either a separate or a related system to capitalism.

8   Ibid., p. 129.
9   Ibid., p. 137.
10 Bebel, *Woman*, p. 9.
11 Ibid., p. 1.

The invisibility of sexual oppression was not total. For in order for this sleight of hand to occur, the concept had first to be recognised. Ironically, the fact that Bebel accepted the existence of sex oppression, if only to then dissolve it into class oppression, gave a status and recognition to the experiences of women and ensured the acceptance of the woman question as an issue for socialists. Indeed, on occasion Bebel was moved to say that, 'it is necessary to treat the so-called Woman Question separately',[12] and this was an important aspect of the appeal of *Woman*.

This was the ambivalence at the heart of the socialist construction of the woman question. Socialist theory both recognised and then effectively shelved the question. Moreover, Engels and Bebel's undeveloped arguments were cited by other socialists to legitimise very different interpretations of the woman question. For example, the 'founding fathers' could be represented as endorsing the view that the woman question was a discrete and important matter which socialists must address. They could also be presented as supporting the view that the class struggle was the only issue for socialists, and that therefore the woman question was irrelevant. These ambiguities set the framework for the SDF's own understanding of the woman question.

While the sex/class analogy was the most important aspect of Engels and Bebel's work for the socialist construction of the woman question, other themes from *Woman* and *Origin* highlighted the particular way in which the woman question came to be understood. Throughout *Woman*, Bebel explored the social construction of gender. He argued, for instance, that

woman stands, through custom and education, as well as the freedom allowed her by law, behind the workingman. To this, another circumstance is added. Conditions, lasting through a long series of generations, finally grow into custom; heredity and education then cause such conditions to appear on both sides as 'natural'.[13]

This argument was a radical challenge to the commonsense of the period and, in making it, Bebel acknowledged the possibilities for change. In the same way the anthropological evidence used in *Woman* suggested that women had not always been oppressed and that therefore their condition was not immutable. This positive aspect of *Woman* was part of its widespread appeal.[14]

Despite challenging what Bebel termed, 'the twaddle about the

12 Ibid.
13 Ibid., p. 9.
14 The same kind of argument can be made on Engels' behalf. See R. Delmar, 'Looking Again at Engels's "Origin of the Family, Private Property and the State"', in

'natural calling' of woman',[15] neither he nor Engels took the next step and criticised the sexual division of labour itself. Engels saw the sexual division of labour as biological in origin, for the 'first division of labour is that between men and women for the propagation of children'.[16] Yet he argued this division was not the basis for social inequality. Primitive society did not have an absolute identity of sexual roles but, so he argued, it did equally respect them. Hierarchy came with the onset of class society. But this was an argument about the value attached to the sexual division of labour; it did not question the division itself. Engels assumed that the sexual division of labour is natural and that therefore childcare, for example, would always be woman's role. It was just that under socialism, woman's role in society would be respected once again and be deemed equal in value to the man's contribution to the community.

Bebel agreed with Engels and argued that primitive society meant 'equality for all'. He even went further and suggested that something approaching a matriarchy characterised this early society.[17] Yet when he described present society, he too assumed the inevitability of a sexual division of labour, as, for instance, in the description of woman's 'calling as mother and rearer of children'.[18] Bebel discussed the relative contribution of 'nature' and 'nurture' to the sexual division of labour in more depth than Engels, but in the final analysis his conclusions amount to a plea for women's penetration of the public sphere rather than a challenge to the sexual division of labour.[19] Woman should not be confined to her traditional role, but she would not be able to do more than supplement it. Woman would still be the child-rearer in a socialist society.

Bebel and Engels' limited challenge to 'the natural' and the presence of the sex/class analogy in their theories affected the strategies that they recommended for the emancipation of women. There is some suggestion of inevitability in Bebel's assertion that 'no power on earth can prevent' women's emancipation and equality between the sexes.[20] Yet he gives much greater emphasis to the part woman must play in her own emancipation. For although women could not hope for their freedom

J. Mitchell and A. Oakley (eds.), *The Rights and Wrongs of Women*, Penguin, 1976, p. 287.

[15]   Bebel, *Woman*, p. 182.
[16]   Engels, *Origin*, p. 129.
[17]   Bebel, *Woman*, pp. 30, 24.
[18]   Ibid., p. 122.
[19]   Ibid., p. 182. Some commentators see no ambiguity in Bebel's presentation of the sexual division of labour. See, for example, R. J. Evans, *The Feminists*, p. 157.
[20]   Bebel, *Woman*, p. 349.

until after the revolution, they had to be persuaded to contribute to the present class struggle. Passivity would not bring the days of freedom any closer. Bebel, therefore, exhorted:

To woman also in general, and as a female proletarian in particular, the summons goes out not to remain behind in this struggle in which her redemption and emancipation are at stake. It is for her to prove that she has comprehended her true place in the Movement and in the struggles of the present for a better future; and that she is resolved to join. It is the part of the men to aid her in ridding herself of all superstitions, and to step forward in their ranks. Let none underrate his own powers, and imagine that the issue did not depend on him.[21]

To underline the fact that women had to take action for themselves rather than expect action to take place on their behalf, Bebel went a step further and warned that 'women should expect as little help from the men as workingmen do from the capitalist class'.[22]

Sheila Rowbotham has interpreted this as putting 'the oppressed firmly in charge of their own liberation',[23] but that would have smacked too much of feminism for Bebel. The duty of socialist women was not to divert energy from the class struggle by autonomous action, as women did in what was termed the bourgeois women's movement. In order to distinguish socialism from its potential rival, feminism, it was important for socialists to challenge the view that sex and class oppression were distinct, or even unrelated, oppressions which demanded separate solutions. It would be too crude to see the socialist construction of the woman question as nothing more than the pragmatic response of one movement concerned to recruit at the expense of a competing ideology. But part of the complexity of the evolving relationship between socialism and feminism has been, and continues to be, the nature of the original socialist construction of the woman question.

Engels shared Bebel's belief that as a prerequisite for emancipation women should participate in waged work and thus become full members of the class.[24] There would then be no ambiguity about women's oppression for as members of the proletariat, theirs would be class oppression. For Engels, history is made in the public sphere, in the area of production, and until women are part of that they are invisible to history. Yet as Moira Maconachie has commented, by a sleight of hand, Engels, while placing family within history, also confined women within the family and thus displaced women from history.[25] In addition Engels

[21]   Ibid., p. 378.
[22]   Ibid., p. 121.
[23]   S. Rowbotham, *Women, Resistance and Revolution*, Pelican, 1974, p. 81.
[24]   Engels, *Origin*, p. 221.
[25]   M. Maconachie, 'Engels, Sexual Divisions and the Family', *University of Kent Women's Studies Occasional Papers*, 1, 1983, p. 11.

did not clarify the role of a socialist party in women's penetration of the labour market for, unlike Bebel, he did not directly address the political implications of the woman question. Engels' focus is much wider, emphasising the broad sweep of societal development. But even his recommendation has some ramifications for socialist politics, as it suggests that socialists should take a firm stand against those who oppose women's, including married women's, labour.

In conclusion, the socialist construction of the woman question, particularly Bebel's *Woman*, paradoxically marginalised women within contemporary socialist concerns while also drawing them more firmly into the socialist arena. There now was a 'woman question', but its resolution had to await that of the social question. The duty of women who wanted emancipation was to join in the class struggle, in order to achieve a socialist society in which the woman question, so it was promised, would be addressed. In a sense, there was no sex question under capitalism, only one of class, and to engage in sex issues, that is feminism, would only delay the achievement of socialism and thus the resolution of the woman question. In this way women's issues were marginalised by socialists. Merely by engaging in the class struggle in capitalist society, women were doing as much as was necessary at that historical juncture to gain their freedom in the long term.

This argument rested on one work which only incidentally addressed women's oppression and another which did so, but in a less than rigorous manner. The legacy of the founding fathers was thus an ambiguous one. They appeared to collapse sex into class oppression, and built the rest of their arguments on this assumption: yet the sex/class analogy was never fully explored or justified. This was the limitation of these texts. Their ambiguity provided grist to the mill for the very different practical interpretations of the relevance of the woman question to socialists.

The reception of 'The Origin of the Family' and 'Woman and Socialism' in the British socialist movement

Whatever the shortcomings of the theoretical analyses provided by Bebel and Engels, their use by British socialists depended upon access to *Origin* and *Woman*. How aware of these works were British socialists before World War I? Both were published originally in German, and their availability to a British audience obviously depended upon their translation and cheap mass publication. They also had to be publicised and recommended to a potential audience. Prior to World War I, the two books enjoyed different fortunes in these respects.

Of the two books, *Woman* had by far the greater impact across the Second International in this period. Not only did it have an extraordinary volume of sales, going through five dozen German editions before 1914,[26] but it was also the most popular book borrowed from German workers' libraries in the same period.[27] In contrast, *Origin* had a much more limited audience.[28] This same pattern was borne out throughout the countries of the Second International for *Woman* was translated widely. Once Daniel De Leon, leader of the American Socialist Labour Party, had translated *Woman* in 1903, 'it immediately became the most popular book on the subject for generations of [American] women activists'.[29]

Many women socialists testified to the inspiration and influence of *Woman*. Ottilie Baader remembered:

Although I was not a Social Democrat I had friends who belonged to the party. Through them I got the precious work. I read it nights through. It was my own fate and that of thousands of my sisters. Neither in the family nor in public life had I ever heard of all the pain the women must endure ... Bebel's book courageously broke with the old secretiveness ... I read the book not once but ten times.[30]

She said the book brought 'hope and joy to live and fight'. Many emphasised that the book's assurance of liberation in a future society was in itself an inspiration; 'it forged the most unshakeable belief that tomorrow's dawn would also bring women deliverance'.[31] For Clara Zetkin, *Woman* was 'more than a book, it was an event, a deed'.[32] The numerous personal testimonies also came from beyond Germany; for Alexandra Kollontai, Bebel's book was the 'woman's bible'.[33]

For many women Bebel's book had a significant effect on them and their politics. But did the huge sales of *Woman* indicate a more

---

[26] J. H. Quataert, *Reluctant Feminists: In German Social Democracy 1885–1917*, Princeton University Press, Princeton, New Jersey, 1979, p. 236.

[27] H. J. Steinberg, 'Workers' Libraries in Germany before 1914', *History Workshop Journal*, 1, 1976, p. 174.

[28] Ibid., pp. 166–80.

[29] M .Tax, *The Rising of the Women: Feminist Solidarity and Class Conflict, 1880–1917*, Monthly Review Press, New York, 1980, p. 37.

[30] Ottilie Baader quoted in J. H. Quataert, 'Unequal Partners in an Uneasy Alliance: Women and the Working Class in Imperial Germany', in M. J. Boxer and J. H. Quataert (eds.), *Socialist Women: European Socialist Feminism in the Nineteenth and Early Twentieth Centuries*, Elsevier, New York, 1978, p. 120.

[31] Wilhelmine Kähler quoted in Quataert, *Reluctant Feminists*, p. 7.

[32] Clara Zetkin to the SPD Party Congress in 1896 quoted in H. Draper and A. G. Lipow, 'Marxist Women versus Bourgeois Feminism', *Socialist Register*, Merlin Press, 1976, p. 197.

[33] From Kollontai's introduction to the first unabridged Russian translation of *Woman* in 1918 (C. Porter, *Alexandra Kollontai*, Virago, 1980, p. 36).

widespread commitment to the woman question? Jean Quataert doubts whether the book's great popularity had any direct correlation with a feminist awakening. She acknowledges that *Woman* 'crystalised felt sentiments at crucial times in some women's lives' and that it 'provided the activists with emotive myths so crucial in mobilizing and sustaining social groups'. However, she also warns that it was read for its historical and anthropological material as an indictment of capitalism rather than as an analysis of the woman question.[34] This is borne out by the kind of books that were borrowed alongside *Woman* in German workers' libraries. These tended to be natural science and history along with many novels, rather than any other works relating specifically to women. Bebel's account of the progressive development of society and his picture of the future appealed to many readers and fitted in with other SPD literature and such internationally popular works as Bellamy's *Looking Backward*.[35] Harry McShane makes a similar point in relation to *Origin*, which he remembers some socialists reading in this period. He notes that they were more interested in tracing the origins of society than they were in the woman question. Indeed, 'the other argument passed them by'.[36] Thus while Bebel's book, in particular, gave to woman the 'courage to follow her conscience', as Mathilde Wurm wrote,[37] for many other readers, particularly men who could not make the same personal identification, these books offered socialist accounts of society's potential for change rather than a direct plea for women's emancipation.

What then was the effect of *Origin* and *Woman* on the British socialist movement? The first problem was one of availability. The initial English translation by Harriet Adams Walther of *Woman* was made from an unrevised edition of *Woman in the Past, Present and Future*. Since this was published in 1885, for a considerable period the only available English text of *Woman* was drawn from Bebel's least developed version of what was to be a much revised and extended book. The second translation was produced in 1893 from the German ninth edition but without consultation with the author.[38] Although several editions of this were produced before 1914, copies do not seem to have been easily accessible. The price was one problem; in 1906 *Woman* in paperback

---

[34] Quataert, *Reluctant Feminists*, p. 236.
[35] H. J. Steinberg, 'Workers' Libraries', pp. 176–7; E. Bellamy, *Looking Backward*, Signet, New York, 1960.
[36] H. McShane and J. Smith, *Harry McShane: No Mean Fighter*, Pluto, 1978, p. 35.
[37] Mathilde Wurm in *Gleichheit*, February 1910 quoted in Quataert, *Reluctant Feminists*, p. 7.
[38] Y. Kapp, *Eleanor Marx: Volume II: The Crowded Years, 1884–1898*, Lawrence and Wishart, 1976, p. 83.

cost ninepence and was later advertised at a shilling.[39] Moreover, for considerable periods *Woman* does not seem to have been in print. SDFer T. A. Jackson, in describing his search at the turn of the century for Marxist books, including secondhand and remaindered ones, mentions that 'he got hold of a poor translation of Bebel's *Woman*'.[40] It does not seem to have been easy to find. When F. Keddell wrote the Fabian tract, *What Socialism Is*, he had to read Walther's translation at the British Museum.[41]

From about 1903 American Kerr and Co. editions of socialist texts became available cheaply in Britain. Among the previously unavailable works now obtainable was the first English translation of *Origin*[42] and, perhaps, De Leon's translation of *Woman* which was published in New York in 1904. By this and other means, the availability of both books improved, so that by 1914 they were fairly easily obtained; at least by those with access to the socialist press or party bookstalls. They were therefore not available to the browser or the casual reader.

Thus, it was important for the dissemination of *Origin* and *Woman* that they be widely publicised to their potential audience. Bebel's book succeeded to a degree in this respect, attracting reviews and references across the spectrum of socialist opinion. Annie Besant favourably reviewed *Woman* in her journal *Our Corner*, pronouncing it 'instructive and useful'.[43] Edward Carpenter quoted Bebel in *Woman, and Her Place in a Free Society*, as did Mrs Wolstenholme Elmy in her ILP pamphlet, *Woman – The Communist*.[44] Havelock Ellis in 1884 called in the journal *Today* for an English translation of Bebel's 'clear and outspoken' book.[45] While the *Labour Leader* advertised *Woman*, readers of *Clarion* were recommended to read Bebel and the Fabian's *Guide to Books for Socialists* listed it as one of the best general books on women.[46] Lest it be thought that *Woman* was well known to socialists, it should be noted that these are most of the references to this work over a period of twenty-five years.

[39] *Justice*, 26 May 1906; *Labour Leader*, 3 July 1908.
[40] T. A. Jackson, *Solo Trumpet*, Lawrence and Wishart, 1953, p. 60.
[41] F. Keddell, *What Socialism Is*, Fabian Tract, 4, 1886 described in R. Weintraub (ed.), *Fabian Feminist: Bernard Shaw and Woman*, Pennsylvania State University Press, University Park, 1977, p. 92.
[42] Jackson, *Solo Trumpet*, p. 67; T. A. Jackson, 'We Don't Know how Lucky We Are: Selling Red Books Thirty Years Ago', *Daily Worker*, 7 February 1935; Macintyre, *A Proletarian Science*, p. 92.
[43] *Our Corner*, August 1885, p. 98. See appendix 5 for a brief biography of Annie Besant.
[44] E. Carpenter, *Woman, and Her Place in a Free Society*, The Labour Press Society, Manchester, 1894, p. 25; E. Wolstenholme Elmy, *Woman – The Communist*, ILP, 1904, p. 6.
[45] *Today*, October 1884, p. 352.
[46] *Labour Leader*, 3 July 1908; *Clarion*, 2 November 1895; *A Guide to Books for Socialists*, Fabian Tract, 132, 1907, p. 5.

The notoriety occasioned by James Connolly's reaction to De Leon's translation of *Woman* gave the book more attention in America, and thus, through the Socialist Labour Party, in Britain. Connolly objected to what he saw as *Woman*'s 'quasi-prurient revelations of the past and present degredation of womanhood'. He doubted whether such a book could bring women to socialism. It was therefore ironic, given Connolly's claim that hundreds of women had been repelled by Bebel's book,[47] that in 1912 Mrs Bridges Adams chose the name 'Bebel House' for her Working Women's College.[48] She clearly thought that not only would Bebel and his association with women's emancipation be familiar to potential supporters in the labour movement, but that *Woman*'s reputation would not harm her attempts at fund-raising.

Attention was also directed to Bebel's book by the review essay by Edward and Eleanor Marx Aveling which originally appeared in the *Westminster Review* and was subsequently published in 1886 as the pamphlet, *The Woman Question*. This interpreted Bebel for an audience who might be unable to obtain *Woman* itself. The Avelings summed up Bebel's main thesis simply: 'the [woman] question is one of economics'.[49] Like Bebel, they were therefore very critical of feminists who were seen as being essentially bourgeois; that is, who did not recognise that the woman question was an economic question, and who believed that changes could take place within the framework of capitalism. In this the Avelings go further than Bebel. They also moved beyond him in granting some recognition to patriarchy and, less ambiguously than Bebel, by presenting a strategy of an alliance between parallel movements of the oppressed. The Avelings gave a stronger identity to the woman question, but, in the final analysis, kept its solution firmly tied to socialism rather than to feminism. They referred to many of Bebel's points on, for example, marriage and prostitution, while giving particular emphasis to the woman question as a class issue. Men and women should work together to achieve socialism, which would end their oppressions. The Avelings interpretation of Bebel was of no little consequence, for by 1887 their pamphlet, *The Woman Question* was in its fourth edition.[50]

[47] *The People*, 9 April 1904 reprinted in *The Connolly De Leon Controversy*, Cork Workers Club, Cork, nd, p. 9.
[48] *Justice*, 13 January 1912; W. W. Craik, *The Central Labour College, 1909–29*, Lawrence and Wishart, 1964, pp. 102–3.
[49] E. M. and E. Aveling, 'The Woman Question', *Westminster Review*, January 1886, pp. 208–9. The article was printed as a penny pamphlet by the Twentieth Century Press and advertised in *Justice* (*Justice*, 8 July 1905). This has been republished, edited by J. Müller and E. Schotte as *Thoughts on Women and Society*, International Publishers, New York, 1987.
[50] Y. Kapp, *Eleanor Marx*, vol.2, p. 83.

The significance of Engels' *Origin* prior to 1914 is much harder to assess. Readers could react very positively, as for example Margaret McCarthy who remembered being excited by the book in the 1920s:

Through Engels I felt I was reaching back to ancient, fascinating social institutions, a wonderful *Alice through the Looking Glass* sort of world where, under the matriarchy, woman the mother, the queen, the priestess was recognised, honoured and adored, and the role of woman and man was a reversal of what we know today.[51]

Yet *Origin* was rarely cited and did not feature in the Fabian's *Guide to Books for Socialists* or in the SDF Women's Education Committee's booklists. It seems generally to have been far less well-known than *Woman*.

To what extent do these general comments regarding Bebel and Engels' works apply to the SDF? In keeping with the general pattern, *Woman* got more attention than *Origin* within the SDF press; the former was advertised prior to publication and advertisements for it appeared occasionally throughout the SDF's lifetime.[52] More significantly *Woman* was reviewed on three separate occasions in *Justice*.

The two notices of the first English translation were favourable, the reviewer urged that the book be read widely and regarded as particularly valuable the sections on 'the natural sexual passion and the terrible evils which result from its suppression and mere property marriage'. Emphasis was given to Bebel's conclusion that 'we have no idea of what women may be capable of in better arrangements' as 'the difference between man and woman is far less than we are in the habit of supposing'.[53] In the second notice, Bebel's chapter on the Future was condemned as 'short and useless', although it was admitted that this was an area in which prediction was pointless, as 'it is of course quite impossible to say what stipulations women, when enfranchised fully, will make for their own protection'.[54] Nevertheless, this was one of the sections which Bebel greatly expanded in future German editions.

Ten years later, Belfort Bax took the occasion of the publication of the Jubilee edition of *Woman* in Germany to re-review the book. Since Bax never accepted the analogy between sex and class, it was not surprising that he damned by faint praise: 'without being able to lay claim to any special originality, the book, in its present shape, contains a quantity of industriously collected material, of use to Socialists, on a variety of economical and social topics, and, as a compilation, is in many respects

[51] M. McCarthy, *Generation in Revolt*, Heinemann, 1953, p. 100.
[52] *Justice*, 11 April 1885; 2 November 1907; 3 April 1908.
[53] *Justice*, 20 June 1885.
[54] *Justice*, 4 July 1885.

good'.[55] He described the main argument as 'a piece of special pleading based on a theory of the identity of object of the Proletarian movement and the so-called Women's Movement'. Moreover, Bax's view did not go unnoticed, for the SPD's *Sozialdemokrat* commented on Bax's review. Bebel himself expressed 'pain for the welfare of [Bax's] Social Democratic soul'.[56]

In 1906 the fourth English edition of *Woman* was reviewed in *Justice*. Here was the clearest evidence yet of the work's influence on the socialist construction of the woman question, for it was noted that 'To Socialists the woman's question calls for no independent consideration apart from the workman's question'. It was suggested that the woman question, which was defined as 'the economic dependence of woman upon man', was receding into the background as more women entered the labour market, thereby opening the way for class-conscious women. The reviewer recommended *Woman* as particularly good propaganda to give to those who were not yet converted to socialism.[57] Thus over twenty years after the first English edition of *Woman*, Bebel's book was still regarded within the SDF as a useful and relevant text.

None of this shows the extent to which Bebel was read by SDFers. One indication is the number of times that Bebel was cited within *Justice* and *Social Democrat*, although one must recognise that it was not the practice to heavily reference articles and letters. S. Gardner in a letter to *Justice* recommended *Woman*. Dora Montefiore did likewise in her pamphlet for the SDF Women's Education Committee (WEC), *The Position of Women in the Socialist Movement*. She advocated that every socialist woman should study Bebel's book, although she noted that by 1909 some of the biological and sociological material was out of date. Nevertheless she urged *Woman* on her readers, 'It will awaken and stimulate thought, and open out many by-ways of study and inquiry, which will help to develop consciousness'.[58] The WEC also recommended *Woman* on its reading list for advanced Women's Socialist Circles to study and discuss. The book also formed the subject of several branch lectures.[59]

A reference might indicate no more than a passing acquaintance with the work, but a direct quotation demonstrated rather more. Dora Montefiore and Edith Swift both used quotations from Bebel in articles

---

[55] *Justice*, 17 August 1895. See appendix 5 for a brief biography of E. Belfort Bax.
[56] *Justice*, 30 November 1895.
[57] *Justice*, 26 May 1906.
[58] *Justice*, 2 June 1894; D. B. Montefiore, *The Position of Women in the Socialist Movement*, Twentieth Century Press, 1909, p. 1. See appendix 5 for a brief biography of Dora Montefiore.
[59] *Justice*, 6 August 1910; 14 December 1901, 15 February 1908.

in *Social Democrat*,[60] while R. B. Kerr quoted from *Woman* to sustain his argument that socialists had to recognise that the class war *and* the sex war had come to stay.[61] Moreover, the use of quotation assumed that readers of *Justice* and *Social Democrat* would have recognised the general significance of the book.

Criticism of Bebel also aided publicity and spurred readers to take up the text. Bax's hostility seems to have done as much as the socialist women to promote *Woman*. He described the first edition as containing 'a precious lot of Woman and precious little Socialism', although he admitted that in later editions the balance altered. He thought the book was 'full of violent prejudice' and was 'one-sided' with its 'blind worship of the other sex'.[62] Bax's vehemence in itself made *Woman* seem a more tantalising read.

It is hard to conclude that Engels's *Origin* was as important amongst the SDF as Bebel's *Woman*. Bax attacked *Origin* as vehemently as he criticised Bebel, and for the same reasons.[63] Yet Bax's attention to *Origin* was unusual, and although R. B. Kerr also quoted Engels, there is little sense within the SDF press of a general familiarity with the book. Indeed, some writers quoted Morgan's *Ancient Society*, the work forming the basis for *Origin*, either because they were not familiar with Engels or simply through preference.[64] *Origin* was neither as accessible nor as well publicised within the SDF as the work of Bebel.

It is reasonable to conclude that the work of the founding fathers was assimilated within the SDF at least to the extent that it set the framework for the organisation's understanding of the woman question. However, of the two books *Woman* was the more influential as a text which spoke directly to the experiences and frustrations of many women socialists or proto-socialists. The way in which the socialist construction of the woman question suggested by these volumes shaped the SDF's understanding of the question forms the subject of the next chapter.

---

[60]   *Social Democrat*, February 1901, p. 49; November 1909, p. 500.
[61]   *Justice*, 16 March 1907. Dora Montefiore also used this quotation in an early letter to *Clarion*, 23 October 1897.
[62]   *Social Democrat*, March 1909, p. 114; December 1902, p. 361; July 1897, p. 205.
[63]   *Justice*, 28 November 1896.
[64]   For example Zelda Kahan in *Social Democrat*, December 1909, p. 539, although she later wrote a book on Engels which contained a chapter on *Origin* (Z. Kahan Coates, *The Life and Teachings of Friedrich Engels*, Lawrence and Wishart, 1945). Similarly H. M. Hyndman cites Morgan rather than Engels (Hyndman, *Further Reminiscences*, p. 300).

2   The SDF's understanding of the woman question

This chapter places the woman question within the SDF's under-standing of socialism in order to explain how SDFers arrived at their ambivalent position on the relationship between sex and class. Together with an exploration of the range of arguments used within the SDF concerning the nature of women's condition under capitalism and its political implications, this provides a picture of the SDF's understanding of the woman question.

To understand the SDF's position on the woman question one must place it within the wider context. The party's understanding of socialism was essentially an orthodox Second International Marxist one;[1] that is, the crucial divide in society was economic, essentially one of class, and everything else was secondary. This premise led to a narrow definition of the issues which were regarded as crucial to socialist politics. In contrast, a wide variety of other debates, such as those over religion, teetotalism and feminism, were defined as peripheral. As the SDF's columnist, the Tattler, emphasised:

Socialism deals only with the economic question and however much any of us may speculate on the changes in sexual relations that may result from changed economic conditions, the individual making them is responsible for such speculations, and they are to be in nowise regarded as part of socialist teaching.[2]

Anything beyond the strictly economic was a matter for the individual conscience, and as such could not be used to impugn anyone's socialist credentials. Thus, for example, Belfort Bax was able not only to have his misogynist views printed in *Justice*, despite opposition from women and men, but also to have his right to do so defended editorially.[3] Although this policy might alienate potential women members, this was seen by the party as merely a side effect of a sound political principle.

---

[1]   See G. D. H Cole, *Marxism and Anarchism*, p. 410; W. Wolfe, *From Radicalism to Socialism: Men and Ideas in the Formation of Fabian Socialist Doctrines, 1881–9*, Yale University Press, New Haven, 1975, pp. 98–100.

[2]   *Justice*, 21 September 1895.

[3]   *Justice*, 10 August; 2 November; 21 December 1895.

The SDF did, of course, have a political programme. The centrality of their economic analysis of class society to their socialism did not preclude a politics which sought democratic and social reforms. Although there were to be secessions from the SDF over the years on this issue, for example by the Socialist League in 1884 and the Socialist Labour Party in 1903, the main body of the party saw engaging in political campaigning and electioneering as a means not only to propagandise for socialism but also to campaign for short term gains for the working class as a whole. Examples included the eight-hour day, public provision of low cost housing and the nationalisation of the railways.[4] These 'stepping stones to a happier period' were seen as progressive demands which would 'palliate the evils of our existing society'.[5] The SDF were therefore not Marxists who argued for the immiseration of the proletariat as a spur to creating a revolutionary class and an end to capitalism. The party assumed that support for specific social reforms would further its ultimate goal of achieving a socialist society as they would result in a more energetic and healthier working class as well as help to shift the balance from the private to the public sector.[6] In order to promote these palliatives the SDF also included within its overall programme a series of democratic reforms which had been transferred directly from the party's Radical predecessor, the Democratic Federation. These included adult suffrage, payment of MPs and abolition of the House of Lords. Neither aspect of the SDF's programme – the palliative social reforms or the radical democratic policies – included any demand which could be termed a 'women's issue'. Why not?

There are two aspects to this question. The first focuses on why what was essentially a democratic programme derived from Radicalism could not include demands specific to women. Such an argument fails to recognise the extent to which the Radical agenda was itself a deeply gendered one, as recent discussion of the formative concept of citizenship and the 1867 Reform Act has shown.[7] In addition, Dorothy Thompson and Anna Clark, in their different ways, have shown how women were marginalised from the discourse of Radicalism[8] – although

4   Collins, 'The Marxism of the SDF', p. 57.
5   Ibid.
6   Ibid, pp. 58–9, 64.
7   The panel on '1867' at the 1995 Social History Society Conference at York explored the gendering of citizenship at this key moment with thought-provoking papers from Keith McClelland, Jane Rendall and Catherine Hall. For published accounts of these arguments, see C. Hall, 'Rethinking Imperial Histories: The Reform Act of 1867', *New Left Review*, 208, 1994 in which she also refers to recent work by McClelland and Rendall, pp. 10 (fn. 9), 24 (fn. 55).
8   D. Thompson, 'Women and Nineteenth Century Radical Politics: A Lost Dimension',

this is an issue which has been ignored by those revisionist political historians who seek to emphasise the Radical antecedents of socialist and labour organisations and the importance of continuities of Liberalism within working-class politics.[9] It certainly seems that Radicalism, in all but its exceptional form of Owenism, was no more able to place women at the heart of its politics than socialism.[10] Thus whatever the assessment of the overall influence of Radicalism on the SDF over the latter's lifetime, the party's programme was informed by a tradition which saw no reason to identify women as a separate social group with particular needs or requiring particular rights.

This links to the second aspect of this question. The reason why the SDF had a political programme at all was to advance the interests of the working class which, in turn, would enable the class as a whole to participate in, and benefit from, the end of the economic system which oppressed them. Any identification of a separate political agenda for women was seen as detracting from the key issue of class. For the SDF there was no logic in extending the radical agenda to an inclusion of separate interest groups such as women, for as members of the working-class women would benefit from such reforms. Sectional demands would only weaken class solidarity.

There were therefore pragmatic grounds for the marginality of a range of contentious issues prominent amongst which was the woman question. As these matters were characterised by an absence of consensus, it was thought better not to give time to the 'conscience' issues such as teetotalism, religion and vegetarianism; they only diverted energies from the current economic question. So, 'it is the economic conditions we have to attack and ... when these have been changed these abstract questions will settle themselves'.[11] Women, for example, were being asked to wait until after the revolution when the substance of the woman question would be addressed. The danger was thought to be clear, 'it threatened a division in our ranks by directing the attention of women from the real enemy, capitalism, to an imaginary enemy, an abstract "brute man"'.[12] Hence, the SDF's narrow definition of socialism dovetailed neatly with a pragmatic concern to marginalise

---

in J. Mitchell and A. Oakley (eds.), *The Rights and Wrongs of Women*; A. Clark, 'The Rhetoric of Chartist Domesticity: Gender, Language and Class in the 1830s and 1840s', *Journal of British Studies*, 31, 1992.

[9] See E. F. Biagini and A. J. Reid (eds.), *Currents of Radicalism: Popular Radicalism, Organised Labour and Party Politics in Britain, 1850–1914*, Cambridge University Press, Cambridge, 1991.

[10] For women and Owenism, see B. Taylor, *Eve and the New Jerusalem*.

[11] *Justice*, 28 December 1895.

[12] *Justice*, 16 May 1896.

'conscience' issues, such as the woman question. To focus on these issues would promote internal disagreement and, it was argued, would divert energy from socialism itself. The solution was a limited but specific manifesto coupled with the democratic right to pursue one's own conscience over private matters. Maximum unity and solidarity could then be maintained.

These general arguments concerning 'conscience' issues were reinforced in the case of the woman question by the founding fathers' construction of that issue. As we have seen, Engels and Bebel's argument was ambivalent. Women's oppression was recognised by them, and then immediately subsumed within class oppression; their construction of the woman question both recognised and then effectively shelved the problem. Yet by providing a theory in which it was possible to conceptualise the woman question, Engels and Bebel set the framework for socialist organisations to develop a relationship with women as potential and actual socialists. No party of the Second International challenged this orthodoxy.[13]

For the SDF, the socialist understanding of the woman question combined with its own narrow economic definition of socialism provided a theoretical basis for an open policy on women's issues. The SDF included individuals with a wide range of views in this area who were permitted to develop and expound their ideas with impunity. Yet no particular viewpoint could officially become party policy.[14] This lack of a clear policy had consequences for women's perception of socialism and their participation in the party.

An official policy of 'no policy' did not, of course, mean that the woman question disappeared. It did mean, however, that a range of factors determined the overall impression of the SDF's viewpoint. Those who already had power and who had access to the media were necessarily favoured. In particular this explains, if it does not excuse, the amount of space given to Belfort Bax and his supporters. They argued forcibly against the founding fathers, proposing not only that women were not oppressed but that they were, in fact, the privileged sex, practically and legally. In theoretical terms, such opinions could be viewed as merely idiosyncratic rather than reprehensible.

The SDF's lack of a policy on the woman question did not have a neutral effect. Bax's position as a key member of the party leadership, and the vociferousness of his attack, meant that feminists and their supporters within the SDF were quickly forced into a reactive position. Some, however, took a more relaxed line. As Herbert Burrows, a leading

---

[13]   See Boxer and Quataert (eds.), *Socialist Women*; Evans, *The Feminists*, ch. 3.
[14]   See *Justice*, 21 September 1895; 28 December 1895; 6 February 1897.

opponent of Bax, explained when he was once again accused of failing to rise to Bax's bait, 'There are certain things a man does not do, and one of these is to argue with a madman.'[15]

The lack of access for rank-and-file women to the socialist press and the negligible representation of women in the SDF's leadership minimised the initial response to Bax and his allies. The apparent lack of a vigorous counter-argument to Bax's variations on a theme of misogynism meant that Bax seemed to set the parameters for the debate. This in turn distanced women, and indeed sympathetic men, from the party.[16] For example, Catherine Davidson argued that if Bax's views were upheld by the party, then women had no place in the SDF and should resign forthwith. But if his views were not those of the party then they should not be published in *Justice*.[17] Some men also complained of Bax's continued ability to use the socialist press to insult women, particularly socialist women, and suggested that the solution lay in the hands of women SDFers.[18]

Without a re-evaluation of the socialist perspective on the woman question, there could be no advance on *Justice*'s liberal editorial position. The editor argued, 'I do not intend ... to be a party to creating any division whatever in our ranks about a matter which does not affect the material basis of Socialism, and over which, it seems to me, socialists might agree to differ, or at least discuss calmly and without malice.'[19] Yet the language and themes of one of the most significant SDF debates on the theory of the woman question suggested otherwise. Under the heading 'The Cult of Abstractions', a leader in *Justice* by Belfort Bax provoked a discussion which raged over the last months of 1895. Bax used the woman question to argue against socialism fetishising abstract concepts, such as equality. He felt that 'in pursuance of his fetish, abstract equality, the woman-sentimentalist is prepared to ignore all considerations of practical utility to the Commonweal'; his objection to equality was that he did not believe that women could ever be equal to men. Bax ridiculed the feminist, whom he assumed to be male, for espousing such a view. He countered that:

True equality involves that division of functions between the sexes best adapted for furthering the general well-being. This division must in the nature of things be subordinate to the physiological and the resultant psychological – ie. to the natural or organic as distinguished from the economic or social – abilities or

---

[15] *Justice*, 2 November 1895. See appendix 5 for a brief biography of Herbert Burrows.
[16] See *Justice*, 18 January 1908.
[17] *Justice*, 9 April 1910.
[18] *Justice*, 26 March 1910.
[19] *Justice*, 20 February 1897.

disabilities of the female sex. If it can be shown by science now, or if experience shows in the future, that women, owing to (dare I suggest the blasphemy?) inferior average mental capacity, liability to hysteria in the protean forms of that little-understood but widely spread morbid condition, are in general not so well fitted as men are for political, administrative or judicial functions, then to force women promiscuously into these functions, and thus sacrifice social welfare on the fetish formal Equality will be just as reasonable as the procedure of the Anarchist, who is prepared to immolate social progress and mankind in general on the altar of the fetish formal Liberty.[20]

Quite apart from the immoderation of his language, Bax here raised many of the issues which were to divide SDFers in their discussions on the woman question. These included whether women were oppressed, the meaning and desirability of sexual equality and the origins of sexual inequality (natural or social).

The tone of Bax's language was, however, important. His description of any 'cult' of an 'abstraction' – that is the 'conscience' issues of socialism – as 'fads' both trivialised the woman question and underlined its marginality from the central concerns of socialism. Certainly, the perception of the woman question as a 'fad' was often used as a way of curtailing debate; there was little point in giving time to something defined as irrelevant.[21] While the language used by Bax and his allies was important, more so were the areas of substantial disagreement on the woman question which surfaced within the party. The contradictory views produced a very ambiguous picture of the party's attitude to the woman question. These were, of course, founded on the ambiguities inherent in the theoretical construction of the woman question.

The sex/class analogy

For all socialists, the woman question was about the relationship between class and sex, and therefore a central area of dispute for SDFers surrounded these categories. In particular the debate focused on whether an analogy could be drawn between sex and class, as both Engels and Bebel had implied. As outlined in the previous chapter, the sex/class analogy was a highly ambiguous and underdeveloped concept in Engels and Bebel's writings. It was interpreted in various ways by SDFers, but no consensus was reached. This failure to agree had diverse ramifications for the SDF's discussion of strategy in relation to women.

For some, the most telling aspect of the sex/class analogy was the

---

[20] *Justice*, 19 October 1895.
[21] Examples of the editor curtailing debate on the woman question can be found in *Justice*, 28 December 1895; 5 March 1904.

assertion that woman was the proletarian in the home. One correspondent to *Justice* called herself 'Proletarian in the Home', and agreed with Clara Zetkin and Engels' description of woman's condition.[22] Another wrote that 'Engels was right when he said that woman is the proletariat – a slave, as I take it – of the home',[23] and concluded that women's and men's fight was the same, for male members of the proletariat were also slaves.

Others took the sex/class analogy further, making a direct analogy between class and sex. For example:

Man collectively treats woman as the capitalist treats both by witholding the means of subsistence as far as possible and so forcing the weaker party to accept what terms are offered. As a rule he is as much opposed to the emancipation of woman from his domination as the capitalist is to the emancipation of labour from the domination of capital.[24]

This made much more explicit men's responsibility for women's oppression, an aspect of the original analogy which its creators had skirted around. The same analysis was adopted by others. For instance, in 1907 G. Wilson of the WSPU maintained that 'from the highest to the lowest grade, women's labour is exploited by men'. In describing women as a class,[25] Wilson took a step beyond the dominant socialist understanding of the woman question. Such reasoning had strategic implications which were unacceptable to socialists. The Tattler, for example, argued: 'What I am especially concerned about is to protest against the endeavour to create a sex antagonism where there should be co-operation; to make out that women, as such, have interests apart from those of men, and to set up a solidarity of women against the solidarity of the working class.'[26] Women, specifically working class women, might share the same interests as the class as a whole, and even suffer their own particular oppression; but, for most socialists, they did not, and could not, constitute a separate class. Certainly, there was no room in Marxist analysis for women to constitute a class.

It is worthwhile to explore in a little more detail the implications of regarding women as a class. If women were a class, then an alliance with the proletariat, which the sex/class analogy was designed to promote, would mean a clash of interests: women would have to work with their male oppressors. Some socialists recognised the force of this argument, suggesting that there was both a class and a sex war. R. B. Kerr cited a

[22] *Justice*, 28 November 1896.
[23] *Justice*, 9 January 1897.
[24] *Justice*, 10 August 1895.
[25] *Justice*, 5 January 1907; also, 2 February 1907.
[26] *Justice*, 9 February 1907.

range of evidence: maternity, the second most essential industry after production, was not paid; the double standard of sexual morality; the multitudes of women condemned to unwilling celibacy or to unwilling motherhood; and the high incidence of rape. All these suggested that, 'it is as vain to tell women not to speak of the sex war as it is to tell workmen not to speak of the class war. Both agitations have come to stay and Socialists will do well to face the fact.'[27] M. M. A. Ward also shared this perspective although her understanding of class was not a precise one. Her argument was that:

The so-called 'sex war' is an outcome of conditions of injustice which lead to bitterness and recrimination. Just as unnatural economic conditions make one class of human beings bitter against another class, so do artificial relations between men and women promote dissensions which lead to unreal antagonisms. Thus we have the anti-feminist man and his corollary the woman who talks of 'sex war'. These types are excrescences which will only be got rid of when a just and rational basis of society has been evolved through the knowledge and inspiration of Socialism.[28]

Here the sex/class analogy was used in the sense of the founding fathers, for she saw both sets of 'unnatural' and 'artificial' relations being resolved in a socialist society.

J. B. Askew re-examined the concept of class war 'in view of the tendency to substitute the sex war of woman striving for her emancipation from the tyrant man'. He asked whether a sex war existed, and, if it did, whether it was more important than the class struggle. His conclusion made explicit what many SDFers already assumed; that the sex war was 'confined to certain sections of the bourgeoisie' and 'any attempt to direct the policy of working women on this basis will simply be to play into the hands of the enemies of their class'.[29] Proletarian men and women should work together for socialism and ignore any calls for sex solidarity. Quelch made this perfectly clear: 'The interests of working class women are those of their own fathers, brothers and husbands; not those of the plutocratic and aristocratic women, who exploit them.'[30]

This was also a view shared by socialist women. For example, Dora Montefiore spoke against sex war and for human emancipation:

Some women at the present time are interpreting things wrongly; they feel and resent much of the burdensome economic inheritance of the past; and forgetting that it presses almost as heavily on unprivileged men, they try to stir up a sex-war

27 *Justice*, 16 March 1907.
28 *Justice*, 30 March 1907. See appendix 5 for a brief biography of M. M. A. Ward.
29 *Justice*, 25 January 1908.
30 *Social Democrat*, July 1910, p. 292.

instead of preaching class-war ... they are making the fundamental mistake of stirring up an hysterical form of feminism, instead of setting before the people an understanding and reforming scheme of humanism.[31]

However, unlike some prominent SDFers, Montefiore's understanding of the sex/class analogy was to give primacy to the class struggle whilst ensuring that women had an equal role within it. Other SDFers not only doubted women's equal role in the struggle for socialism but disputed the sex/class analogy which underlay it.

Belfort Bax was, of course, the principal opponent of the sex/class analogy. Rather than adapting or modifying it, Bax questioned its fundamental assumptions. He was to call the analogy 'false', 'specious' and 'preposterous' for its attempt to link a biological category with an economic one, that of class.[32] This was particularly reprehensible, as he contended that 'feminist dogma has been smuggled into the [socialist] movement on the strength of a false analogy'.[33] Bax felt no need to explain what the strategic consequences were of this denial of a fundamental concept of the woman question; for him, it seemed as though women had no reason to participate in the fight for socialism.

The Tattler, a pseudonym which seems to have cloaked the identity of *Justice*'s editor Harry Quelch, was also a crucial participant in this debate.[34] Through his weekly column 'Topical Tattle', he sustained and gave even greater currency to Bax's rejection of the sex/class analogy. Not only did he repeatedly deny the veracity of the analogy but he blamed 'women's righters' for originating it, thus distancing the whole debate from socialism itself.[35] The Tattler was clear that 'Women are not a class, and the relations between men and women are not the relations existing between classes'. He argued that class divisions were 'superficial, material, social and artificial', whereas differences between the sexes were 'natural, fundamental, physiological'. Therefore, according to the Tattler, 'it should be understood that the claim of women to the suffrage is not the same thing as the claim of a class to be enfranchised from social, political or economic subjection'.[36]

However, such a rebuttal was specious, for the sex/class analogy was not concerned with whether sex was analogous to class but whether sex oppression was in any way analogous to class oppression. The Tattler

---

[31]   D. B. Montefiore, *Some Words to Socialist Women*, Twentieth Century Press, 1908, p. 13.

[32]   *Justice*, 28 November 1896; *Social Democrat*, July 1897, p. 202.

[33]   *Justice*, 8 February 1902.

[34]   See T. A. Jackson, *Solo Trumpet*, p. 62. See appendix 5 for a brief biography of Harry Quelch.

[35]   *Justice*, 31 October 1903; 21 January 1905.

[36]   *Justice*, 15 December 1906.

might have been correct to say that sexual difference was 'natural, fundamental, physiological' but it is very different to argue that gender difference and, specifically, sexual oppression is also 'natural'. Yet this was no accidental slip; both Bax and the Tattler refused to recognise that women suffered any oppression specific to them as a sex. Indeed, they claimed that women were a privileged group in society despite their inferiority to men. The opponents of Bax and the Tattler focused on these broader points rather than the Baxian opposition to the sex/class analogy itself.

In summary, the sex/class analogy was clearly a familiar, if disputed, term for SDFers. In their attempts to clarify it, various positions were espoused: sex was equated with class; sexual oppression was seen as broadly similar to class oppression; and sexual oppression was regarded as part of a broader class oppression. With no possibility of arbitration from an official party position the exact nature of the analogy remained obscure and it was possible for SDFers entirely to deny its validity. At best, the sex/class analogy remained a contested concept, a matter for the individual decision of SDFers, rather than one upon which the organisation as a whole took an unequivocal stand.

Woman's oppression as a sex

The question, of whether women were oppressed as a sex, and what that meant were also disputed within the SDF. Party members used a range of terms to describe women's condition – 'disabilities', 'dependence' and 'degradation' to 'subjection' and 'slavery'[37] – but applied them with little consistency or rigour. Nor was there any discussion of whether describing woman's condition as, for example, 'dependence' would have a particular ramification for strategy. In all of this, SDFers were, of course, following the example of the founding fathers. However, the dispute within the SDF was over a more fundamental question. Did women suffer from specific oppression as a sex?

Whatever their language, a significant number of SDFers accepted the argument that women suffered oppression in addition to that of class. Mary Gray pointed out that 'women are more enslaved than men today' while J. Sketchley believed that 'woman has ever been the victim of tyranny in all its forms'.[38] However, this was denied by a vocal and influential group of SDFers. The Tattler, of course, used his weekly column in *Justice* to deny the existence of sex subjection. He was

---

[37] *Justice*, 21 June 1890; 10 August 1895; 16 July 1887; 18 April 1896; 18 March 1893.
[38] *Justice*, 17 September 1892; 29 December 1906. See appendix 5 for a brief biography of Mary Gray.

partnered by Bax who also had much greater access to *Justice* than most SDFers. Between them, they created the impression of a substantial volume of objection to the woman question. This coloured others' perception of the party, both then and now.

The Tattler objected to any suggestion that women were subjected to men, and the inference that men as a group were responsible for women's condition.[39] He argued that any talk of sex subjection was 'mere cant and humbug' and 'so much nonsense'.[40] For him, the economic system was responsible for everything, even differential oppression, for women's oppression was a matter of degree not of form.[41]

The Tattler's conclusion that women's oppression was fundamentally a class issue was undeniably part of the founding fathers' construction of the woman question. His persistent presentation of this aspect of the question, helped to make the woman question invisible. Yet his perspective went even further than this. For coupled with the Tattler's critique of sex subjection went a broader claim which derived from Bax rather than from Bebel or Engels; namely that women were dominant or privileged. The Tattler asserted that 'So far from the condition of the women being the fault of the men, the very reverse is the case. They dominate the men, and make blacklegs and cowards of them.'[42]

The Tattler assumed the notion of privilege in much of his writing on women. He argued, for example, that, 'before equality can be secured, [woman's] privilege must be surrendered and worship must be given up'.[43] Women's numerous privileges included those in criminal and civil law, their exemption from military service, and the right of maintenance from a husband.[44] Moreover, this privilege extended across the boundaries of class: 'the working woman is quite as much privileged against the working man as the middle class woman against the middle class man'.[45] It was therefore unjust, so Bax argued, to increase their dominance by giving women the vote as well. Bax thought that feminists were trying to sustain this position of a 'sex aristocracy'.[46]

There were, of course, refutations of Bax. Yet views such as those of M. M. A. Ward – 'Women do not want privileges – they demand

[39] For example, *Justice*, 22 June 1895.
[40] *Justice*, 17 March 1894; 29 June 1895.
[41] *Justice*, 30 January 1897.
[42] *Justice*, 12 May 1894.
[43] *Justice*, 26 May 1894.
[44] *Social Democrat*, September 1904, p. 545. See also *Social Democrat*, March 1909, pp. 117–18. But 'KC' criticised Bax because his description of woman's condition did not apply to working-class women (*Justice*, 3 August 1895).
[45] *Justice*, 24 August 1895.
[46] *Justice*, 23 January 1897.

rights'[47] – made far less impact than Bax's. The SDF's understanding of the woman question ensured that a wide range of views on the nature and extent of women's oppression could be voiced within the party with no apparent distinction being made between each point of view. Yet the hierarchical nature of power within the SDF meant that the views of some, such as Bax and the Tattler, had a greater influence within the party than those of rank-and-file members.

Sexual equality

Just as there could be dissension over such a fundamental concept as women's oppression, so the meaning of sexual equality was also in doubt. Despite the fact that the social, political and economic equality of the sexes formed part of the SDF Programme there was no consensus as to the meaning of the phrase or, indeed, to what it committed the party.[48] Some seemed directly to flout this part of the Programme, while others felt that the party's commitment was clear and that reneging on it would be detrimental to socialism itself; 'Are we to have Socialism for men and still slavery for women?',[49] asked one correspondent to *Justice*. For these writers the concept of equality of the sexes was clear enough.

For others, however, the term was still in need of clarification. Some SDFers sought to define 'equality' more closely as the equality of value and opportunity that they took from Engels and Bebel's analysis of primitive society. In this interpretation 'equality' was not the same as 'identity'. Rather, the sexes would 'be on an equal plane' but the sexual division of labour would remain unchallenged. A leader in *Justice* elaborated this argument:

We do not for a moment admit the absurd theory that women are in every way equal to men ... [I]t would surely be a very dangerous principle to set up that social and political equality is to depend on absolute physical and mental equality ... Social, or Socialist, equality does not mean that everyone shall do precisely the same thing ... but that each shall do what he or she can best do for the common good, and that all shall be socially equal, no matter what the duty of each may be.[50]

Like Engels and Bebel, most of the proponents of this argument did not challenge the sexual division of labour which was at the root of such a

---

[47] *Justice*, 2 March 1907. See also *Social Democrat*, October 1904, pp. 597–601.
[48] *Justice*, 9 August 1890. The *Programme and Rules of the SDF* (Twentieth Century Press, 1894) included in the party's object 'the establishment of Social and Economic Equality between the Sexes' (p. 1). This remained in subsequent editions of the *Programme and Rules*, for example 1895, 1904, 1906.
[49] *Justice*, 9 February 1901; also 25 October 1902.
[50] *Justice*, 13 February 1897; also 23 January 1909.

differentiation of roles. Thus women were likely to continue to adopt a traditional role under socialism, although greater value would be attached to childcare, for example. Herbert Burrows was unusual in opposing this argument in his SDF pamphlet, *The Future of Woman*. He argued against strongly differentiated gender roles, noting that 'there will be no further question as to whether women shall always make beds and men always bake bread'. He did not believe that woman would be handicapped under socialism by her duties as wife and mother. In particular, he did not believe that the chief end of woman's life would be motherhood, although he admitted that this was an issue that was not agreed upon even by 'advanced women's advocates'. Nor did he believe that 'the woman of the future will find her chief glory in the pan, the dishcloth, and the scrubbing brush'.[51] Burrows' argument was unusual, but it showed that it was possible to challenge the sexual division of labour within the argument for sexual equality.

Yet there were, however, a few vocal dissenters from this analysis who were unable to accept that women could be equal, even when equality was defined in terms of equal value. Evacustes A. Phipson argued that even in an economically equitable socialist society, there could be no sexual equality. Man would always be superior; 'Not only would he still be physically stronger, probably also mentally, but a vastly larger proportion of women's time would be occupied in sex matters, in endeavouring to attract lovers by dress etc., in preparing for, bearing and rearing children, and in ailments and diseases peculiar to females'.[52] Phipson believed that sexual differences were innate, and no matter how much social differences were altered, these 'natural' differences would remain and preclude any real equality. Similarly, Bax did not believe that sexual equality was possible, because of what he saw as the immutable inferiority of women.[53] He even suggested, sarcastically, that the SDF Programme be amended so that it was clear that 'the word "equality" is to be understood in a non-natural sense, as implying "all the kicks" for the brute man and "all the halfpence" for the angel woman'.[54]

Bax and others were able to publish their prejudices and yet still remain Social Democrats. Implicitly, they rejected the Programme's demand for sexual equality; but they never baldly stated their opposition, merely suggesting that it was unrealisable and unimportant. The socialist

---

[51] H. Burrows, *The Future of Woman*, Twentieth Century Press, 1909, pp. 4,7,8.
[52] *Justice*, 16 January 1904.
[53] See for example Bax's essay 'Feminism in Extremis', *Social Democrat*, December 1902, pp. 361–6.
[54] *Social Democrat*, March 1909, p. 119.

construction of the woman question allowed them the space to exercise their conscience, and effectively to undermine what was generally regarded as a basic tenet of socialism, that of equality between the sexes.

Nature or nurture?

Fundamental to any debate on sexual equality was the question of the origin of women's condition, specifically whether it was natural – that is, biological in origin – or a product of nurture – that is, socially conditioned. Underlying the disagreements within the SDF were radically different views on this matter. Following Bebel and Engels, whose major contention was that the woman question was not a biological one, many SDFers cited historical and anthropological evidence in their argument that women's position was socially constructed. Edith Lanchester, for example, said, 'Custom and superstition separates the sexes and breeds confusion'.[55] Dora Montefiore explained how women might be perceived as inferior:

Presume a class or a sex unsuitable for certain functions, withhold from them suitable education, legislate for them so that they shall have no chance of ever fulfilling these functions, and give them a religion which teaches them at every turn they are marked out by divine law for the suffering of oppression and of disabilities, and it will not be surprising if general unsuitability for the fulfilling of these certain functions is the result.[56]

Many women SDFers understandably shared this view,[57] for socialism had little to offer them unless there was a possibility of change in women's condition. A majority of male members of the party also used this argument; but, once again, a small vocal group dissented.

Bax emphasised biological difference as the root of woman's condition, assuming as a consequence that these were immutable characteristics. In fact, he saw women as the personification of biology: 'Sex is an attribute of man, it is the substance of woman. Man has a sex but woman is a sex.'[58] Bax argued, therefore, that women were not only constrained by their biology but also confined by it to a position that suited their inferior capacities. He was joined in this stance by F. J. Gould, who elaborated on the biological factor which determined women's inferiority – her reproductive capacity. He argued that her

---

[55] *Justice*, 10 October 1896; also *Social Democrat*, December 1909, p. 538. See appendix 5 for a brief biography of Edith Lanchester.

[56] *Social Democrat*, May 1901, p. 138.

[57] See for example Kathleen B. Kough (*Social Democrat*, October 1907, p. 599) and 'Hopeful' (*Justice*, 23 September 1893).

[58] *Social Democrat*, June 1901, p. 168.

childbearing function 'makes peculiar demands upon her physique and lessens her ability for muscular or intellectual achievement'.[59]

Bax and his supporters' persistent argument that women were innately inferior brought a sharp rebuke from Burrows. He commented that under socialism 'This old, wretched idea of the Baxites that men and women must ever remain in the same grooves will be utterly exploded as a relic of the stupid past'.[60] The Baxian argument supported the status quo in terms of sex roles and painted a negative picture of woman's capacities including her capacity for change. Burrows' opposition might have been expressed in an unusually strong tone, but amongst the rest of the SDF there was agreement that essentially women's position was socially conditioned and therefore mutable. This latter position, indeed, was the one set out in *Woman* and in *Origin*. Bax's views ran counter to the whole spirit and tradition of the woman question, and it was therefore all the more remarkable that they should be so freely expressed. The lack of any sustained opposition to them from within the leadership of the SDF is comprehensible only because such views remained notionally the private views of individual SDFers.

Feminism

The woman question remained an issue for the SDF throughout its existence, for socialists were not expressing their views in a vacuum. They had a rival – feminism. This was a rivalry in both ideological and organisational terms. Feminism provided an alternative explanation of, and strategies to overcome, women's oppression, as well as offering a competing organisational focus for women. Crudely, it might seem that one movement defined itself primarily in terms of class while the other defined itself in terms of sex. But socialists were not willing to concede all the ground on sex to feminism, hence the socialist construction of the woman question. Neither Bebel nor Engels was opposed to the fight for equal rights for women. However, as we have seen, Bebel, in particular, provided the theoretical grounds for the Second International to develop an increasingly hostile attitude to what was termed 'bourgeois' feminism.

The SDF's attitude towards feminism developed as the feminist movement evolved. Like other parties in the Second International, it viewed feminism as a movement to benefit bourgeois women. Eleanor

---

[59] *Social Democrat*, June 1909, p. 251. In contrast to Gould, F Askew argued that it is woman's biology which makes her superior. In particular he cited her capacity for endurance as well as reproduction (*Social Democrat*, October 1904, p. 594).

[60] Burrows, *The Future of Woman*, p. 4.

Marx, for example, described the 'so-called "Women's Rights" question' as 'a bourgeois idea', while Enid Stacy described it as a 'middle class fad'.[61] Both Marx and Stacy felt that only socialism could address the reality of working-class women's lives and accord them true equality.

Other SDFers indulged in more personal attacks on feminism. 'The Sage of the Northern Heights' – a pseudonym which concealed the identity of a patronising rather than wholly misogynic man – described the feminist movement of 1894. He observed that the women's movement was growing and 'bids fair to bring about some great results', but he added that this would not affect working-class women. He described feminists as being chiefly single, lower-middle-class women, who, unable to find a husband 'eke out a living the best way they can. Dispirited in life, educated, and proud, they resent bitterly their social position, and they are calling out for freedom'.[62] Yet at this stage the 'Sage' could still see a role for such women in the socialist movement, provided they could accept the principles of collectivism.

Such magnanimity could not survive the polarisation of the two movements. By 1907, Kathleen B. Kough was able to say categorically that 'SDF women are strongly opposed to the "feminist" movement'.[63] Earlier, a report of the 1899 Women's International Congress, which appeared in *Justice* under the heading 'Futile Feminism', contained this disparaging picture of the delegates: 'women with smart frocks and indefinite ideas, whose chief pleasure was the talking of namby-pamby platitudes'.[64] Bax, always more vitriolic on this matter, wrote of 'the shrieking brotherhood and sisterhood' and of 'the rabid feminist' and 'his pet sex'.[65] He persisted in assuming that feminists were men, for surely such inferior creatures as women could not provide their own advocates? However, this was a fairly idiosyncratic approach within the SDF. Most of the debate between socialism and feminism came to focus on feminists' supposed espousal of 'sex antagonism' and 'sex war'.

There was some feeling that feminism exacerbated sex difference into sex antagonism. Thus Beatrice Browning wrote of 'a false campaign for women's rights, which is, in my opinion, setting up sex distinctions instead of making for equality'.[66] Even Dora Montefiore, who by today's criteria would be described as a feminist, wrote of women who 'try to stir

[61] *Justice*, 23 November 1895; 13 October 1894. See appendix 5 for brief biographies of Eleanor Marx and Enid Stacy.
[62] *Justice*, 18 August 1894.
[63] *Report of First International Conference of Socialist Women*, 1907, p. 30, in G. Tuckwell Papers, File 353. See appendix 5 for a brief biography of Kathleen Kough.
[64] *Justice*, 8 July 1899.
[65] *Social Democrat*, February 1901, p. 101; March 1909, p. 116.
[66] *Justice*, 25 October 1902.

up a sex-war instead of preaching class-war'.[67] This view did not, however, go unchallenged. Louisa Thomson Price denied that the feminist movement was about sex war. 'It is merely the outcome of the fact that woman has at last realised that the economic and political degradation of one sex means the gradual degeneration of both.'[68] Nevertheless, for most SDFers feminism was a movement that had to be opposed because it could divide the working class. This in itself made the woman question important.

Underlying Bax's hostility to all aspects of the woman question was a belief that its existence was evidence that 'feminist dogma has been smuggled into the movement'.[69] But Dora Montefiore denied this: 'It is not ... as a "feminist dogma" that the Woman Question has taken its right place in the Socialist demand, but as a "human dogma", and as part of a great evolutionary demand for the social, economic and political freedom of every human being'.[70] Only by socialists recognising that half the working class was female, and thus including their liberation within that of the class, could they hope to appeal to women who might otherwise seek support for their emancipation from feminists. The woman question was the theoretical domain where this rivalry was played out within the SDF. Not surprisingly, the practical strategies which flowed from this debate were shaped by the many dissensions within the party.

Strategic implications of the woman question

The strategic implications of the woman question concerned the relationship between women as a sex and the proletariat as a class. Essentially the issue was, where should working-class women put their energy? Amongst the SDF, understandably, there was no argument for complete separatism for women. However, given the dissensions over the woman question, there were varying degrees of encouragement given to women to involve themselves in the class struggle.

Many SDFers chose to emphasise women's responsibility within the class struggle. The Tattler pointed out that socialists did not ask workers to appeal to capitalists for freedom but, rather, argued for workers' determined self-organisation. He believed that women should do like-wise.[71] But the Tattler wanted it both ways, for he taunted women that

[67]   Montefiore, *Some Words to Socialist Women*, p. 13.
[68]   *Justice*, 25 September 1909.
[69]   *Justice*, 8 February 1902.
[70]   *Social Democrat*, April 1909, p. 151.
[71]   *Justice*, 21 April 1894.

'if they are not inferior, then ... they can do as much as men to secure their emancipation'.[72] This left the male socialist untouched by any criticism that a party which permitted misogynism might not seem the most appealing organisation to join if one were a woman. It was left to others to make the point; as J. W. Wood wrote, 'When Socialists learn to treat women now, as they will have to treat them in the coming commonwealth, they will be found responsive'.[73] For others, the strategic implication of the woman question was that men and women should work together in the fight against capitalism. This was to be 'a combined attack by both men and women on the economic conditions which enslave them' partly to forestall separatism.[74] Yet often this partnership sounded as though it had little to offer women in the short term. Take, for example, the implications behind T. Relton's statement, 'With the freedom of men will come the emancipation of women, and not before'.[75] Nevertheless, many women espoused such a partnership, as for example 'Jill' who wrote in the column 'A Woman's Point of View', 'Let us fight shoulder to shoulder, brother-man and sister-woman against the common foes – Capital and Privilege – each for all and all for each. The woman's cause is the man's, the man's cause is the woman's.'[76]

Yet for some SDFers such rhetoric did not go far enough. It had to be understood that 'without a conscious participation of the women in the class struggle of the proletariat against the bourgeoisie you will never see ... the realisation of socialism'.[77] I. D. Pearce called for woman's self-activity in the class struggle because 'it is not for men to say what women shall or shall not be "allowed" to do, but, actually, a necessity that women shall find out for themselves what faculties and capabilities they possess and develop them at whatever cost'.[78] Others argued for women's participation for the sake of socialism itself, believing that the revolution could not be achieved without the aid of women.[79] Dora Montefiore underlined this point in one of her pamphlets for the SDF's Women's Education Committee:

Nothing but a social and economic revolution, in which women themselves take a conscious and active part, can make for their complete emancipation. For this reason, we militant women strongly protest against the idea that Socialism can

[72] *Justice*, 7 July 1894.
[73] *Justice*, 14 April 1894.
[74] *Justice*, 26 May 1894. For opposition to separatism, see *Justice*, 13 May 1899.
[75] *Justice*, 8 November 1902.
[76] *Justice*, 19 January 1907. See also Annie Oldacre in *Justice*, 16 April 1904.
[77] *Justice*, 28 November 1896.
[78] *Justice*, 4 October 1902.
[79] *Justice*, 28 March 1896; 4 April 1909.

be given to us by men ... Socialism given to us would be only an added slavery. It is in working for our own emancipation that we shall gain that inner freedom, that sense of striking off our own chains, that really frees the individual.[80]

Certainly, any idea that women should wait passively until after the revolution was anathema to many of the women activists in the SDF. Margaretta Hicks felt that was 'worse than waiting for Heaven. Unless we do and say something now we shall all be dead and buried before any improvement is made. The revolution will come when we have worked for it.'[81]

For these women, the socialist construction of the woman question – even as it was interpreted within the SDF – integrated women into the socialist project, and demanded their full participation as equals in the struggle. These women demanded to be taken seriously; but, on occasion, the SDF's understanding of the woman question could militate against their participation in the party. The freedom permitted all party members to view the woman question as a 'conscience' issue, allowed some to air 'private' thoughts on women and their condition which ranged from the patronising to the misogynic. Consequently, there was little need for the principal opponents of the woman question, who deemed women to be naturally inferior and actually privileged, to express an opinion on the strategic implications of their argument. They merely implied that socialism was a man's world, and that woman could best support it from within her own domain, the home and the family.[82]

To sum up, the most important implication of the SDF's construction of the woman question was that it made a virtue out of the political vacuum it created around women. As a 'conscience issue', the woman question provided no measure for socialist practice in relation to women. As a consequence, it allowed all sorts of assumptions about women to gain credibility. It is important to recognise that this was not purely the result of individual prejudice and misogynism; it was rooted in the ambiguities of the theory itself. The particular combination of theoretical positions ensured that the woman question was not integrated into socialism itself. On the one hand, there was the SDF's limited economic definition of socialism which itself marginalised women. Added to this were the theoretical ambiguities of the woman question, in particular the paradox whereby women's oppression was recognised but immediately buried within the larger class question. The result was a continuation of the status quo both in ideological and

---

[80] Montefiore, *The Position of Women in the Socialist Movement*, p. 8.
[81] *Justice*, 6 April 1895. See appendix 5 for a brief biography of Margaretta Hicks.
[82] See, for example, *Justice*, 27 January 1900.

organisational terms. Moreover, those who benefited from this circumstance had recourse to a theoretical justification for the absence of a
party line on the woman question.

The SDF's construction of the woman question enabled its members
to hold a variety of different views on all the issues which formed it. In
this the woman question was no different from other 'conscience' issues
such as religion or teetotalism. However, the woman question was, in
strategic terms, more important than any other. It concerned a much
larger group in the population and a range of assumptions which were
fundamental to the way in which a whole sex might relate to socialism.
The absence of any agreed guiding principles for the woman question
meant that misogynism was no bar to membership of the party.

If these prejudices and assumptions had remained the dark secrets of
individuals, then the woman question would not have been as significant
an issue for socialists as it undoubtedly was. The fact that men
predominated within the party hierarchy, and within the pages of the
SDF press, gave individual men the opportunity repeatedly to express
their private views on women. Moreover, the party's analysis of the
woman question ensured that they were beyond official criticism or
sanction. It therefore became possible for a relatively small group of
opinionated men to dominate internal discussion within the SDF on the
substance of the woman question and, perhaps even more importantly,
to appear to be the voice of the whole party on these matters. The fact
that there was no party position on this question of individual conscience
became obscured to those outside the party, and even to some within it,
when persistent and loud voices proclaimed woman's inferiority, her
privilege and her limitations.

However, the party was officially committed to sexual equality in its
programme and needed to recruit women to the socialist cause if the
battle to end class society was ever to succeed. In that sense the woman
question could not be shelved, and in reality it rarely remained merely a
matter of private conscience. There were always members of the SDF
who recognised woman's oppression and argued for her emancipation as
an essential part of socialism. However, without a party position on the
woman question, they had few weapons other than argument against the
persistence of sexist assumptions about women, their capacities and
potential. The theoretical basis, derived from the founding fathers, for
the contention that working class women should identify with their class,
rather than their sex, was never fully explored. The practical effect of
this political vacuum around women will become apparent in part II,
where particular aspects of the woman question will be explored in more
detail.

3 Understanding the SDF and the woman question

There were various influences upon the SDF's construction of the woman question. The formulation of the founding fathers was crucial, as was the SDF's narrowly economic definition of socialism. But precisely because the woman question was understood as a matter of private conscience, the whole issue was also influenced by key individuals.

The figure who is most heavily associated with the SDF and the woman question is the misogynist Belfort Bax. Although Bax often seemed to set the terms of debate for the woman question within the SDF, the party was also part of the Second International. Within the Second International, the crucial influence on the woman question was that of Clara Zetkin. How did she affect the SDF's understanding of the woman question? This chapter explores the influence of Bax and of Zetkin in two separate studies. A third case study explores the similarities and differences in the ways in which the SDF understood and organised around the categories of race and sex. Together these studies clarify further the ways in which the SDF constructed the woman question.

The paradoxical Mr Bax

Ernest Belfort Bax was a prominent and long-standing member of the SDF who had a profound influence on his party's understanding of the woman question.[1] The fact that one individual could have such an effect on a wide-ranging set of issues is noteworthy in itself; but when that individual was also a well known misogynist, an explanation is required of his influence and its effect. Why was Bax not only tolerated but

---

[1]   For Bax, see his autobiography, *Reminiscences and Reflexions of a Mid and Late Victorian*, Augustus M. Kelley, New York, 1967, first published 1918; J. C. Cowley, 'The Life and Writings of Ernest Belfort Bax', PhD, London University, 1965; R. Arch, *Ernest Belfort Bax, Thinker and Pioneer*, Hyndman Literary Committee, 1927; J. Cowley, *The Victorian Encounter with Marx. A Study of Ernest Belfort Bax*, British Academic Press, 1992.

viewed as a friend by Engels, Eleanor Marx and William Morris? By what means did he sustain his influence within the SDF?

Bax was particularly important to the SDF's theorising of the woman question as he was a philosopher and writer. He has been termed the 'brain of the SDF'.[2] His writings on socialism concentrated on socialist morality and ethics from what he understood as a marxist perspective.[3] Cowley, Bax's biographer, has argued that Bax's main contribution was his attempt to formulate a theory of ethics which fitted into the marxist view of the world. In particular, Cowley stresses Bax's belief that the moral confusion and hypocrisy of bourgeois Victorian England made it necessary for marxists to state clearly what moral principles socialism offered the contemporary world. They also had to determine, so Bax believed, the ethical grounds for urging the proletariat to fight together to overthrow capitalism.[4] These interests meant that Bax was particularly concerned about issues which were part of the private sphere and this brought him into the domain of the woman question.

Bax argued against the prevailing view in the SDF, that 'conscience' issues were best not discussed as they were incapable of resolution by the party and would only exacerbate divisions within it. Bax was therefore in the curious position of arguing for discussion of the 'conscience' issues whilst opposing the very existence of the woman question. He could not accept any of the premises on which the founding fathers' formulation rested. But unlike many other SDFers, who fought shy of any lengthy disputations on the woman question, Bax relished such opportunities.

Bax's readiness to intervene in any discussion of the woman question was not merely a desire to provoke. His interest in socialism was almost exclusively an intellectual one, and he therefore courted debate, particularly on the page, as he was not a good public speaker.[5] E. P. Thompson's description of Bax gives some of the flavour of the man:

there *was* something funny about Belfort Bax. The truth is that he was an owl. There was a good deal in him of the music hall professor – the sudden fits of utter abstraction, the completely unpractical cast of mind, the essential lack of proportion which revealed itself in a blank absence of the sense of humour. His

[2]   C. Tsuzuki, 'The "Impossibilist Revolt" in Britain', *International Review of Social History*, 1, 1956, p. 379.

[3]   For example, *The Religion of Socialism*, Swan Sonnenschein, 1891, third edition, first published 1885; *The Ethics of Socialism*, Swan Sonnenschein, 1889; *Outlooks from the New Standpoint*, Swan Sonnenschein, 1891.

[4]   Cowley, 'Belfort Bax', p. 67.

[5]   T. P. O'Connor's obituary of Bax, *Sunday Times*, 28 November 1926. Also see C. Tsuzuki, 'Impossibilist Revolt', p. 379.

best work was done when Morris was at his elbow to bring him down to earth with a bang out of his naive ruminations.[6]

Henry Salt remembered Bax, 'the philosophic revolutionist', as a paradoxical man 'whose threatful attitude towards society was in a somewhat strange contrast with his own personal apprehensiveness'.[7] Despite the strong feelings he provoked, Bax seems to have kept aloof from the rank and file of the party and from people generally. He never had any close acquaintance with the workers, although a few of his close friends were working men, such as Mahon, Lane and Quelch.[8] Engels stressed Bax's 'unacquaintance with the world', his 'hermit-like simplicity'; he was a 'bookworm' and a 'hunter of philosophical paradoxes'.[9] Bax therefore developed his ideas within a virtual social vacuum: there was no test against political practice, little direct opposition, or even stimulation after Morris's death. This explains the force of language he used against opponents in *Justice*. He taunted in order to gain a response; but his isolation fed an arrogance which could not be swayed by the arguments of lesser mortals. The fact that many supporters of the woman question, such as Burrows and Eleanor Marx, refused to debate with Bax on his own terms only increased his frustration, and his arguments showed little development after the turn of the century.[10]

How, then, did Bax's anti-feminist thought fit with the body of his writing? Some historians, such as Meier, see Bax as merely inconsistent.[11] Cowley goes even further. He suggests that Bax's anti-feminism was a profound personal obsession which was almost completely irrational and bore no relation to the rest of his thought; Cowley concludes that there is no hint of anti-feminism within Bax's historical works or in his writings on socialist ethics.[12]

Was Bax's misogynism no more than an unfortunate aberration? Many contemporaries of high repute were very positive about Bax. Engels wrote of Bax's 'largeness of view', that he was 'very talented and understands something'. This was a compliment indeed from such a stern critic of British socialism.[13] Bax was particularly close to William

---

[6] E. P. Thompson, *William Morris: Romantic to Revolutionary*, Merlin, 1977, p. 373.

[7] H. S. Salt, *Company I Have Kept*, Allen and Unwin, 1930, p. 65.

[8] J. C. Cowley 'Belfort Bax', p. 122; W. Wolfe, *From Radicalism to Socialism*, p. 95.

[9] Engels to Laura Lafargue, 9 August 1887; Engels to Sorge, 29 April 1886 quoted in P. Meier, *William Morris: The Marxist Dreamer*, vol. 1, Harvester, Sussex, 1978, p. 225.

[10] S. Pierson, 'Ernest Belfort Bax (1854–1926): The Encounter of Marxism and Late Victorian Culture', *Journal of British Studies*, 12, 1, 1972, p. 56.

[11] Meier, *William Morris*, I, p. 225.

[12] Cowley, 'Belfort Bax', pp. 92–7.

[13] Engels to Laura Lafargue, 9 August 1887 quoted in Meier, *William Morris*, I, p. 225; Engels to Bebel, 18 August 1886, quoted in Thompson, *William Morris*, p. 422.

Morris in the early years of the Socialist League, through collaborative writing and as family friends. Meier concludes that Morris took Bax very seriously and that Morris felt he owed much of his understanding of Marxism to Bax.[14] Eleanor Marx also had a high opinion of Bax – he 'is excellent in all respects' – and she recommended him to others as a personal friend.[15] They too worked together in the Socialist League, as well as in the SDF, and in various journalistic ventures.[16] So how could individuals such as these not only work with but be close friends with a misogynist like Bax?

Eleanor Marx seems to have shared the view of historians that 'Bax – reasonable on many points is quite mad on others'.[17] This was sufficient for her to tolerate Bax into the mid-1890s. Similarly, May Morris remembered her father poking fun at Bax for his misogynism although she seems to have found Bax more disturbing. Certainly she had plenty of reason to feel so: she told this story about Bax – 'The papers reported one day the fall of a woman from Clifton Suspension Bridge when somehow or other her neck was not broken. Bax's comment was triumphant; she was the lower organism; man the higher animal, would have been killed.'[18] Bax, as everyone commented, did not have a sense of humour[19] and seriously believed that women were inferior to men.

Bax's opposition to feminism became more entrenched in the mid-1890s, from the 'Cult of Abstractions' debate onwards.[20] Bax was able to be the respected friend of leading socialists, not known for their anti-women views, partly because these friendships predated his most virulent anti-feminism. Engels, Eleanor Marx and Morris knew him best before then, when Bax was a member of the Socialist League; he resigned from the SDF in December 1884 and rejoined in 1888. During this period the influence of Morris, in particular, seems to have softened the edges of Bax's anti-feminism. Later he was able to give full rein to his prejudices and in so doing reaped Eleanor Marx's wrath.[21] But by the time of the 'Cult of Abstractions' debate in the autumn of 1895,

---

[14] Meier, *William Morris*, I, p. 226.
[15] Eleanor Marx to Laura Lafargue, 17 March 1884 quoted in O. Meier (ed.), *The Daughters of Karl Marx: Family Correspondence, 1866–98*, Penguin, 1984, p. 176; Y. Kapp, *Eleanor Marx*, II, p. 57.
[16] Ibid., pp. 33, 362, 366.
[17] Eleanor Marx to Laura Lafargue, 23 April 1886 quoted in Kapp, *Eleanor Marx*, II, p. 91.
[18] May Morris, *William Morris, Artist, Writer, Socialist*, II, Basil Blackwell, Oxford, 1936, II, p. 174.
[19] H. W. Lee and E. Archbold, *Social Democracy in Britain*; Meier, *William Morris*, I, p. 225; Thompson, *William Morris*, p. 373.
[20] Cowley, 'Belfort Bax', p. 103.
[21] Kapp, *Eleanor Marx*, II, p. 637.

Engels was dead and Morris was seriously ill.[22] While Morris and company may have moderated the public expression of his views, there is no doubt that Bax was always a misogynist. Without those whom he respected to mock and question his extreme views, there was no restraint on Bax's part. By the mid-1890s, the passive tolerance of some of his SDF colleagues only exacerbated his misogynist tendencies.

Yet given that Bax's misogyny was not explicitly shared by many SDFers, how did he manage to make such an impact on the party's discussions of the woman question? Bax certainly had greater access to the SDF presses than most other party members. His close friendship with Harry Quelch, who was editor of *Justice* from 1892 as well as manager of the party's press, aided the publication of his views.[23] Indeed, Bax's role as a freelance journalist gave him an undoubted advantage over rank and file SDFers in his contacts with, and access to, the socialist and non-socialist press. Moreover, because he lived on inherited income,[24] Bax did not have to trim his views for any editor. His confidence in print was reflected in his increasingly rhetorical and bombastic tone, what Rebecca West termed as 'Mr Bax's habit of writing at the top of his voice'.[25] To this was added his style – often abstruse, 'heavy and sometimes almost unreadable'[26] – which was influenced by his interest in German philosophy. This style and form of argument were peculiarly intimidating to the unpracticed; when it came to the woman question, Bax's manner of presentation was complicated further by an irrational form of argument.[27] Many of the more experienced of his opponents felt that as Bax set the terms of debate, there was little point in trying to out-Bax Bax; to debate with the man was to appear to sanction the rationality of his position – for who would argue with an irrational person?

Bax's anti-feminist writings continued to be printed in SDF presses presumably because they were provocative, and therefore good copy. The rationale must have been that provocation could be afforded on such a marginal matter as – on the SDF's understanding – it could not damage socialism itself. Bax's misogyny was tolerated as the weakness of a good Social Democrat which was more laughable than reprehensible.

22   This debate took place in *Justice* from October to December 1895 (see chapter 3). Engels died on 5 August 1895 and William Morris died 3 October 1896, having been ill for some time.
23   Bax (ed.), *Harry Quelch, Literary Remains*, Grant Richards, 1914, p. 19.
24   Bax was left £400 a year by his father in 1882. Nevertheless he found his finances somewhat stretched by his family responsibilities. He had six children during his first marriage (Cowley, 'Belfort Bax', p. 50).
25   *Clarion*, 21 November 1913.
26   Meier, *William Morris*, I, p. 226.
27   See, for example, Victor Grayson's comments in *Woman Worker*, 12 June 1908.

As a long-time member of the leadership of the SDF Bax's position seemed unassailable. There were, however, various attempts by rank-and-file members to censure Bax for his anti-feminism.[28] The publication of Bax's *The Legal Subjection of Men* by the Twentieth Century Press was particularly criticised, for example by Burrows:

That pamphlet was lauded and boomed in *Justice* by an editorial review; it was advertised as no socialist book has ever been advertised before, not even Hyndman's 'Economics' ... and it is being sold by some of our branches and stamped with their stamp ... Show me the vegetarian or vaccination pamphlet that has ever been thrust down our throats like this. I say deliberately that a persistent attempt has been made and is being made to put forward the pamphlet as an SDF book, as voicing that is, SDF opinions.[29]

As this was not, and could not be, SDF policy then surely, Burrows argued, it should not be allowed to be mistaken for it. Yet it seemed that the best that could be hoped for by way of denial was Quelch's repeated assertion that publication by what was seen as the SDF's publishing house was not an endorsement of any work as party policy or even as part of socialism.[30] Yet despite such denials, it was all too easy for Bax's views to be represented as those of his party.

Even if Bax's misogyny might not have coloured all of his thought in the eyes of fellow SDFers, his misogyny coloured their socialism in the eyes of many contemporaries. Subsequently, historians have taken a similar view.[31] Whether Bax's misogyny should be judged as merely an aberration depends on whether his views can be dismissed as a joke or a hobby horse, as several male historians feel able to do,[32] or whether it is felt such a taint cannot but have infected all of his thinking. Cowley insists that Bax's anti-feminism was a phobia or personal obsession which was kept in a watertight compartment separate from his views on socialism.[33] In contrast, Robert Arch, Bax's first biographer, concludes 'On this subject he was opposed to the overwhelming majority of Socialists both here and abroad, and his attitude, extraordinarily bitter as it was, alienated many, and maimed his otherwise magnificent work'.[34]

[28] See protests from Brixton SDF (*Justice*, 26 October 1895) and Willesden SDP (*Woman Worker*, 30 December 1908).
[29] *Justice*, 20 February 1897. See also *Justice*, 4 January 1908.
[30] See *Justice*, 24 November 1906. For the Twentieth Century Press, see *Justice*, 15 June 1907; J. M. Bellamy and J. Saville (eds.), *Dictionary of Labour Biography*, 8, Macmillan, 1987, pp. 204–8.
[31] For a contemporary example, see *Justice*, 23 January 1909 while the representation of the SDF as anti-feminist can be seen in O. Banks, *Becoming a Feminist; The Social Origins of 'First Wave' Feminism*, Wheatsheaf, Brighton, 1986, p. 23.
[32] For example, Thompson, *William Morris*, p. 374.
[33] Cowley, 'Belfort Bax', p. 93.
[34] R. Arch, *Ernest Belfort Bax*, p. 21.

Bax was therefore a paradoxical figure from many perspectives. He was the philosopher in the SDF who had had the closest relationship to Engels and he was the vehicle whereby others learnt of Marxism. He was deeply committed to rational argument, and yet was unable to apply such a standard to the woman question. As an exponent of historical materialism, he was nevertheless able to overlook the economic roots of modern feminism. Yet his concern for an ethical dimension to Marxism meant that he focused on the 'conscience issues' of the SDF, arguing for their centrality in socialism whilst simultaneously denying the existence of the woman question. His obsession with bourgeois hypocrisy centred on the family; in relation to that, and marriage itself, he adopted a libertarian position where he found himself agreeing with – or even being more radical – than the feminists he so opposed. Despite being out of step with most SDFers over the woman question, and certainly over his misogynism, Bax nevertheless managed to set the agenda for many of the SDF's discussions. The SDF's understanding of the woman question gave Bax the space to pursue his paradoxical position as socialist and misogynist.

Clara Zetkin, the International and internationalism

Clara Zetkin[35] has been described as, after Engels and Bebel, the principal socialist theoretician on the woman question.[36] Zetkin's pre-eminent reputation within the Second International, along with that of the German Socialist Women's Movement, which she led, heavily influenced the SDF's understanding of the woman question.

Zetkin's contribution to the theorising of the woman question was to clarify further the relationship between sex and class. Moreover, she translated Engels and Bebel's work into a practical strategy for the socialist movement in relation to women. In particular she set out to show that the interests of proletarian women lay with their class and not with the bourgeois women's movement. Her pamphlet *The Question of Women Workers and Women at the Present Time*, published in 1889, has been described as 'both the most important product of the literature of women's emancipation and the guideline for the ensuing policy of Social Democracy on the woman question'.[37] In it, Zetkin set out clearly all the

---

[35] For Clara Zetkin (1854–1933), see K. Honeycutt, 'Clara Zetkin: A Left-Wing Socialist and Feminist in Wilhelmian Germany', PhD, Columbia University, 1975. For a portrait of Zetkin through her close friendship with Rosa Luxemburg, see E. Ettinger, *Rosa Luxemburg: A Life*, Harrap, 1987, particularly pp. 100–2.

[36] Honeycutt, 'Clara Zetkin', p. 5.

[37] W. Thönnessen, *The Emancipation of Women: The Rise and Decline of the Women's Movement in German Social Democracy, 1863–1933*, Pluto, 1973, p. 44. Karen

arguments on the woman question thus far, underlining the intimate connection between women's and proletarian emancipation. But this clear and popularised exposition of the woman question was not translated into English and therefore its considerable impact in Germany was limited amongst SDFers to those readers of German who were able to acquire a copy.

Awareness among the SDF of Zetkin's position on the woman question might have been furthered by her speech to the 1889 Paris International where she again argued that working women could expect nothing from the bourgeois women's movement.[38] However, the speech's impact on the SDF was limited by the fact that the party was absent from this meeting of the International, as their representatives attended the rival Possibilist Congress.[39] In contrast, Zetkin's speech on women to the 1896 SPD Congress was reported in *Justice* by Eleanor Marx. She devoted a whole column to Zetkin's speech because, she argued, this was the best exposition to date on the theory and practice of the woman question.[40]

In this speech Zetkin differentiated between women's experiences of oppression on the basis of class. This constituted an important clarification of the woman question. Zetkin distinguished between three classes. The woman of the upper class, she argued, could develop her own individuality, but as a wife was still dependent upon a man. But it was amongst the middle class that 'the true struggle against man' existed. As Zetkin elaborated, 'The women of this class are sick of their moral and intellectual subjugation. They are Noras rebelling against their dolls' homes. They want to live their own lives, and economically and intellectually the demands of the middle class woman are fully justified.'[41] This is a much more sympathetic account of middle class women's oppression than many male socialists gave. Nevertheless, Zetkin suggested only that there was nothing inherently wrong about such demands from the perspective of the middle-class women who made them. But, she argued,

Honeycutt translates the pamphlet as *The Working Women Question and the Women Question of Today* (Honeycutt, 'Clara Zetkin', p. 72).

[38] Honeycutt, 'Clara Zetkin', p. 92. See also R. J. Evans, 'Theory and Practice in German Social Democracy, 1880–1914: Clara Zetkin and the Socialist Theory of Women's Emancipation', *History of Political Thought*, 3, 2, 1982, pp. 285–304, esp. p. 291.

[39] For the reasons for the divided Congress and the effect on the SDF, see Tsuzuki, *H. M. Hyndman*, pp. 114–18; G. D. H. Cole, *History of Socialist Thought, vol.3: The Second International, 1889–1914*, Macmillan, 1956, pp. 7–8.

[40] *Justice*, 7 November 1896. For a full translation of Zetkin's speech, see H. Draper and A. G. Lipow, 'Marxist Women versus Bourgeois Feminism', pp. 192–201.

[41] *Justice*, 7 November 1896.

problems arose when these demands were presented as being for the benefit of all women.

As for the proletarian woman, Zetkin argued that she had been 'drawn into the vortex of capitalist production' as cheap labour. This had brought her economic independence, but at a price for her and her family – 'neither as a person nor as a woman or wife does she have the possibility of living a full life as an individual'.[42] Zetkin explained the difference between the focus for proletarian woman's emancipation and that of middle-class women; unlike the middle-class woman, the proletarian woman did not have to fight the men of her class but instead worked with them in the struggle against the capitalist class. Zetkin carefully added that working-class women approved the demands of the middle-class women's movement 'but only as a means to the end that she may be fully armed for entering into the working class struggle along with the man of her class'.[43] Thus although the primacy of class for proletarian women was underlined, commitment to women's rights was not dismissed out of hand as merely bourgeois. Such demands were distinguished as a means rather than an end. Herein lay the significant difference between the movements calling on proletarian women's allegiance on the basis of *either* her sex *or* her class.

Zetkin emphasised in a part of her speech which was not quoted in Eleanor Marx's account, '[T]here is no such thing as a "women's movement" in and of itself ... [A] women's movement only exists within the context of historical development and ... there is therefore only a bourgeois and a proletarian women's movement, which have nothing more in common than does Social Democracy with bourgeois society'.[44] This seems to be an acknowledgement of a specific proletarian woman question. Yet this runs against the tenor of the founding fathers and of Clara Zetkin herself who, in arguing for the differential experience of proletarian and bourgeois women, implied that patriarchy was limited to the bourgeois class. Zetkin's use of the term 'independence' to describe working-class women of her day ignored both the reality of waged work for women – with no equality in pay, it cannot be said to have produced equivalent economic independence for men and women – and also rendered invisible those women who were not part of the labour force. Yet the thrust of her argument did not dwell on these issues but on the woman question as a class question; and hence the

[42] Clara Zetkin in Draper and Lipow, 'Marxist Women versus Bourgeois Feminism', p. 196.
[43] *Justice*, 7 November 1896.
[44] Honeycutt, 'Clara Zetkin', p. 194.

need for systematic propaganda among proletarian women as a necessity for the socialist movement.

This 'brilliant speech' was never published verbatim in English during the lifetime of the SDF. Nevertheless, Clara Zetkin's contribution to the woman question was recognised within the party.[45] Zetkin's influence was undoubtedly reinforced by her identification with the most successful socialist women's movement of the Second International. The German experience showed in practice that clear delineation from the bourgeois women's movement, and deliberate socialist propaganda amongst women, could produce a strong and active socialist women's movement. Hence when the SDF needed to counter bourgeois feminism – in the shape of those women fighting for limited women's suffrage – the party turned naturally to Clara Zetkin's words, publishing one of her speeches as the pamphlet *Woman Suffrage*.[46]

Again Zetkin distinguished between the socialist and the bourgeois women's movement, emphasising that 'Between these two classes there yawns an antagonism of interests which no talk about the universal sisterhood of women can bridge over.'[47] This position has lead Jean Quataert to describe German Social Democratic women as 'reluctant feminists', who faced persistent tensions between their loyalty to class and sex but for whom, ultimately, feminism was a secondary concern overshadowed by the larger task of the class struggle.[48] Although this message of the primacy of class even on women's issues was the one that the SDF took from Clara Zetkin, she provided another through the practical example of the German socialist women's movement.

Although the membership of the German socialist women's movement had reached nearly 175,000 by 1914,[49] Clara Zetkin and other socialist women had developed their practice in what initially seemed to be unpropitious circumstances. Women were barred from joining political parties in most parts of Wilhelmine Germany until 1908. Yet

[45]   See, for example, *Justice*, 28 November 1896; 9 January 1897.

[46]   Originally titled *Woman Suffrage and Social Democracy*, *Woman Suffrage* was a translation of Clara Zetkin's speech to the Socialist Women's Conference at Mannheim in 1906. It was advertised in the women's column of *Justice* (e.g. 3 April 1909) and in the pamphlet *Some Words to Socialist Women*. It was also being read: the secretary of Blackburn Women's Circle read *Woman Suffrage* to the group when another speaker did not arrive (*Justice*, 16 April 1910).

[47]   C. Zetkin, *Woman Suffrage*, Twentieth Century Press, 1907, p. 3.

[48]   Quataert, *Reluctant Feminists*, p. xi.

[49]   For a table of the membership of the SPD women's movement, 1905–14, see R. J. Evans, 'Politics and the Family; Social Democracy and the Working Class Family in Theory and Practice before 1914' in R. J. Evans and W. R. Lee (eds.), *The German Family*, Croom Helm, 1981, p. 283. For the SPD women's movement, see Honeycutt, 'Clara Zetkin'; Quataert, *Reluctant Feminists*; Thönnessen, *The Emancipation of Women*; Evans, 'Politics and the Family'; Evans, *The Feminists*, pp. 159–65.

in the years of illegality, the German socialist women's movement was able, with the sanction of the SPD, to sustain an independent existence. Zetkin's 1896 speech, in particular, had allayed fears that this might be a separatist or 'feminist' enterprise, for she had insisted on the unbridgeable class gulf between feminists and socialists. The party therefore backed the necessary autonomous organisation of women. The women had their own newspaper, *Gleichheit* ('Equality'), which Zetkin edited, their own organisers and congresses. After 1908 when the legal constraints on women's full membership of the party were removed, the SPD attempted to integrate and limit their women's movement. Despite a rhetorical commitment to the woman question, the party as a whole was not particularly supportive to its own women's organisation and wanted it to fulfil a subordinate rather than equal role. This gulf between revolutionary theory and a practice which fell well short of that, was not particular to the woman question but was characteristic of the SPD as a whole, and indeed of Second International socialism.[50]

This gap between theory and practice formed the context for the evolution of the SDF's own politics. The SDF could see that there was a proletarian women's movement *within* the SPD which produced a woman-focused socialism where class was still the defining feature but gender was not entirely obliterated. They could also see that, in terms of numbers, this was a remarkably successful way to organise women in relation to a socialist movement. Thus the practical ramifications of Zetkin's contribution to the theory of the woman question, in the shape of the German socialist women's movement, provided an example to the SDF if they chose to follow it and an inspiration to many of its women members.

Why should the experience of another country's socialist movement be of particular significance to the SDF? The key was, of course, the domination of the Second International by Zetkin's party, the Social Democratic Party (SPD). The relationship of the SDF with the SPD was like that of a younger to an elder sibling; there was respect and interest in their work but there was also some resentment at their success and dominance at all family occasions. *Justice* reported on the SPD more than any other socialist organisation; covering its congresses and its election results as well as the activities and the deaths of German Social Democrats. Such coverage symbolised internationalism amongst British Social Democrats which was only seriously disputed in the years

---

[50] See G. Roth, *The Social Democrats in Imperial Germany*, Bedminster Press, Totowa, New Jersey, 1963; W. L. Guttsmann, *The German Social Democratic Party, 1875–1933; From Ghetto to Government*, Allen and Unwin, 1981.

immediately before 1914.[51] Most importantly, it assured that SDF women would be aware of their sisters within the SPD.

The SDF's internationalism has been obscured by the retrospective representation of the party as the creature of Hyndman. Although Hyndman's relationship with the SPD was never a very happy one – he criticised them for being too doctrinaire – his views were far from typical.[52] The growth of his national chauvinism in relation to Germany affected the party, but he did not speak for the party as a whole. Women, in particular, might well have been more internationally minded partly because they regarded the theory and practice of the SPD on the woman question as a positive model rather than as a rival. Certainly, some women members of the SDF played an important role in sustaining the party's internationalism. During her lifetime, for example, the international reports in *Justice* relied heavily on the contributions of Eleanor Marx. Marx's extensive international contacts, and her facility with languages, meant that she was often called on to translate texts and at international meetings. A decade later, Dora Montefiore filled a similar role. Although she did not have the same socialist pedigree as Eleanor Marx, her extensive travels and fluency in several languages gave her an entrée into international socialist and feminist circles which was reflected in her domestic journalism.[53]

The links between SPD and SDF women were enhanced by personal networks. In addition to Eleanor Marx, by 1905 *Justice* was able to name three women in particular as 'home grown Social Democrats [who] enjoy great and world-wide reputations' – Dora Montefiore, Rose Jarvis and Mrs Despard.[54] Of these, the most important was undoubtedly Dora Montefiore, a friend of Clara Zetkin and Alexandra Kollontai.[55] All three were part of an international network of socialist women whose mutual friendship helped to reinforce their commitment to internationalism. Montefiore's own internationalism featured strongly in her writing for the SDF press, particularly 'Our Women's Circle' which she edited in *Justice* from March 1909 to the end of 1910; this showed

[51] For BSP debates on militarism, see Kendall, *The Revolutionary Movement in Britain*, pp. 46–62; Tsuzuki, *H. M. Hyndman*, pp. 194–215.

[52] Tsuzuki, *H. M. Hyndman*, pp. 122–5, 206–8. Ironically, even Keir Hardie agreed with Hyndman on this, see K. O. Morgan, *Keir Hardie, Radical and Socialist*, Weidenfeld and Nicolson, 1975, p. 183.

[53] Kapp, *Eleanor Marx*; D. B. Montefiore, *From a Victorian to a Modern*, E. Archer, 1927. See appendix 5 for brief biographies of Rose Jarvis and Charlotte Despard.

[54] *Justice*, 22 April 1905. Dora Montefiore was also profiled as a great internationalist in *Social Democrat*, August 1911, p. 373.

[55] For example, it was Dora Montefiore who invited Clara Zetkin to Britain in 1909. For an account of this visit when Clara Zetkin was accompanied by Alexandra Kollontai, see Porter, *Alexandra Kollontai*, pp. 164–8. See also *Justice*, 1 May 1909.

examples of other socialist women's practice, particularly from Germany as well as from America and Russia.[56]

With the establishment of the Socialist Women's International in 1907, Britain had its own Socialist Women's International Bureau. As the ILP refused to participate this became principally a SDF organisation.[57] Dora Montefiore played a key role in the Bureau communicating directly with Clara Zetkin who, as Secretary of the Socialist Women's International, linked its national sections through *Gleichheit*. From 1907, pieces by Zetkin and others taken from *Gleichheit* appeared in *Justice*.[58] Similarly, Dora Montefiore contributed a piece for *Gleichheit* in honour of Bebel's seventieth birthday.[59] Yet all this was occurring at a time when, according to historians, the national party was becoming increasingly chauvinistic. The internationalism of SDF women was clearly far from typical. Indeed, Dora Montefiore resigned in 1912 from what had become the BSP because of the growing chauvinism of her own party; she rejoined, in 1916, when the pro-war Hyndman and his supporters left. Like other SDF women, Dora Montefiore was involved in anti-militarist activity. This seems to have linked many women across the International, pre-eminent amongst whom was Clara Zetkin.[60]

Zetkin, as we have seen, was an extraordinarily important figure for women in the Second International. She represented the strongest socialist women's organisation in the International which both inspired and also provided a practical example to socialist women in other countries. She was also personally responsible for the inauguration and co-ordination of the Socialist Women's International which helped to share experiences and strategy across national boundaries. Most importantly she provided the synthesis of the founding fathers' theory and practical experience which produced the SPD's and the

[56] For international reporting in 'Our Women's Circle', see *Justice*, 15 May 1909; 29 May 1909; 12 June 1909; 14 May 1910; 11 June 1910.

[57] For the ILP's view of the Socialist Women's Bureau (British), see Johnson to Hendin, 19 October 1907, Francis Johnson Papers, 1907/238 and Johnson to Hendin, 12 May 1908, Francis Johnson Papers, 1908/183. The Bureau included representatives from the SDP, the Women's Committee of the SDP, Fabian Society, Clarion Scouts, Teachers' Association and the Adult Suffrage Society (*Justice*, 10 August 1908).

[58] For *Gleichheit*, see *Justice*, 3 July 1909; 29 January 1910. Examples of Zetkin's writing are in *Justice*, 1 May 1909; 9 October 1909.

[59] *Justice*, 26 February 1910.

[60] For socialist women's anti-militarist activities during the First World War, see Thönnessen, *The Emancipation of Women*, pp. 75–9; A. Balabanoff, *My Life as a Rebel*, Indiana University Press, Bloomington, 1973, pp. 130–3; Porter, *Alexandra Kollontai*, pp. 210–1. The role of socialist women in anti-militarism in this period has not yet been fully acknowledged, see, for example, A. Wiltsher, *Most Dangerous Women: Feminist Peace Campaigners of the Great War*, Pandora, 1985. This could be because their socialism, and particularly their support of adult suffrage, has marginalised them from some current definitions of feminism.

International's understanding of the woman question. Zetkin clarified the question of loyalties for proletarian women, by stressing the primacy of class and thus of socialism, as against sex and therefore bourgeois feminism. Her ideas illustrated the dilemmas faced by SDF women in understanding the complex relationship between sex and class. Her practice indirectly affected SDF women in their own attempts at organisation, and directly impinged upon them through the Socialist Women's International and, more particularly, through the person of Dora Montefiore.

A comparative case: race

One of the themes of this book is the way in which socialists, specifically the SDF, understood the categories of sex and class, and the relationship between them. By examining the party's treatment of a further category, that of race, an assessment may be made on the degree to which their analysis of the woman question was idiosyncratic.

Race was drawn into the discussions of the woman question in relation to the concept of equality. In this period, many socialists and non-socialists shared the patronising assumption that there were lower races who were like children compared to white Europeans.[61] Such fundamental differences precluded any form of real equality and led to the recommendation for separate development. For example, it was argued in *Social Democrat* that 'Socialism is a doctrine proclaiming the fundamental identity for a common socio-political life of the men of the progressive races', but this excluded 'the negroid branch of the human family' on the grounds of 'an organic difference of a deep-lying, if not fundamental, character'.[62]

In Bax's original 'Cult of Abstractions' article, which questioned the validity of absolute equality, the issue of race was addressed alongside that of sex. Bax argued against absolute racial equality as well as against formal sexual equality. He argued that black people had a right to follow their own social development in areas where they were indigenous. Indeed he insisted, 'This, and not the futile attempt to combine in a single organised community on a basis of equal political rights, two entirely disparate and antagonistic racial elements is the form that true and real, as opposed to sham and abstract, equality must obviously

---

[61]   For the broader context of contemporary ideas about race, see C. Bolt, *Victorain Attitudes to Race*, Routledge and Kegan Paul, 1971; G. Jones, *Social Darwinism and English Thought: The Interaction between Biological and Social Theory*, Harvester, Brighton, 1980, ch. 8; P. B. Rich, *Race and Empire in British Politics*, Cambridge University Press, 1986, esp. ch. 1.

[62]   *Social Democrat*, September 1904, pp. 535–6.

take'.[63] Bax believed that, like the sexes, there was a natural hierarchy among the races based on organic difference. Moreover, Bax assumed that his views on racial difference were less contentious to his comrades than those on sexual difference. He therefore used race to reinforce his arguments on sex.

A good example was Bax's implacable opposition to women's enfranchisement. He had argued that the way to solve the 'negro question' in America would be to exclude blacks from the franchise in 'white' states, whilst handing over the whole of the government of the southern states to the 'negro' (male, presumably) to the exclusion of the white population. This proposal was challenged by W. H. Humphreys. However, interestingly, Humphrey's challenge was based on a contradiction in Bax's position on the race and woman questions; he was not concerned with Bax's racist assumptions. Humphreys suggested that if Bax's solution to the 'negro problem' were applied to the sex problem, it would justify women's enfranchisement and disenfranchise men, who constituted a minority to the female majority in the population.[64] Bax did not use this argument again!

Significantly, Bax's analysis treated 'race' as a far more important concept than that of 'sex'. Indeed, class and race were categories which he recognised for political analysis; sex emphatically was not. Furthermore, and characteristically, Bax's analysis of racial oppression was almost entirely in the abstract. He had no conception of the particular ways in which class, race and sex oppression interact and reinforce one another.

The issue of race was addressed in this period most frequently in relation to the Jewish question.[65] Studies by Cohen and others reveal the pervasiveness of anti-semitism amongst British socialists of this period, including the SDF.[66] The SDF's anti-semitism provides another way of illustrating the similarities and differences between the party's treatment of sex and race.

[63]   *Justice*, 19 October 1895. For a comparison with the assumptions of Marx and Engels, see D. Paul, ' "In the Interests of Civilization": Marxist Views of Race and Culture in the Nineteenth Century', in M. C. Horowitz (ed.), *Race, Class and Gender in Nineteenth Century Culture*, University of Rochester Press, Rochester, New York, 1991.

[64]   *Social Democrat*, October 1904, p. 597.

[65]   For an exploration of the contemporary labour movement's attitudes to race, see K. Lunn, 'Race Relations or Industrial Relations?: Race and Labour in Britain, 1880–1950', in K. Lunn (ed.), *Race and Labour in Twentieth Century Britain*, Frank Cass, 1985.

[66]   S. Cohen, *That's Funny You Don't Look Anti-Semitic: An Anti-Racist Analysis of Left Anti-Semitism*, Beyond the Pale Collective, Leeds, 1984, esp. pp. 19–36; P. D. Colbenson, 'British Socialism and Anti-Semitism, 1884–1914', PhD, Georgia State University, 1977.

Like the woman question, the Jewish question was seen by many SDFers as an economic issue. A distinction was made between rich and poor Jews. Often, the Jewish capitalist was identified as 'par excellence the personification of international capitalism'.[67] Jews, like women, were stereotyped by the SDF. Jews were either 'imperialist financiers' or 'lumpen scabs', and this was reinforced by the campaigning and often virulent debates which led to the Aliens Act of 1905. There was a significant strand amongst SDFers – and socialists in general – which held that attacking capitalism and attacking Jewry were interchangeable parts of the economic analysis of socialism. Bebel called this the 'socialism of fools'.[68] Both Hyndman and Quelch, however, displayed these prejudices but denied that they were anti-semitic. For them, attacking capitalist Jews, or bourgeois women, was only about class and not about race or gender.

A comparison of reactions to displays of anti-semitism or misogynism by SDFers reveals both parallels and some significant differences. Anti-semitism attracted strong reactions from members, particularly but not exclusively Jewish SDFers, who argued firmly that the equation of international capitalism with Jewry was unequivocally anti-semitic. Anti-semitism, they pointed out, should be anathema to socialism. This issue came to a head during the Boer War, when SDF opposition to the war provided Hyndman with the space to argue that it was the product of an international Jewish conspiracy.[69] In response J. B. Askew argued that the editorials of *Justice* should not be used to propagate members' 'individual fads and fancies – much less to make remarks which can hardly fail to be offensive to a large section of our comrades'. He warned against 'substituting futile racial bickering for the class war'.[70] For some weeks, the only correspondence published was highly critical of the identification of the SDF with anti-semitism. As M. Shayer wrote, '*Justice* is on the high road to real anti-semitism ... We accept your assurance of your good sentiments, but *Justice* cannot be judged by that; it must be judged by what you write in it'.[71]

Hyndman and Quelch's response to this criticism shared many of the characteristics of the discussions over the woman question. There was, for instance, the claim that rather than being anti-semitic, the article or comment in question was merely 'a statement of facts'.[72] Then there was the disingenuous denial of anti-semitism followed by a repeated

[67] *Justice*, 9 September 1899.
[68] Quoted in Cohen, *That's Funny You Don't Look Anti-Semitic*, p. 9.
[69] For example, 'The Jews War on the Transvaal', *Justice*, 7 October 1899.
[70] *Justice*, 9 September 1899.
[71] *Justice*, 7 October 1899.
[72] See the editorial comment in *Justice*, 9 September 1899.

avowal of the offending sentiments. Hyndman even resorted to claims of personal friendship with Jews in his own defence. All these strategies find their parallel in responses within *Justice* to criticism over the patronising attitude of some SDF men towards women.

Other attitudes expressed towards critics of anti-semitism within *Justice* also have a familiar ring. One was the rehearsal of the detail of the prejudiced stereotype, followed by a denial that the writer actually believed this. Most space was thus given to the repetition of the prejudice, rather than to the denial. This tactic was often linked with the assumption that there was some truth in the stereotype, and that the oppressed group in some way brought vilification upon themselves. For example, from the front page of *Justice*: 'We do not aver that the Jews have themselves to thank to a great extent for the bitter feeling against them ... They are exceedingly purse-proud when wealthy, very arrogant, very unscrupulous and very clannish'. This piece continued in a defensive tone which was also often used in relation to the woman question. The writer complained that somehow Jews were thought to be beyond criticism, for 'if anyone says anything against the Jews he is immediately accused of prejudice, of race hatred, of heaven knows what'.[73] This hardly constituted a prelude to self-criticism. Indeed, there was even the suggestion that Jews, like women, were too sensitive to these matters; they were urged 'not to be so thin-skinned over such a trifle, or so narrow'.[74] Once again the victim was to blame.

It was not just the tone and attitudes reflected in the response to criticism of anti-semitism which bore a strong likeness to those marshalled against the proponents of the woman question. Some of the arguments used by the critics also show a strong similarity. It was argued, for instance, that senior members of the party abused their positions of influence so that their personal views were printed. These could then be mistaken for party policy. Thus J. B. Askew could have been writing about the woman question when he stated in the Jewish question debate, 'I think that it is a serious question for the SDF how long they can with impunity allow their organ to be made a playground for certain eminent members to air their fads in, and to endanger the whole cause of Social Democracy thereby.'[75]

It was also the case that Hyndman and Quelch's anti-semitic remarks were printed without comment, but those that were printed in opposition 'find that notes by the editor are invariably appended, the apparent

73 *Justice*, 26 August 1899. See also *Justice*, 28 October 1899.
74 *Justice*, 4 November 1899.
75 *Justice*, 14 October 1899.

object being to discredit the writers opinions'.[76] This also happened to critics of the representation of women within *Justice*. But here there was a difference, explained by the different degrees of access enjoyed by the principal opponents in each question. Those who opposed anti-semitism within *Justice* included Theodore Rothstein and Belfort Bax, who were both influential in the party. Although their letters appeared alongside equally vehement ones from rank-and-file SDFers, their undoubted influence with the SDF leadership gave a greater force to their intervention. With the woman question, where the marginality of women within the organisation minimised their access to the centres of decision making, women's opposition in the press appeared to be much more muted.

There were parallels too, between the arguments made by the critics of anti-semitism within *Justice* and those made by feminists. Speaking from their own experience, opponents challenged the economic analysis that some SDFers made of Jewry, pointing out that race prejudice affected all Jews, rich or poor. The effect of campaigns against capitalist Jews would only rebound on poor Jews, whom the SDF maintained they supported. As one member wrote, 'I have seen with my own eyes that the result of such an agitation was the loss of life and property of the poor Jews'.[77] Therefore the SDF would have to choose whether it was for international Social Democracy or for race prejudice; the two were mutually exclusive.[78] Rothstein spoke for all the critics when he said that anti-semitism constituted 'an indelible stain on English Socialism'.[79] Nor was claiming merely to reflect the commonly held assumptions of the time any defence, for the critics argued that to claim to be socialists, SDFers had 'to rid themselves of the race prejudice they have imbibed with their mother's milk'.[80] Such opposition to the anti-semitic tone of *Justice* appears effectively to have curtailed further excesses from being published; there were few anti-semitic letters in *Justice* after 1899.[81] Anti-semitism became far less publicly acceptable than mere misogynism. But this is not to argue that both were not part of the fundamental assumptions of many SDFers. It merely implies that the opponents of anti-semitism had more of an effect on limiting the public utterances of the SDF's more anti-semitic members.

Opponents of anti-semitism were able to make this a central matter at

---

[76] *Justice*, 11 November 1899.
[77] *Justice*, 7 October 1899. For Rothstein's exposition of the workings of anti-semitism see *Justice*, 21 October 1899.
[78] *Justice*, 14 October 1899.
[79] *Justice*, 28 October 1899.
[80] *Justice*, 7 October 1899.
[81] See, for example, *Justice*, 4, 11 November 1899.

the 1900 SDF Annual Conference. This was an important achievement but one which was unmatched by any equivalent action with regard to anti-women attitudes. The attack on the anti-semites within the party took the form of a resolution. This reflected its unlikely parentage, for Quelch was involved in its drafting with the Jewish socialist Joseph Finn, John Spargo and Herbert Burrows. The resolution which was adopted by the Conference did not constitute as clear a statement as the critics had demanded.[82] For example, it included references to international capitalism in a manner reminiscent of some of the criticised remarks of Hyndman and Quelch. Nevertheless, it went some way towards the complete rejection of anti-semitism; without, however, making it an offence for which an SDFer could be expelled from the party.

The report of the Conference in *Justice* reflected some of the membership's ambivalence.[83] But the Conference's decision was an important recognition at an organisational level that anti-semitism was a problem with which socialists had to deal. This was a sharp contrast to the policy on the woman question. There was little comparable recognition at a party level of the damage that the pervasive attitude to women expressed in SDF publications had on women, or on their perception of the SDF and of socialism.

This difference between the way in which race and sex were treated by the SDF was partly a consequence of the way in which Jewish members organised within the party. The SDF had separate Jewish branches where Yiddish was used.[84] This was partly due to the concentration of Jewish members within certain geographical areas, such as the East End of London; but it was also a recognition of a pre-existing tradition of separate organisation in, for example, the Bund and in Jewish trade unions. On the other hand, the positive and pragmatic arguments for separatism were reinforced from a much more negative perspective by the prejudice of some SDFers, who argued for separate organisation for those of an 'alien race'. This kind of argument suggested that as the SDF was principally a propagandist organisation, large numbers of a 'foriegn element' amongst its membership might 'repel or cause the newly awakened to hesitate about joining us on account of language troubles for fear of the alien'.[85]

The argument for separate but equal branches for Jewish members never carried the same force when applied to women members. They

[82] *Justice*, 11 August 1900.
[83] Ibid.
[84] For example Whitechapel SDF was a Yiddish speaking branch (*Justice*, 24 March 1894).
[85] *Justice*, 30 March 1907.

were never able to achieve separate yet equal organisation. The Women's Socialist Circles, formed from 1904, were attached to existing branches rather than having the status and recognition of branches in their own right. Women's desire for self-organisation was thwarted by the fear, amongst the male party leadership, that separatism was a manifestation of feminism. Moreover, Jewish members were, in some respects, more fortunate that the practical questions of geography and language combined with the prejudices of others to sustain their traditions. In contrast, women were not concentrated in any particular area, nor was language a problem; with little tradition of any form of organisation, prejudice could dictate their position and form of organisation.

In summary, there were many similarities between the tone and the type of response made by the SDF to the problems of race and sex. The similarities consisted of the hold enjoyed by a few individuals over the party press, and their use of it to parade their own prejudices. The anti-semites and sexists also share similar reactions when criticised for positions which, theoretically at least, were recognised as incompatible with socialism. The principal difference is demonstrated by the coherence and vehemence of the opposition to anti-semitism in the Boer War period, contrasted to the more muted, but long-lived complaint, that the party's theory and practice on the woman question were out of alignment. In the wider society of the time, it would have been futile to speculate on the relative power of Jews as against women, for the two groups were fractured by race, sex and class and were not comparable. Yet within the SDF, anti-racist[86] members were more successful in making their case heard than the anti-sexists. This reflected the relative power of the particular SDFers involved. Anti-semitism remained something which the majority of socialists did not want to be openly associated with, despite the anti-semitic feelings of many. There was, by comparison, no critical mass of the membership which felt that the party's attitude to women might equally undermine its socialist credentials. At its crudest, it was felt that anti-semitism might deter more potential members than it recruited. Misogynism was not regarded so seriously partly because those who might be alienated were already perceived as problems for socialism.

[86] In this case anti-racist is understood as those who fought anti-semitism for there was no real consciousness of black racism within the SDF, or beyond. The question of anti-Irish chauvinism was viewed as a separate matter. Geoffrey Bell notes that Hyndman may have been anti-German and anti-Jewish but he was not a chauvinist on Ireland (G. Bell, *Troublesome Business: The Labour Party and the Irish Question*, Pluto, 1982, pp. 2–3). It seems that at this period only those who were committed to opposing anti-semitism perceived their fight as one against racial prejudice.

Clearly the SDF's handling of the woman question was not unique. Some of the responses of the party hierarchy, and of individual members, were similar to those found in other areas which caused the SDF problems. However, the particular configuration of issues which made up the woman question combined with the party's theoretical understanding of it to produce a pattern of responses specific to this question.

Part 2

The SDF and the woman question: the theory and practice of the party on aspects of the woman question

4　The politics of the private sphere

The dividing line between the 'public' and 'private' was of crucial importance for the SDF's analysis of the woman question. The division marked the limit of political activity, although it was a distinction that was both historically and culturally specific.[1] The private sphere of the family, personal relationships and individual conscience provided an inner sanctum which was supposedly free from political dispute. This masculine model of politics was least satisfactory when confronted with elements of the private sphere which had, even temporarily, entered the public domain. Given the party's reliance on such a clear distinction between public and private, the ways in which issues defined as 'private' were perceived by SDFers, and the means by which these issues penetrated the public sphere, need to be examined more closely. This chapter, therefore, examines several aspects of the so-called private sphere – the family, marriage and 'free love' – and the conditions under which SDFers discussed them.

Socialism and the family

The family is often taken to be a symbol for the whole private sphere. The paradoxical way in which the SDF perceived the family was characteristic of other contemporary socialist organisations. Although socialists as a whole were publicly identified with the abolition of the family, individually they not only relied heavily on support from their families but also used positive familial images as part of the language of socialism.

By the time the SDF was founded, socialism and communism already had established certain characteristics in the public mind. The SDF thus inherited deeply rooted, common-sense assumptions about socialism.

---

[1]　For a discussion of the history of the public/private concept, see Elshtain, *Public Man, Private Woman*. See also the Introduction to S. M. Reverby and D. O. Helly (eds.), *Gendered Domains: Rethinking Public and Private in Women's History*, Cornell University Press, Ithaca, NY, 1992, pp. 1–24.

One of the 'vices' most commonly attributed to it was the abolition of the family. This phrase conjured up yet more demons, for it suggested that socialism would mean the end of marriage and the introduction of a community of women. Nothing would be safe from the socialists' attentions: if that bastion of privacy, the family, were to be destroyed, then clearly socialism threatened the whole fabric of society. The 'abolition of the family' therefore symbolised in one brief phrase all that was most subversive about socialism, not just with regard to society as a whole, but, more powerfully, to individuals themselves.

The association of socialism with the abolition of the family goes back to the Utopian Socialists. Robert Owen's *Lectures on the Marriage of the Priesthood of the Immoral World* inadvertently provided the ammunition for a very resilient stereotype of socialism. Owen denounced the family and advocated 'marriages of Nature' in the New Moral World. This provided anti-socialists with the basis for their effective propaganda. By the late 1830s, merely mentioning socialism was sufficient to evoke in most people's minds 'a system behind which all took refuge who wished to cast off the restraints of society and make free with his neighbour's wife and chattels'.[2] It became commonplace to associate socialism with immorality and worse.[3] This sensationalism lingered in the memory far longer than the less publicised explanations, or denials. Socialism and the abolition of the family were apparently irretrievably entwined in the public mind.

Writing in 1848, Marx and Engels included a section in the *Communist Manifesto* to clarify this issue.[4] Their argument focused on the bourgeois form of the family which, they argued, would disappear when its material base no longer existed. This was not to be enforced destruction – tearing babies from their mothers' arms – as the word 'abolition' implied. Rather, it would form part of the evolution of society. However, the nuances of even this position could easily be misrepresented.

What inheritance did this leave succeeding socialist organisations, such as the SDF? The assumption that socialism had been added in the popular consciousness to the seditious demons threatening the heart of the nation, the family, shaped the perceptions of potential socialists and, in turn, constrained subsequent socialist propaganda. The problem was made worse by the fact that some socialists did advocate the abolition of the family; but socialists as a whole could not agree on the matter and,

[2]   Thomas Frost quoted in Taylor, *Eve and the New Jerusalem*, p. 185. See also J. Saville, 'Robert Owen on the Family and the Marriage System of the Old Immmoral World', in M. Cornforth (ed.), *Rebels and their Causes*, Lawrence and Wishart, 1978.
[3]   Taylor, *Eve and the New Jerusalem*, p. 187.
[4]   K. Marx and F. Engels, *The Communist Manifesto*, Penguin, 1967, p. 100.

more importantly, did not see why they should agree. Thus, as a group, socialists were ill-equipped to deflect attacks.

Within the SDF, there were essentially two diametrically opposed approaches to the family. For some, socialist society would see the abolition of the family; not in the sense of the violent stereotype of the critics, but rather in a way that would expand individual freedom and provide collective alternatives for some of the functions of the family, such as childcare. For others, socialism would bring a purified family form, no longer distorted by capitalism. Paradoxically, both views could be derived from the founding fathers of socialism. This, of course, meant that, like the woman question as a whole, any doctrinal dispute over the family could only be inconclusive. However, there were few such debates within the SDF. This was partly because of SDFers' understanding of the woman question. But it was also because the principal disagreement over the family centred on the nature of a future socialist society, about which it was agreed that detailed speculation would be fruitless. Debate thus tended to settle on safer subjects; a general condemnation of the effect of capitalism on the family, and of the hypocrisy of the bourgeois sanctification of that institution.

Much of the ambivalence that characterised the SDF's public position on the family was to be found in the writings of the theorists of the woman question. Although, as we have seen, the family was theorised within Engels' and Bebel's writings, the manner in which this was done provided the basis for various interpretations. The founding fathers' perception of the family as an economic unit, through which property is accumulated and inherited, meant that the family was discussed in terms of its function in society as a whole. The family was not discussed in terms of individual's experience; its internal power relationships and, more specifically, the sexual division of labour.

The founding fathers argued that in a socialist society, the economic role of the family would have ended and its specific tasks would have to be socialised.[5] Although the family's social functions would now be met in other ways, it was not so clear what would happen to the complex of personal relationships which also constituted the family. It was the abolition of *this* family which haunted socialists.[6] Nevertheless, some SDFers had no qualms in arguing for the abolition of even this family. E. E. Williams, for example, argued that what he called 'the domestic stud farm' had outlived its usefulness and was neither 'a permanent or a particularly heaven-sent organisation'.[7]

---

[5] Engels, *Origin*, p. 139.
[6] See, for example, 'A Woman's Point of View', in *Justice*, 26 January 1907.
[7] *Justice*, 25 June 1892.

Those arguing for the total abolition of the family drew on the virtually consensual socialist condemnation of the bourgeois family; but then so did those who envisaged this degenerate type metamorphosing into a pure form. The founding fathers' assumption that there was nothing inherently oppressive about the family form was shared by many socialists.[8] De Leon, for example, argued that in contrast to the perilous condition of the contemporary working-class family, the monogamous family would 'bloom under Socialism into a lever of mighty power for the moral and physical elevation of the race'.[9] Clearly, it was impossible for SDFers to envisage a distorted and degraded family without already having an ideal freed from the taints of capitalism. However, there was little public discussion of the nature of this ideal form.

Divided though they might be as to the exact nature of the family under socialism, most SDFers were agreed that its distorted and decaying form under capitalism was sustained by bourgeois hypocrisy. Yet when it came to their practical attitude towards, and experience of, the family a much less critical position was adopted. There is little evidence to suggest that SDFers' practice amounted to self-conscious prefiguration. This was only to be expected, precisely because they lacked any clear idea of an alternative.

So what was the SDF's practical relationship to the family as an institution? One of the most comprehensive articulations of the role of the family for a socialist was Clara Zetkin's, who said:

it is out of the question that the task of socialist women's activity should be to alienate proletarian women from duties as wives and mothers; on the contrary it must operate so this task is fulfilled better than before, precisely in the interests of the proletariat. The better relations are in the family, and the more effectively work is done in the home, so much the more effective is the family in the struggle. The more the family can be the means of educating and moulding its children, the more it can enlighten them and see to it that they continue the struggle for the emancipation of the proletariat with the same enthusiasm and devotion as we in the ranks ... Thus many a mother and many a wife who imbues husband and children with class consciousness accomplishes just as much as the woman comrades whom we see at our meetings.[10]

SDFers were not usually as forthright; but it is clear that this view was not significantly contested. Indeed, this quotation comes from a speech which became the principal statement on the woman question for the

---

[8] For a similar argument concerning Marx's assumptions about the family, see Elshtain, *Public Man, Private Woman*, p. 187.

[9] D. De Leon, Preface to A. Bebel, *Woman*, p. xvii. For the effect of De Leonism on the SDF, see C. Tsuzuki, 'The "Impossibilist Revolt" in Britain', pp. 377–97.

[10] Clara Zetkin quoted in H. Draper and A. G. Lipow, 'Marxist Women versus Bourgeois Women', pp. 199–200.

whole of the Second International. To this extent, Clara Zetkin's position was the SDF's official policy, even if it was endorsed unenthusiastically. Overall, this position sought to mobilise the family without challenging either the institution, or the sexual division of labour within it.

The key assumption was that the family would form a bulwark for a socialist against a hostile world.[11] It would fulfil its conventional role, but in support of the party rather than just the individual. Moreover, it was assumed that the family, specifically the wife, should provide the necessary care and support to free the, usually male, activist for political struggle. For the SDF, this assumption became most apparent in its continued concern over the failure – as it was argued – of the socialist's wife to be a 'socialist wife'; that is, to nurture and support the class warrior and even, but not necessarily, become actively involved herself. Socialists, therefore, saw the family as a form of support rather than an institution which should be practically challenged. It was almost inevitable that this perception would then be reflected in many SDFers' assumptions about women, their potential for politicisation, their interests and capacities.

Familial assumptions were also reflected on a broader scale in the way socialist parties were organised. Most Second International parties attempted to emulate the extensive socialist culture the German socialists had built up,[12] and although the SDF was not so successful in creating an all embracing subculture, the range of its activities also incorporated a family model. The SDF was considerably less self-conscious than the SPD in its appeal to the party as a family, but they too had their youth (Socialist Sunday Schools) and women's (Women's Socialist Circles) movements. The status of these groups in the party reflected the sexual division of labour within the patriarchal family. They had little power, echoing the subordinate position of women and children in the family; they were there to be supportive of 'full' members of the party. Solidarity and loyalty, often in a very paternalistic form, were the key in the party, as in the family.

Although this similarity between the family and the party left little room for a critique of the former as an institution, there were positive

---

[11] See, for example, Evans, 'Politics and the Family', particularly pp. 273–4, 277. See also J. Humphries, 'Class Struggle and the Persistence of the Working-Class Family', *Cambridge Journal of Economics*, 1, 3, 1977, pp. 241–58.

[12] For the SPD's socialist subculture, see G. Roth, *The Social Democrats in Imperial Germany*; Guttsmann, *The German Social Democratic Party*; Nettl, 'The German Social Democratic Party, 1890–1914, as a Political Model', *Past and Present*, 30, 1965; Evans, 'Introduction: The Sociological Interpretation of German Labour History' in R. J. Evans (ed.), *The German Working Class, 1883–1933*, Croom Helm, 1982.

features for women in this arrangement. The benefits of the actual and metaphorical family to individual socialist men and to socialist parties respectively are obvious. Yet for socialist women, and women in the families of socialist men, there could also be equivalent benefits, such as mutuality, support and protection against a hostile world. For women, this might count for more than their inferior position in the party hierarchy. Certainly, Quataert has argued that a socialist subculture, such as that surrounding the SPD, offered psychological and material protection to its female members and compensated for the hardships of life.[13] If this were the case, the family would be better able to provide support for a socialist project if its very basis were not under attack. Here is a salutary reminder of the difference between the theoretical construction of a 'question' and the perceptions of those living that issue. For many socialist women, the conventional family was an important element in bringing them to, and then sustaining their involvement in, socialist politics.

To summarise, there was little space for the SDF to develop any sustained critique of the family. This was a product of their theoretical understanding of the woman question, and the role of the family within that, coupled with their pragmatic recognition of the importance of the family to individual socialists and to the party. It was argued that radically criticising 'the family' would only unsettle the smooth facade of solidarity, and could undermine it altogether. There was certainly a fear that any sustained discussion would not only be inconclusive, and hence unfruitful, but would feed the prevailing myth that socialism meant abolition of the family.

The SDF's own ambivalence around the family became most apparent when they were forced to confront as an organisation the specific issue of marriage and 'free love'.

Marriage and 'free love'

As we have seen, the family was the site of many of the contradictions of the SDF's understanding of the woman question. It was the sphere most clearly identified with women and women's interests in the eyes of SDF theorists, yet it was also an area where socialists felt vulnerable to misrepresentation by their opponents. SDFers were anxious that conventional prejudices could jeopardise their political, and particularly their electoral, prospects. They were therefore very sensitive to

[13] Quataert, *Reluctant Feminists*, p. 5. This is a particularly optimistic account of the German socialist women's movement, emphasising the positive value of women's experience of the socialist subculture and their role within it.

pronouncements by other party members which attempted to prescribe 'private' practice. This was particularly clear in the reverberations surrounding the Edith Lanchester Case, which will be discussed later in this chapter. These highlighted socialists' ambivalence on the issue of marriage and 'free love'. They also indicated the problem that parties of the Second International, such as the SDF, had with prefiguration, both as a concept and as a part of socialist practice.

The issue of marriage, whether in its contemporary form or its possible developments under socialism, was addressed by the SDF largely in terms of the debate raised around 'free love' unions. This issue illuminated the SDF's practical understanding of the relationship between the private and the public spheres. It provides a means to analyse on whose terms 'free love' was debated within the SDF; the extent to which the personal became political; and the effect this had on the woman question itself.

Socialist theorists of the woman question took marriage as emblematic of women's general condition. They argued that the economic exploitation which characterised capitalism permeated the most personal of relationships, ignoring any boundary between the public and private spheres. Hence a distinction could be drawn between bourgeois and proletarian marriage. Bourgeois marriage was nothing more than prostitution;[14] it was essentially an economic transaction, and had nothing to do with love.

Although Engels reduced bourgeois marriage to an economic relationship, he did not view all marriages in this light. The absence of private property coupled with women's economic independence through paid work meant, he argued, that proletarian marriage was a matter of affection rather than economics.[15] Indeed the founding fathers concluded that, aside from a little wife-beating, proletarian women were considerably less oppressed in marriage than their bourgeois sisters!

This sentimental picture of proletarian marriage highlights the weakness in Engels' analysis, which he shared with Bebel. The description of marriage as an economic relationship amongst the propertied classes failed to describe the reality of the experience of emotional relationships. Neither of the founding fathers recognised other dimensions of power between the partners in a marriage, whatever their economic class. The problem was not marriage but property; hence a future socialist society would provide the conditions for love and marriage to flourish uncorrupted by economic exploitation. Bebel suggested that socialism would mean that women like men would be completely free in their

[14] Engels, *Origin*, p. 134.
[15] Ibid., p. 135.

choice of partner.[16] He emphasised that socialist marriage would be a private matter, unregulated by the state. It was, of course, assumed by Engels and Bebel that people's personal relationships would continue to be monogamous and heterosexual,[17] although freed from economic coercion and bourgeois hypocrisy.

The socialist theorists of the woman question therefore had a complex position on marriage in capitalist society. On the one hand, there was an emotive picture of a relationship based on compulsion, not love; and, on the other, that marriage itself was not the problem but the economic pressures which corrupt it. As with the discussion concerning the family, the founding fathers' position could be used not only to support marriage but also to substantiate an anti-marriage position. For example, the suggestion that in a socialist society, state endorsement of marital relationships might not be necessary lent credence to the 'free love' position.

Notwithstanding these ambiguities, the SDF's general understanding of the woman question meant that whatever the founding fathers had to say, there was scope for the party to reflect a wide range of views on marriage. This was obviously a personal rather than a party matter; the epitome of a 'conscience' issue. The debate centred on those who argued for and practised 'free love' in opposition to the institution of marriage. A 'free love' union was an agreement between a man and a woman to live together in a sexual relationship without benefit of state or church blessing. However, the term had by the 1880s a number of other popular connotations. Although it was seen by some as a private matter which was only the business of the adults concerned, for others 'free love' meant promiscuity counterposed to Holy Matrimony.

'Free love' unions, as self-conscious acts, were not common. There was a much longer tradition amongst the working class of common-law marriage, usually because one partner was not free to marry;[18] this was

16 Bebel, *Woman*, p. 343.
17 The founding fathers were products of their time and therefore assumed heterosexuality as the 'norm' in all their discussions of present and future personal relationships. Bebel refered to male homosexuality as an 'unnatural passion' (ibid., p. 37) and to lesbianism as 'this aberration' (p. 38). Engels wrote of that 'abominable practice of sodomy' (Engels, *Origin*, p. 128). Even in such enlightened circles as the 'Men and Women's Club', formed in 1885 to discuss the sex question, 'all participants treated heterosexual feelings and identity as unquestionable and inevitable, variable only in its intensity between male and female' (J. R. Walkowitz, 'Science, Feminism and Romance: The Men and Women's Club 1885–1889', *History Workshop Journal*, 21, 1986, p. 37).
18 B. Taylor, *Eve and the New Jerusalem*, pp. 197–202 for Owenite 'free lovers' and for the attacks on Owenism for its supposed sexual immorality; pp. 193–6, 198 for examples of reasons for resistance to legal marriage in the first half of the nineteenth

not perceived as unregulated promiscuity, but marriage in all but legal terms. In contrast, 'free love' had been self-consciously adopted and sustained among some Owenites and other radical groups, particularly anarchists.[19] It was thus easy for the association of apparently subversive behaviour and subversive politics to become a strong one in the public mind. For example, the Dean of St Paul's Cathedral preached a sermon on Eleanor Marx and Edward Aveling shortly after her suicide, using them as an example of the dangers of socialism and 'free love'.[20] 'Free love' seemed dangerous, and came to represent all sorts of fears which bore little relationship to the quiet mundanity of many such unions.[21]

A tendency to understand 'free love' unions in a sensationalist way was exacerbated in the 1890s by the publication of Grant Allen's *The Woman Who Did*.[22] The notoriety of this novel can be gauged from the fact that it 'remained for many years the type of "daring" novel that one would not allow one's daughters and servants to read'.[23] This sort of reaction, of course, ensured widespread demand; so great, in fact, that the book went through twenty editions in one year.[24] The novel's heroine, Herminia Barton, rejects marriage on principle, choosing to enter into a 'free love' union with her lover. A child is conceived, but the lover dies and Herminia is forced to raise her child alone. As an adult, her daughter marries and, on discovering her mother's story, renounces her for her depravity. Herminia commits suicide. The novel was popularly seen as representing feminist criticisms of marriage, although, of course, the tale is hardly an exhortation to go and do likewise, and it was understandably condemned by feminists such as Millicent Garrett Fawcett.[25] The publication of the novel, and the resulting furore, meant that 'free love' was, by the 1890s, a familiar and sensationalised topic in

century. See also I. Minor, 'Working Class Women and Matrimonial Law Reform, 1890–1914', in D. E. Martin and D. Rubinstein (eds.), *Ideology and the Labour Movement*, Croom Helm, 1979, pp. 103–24, particularly p. 114; L. A. Tilly and J. W. Scott, *Women, Work and Family*, Holt, Rinehart and Winston, New York, 1978, pp. 96–8; J. R. Gillis, *For Better, For Worse: British Marriages, 1600 to the Present*, Oxford University Press, 1985, ch. 7.

[19] M. S. Marsh, *Anarchist Women, 1870–1920*, Temple University Press, Philadelphia, 1981; H. D. Sears, *The Sex Radicals*, Regents Press of Kansas, 1977.

[20] J. S. Lohman 'Sex or Class? English Socialists and the Woman Question, 1884–1914', PhD thesis, Syracuse University, 1979, p. 47.

[21] Many 'free love' unions were long-term stable relationships, for example Helena Born and William Baillie, Eleanor Marx and Edward Aveling, and indeed Edith Lanchester and James Sullivan.

[22] G. Allen, *The Woman Who Did*, John Lane, 1895.

[23] S. Hynes, *The Edwardian Turn of Mind*, Princeton University Press, Princeton, New Jersey, 1968, p. 182.

[24] E. Trudgill, *Madonnas and Magdalens*, Heinemann, 1976, p. 242.

[25] M. Garrett Fawcett, 'The Woman Who Did', *Contemporary Review*, 67, 1895, p. 630.

the press.[26] SDF members' views on marriage and 'free love' were formed and sustained within this broad context, as well as in relation to the founding fathers' analyses.

Within the SDF, marriage and 'free love' were discussed occasionally and a variety of views were expressed on the subject. Harry Quelch, for example, clearly echoed Engels when he wrote, 'the fact that many marriages are the result of mutual affection does not alter the fact of the dependence of women, and where they are not, the union simply means prostitution though it be stamped with legality'.[27] At least Quelch's reference to 'mutual affection' suggested a more recognisable portrait of marriage than Engels' theoretical construction.

None the less, one view of marriage within the SDF did see it as an essentially economic relationship. Marriage was described by several members as a woman's career or profession. *Justice*'s columnist, the Tattler, for example, put forward the not uncommon view among male socialists that 'So long as marriage is a career for women, as it is today, when a woman gets married she should abandon other careers to her less fortunate sisters.'[28]

But not all SDFers wrote of marriage as a uniform institution. Many, like Engels and Bebel, made a distinction between bourgeois and proletarian marriage. However, the distinction was not always made on similar grounds. S. Gardiner, for example, described marriage for middle class women as 'a duty to the family, which must be performed as soon as possible, because each year takes from her commercial value'. She then went on to paint a rather different picture to that of Engels of the reality of working class marriage: 'A working class man, as a rule, wants a slave when looking for a wife; someone to minister to his wants, and make his life a little more comfortable; and even when a young couple do begin well, the wife soon loses touch with her husband when the babies arrive and duties multiply.'[29] Hence, by implication, marriage for women was an institution which limited and restricted their individuality and denied their economic independence. Indeed, for other SDFers, the marriage question was explicitly concerned with gender rather than class; 'marriage is nothing more or less than a bogey invented by man to enslave woman and so enable him to appropriate surplus value'.[30] This particularly direct economic explanation was, however, most unusual.

---

[26] There were, for example, references to Grant Allen's novel in the coverage of the Lanchester Case in 1895. See *Labour Leader*, 2 November 1895.

[27] *Justice*, 16 July 1887.

[28] *Justice*, 13 January 1900.

[29] *Justice*, 23 June 1894.

[30] *Justice*, 10 August 1895. This is a very similar argument to that made by C. Delphy,

Some SDFers took the view that the legal aspect of the question, marriage versus 'free love', was less important than the nature of the relationship itself.[31] Yet there was also a strand of thought amongst socialists that was considerably less ambiguous about the legal institution of marriage. For them, marriage provided 'economical and social protection for the woman' without which 'the man will in the name of freedom and free union exercise rights, but towards which he will have no duties'.[32] Engels had suggested that the original impetus behind monogamous marriage in primitive society was women's 'longing for the right of chastity, of temporary or permanent marriage, as a way of release'.[33] Such views were based on the widely held assumption that male sexuality was unrestrained whilst women's sexuality was passive. 'Free love' was therefore seen as sexual liberty for men without any responsibility; it was indistinguishable from promiscuity, in contrast to the more common socialist association of marriage with prostitution. Some of those who argued for this position clearly saw themselves as social purists.[34] This vision of 'free love' as promiscuity remained a thread throughout socialists' discussion of marriage, for example, Robert Blatchford saw 'free love' as 'A succession of transient amours, which shall leave one jaded, disillusioned and unmated'.[35] From this perspective it was hard to understand why a woman would advocate 'free love'.

Although there might be debate amongst SDFers on the theory of marriage, there was little equivocation when it came to their practice. Most SDFers had traditional marriages. Hyndman, Quelch and Bax were all married and both Bax and Hyndman were sufficiently uncritical of the institution to re-marry after the deaths of their first wives.[36] When

Close to Home: a materialist analysis of women's oppression, Hutchinson, 1984, particularly 'The Main Enemy', pp. 57–77.

[31]   Justice, 3 November 1894.

[32]   Justice, 23 November 1895.

[33]   Engels, Origin, p. 117.

[34]   Social purity was a crusade against sexual vice and the double standard. For an exposition of social purity by one of its leading evangelists, see Josephine Butler, 'Social Purity', reprinted in S. Jeffreys (ed.), The Sexuality Debates, Routledge and Kegan Paul, 1987, pp. 170–89. Social purity was a very important strand in Victorian and Edwardian feminism. See E. J. Bristow, Vice and Vigilance: purity movements in Britain since 1700, Gill and Macmillan, Dublin, 1977; Weeks, Sex, Politics and Society, pp. 81–95; F. Mort, 'Purity, Feminism and the State: Sexuality and Moral Politics, 1880–1914', in M. Langan and B. Schwartz, Crises in the British State 1880–1930, Hutchinson, 1985, pp. 120–1; S. Jeffreys, ' "Free from all Uninvited Touch of Man": Women's Campaigns around Sexuality, 1880–1914', Women's Studies International Forum, 5, 6, 1982, pp. 629–45; J. R. Walkowitz, Prostitution and Victorian Society, Cambridge University Press, Cambridge, 1980, esp. part II; Levine, Victorian Feminism, ch. 6; Kent, Sex and Suffrage in Britain.

[35]   Clarion, 10 March 1911.

[36]   Hyndman's first wife Matilda died on 1 July 1913 and he then married Rosalind

a correspondent to the woman's column in *Justice* asked for socialists' opinions on legal marriage, she was given the examples of Hyndman, whose wife 'throws herself as wholeheartedly and enthusiastically as he does into the work of socialist propaganda', and the happily married Watts, Bax and Quelch.[37]

In a series of pen portraits of leading SDFers in *Social Democrat* there was certainly no mention of 'free love' unions, although the portraits do give an interesting insight into some SDFers' marriages. The portrait of J. Horsfall of Nelson SDF noted 'the self-sacrificing spirit of our comrade's partner in life, who has aided us materially by the encouragement and assistance she has given, and by a broad-viewed toleration in his home life too seldom met with from socialist wives'.[38] Other SDFers seemed to have had wives in the same mould as Mrs Horsfall; Mrs Wilson, wife of G. H. Wilson of Reading SDF, 'joined the branch a few months after himself, so he has been free from domestic opposition from which so many suffer'.[39] Similarly *Social Democrat* commented that, 'undoubtedly much of [George] Lansbury's success has been due to his wife's ready acquiescence, if not active participation, in his public work'.[40] The praise here was for recognisably traditional marriages. They have, moreover, to be understood in the context of the widely held assumption, as the Horsfall portrait in particular suggests, that wives could be a real and effective block to their husband's political activity. These SDF wives were congratulated on their acquiescence, self-sacrifice, toleration and lack of domestic opposition; qualities that were based on the familiar sexual division of labour.

There were few women SDFers included in this series. But when Mary Gray (of Battersea SDF and the SDF Executive) was the subject of such a portrait, the nature of her marriage was dealt with in a much more distant manner. For although her husband was mentioned, it was in terms of his job, and there was no passage on his practical and moral support for her work.[41] Indeed, there was no male equivalent to the concept of 'socialist wife', nor any detail on how the Grays organised their marriage to cope with her unusual political activity. Once again,

Travers in May 1914. E. Belfort Bax married a governess in 1877 and they had six children. His first wife died in 1890 and in 1897 he married a woman from a German middle-class family. Bax's children saw little of their father and step-mother, who travelled everywhere together, and were, by all accounts, devoted to one another (Cowley, 'Belfort Bax', p. 95).

37   *Justice*, 9 January 1909.
38   *Social Democrat*, June 1899, p. 164.
39   *Social Democrat*, July 1899, p. 198.
40   *Social Democrat*, January 1900, p. 4.
41   *Social Democrat*, November 1899, pp. 323–5.

the SDF's theoretical commitment to sexual equality failed to affect even the most mundane aspects of its practice.

As a certain general notoriety attached to 'free love' unions, it is not perhaps surprising that little evidence of them is apparent in party accounts of members' lives. Even when the names of those known to be living in 'free love' unions were referred to in *Justice* or *Social Democrat*, no mention was made of this fact. Thus Eleanor Marx was always described as Aveling's wife, and Edith Lanchester was never referred to as living in a 'free love' union. It is therefore hard to gauge how many other SDFers contemplated living, or even lived, in a 'free love' union. T. A. Jackson lived with Katie Hawkins although they did eventually marry – he said for the sake of the children. Katie Hawkins, herself a suffragette and socialist, made her ambivalence about the institution of marriage clear by choosing to keep her own name after marriage.[42] Elizabeth Wolstenholme Elmy, a correspondent to *Justice* although never a member of the party, lived with Ben Elmy. It was only when she became pregnant that they were persuaded to marry by some of her suffragist friends.[43] Other socialists also lived together before marriage but did not do so openly, such as the ILPers Mary MacArthur and W. C. Anderson.[44]

The most well known SDF members who lived in a 'free love' union were Eleanor Marx and Edward Aveling.[45] The relationship was not seen by Eleanor Marx as a self-conscious rejection of the institution of marriage, but a pragmatic decision forced upon them by the fact that Aveling was already married. Like many other socialists, Eleanor Marx took this aspect of the woman question to be a private matter, separate from her public political practice. Yvonne Kapp points out that Eleanor Marx did not regard the domestic hearth as the centre of women's struggle, and that she was therefore not politically interested in the 'free love' campaign. As 'she had no wish either to strike a challenging blow for free love or to be seen as conducting some furtive liaison', she announced her intentions to her family and to friends when she decided to live with Aveling in 1884.[46] From then on she added his name to hers and talked of him as her 'husband'. But if Eleanor Marx

[42] V. Morton and S. Macintyre, *T. A. Jackson*, Our History, 73, 1979, p. 8. For a similar dilemma see H. G. Wells, *Experiment in Autobiography*, II, Faber and Faber, 1984, p. 438.

[43] Walkowitz, *Prostitution and Victorian Society*, p. 123.

[44] F. Brockway, *Towards Tomorrow*, Hart-Davis, 1977, p. 26.

[45] Eleanor Marx and Edward Aveling were early members of the SDF, who left to form the Socialist League in December 1884 and rejoined the SDF in 1896. For their relationship, see Kapp, *Eleanor Marx*, II; R. Brandon, *The New Women and the Old Men*, Secker and Warburg, 1990, esp. ch. 4.

[46] See Kapp, *Eleanor Marx*, II, pp. 15–21.

was not an evangelist for 'free love', her decision does at least reflect an indifference to the institution of marriage. She was certainly not critical of friends who also lived in 'free love' unions, such as Edith Lanchester, who had been her secretary. Although there is no evidence that Eleanor Marx communicated with Edith Lanchester during the public furore of the Lanchester Case, she did give Edith practical support later in 1897 by having her to stay during her first, determinedly unmarried, confinement.[47]

It is hard to judge what other socialists thought of the Marx-Aveling union; although, for example, Havelock and Edith Ellis cited the experience of Eleanor Marx and Edward Aveling as their reason for becoming legally married, despite their own indifference to the institution.[48] Opinions of the Marx-Aveling union were undoubtedly coloured by Eleanor's choice of partner, with his poor reputation in relation to women and money, and by her eventual suicide.[49] As we have seen, the marital practices of most SDFers seem to have been untouched by this and other examples of 'free love' unions. If anything, it could be argued that these few notorious cases served to warn other socialists of the dangers of 'free love' unions.

It does appear that most SDF marriages were conventional. Certainly, there was no desire to draw attention to any relationships that were not. The SDF's presentation of marriage and 'free love' reflects a reluctance to advocate anything which might be seen to tarnish the image of socialism. Yet, at the same time the theory of socialism suggested a critique of certain aspects of contemporary marriage. By identifying the oppressive aspects of marriage as traits of the bourgeoisie, it was all too easy for SDFers to distance this critique from their actual practice. These contradictions and uncertainties became most apparent in the Lanchester Case.

The Lanchester Case

The whole question of 'free love' might have stayed firmly hidden as a matter of 'private conscience' but for the occasions when the 'private' was inexorably sucked into the public world. Such events exposed the

---

[47]   Ibid., p. 679.
[48]   V. Brome, *Havelock Ellis*, Routledge and Kegan Paul, 1979, p. 79.
[49]   Many leading socialists believed that Aveling had, in effect, murdered Eleanor Marx. His behaviour, including a secret marriage, was thought to have driven her to suicide. See *Justice*, 30 July 1898; *Labour Leader*, 30 July 1898. This only added to Aveling's already poor reputation in socialist circles in relation to women and to money. These feelings ensured that publicly Aveling was not deeply mourned, unlike Eleanor Marx who acquired an almost saintly aspect.

attitudes of the SDF. The most significant event in this context was the Lanchester Case, of October 1895.

The Lanchester Case was a *cause célèbre*. It concerned a young woman who announced her intention of living in a 'free love' union, and whose family therefore kidnapped her and had her committed to an insane asylum. It was only through the assiduous campaigning of her lover and friends that she was released. The case was of further sensation as the central character, her lover and friends were all socialists; indeed they were all SDFers.

The events themselves were certainly extraordinary.[50] The central character was Edith Lanchester, then aged twenty-four, an educated woman of middle-class background.[51] She had joined the SDF in 1892 and had engaged in a wide range of public propaganda work, including standing unsuccessfully for the London School Board in 1894 in West Lambeth. She had become sufficiently well known within the party to be elected to the SDF Executive in 1895. From 1893 she lodged in Battersea with a working-class family, that of another leading SDF woman, Mary Gray. It was here that the events that become known as the Lanchester Case began.

Through the course of her political activity Edith Lanchester had met a working-class man, James Sullivan, who was also an active member of Battersea SDF.[52] The discrepancy in their class backgrounds was considered at the time to be an important aspect of the Case. The two fell in love and decided, as they were opposed to the institution of marriage, that they would live together in a 'free love' union. They made known their intentions, announcing that the union would begin on 26 October, 1895. On October 25th Edith's three brothers, her father and a Dr Blandford,[53] a leading mental specialist, called at her lodgings. Dr

---

[50]   Accounts of the Lanchester Case vary in detail and I have re-constructed the events from the consistent aspects of the various sources, see *The Times*, 30 October 1895; E. Lanchester, *Elsa Lanchester Herself*, Michael Joseph,1983, pp. 1–5; *The Labour Annual*, 1896, p. 60; D. Rubinstein, *Before the Suffragettes: Women's Emancipation in the 1890s*, Harvester, Brighton, 1986, pp. 58–62; *British Medical Journal*, 2 November 1895, pp. 1,114–5, 1,127–8; *The Lancet*, 2 November 1895, pp. 1,175–6.

[51]   Edith Lanchester (1873–1966) trained to teach but had to leave that profession after a year as her socialist convictions had led to conflict. She then retrained in typing and shorthand and one of her subsequent jobs was as a secretary to Eleanor Marx. For a slightly jaundiced account of Edith's life see her daughter's autobiography, Lanchester, *Elsa Lanchester Herself*.

[52]   For an account of Battersea SDF at this period see W. S. Sanders, *Early Socialist Days*, Hogarth, 1927. See appendix 5 for a brief biography of James Sullivan.

[53]   Dr George Fielding Blandford had been involved in an earlier case of wrongful confinement, that of the spiritualist Louisa Lowe, although in this case Lowe owed her release to Blandford (A. Owen, *The Darkened Room: Women, Power and Spiritualism in Late Victorian England*, Virago, 1989, pp. 192–3).

Blandford had been told that Edith 'intended to go at once and live in illicit intercourse with a man in a station of life much below her own'.[54] The doctor discussed the marriage question with her for half an hour, in which time Edith Lanchester made clear that she was opposed to marriage, regarding it as immoral and that it only resulted in women losing their independence. She said that she intended to live with Sullivan, saw nothing wrong in that and would not marry him even if he had wished to get married. Dr Blandford and Edith also discussed the effect that having children would have on such a union, the likelihood that she might be deserted, and the resulting economic consequences. Even from Blandford's account of the case, it is clear that Edith argued with assurance and clarity, having thought through her decision. Nevertheless, Blandford concluded that Edith was of unsound mind for the following reasons:

I was informed that there was insanity in her family, her grandmother and an uncle having been insane; that she had always been eccentric, and had lately taken up with Socialists of the most advanced order. She seemed quite unable to see that the step she was about to take meant utter ruin. If she had said that she contemplated suicide a certificate could have been signed without question; I considered that I was equally justified in signing one when she expressed her determination to commit this social suicide. She had a monomania on the subject of marriage, and I believed her brain had been turned by Socialist meetings and writings, and that she was quite unfit to take care of herself.[55]

Without hesitation, Blandford signed the necessary certificate for the Lanchester family, although Edith was not informed of this. As she attempted to leave for work, her eldest brother announced that he was going to take her home. She refused and called out for Mary Gray, who attempted to prevent Edith being forcibly carried out of the house and thrown violently into a carriage. Edith's captors tied her wrists and with the blinds down, took her to a private asylum, The Priory, in Roehampton, where Blandford's certificate ensured her admittance. Although Edith protested her case to the Medical Officer there, it seems that her understandable display of emotion confirmed, in his eyes, Blandford's diagnosis.

Meanwhile Edith Lanchester's friends were not idle. James Sullivan had applied to the South West Metropolitan Court to get Edith released. The magistrate advised Sullivan to go to the High Court and obtain a writ of habeas corpus.[56] Although the magistrate himself could not

[54]   *British Medical Journal*, 2 November 1895, p. 1,127.
[55]   Ibid. The use of the term 'suicide' is particularly powerful as it suggests the fate of the most famous contemporary advocate of 'free love', the heroine of *The Woman Who Did*.
[56]   *The Times*, 28 October 1895.

directly affect Edith Lanchester's incarceration, he did provide the means to publicise what had happened. That night a band of SDFers stood outside the walls of the asylum and sang 'The People's Flag' to reassure Edith she had not been forgotten.[57]

It was not until the afternoon of 28 October that two Commissioners in Lunacy examined Edith at The Priory. They concluded that she had been detained without sufficient cause for she was perfectly sane, if, they thought, somewhat foolish. They therefore ordered her to be discharged on the following Friday. She protested at the delay in her release and managed to persuade Dr Chambers, the medical superintendent, to let her go the next day. In the meantime she was to stay at Chambers' house.

Meanwhile John Burns,[58] who had been a founder member of Battersea SDF but who had broken with the party in the late 1880s and was now Battersea's MP, had seen the publicity about the case in a newspaper. Edith Lanchester was one of his constituents and he wrote on her behalf to the Home Office and the Commissioner of Police. His action certainly speeded up her release, and in some accounts it is seen as the most crucial intervention. His role was explained at the time as one of a public servant rather than 'free love' sympathiser. The *South Western Star* reassured its readers that Burns had acted 'on principle and not out of sympathy with advanced Socialism'.[59]

On the Tuesday John Burns arrived at the asylum, lunched with Edith and when James Sullivan arrived, they all left together for Mary Gray's house. Edith's incarceration had lasted four days. The immediate effect on Edith Lanchester of this experience was to confirm, and even strengthen, the principles to which her family had objected.[60] Until the Case, Edith had had a room at her family's home in Kingston and had visited them about once a week; but now, understandably, she severed all links with her family, particularly her father and brothers.[61] For their part, the members of her family still considered her to be temporarily of unsound mind and maintained that she should have remained in the asylum.[62]

These events should perhaps have been predictable to all concerned.

[57] Lanchester, *Elsa Lanchester Herself*, p. 2.
[58] John Burns (1858–1943) was MP for Battersea from 1892 to 1918. For his relationship with the SDF, see W. Kent, *John Burns: Labour's Lost Leader*, Williams and Norgate, 1950.
[59] Quoted in ibid., p. 74.
[60] *The Times*, 30 October 1895.
[61] *British Medical Journal*, 2 November 1895, p. 1,127; E. Lanchester, *Elsa Lanchester Herself*, p. 32.
[62] Letter from H. J. Lanchester, *The Times*, 31 October 1895.

Yet there could have been a very different outcome but for the furore which led to Edith's release. The incarceration of women in asylums for what were social offences, such as the 'social suicide' of having an illegitimate child, was by no means unknown at this period. There had also been a number of cases of the confinement of women for their unorthodox views, especially for their espousal of spiritualism.[63] Edith Lanchester could have met a similar fate. As it was, she and James Sullivan maintained their opposition to marriage, and their union, which produced two children, lasted until his death in 1945.[64]

At the time, the Lanchester Case raised questions about the state of the lunacy laws, the judgement of individual doctors and, more particularly, the way in which society responded to what was deemed as the deviant behaviour of a woman. Despite the reluctance of the medical profession, then as now, to criticise their own members publicly, both the *British Medical Journal* (*BMJ*) and *The Lancet*'s reports on the Lanchester Case showed real concern for the way in which Dr Blandford had used the law. Yet they, like other commentators, laid the real blame at the door of the socialists who had indoctrinated a gullible young woman. The Case served 'to illustrate the lengths to which ill-advised "morality" doctrines of the Socialistic type would impel young persons who are in other ways harmless and well meaning',[65] even if incarceration in an asylum did not seem to be an acceptable way to deal with the problem.

Interestingly, the *BMJ* recognised that 'the very last thing which practical Socialists would desire would be the popular association of their ideals with a loosening of the marriage tie'.[66] The medical press thus incidentally highlighted the real problems that the Case raised for the SDF. The fact that the Case raised questions of civil liberties made it a matter of particular interest. Indeed, the party sought legal advice from H. H. Asquith QC, MP on whether there was any redress for the wrongful imprisonment of Edith Lanchester, for the assault on Mary Gray during Edith's abduction, as well as whether a libel case was

---

[63]   See E. Showalter, *The Female Malady: Women, Madness and English Culture 1830–1980*, Virago, 1987, esp. part 2; Owen, *The Darkened Room*, chs. 6, 7; P. McCandless, 'Liberty and Lunacy: The Victorians and Wrongful Confinement', *Journal of Social History*, 11, 3, 1978; P. McCandless, 'Dangerous to Themselves and Others: the Victorian Debate over the Prevention of Wrongful Confinement', *The Journal of British Studies*, 23, 1, 1983; S. Humphries, *A Secret World of Sex*, Sidgwick and Jackson, 1988, pp. 64–5; J. Usher, *Women's Madness: Misogyny or Mental Illness*, Harvester Wheatsheaf, Hemel Hempstead, 1991, ch. 4, esp. pp. 72–4.

[64]   Waldo Sullivan Lanchester was born in 1897 followed by Elsa Lanchester Sullivan in 1902.

[65]   *The Lancet*, 9 November 1895, p. 1,176.

[66]   *British Medical Journal*, 2 November 1895, p. 1,128.

possible against Dr Blandford.[67] They were advised that none of the proposed cases would be likely to succeed and they accepted this, knowing that any legal action would have prolonged the notoriety of the Case.

Most importantly, the Lanchester Case prompted a discussion within the SDF on 'free love'. The nature of the discussion showed that without the need to respond to a particular event, many SDFers took the view that such issues were best left alone, for pragmatic and theoretical reasons.

The immediate official response from the SDF to the kidnapping and incarceration of one of their Executive members was somewhat muted:

> Nobody seriously pretended that she was mad, in the ordinary sense of that word; and it is strange that a respected physician like Dr Blandford should have lent himself to what was in effect a family conspiracy to prevent our comrade from taking a course which a father and mother and brothers and sisters would naturally disapprove of under existing conditions. She is lucky to have got out so soon and so easily, and probably what has happpened will lead to some further reform in our lunacy laws.[68]

The inference was one of disapproval of Edith Lanchester's intentions, sympathy for her family's 'natural' reaction, and a sense that she got off rather lightly. Indeed, the instinctive reaction of the leadership was to criticise Edith for focusing such unfortunate attention on the party. *Justice*, therefore, whilst nodding in the direction of socialist rectitude on the marriage question, chastised Edith, before explaining that 'though we are as much opposed to the present marriage laws as a final solution of the relation between the sexes as the most vehement "new woman" can be, we have the right to ask that the question shall not be publicly raised in an acute form by an official member of the SDF, without any conference whatever with other comrades'.

Having emphasised that socialists had to live in 'the world as it is', and having also warned against individual 'anarchistic action or personal revolt', *Justice* concluded, 'we hold that it is better in present conditions that the marriage law should be complied with, no one has the right to interfere with any arrangement that two people of full age come to make in regard to their own persons'.[69] This was hardly a manifesto for 'free love'. The leadership's approach to personal politics was revealed as essentially a pragmatic one; it was certainly not prefigurative. Nevertheless, this did not prevent the organisation of a collection to defray Edith Lanchester's legal expenses, or the organisation of a number of

---

[67] *The Lancet*, 23 November 1895, p. 1,335.
[68] *Justice*, 2 November 1895.
[69] Ibid.

support meetings by SDF branches. Nor did it succeed in limiting the discussion within *Justice* on 'Socialism and Free Love'.

In this correspondence, a range of views can be discerned. They demonstrate not only a lack of unanimity on the marriage question, but also disagreement on the best tactical approach to take to the presentation of a socialist position on the issue. The 'Student of Scientific Socialism' was not alone in arguing:

We are not prepared as an organisation, I presume, to make 'free love' a burning question in our propaganda ... that is about the worst thing we could possibly do ... If *Justice* had allowed it to go forth to the world that as matters stand today the Social Democrats of Great Britain are in favour of a complete renunciation of the legal marriage tie between the young men and young women who join our ranks, in my humble judgement the organ of our movement would have been guilty of a grave dereliction of duty, and the SDF would have been injured in its daily practical work.[70]

Here is one example of a perennial tension within socialist practice: between the pragmatic and the principled presentation of socialist ideas. An example of this, referred to earlier, was the way in which the SDF's position on the family was inhibited by the concession of ground to those who spread the idea that socialism meant the abolition of the family. The party thus spent its time reacting to what was generally seen as a damaging slur, rather than successfully setting its own terms for a discussion on the nature and future of the family.

Why was this choice so compelling? Moving beyond a defensive position proved particularly difficult for socialists when it came to the range of issues most closely associated with the private sphere. As has already been mentioned, there was a view amongst significant sections of the SDF that there was a danger that socialism could be represented as advocating the community of women; that is, that with the abolition of marriage all women would be sexually available to any man. Indeed, socialism had been so represented in the past. It therefore seemed prudent that any action or statement in this area should be carefully considered, so that it could not be twisted to promote further bad publicity. The temptation was therefore to adopt silence as the official position.[71]

This pragmatic recognition of the danger of being identified with 'free love' was reinforced by the theoretical grounding of the woman question. 'Free love' was clearly seen as a 'fad', a matter for the individual conscience rather than the party programme. There was a strong feeling that if any of these 'fads' should stray from the 'private'

[70] *Justice*, 16 November 1895.
[71] *Justice*, 30 January 1904.

into the public sphere, they could rock the foundations of what was understood as socialism. This theoretical underpinning and the pragmatic desire to keep the party united could become closely entwined. Hence there was a recognisable force to Walter C. Hart's question: 'Who does not know of good Socialists outside the organisations who prefer to remain outside rather than be identified with the propaganda of Free Love and other fads?'[72] Understood in these terms, an episode like the Lanchester Case was highly unfortunate, and had to be dealt with in such a way that no one could conclude that 'free love' was sanctioned by the party as socialist practice. There was no room to discuss the rights and wrongs of the matter itself, as that only increased the chances of misrepresentation.

Yet, precisely because of the socialist construction of the woman question, there was indeed, in theoretical terms, an opportunity for the expression of a variety of views on 'free love', and on the tactics which socialists should adopt in relation to it. An issue usually shielded within the private sphere could be, and was, analysed in some depth. In so doing, the pragmatist's tactic, of limiting socialist propaganda to what was thought to be most palatable to those outside the SDF, was challenged.

One of the proponents of this more libertarian position was Belfort Bax, whose misogyny did not make him an obvious supporter of Edith Lanchester – an irony that was noted at the time.[73] Bax was particularly critical of *Justice*'s immediate response to the Lanchester Case. He questioned why socialists had 'to tread so gingerly on the feelings of their "family connections" and other respectable persons'. Just joining the socialist movement was likely to pain 'family connections', yet that was not an acceptable reason for not doing it. Bax argued that 'the first principle of progress is that no action in itself right should be omitted owing to the pain it causes the tender reactionary sentiments of "family connections" or others'.[74] He implied that *Justice*'s response was a reactionary one.

For Bax 'free love' unions were unproblematic; if the couple did not intend to have children, he saw such unions as 'simply a protest against a superstition'. Indeed provided proper provision was made for children, he could see no objection. He felt that attitudes to illegitimacy would only change when more people defied public opinion and refused to get married.[75] This was quite a bold suggestion, particularly when it

---

[72] *Justice*, 20 February 1904.
[73] *Justice*, 23 November 1895.
[74] *Justice*, 9 November 1895.
[75] Ibid.

concerned as emotive an area of the 'free love' debate as the fate of the children of any such union.[76]

Bax took the libertarian position to its natural conclusion when it came to his opinion of what the SDF should advocate regarding personal practice. He said that 'the problem, "to be or not to be" legally married must be decided by each individual for himself or herself'.[77] In many ways this, rather than the immediate official response, was the epitome of the SDF position. It attempted to make a virtue out of holding no single party position and made a plea for the space to voice any view within that vacuum. By castigating the more overtly pragmatic response as reactionary, Bax's position also accrued the appearance of radicalism, by thumbing a nose at conventional morality.

Others were less circumspect in their support for 'free love' unions and clearly rejected the pragmatic approach. 'W'"s response to *Justice*'s initial coverage of the Lanchester Case is one such example; 'I, for one, do not believe in orthodox conceptions of morality, for if I did I would not belong to the Socialists, who are revolutionists.'[78] Unequivocal support was offered by another correspondent to Edith Lanchester herself: 'I think all true Socialists will view with great satisfaction the noble and altruistic example set by Miss Lanchester, in this dark age of hypocrisy and ignorance. To such an extent do these factors prevail, that a frivolous ceremony of red tape, miraculously transforms an immoral into a moral act'.[79] Implicit here is a prefigurative approach to the marriage question. Yet these were muted voices compared to the chorus condemning any association between 'free love' and socialism. Many sympathised with the correspondent who said that 'it is therefore the best thing for the members of the SDF to shut up their bedrooms when going out to party meetings'.[80]

Was the SDF particularly idiosyncratic in its response to the Lanchester Case? The *Labour Leader*, paralleling *Justice*, provided a variety of responses. Keir Hardie, like the SDF leadership, was concerned about the damage the case could do to socialism: 'Enemies of Socialism know that such an escapade as that meditated by Miss Lanchester tends to discredit it among all classes ... the impression such acts make on the outside public ought to be considered.'[81]

76 For discussion of 'free love' unions in relation to children, see, for example, *Justice*, 4 June 1892; 9 November 1895; 21 December 1907.
77 *Justice*, 9 November 1895.
78 *Justice*, 16 November 1895.
79 *Justice*, 23 November 1895; see also *Justice*, 30 November 1895.
80 *Justice*, 23 November 1895.
81 *Labour Leader*, 2 November 1895.

In contrast, Lily Bell[82] took a much less defensive approach, suggesting that 'We are too well used to hearing our principles scoffed at as dreams and illusions'. She focused on the case as an issue of gender – rather than pragmatic – politics. She concentrated in particular on what the case revealed about an adult woman's relationship to her male relatives – 'whether she is to be regarded and treated as if she were part of their property and subject to their will in her actions, or whether she has the right to order her own life in the manner which she believes to be right and best for her'. Although Bell thought it was rather late in the day to be questioning this, she concluded that 'Men are hard to teach, and they part with the idea of masculine authority with great reluctance. One thing is certain, however – such cases as this will do more than anything else to strengthen the feeling of revolt amongst women, and so hasten the time when they shall be able to hold themselves in freedom.' The issue was therefore 'the right of every woman to independent individual action, uncontrolled by her male relatives';[83] the specific question of 'free love' was irrelevant. Lily Bell adopted a libertarian position, as Bax did, but her focus on gender as the crucial issue clearly differentiated her reaction from his, as well as from that of *Justice*.

Other socialists outside the SDF pointed to the double standard in the case; that is, that it was only Edith against whom action was taken. As 'Marxian' asked, 'Where were the outraged relatives of Mr Sullivan?'[84] It was also pointed out that it was inconceivable that events could have occurred the other way around, with a sister taking action against a brother because of his 'immorality'. In the same vein, it was argued that Edith suffered because she was open about her plans, whereas hypocrisy on her part could have been more easily connived at; so, 'had she chosen to go upon the streets and live the life of a common prostitute the chances are that no-one would have troubled her, and she would have been left to live her life in peace'.[85]

The *Clarion* reported the case in a supportive manner: 'Socialists believe that a woman has a perfect right to do what she likes with her own body ... in defiance of priests, laws, custom and cant.'[86] But two

---

[82] The identity of 'Lily Bell' has been disputed. Some historians have assumed that the name cloaked the identity of the *Labour Leader*'s editor, Keir Hardie (for example, K. O. Morgan, *Keir Hardie: Radical and Socialist*, Weidenfeld and Nicolson, 1975, p. 66; Lohman, 'Sex or Class?', p. 179) whereas June Hannam draws on evidence to show that this was the pseudonym of Isabella Bream Pearce (see Hannam, 'Women and the ILP', p. 209). Carolyn Steedman deals with this dispute by using the pronouns 'he/she' when refering to Lily Bell (*Childhood, Culture and Class*, pp. 130,291).

[83] *Labour Leader*, 2 November 1895.
[84] *Labour Leader*, 9 November 1895.
[85] *Labour Leader*, 2 November 1895.
[86] *Clarion*, 2 November 1895.

years after the Lanchester Case in 1897, Julia Dawson raised the matter again in her women's column, arguing that 'when "bonds" of matrimony have to be tackled, we must consider well before we try to break them. There is a Phantom Freedom whose chains are more galling than any fetters forged by matrimony ... Bad as our marriage laws are, they are better than none at all'.[87]

Julia Dawson's position was one part of the spectrum of views on 'free love' which could be found across the socialist movement and within the SDF. But the volume of comment on the Lanchester Case in *Labour Leader* and *Clarion* was considerably less than in *Justice*. Socialists from outside the SDF could afford to be more supportive of Edith Lanchester as their party members were not the principal actors. For the SDF, the fact that Edith Lanchester was a party member, and a senior one at that, was crucial to their response. She was seen as responsible for a link being publicly made between the party and 'free love'. The SDF's official response was therefore concerned to minimise any damage to the party from what was regarded as an unwelcome association with a contentious issue.

Yet, as has become apparent, the SDF's understanding of the woman question meant that they could have no official position on 'free love'. Indeed, as this was a 'conscience' issue, there could be numerous views on it within the party. Pragmatically, the leadership argued that silence was the best policy, but they had no means to enforce this, other than forbidding discussion in *Justice*. They did not do this, and as a consequence a variety of views on 'free love' bubbled to the surface. These views did not have equal status. Certain of them appeared to dominate by virtue of the relative power of their authors within the organisation. Thus the overall impression given by *Justice* was that the Lanchester Case was an embarrassment. It raised a matter that the leadership preferred were not discussed. But if there were to be a discussion, it was felt that the party should not be identified with such contentious and idiosyncratic behaviour as 'free love' unions.

The resonances of the Case were felt for much longer within the SDF than elsewhere. This was not only because the central characters were party members, but also because the controversy that it provoked touched a particular nerve in the debate on what constituted socialist orthodoxy. Thus, having examined the Lanchester Case, it is appropriate to consider the terms under which the debate concerning 'free love' was conducted on further occasions. To what degree did the SDF clarify its ambiguous position?

[87]   *Clarion*, 14 August 1897.

Beyond the Lanchester Case: the SDF's response to 'free love' as a public issue

The reverberations of the Lanchester Case went far beyond the short-term notoriety of the autumn of 1895. 'Free love' continued to be discussed within the SDF when the Case had faded from the national stage. Yet, for a time, the spur for such discussions at a local level was still, in effect, the Lanchester Case. Despite her infamy, Edith Lanchester continued to be an active member of the SDF, maintaining a public profile by speaking at public meetings.[88] Her arrival at a branch could prompt informal discussion around the topic which had become so closely associated with her name. In addition, the subjects upon which Edith chose to speak also provided a more explicit forum for discussion of the marriage question.[89] Edith obviously had a certain curiosity value beyond that of being a female socialist speaker, which she was not afraid to exploit for political ends. The combination of Edith and the marriage question certainly drew the crowds in.

As part of a provincial tour in February 1896, Edith spoke at two meetings for the SDF in Scotland; one in Glasgow and one in Edinburgh, on 'Socialism and Marriage' and on 'Socialism and the Family'. Despite the different titles, the content of the two talks seems to have been the same. The reports of these meetings give an opportunity to compare the different ways in which SDF meetings could respond to the contentious topic of 'free love'.

Caroline Martyn, one of the triumvirate of charismatic leading women socialist speakers of the 1890s,[90] responded very sympathetically to Edith's personality and arguments. In her report of the Glasgow meeting she outlined Edith's persuasive critique of contemporary marriage. Edith unashamedly tackled the traditional objections to 'free love' unions which she had encountered during the Case and which she must have known would have been in the minds of a good number of her

---

[88] Edith Lanchester spoke to London branches, at open air meetings and made provincial speaking tours. In 1896 she reached as far afield as Edinburgh, Southampton, Wigan and Oxford.

[89] Before the Case, Edith Lanchester's main subject was 'Education and Free Maintenance for Children'. After the Case she spoke on 'Women and Socialism', 'Women and Marriage' and 'Women and the Family'.

[90] These were Caroline Martyn, Katherine St John Conway and Enid Stacy. As June Hannam has rightly pointed out historians have highlighted these three popular women speakers and thereby give 'the impression that they were unique, rather than representative of a much broader group' (Hannam, 'In the Comradeship of the Sexes', p. 215). For Caroline Martyn, see her entry in J. M. Bellamy and J. Saville (eds.), *Dictionary of Labour Biography*, 8, pp. 158–60. For Katherine St John Conway, see Thompson, *The Enthusiasts*.

audience. She went on to suggest that the objection that greater freedom would lead to polygamy or promiscuity had no force as the present form of marriage, 'is no bar to the wildest licence'.[91] Instead, she painted a picture of a 'free love' union as a higher form of marriage, where a woman would no longer be a man's property or under his control. Her ideal was a union of souls which, as a purely personal matter, would not need any public ceremony to endorse it.

Threaded through the various reports of Edith's speaking is the sense of the steel of her principle and her unequivocal criticism of the institution of marriage. More importantly, she also presented the marriage question as an item for the current socialist agenda, rather than just for some socialist future. It was because she placed her views within a clear and contemporary socialist context that she angered her socialist opponents as much as the anti-socialists and puritans who could be expected to object. This was particularly apparent in the discussion of the Edinburgh meeting. In a bad-tempered report in *Labour Leader*, which emphasised the opinions of the chair of the meeting, James Connolly,[92] objections were raised not so much at the content of the lecture – which was seen as nothing new – but the way in which Edith 'assumed the representative character and used the phrase "We Socialists" far too much'.[93] She should, it was felt, speak on these matters for herself alone. The report of this meeting characterised the great divide over the relationship between socialism and the marriage question, which was played out not only in the pages of the socialist press but in the day-to-day discussions and meetings of the SDF.

But Lanchester's curiosity value inevitably faded. Although the Lanchester Case was the most important catalyst for SDF discussion of the marriage question and 'free love', it was not the only one. There were other occasions when 'free love' could have been taken up by the SDF as an organisation.

The Bedborough Case

The influence of the Lanchester Case could still be felt on the next event to provoke the SDF's consideration of 'free love'. In 1898, another legal case cast a spotlight onto 'free love' and, although the SDF was no

---

91 *Labour Leader*, 15 February 1896.
92 The *Labour Leader* report may well have been written by Connolly himself. This would explain the particularly sympathetic account given to his views. In contrast, the *Justice* report of the same meeting was considerably more measured (*Justice*, 22 February 1896).
93 *Labour Leader*, 15 February 1896. See also an earlier discusion involving Connolly (*Labour Leader*, 18 January 1896).

longer centre stage, it was caught in the peripheral glare. This particular case concerned George Bedborough and the organisation of which he was secretary, the Legitimation League. Although Bedborough was no socialist, his case, like that of Edith Lanchester, raised libertarian issues about which socialists were concerned.[94]

The Legitimation League had been formed in 1893 in Leeds, by Oswald Dawson, to demand equal rights for illegitimate children. This had a central bearing on the 'free love' controversy. Critics of 'free love' often focused on what were seen as the unfortunate products of a liaison between adults who put principle before the happiness of those unable to defend themselves. Although the League was concerned about all the issues that surrounded 'free love', and drew to it libertarians who were either living in such unions or who wanted to discuss the 'sex question', it remained a very small group. When the League moved to London in 1897 it became a more significant organisation, publishing its own journal, *The Adult*.[95] The focus was now more explicitly on 'free love' and the sex question, with the objects of the League being broadened in June 1897, to include 'educating public opinion in the direction of freedom in sexual relationships'.[96] Its meetings now commanded larger audiences; for example, in 1898 the League's annual meeting in April was attended by 411 people.[97]

Within radical circles the Legimation League was fairly well known and attracted to it many who were interested in the woman question. Some, like George Bedborough, the League's new secretary, had been involved in the journal *Shafts*, which discussed feminist and sexual questions.[98] Moreover, *The Adult* joined the various small journals referred to and advertised within *Justice*, showing that there was an overlap between the socialist and libertarian press both in terms of

---

[94] The Legitimation League had been active in Edith Lanchester's defence in 1895. Bedborough had, with two others, gone so far as to present a case for Dr Blandford's censure before the Royal Commission on Lunacy (Sears, *The Sex Radicals*, p. 256). Phyllis Grosskurth even suggests that Edith Lanchester's release was due to the agitation of Bedborough and other League colleagues (P. Grosskurth, *Havelock Ellis*, Allen Lane, 1980, p. 191). Oswald Dawson, founder of the Legitimation League, wrote a supportive account of the Lanchester Case for the 1896 *Labour Annual* (p. 59).

[95] For a discussion of the milieu which produced *The Adult* and the debates on the sex question, see L. Bland, 'Marriage Laid Bare: Middle-Class Women and Marital Sex 1880s–1914', in J. Lewis (ed.), *Labour and Love: Women's Experience of Home and Family, 1850–1914*, Basil Blackwell, Oxford, 1986, pp. 123–48; Jeffreys, *The Spinster and her Enemies*, ch. 2; J. R. Walkowitz, 'Science, Feminism and Romance'.

[96] N. Brady, 'Shafts and the Quest for a New Morality', MA thesis, Warwick University, 1978, p. 61.

[97] Sears, *The Sex Radicals*, p. 256.

[98] For a discussion of the journal *Shafts* and its context, see N. Brady, 'Shafts and the Quest for a New Morality'.

audience and sentiments. Thus any major events within the League could be expected to have some reverberations within the SDF.

Bedborough was arrested in May 1898 accused of selling an obscene work.[99] This was Havelock Ellis's *Sexual Inversion*, which was concerned with homosexuality. No attempt was made to prosecute the author. It seems clear not only from accounts written with hindsight but also from contemporary comments, that this case was only superficially about obscenity. Scotland Yard believed the Legitimation League to be an anarchist front and sought, successfully, to smash it as an organisation.[100]

The SDF's treatment of the Bedborough case is instructive, as is their view of the organisation central to it, one which openly espoused the politically embarrassing subject of 'free love'. *Justice* did not ignore the case, but the paper did seek to represent it as a matter of free speech rather than as an issue in its own right.[101] *Justice* therefore gave editorial space to publicise and comment positively on the July edition of *The Adult*, as well as carrying adverts for the journal.[102] The SDF showed support for the League, but only as an organisation under attack from the police.

The SDF's response was sparked by a letter to *Justice* in July 1898 which called for support for Bedborough on the grounds that freedom of the press was threatened. When the Free Press Defence Committee was set up to defend Bedborough, it was commented on favourably by the Tattler, and leading SDFers were amongst the well-known radicals who put their names to it.[103] It seems that most of the luminaries did no more than lend their names to the cause whilst others, less illustrious, actually did the work of the pressure group. In supporting the Defence Committee, there was no suggestion that this also entailed identification with the goals of the Legitimation League. Defining the matter as one of freedom of the press suited the SDF's own dilemmas about the substantive questions of 'free love' and sexual liberty. The Defence

---

[99] For the most thorough and colourful account of the Bedborough Case, see A. Calder-Marshall, *Lewd, Blasphemous and Obscene*, Hutchinson, 1972, part 5.

[100] See, for example, *Justice*, 18 June 1898. Scotland Yard destroyed the Legitimation League in the interval between Bedborough's arrest and his trial at the end of October 1898: A. Calder-Marshall, *Lewd, Blasphemous and Obscene*, p. 219; *The Times*, 1 November 1898.

[101] In taking this position the SDF were joined by other socialists such as Julia Dawson (*Clarion*, 9 July 1898).

[102] *Justice*, 9 July 1898. For adverts, see *Justice*, 19, 26 November, 3 December 1898.

[103] *Justice*, 9 July 1898. Supporters of the Free Press Defence Committee included the SDF's H. M. Hyndman, Belfort Bax and Herbert Burrows as well as George Holyoake, Walter Crane, Edward Carpenter, Grant Allen, and G. B. Shaw amongst others (Calder-Marshall, *Lewd, Blasphemous and Obscene*, p. 211; Weeks, *Sex, Politics and Society*, p. 181).

Committee withdrew its support from Bedborough just before his trial when it was realised that his deal with the authorities to avoid jail would mean that there would be no extended court case and therefore no public forum for the issues of censorship.[104]

The Bedborough case was, therefore, not the catalyst for discussion of 'free love' and related matters which it might have been for the SDF. Bedborough was represented within *Justice* as an individual apart from the organisation of which he was a key member. The Legitimation League, the real victim of the case, was barely referred to within the SDF's publications. The only mention of the contentious book itself, *Sexual Inversion*, was in the Tattler's column, where he rehearsed all the favourable reviews that the book had received in the general press, countering the charge of obscenity by stressing the reviewers' comments on the scientific nature of the work.[105] The contrast between the Lanchester and Bedborough cases is striking. As the latter did not touch the SDF as closely as the former, the party was able to follow the general radical approach of the time and to ignore the substance of the matter. The Bedborough case confirms that the SDF did not seize opportunities to discuss the issue of 'free love'. They were reluctant to discuss a matter which was incapable of resolution and which, more importantly, was politically embarrassing.

The Potteries and 'free love'

It was not until the early months of 1904 that the debate over 'free love' broke through again into the pages of *Justice*. The reasons for this are instructive. The Bedborough case might have seemed a likely stimulus to discussion, but the implicit danger of association with the League, and the issue's potential for representation as merely a question of censorship, meant that the 'free love' aspect was easily ignored. This debate was only aired again when there was a less sensationalist atmosphere. In 1904 no potentially compromising court cases were in progress to associate the SDF publicly with 'free love'. Instead, the debate began in response to articles in the Liberal press which had highlighted increasing illegitimacy rates in the Potteries.

From this source, John A. Cross began a discussion in *Justice* which focused on 'free love'. Using the evidence from the Potteries, he made the connection between the increasing economic independence of working women and their corresponding lack of interest in marriage.

---

[104] Bedborough agreed to plead guilty and to sever all his links with the League in return for a non-custodial sentence (*Justice*, 12 November 1898).
[105] *Justice*, 3 September 1898.

Given many socialists' characterisation of marriage as an economic relationship, Cross was not surprised that women who were equal breadwinners with men seemed to see no need for marriage. The Liberal press had represented this apparent rejection of marriage as an example of immorality, particularly when illegitimate children resulted, whereas Cross saw these changes as signs of social progress prompted by economic change. As in many socialist discussions of marriage, he drew attention to the double standard inherent in the slur against the people of the Potteries: 'this "immorality" can never be half so hideous in its social effects as the spurious morality whose cruel tyranny drives so many women to insanity, suicide, procuring abortion and infanticide.'[106] Cross's argument set the tone for the ensuing correspondence, which dealt with the broader question of 'free love' rather than just the specific case of the Potteries.

Most of the correspondence that stretched over the first three months of 1904, until it was curtailed by the editor, came from men who seemed only too eager to argue the abstract merits of socialism combined with, or opposed to, 'free love'. The vehemence of their argument suggests strong, pent-up feelings which breached the SDF's usual defences against such discussions. Many of the arguments covered similar points as the discussions of the 1890s;[107] this was not surprising as nothing had really been resolved. The discussion also revealed a number of socialist men who clearly had no hesitation in pronouncing on women's best interests in this matter. Evacustes A. Phipson, for example, suggested that abandoning the institution of marriage would leave male sexuality unrestrained. Consequently, no woman would be safe and men 'would seek out the youngest possible, until eventually it would be impossible to trust any girl over, say, 9 years of age, out of sight'.[108] If socialism brought 'free love' then, he argued, it would also have to have laws to protect virginity. Phipson's argument says a great deal about how he viewed sexuality, but he was by no means the only correspondent to take this kind of position.

In contrast, Bax vehemently attacked the view that marriage was for women's protection as an example of a feminist – and therefore, to him, a reprehensible – argument. Despite the fact that these arguments were hardly feminist – although the conclusion was one which some feminists would share – Bax railed against this 'attempt to play to the Feminist gallery by trotting out the old legend of the perfidious male monster and the guilelessly innocent and "wronged" female angel'. Generally, he felt

---

[106] *Justice*, 9 January 1904.
[107] See, for example, *Justice*, 16 January 1904.
[108] *Justice*, 30 January 1904.

that Cross had set out the 'only logical and consistent Socialist view on this subject'.[109] This admission was striking; for unlike some other correspondents, Bax felt it was perfectly proper for there to be a socialist view on marriage and 'free love'.

Bax's intemperate language brought the first printed response from a woman correspondent. Many women must have shared Margaretta Hicks's thoughts; 'I did intend to let the masculine gender say what they pleased, and take no notice; but after all, *Justice* is not only for men'. Hicks took the view that Bax's position was not only offensive but atypical of most socialists. She returned Bax's language in kind, revealing in the process how incensed many were by his style as well as his opinions:

No doubt E. B. Bax was a guileless youth who was badly taken in by some damsel, but he might bear it like a man, and not inflict on us his nauseous railings against the purity and innocence of all our girls. It is certainly quite out of order, and a piece of impertinence, to say that to be a 'consistent' Socialist one must agree with him on the marriage laws.[110]

Once again, it seemed that 'free love' could conjure up some unlikely alliances, such as a feminist, Hicks, and anti-feminist Phipson, together on one side, opposed by a misogynist, Bax and a liberal, Cross. The strength of feeling revealed on this issue was often reflected in lurid and sensationalist examples and language, uncommon in *Justice*'s correspondence. But it bears repeating that the debate on 'free love' only surfaced in the paper on a few, particular occasions, partly because of these very emotions. Officially, they were regarded as dangerously misdirected energy. In addition, of course, the party did not feel it could afford endlessly to debate a subject on which there could be no official verdict, and which aroused emotions and alliances which could destabilise the party. So the editor closed the correspondence, for what had started as a comment on changing social practices amongst working people had very quickly become an intra-socialist dispute on dogma. If dogma were now to cover the 'personal' practices of socialists, the damage within and without the party might be considerable. The SDF's leadership had learnt from the Lanchester Case that, when in doubt, the best possible position was none at all, and the best possible comment was silence.

Wells and the Fabian Basis

In 1906, largely as the result of H. G. Wells' intervention, the Fabian Society considered the marriage question in relation to its statement of

---

[109] Ibid.
[110] *Justice*, 13 February 1904.

central tenets known as the 'Basis'. It might be expected that this would cause ripples in the SDF. What was in dispute were, after all, the defining features of socialism, albeit another organisation's 'socialism'. The SDF's position was, of course, that the woman question was not one of these key features. Nevertheless, the discussion of marriage by a rival group could, at minimum, be expected to produce some rehearsal of the SDF's stance and, possibly, to provoke a much wider discussion on 'free love'.

The Fabian Society was not, generally, any more supportive of the woman question than the SDF.[111] Yet the issue refused entirely to die. When the Basis was originally drawn up, Stuart Glennie had attempted to add a clause on marriage and the family; but the opposition of the leading female Fabian of the time, Annie Besant, defeated the proposal.[112] Twenty years later, the issue was resuscitated by H. G. Wells, a short-lived but rather noisy Fabian.[113] Wells was particularly concerned that aspects of the woman question, such as the family and marriage, should be discussed openly and that a commitment to the achievement of women's emancipation be a part of the Basis. As Pease, secretary to the Society and its official historian, commented:

Nobody objected to the principle of this, but many demurred to inserting it in the Basis. We regarded the Basis as a statement of the minimum of Socialism, without which no man had the right to call himself a Socialist. But there are a few Socialists, such as Mr Belfort Bax, who are opposed to women's suffrage, and moreover, however important it be, some of us regard it as a question of Democracy rather than Socialism. Certainly no-one would contend that approval of women's suffrage was acceptance of a part of the creed of Socialism.[114]

Interestingly, in the light of these comments, Wells' proposed amendment – which was to enforce equal citizenship between men and women – was interpreted by supporters and detractors alike as being solely a demand for the suffrage.[115] In other words, it was not suggested that the new Basis should enshrine the broader concept of sexual equality. The proposal nevertheless proved contentious. With the campaigning of key women members of the Society under the leadership of Maud Pember-Reeves, a compromise was reached in January 1907;

---

[111] M. Cole, *The Story of Fabian Socialism*, Heinemann, 1961, p. 127.
[112] E. R. Pease, *The History of the Fabian Society*, A. C. Fifield, 1916, pp. 56,72.
[113] Wells joined the Fabian Society in February 1903, although he took little part in it until 1906. He resigned from the Society in September 1908 (Pease, *The History of the Fabian Society*, pp. 164,181).
[114] Ibid., p. 177.
[115] Technically this would have been a demand for limited women's suffrage as that was all that was required to ensure equality with the existing property qualifications of the male suffrage.

the Basis was amended to include the clause on equal citizenship. Once the suffrage question had been dealt with, in principle at least, there was little general pressure from within the Society to go any further on the woman question, and Wells thereafter proved an uncertain and ambiguous advocate.

The SDF's publications were remarkably quiet regarding this tumultuous episode of the Fabian Society's history. It is true that in general the SDF rarely commented on the internal politics of other socialist groups; to do so might give these groups credibility. More importantly for this particular issue, any suggestion that the fundamentals of socialism should be expanded to include the woman question was anathema to the SDF. But none of these reasons meant that the party was silent on the more general implications of Wells' intervention as a Fabian. In particular, the public association of Wells with both socialism and 'free love' produced a flurry of comment in the SDF press.

Why did this produce a reaction when the amendment of the Basis had not? The recruitment of Wells, already well known as a writer, was obviously quite a coup for the Fabian Society; but it also meant that his particular views, which he never hesitated to publicise, could now be presented as socialist ideas. This had ramifications for all socialists, not just Fabians. In particular, public attention was given to Wells' *Socialism and the Family*. He had offered this to the Fabian Society, but they had declined to publish because of its vagueness. They were particularly unhappy that Wells was free with his criticisms, without offering any practical solutions. This left the Society with no specific recommendations to debate or to disseminate publicly.[116] Wells, undaunted, published elsewhere.

Taken with his novel *In the Days of the Comet* (1906), *Socialism and the Family* seemed to represent a socialist manifesto for 'free love'. In fairness to Wells, he did put considerable energy into denying, in the general and the socialist press, that he had ever advocated 'free love' or the destruction of the family. He argued that *Socialism and The Family* had been misunderstood, and that *In The Days Of The Comet* had never been intended as a socialist utopia.[117] Wells' denials only added fuel to the debate. Through him, socialism came under attack in the general press. Wells' reaction to this onslaught prolonged the dispute; this in turn involved other socialist organisations in the clarification of the matter that Wells had raised. The SDF was one of the organisations to break their usual silence.

Wells' position had caught the attention of the general press partly

[116] Pease, *The History of the Fabian Society*, pp. 175–6.
[117] *Justice*, 19 October 1907.

because of the recent electoral advances of the Labour Party. Their opponents felt a pressing need to meet this threat by rekindling unfavourable stereotypes of socialism.[118] Not surprisingly, the SDF reacted unfavourably to the increasing public identification of socialism with 'free love'. Wells' writing received attention from *Justice* and from *Social Democrat*.[119] One review of *Socialism and The Family* took the, by now well established, position that Wells had every right to express his opinion but that he should not have dogmatised 'in the name of the Socialist movement'.[120] This was sufficient to revive the by now familiar correspondence in *Justice* on 'free love' and socialism.[121]

The SDF's treatment of this episode differed from earlier debates concerning 'free love' in the seriousness with which it regarded the external threat. It seemed to the SDF that its members were being dragged in the mud of innuendo, and that the party might be harmed through misrepresentation. The party poured scorn on the *Daily Express*'s 'Menace of Socialism' campaign.[122] And, in reply, Quelch set out in *Social Democrat* the SDF position on 'free love':

Socialism *does* mean Free Love, but only in the sense that men and women being free, there will be no coercion to force either men or women into relations which are repulsive, or to unwillingly suffer the embraces of another. Socialism does not mean, nor do Socialists suggest, that in the future – as in Heaven – there will be neither marrying nor giving in marriage; nor that there shall be sexual promiscuity or community of wives.[123]

Yet despite the clarity of Quelch's argument disassociating socialism from contemporary advocates of 'free love', his words were used against the SDF as evidence of their advocacy of 'free love'. For example, a 'gutter journal', *Winning Post*, wrote that, 'Comrade Quelch has declared in favour of free love. It seems as though these Socialists do not want to pay for anything.'[124]

Anti-socialists continued to believe that there was mileage to be made from this particular slur while socialists were not sufficiently successful

---

[118] For the anti-socialist crusade of this period, see K. D. Brown, 'Anti-Socialist Union' in K. D. Brown (ed.), *Essays in Anti-Labour History*, Macmillan, 1974, pp. 234–61; *Daily Express*, 20–30 July 1907; J. R. Clynes, *Memoirs, Volume I, 1869–1924*, Hutchinson, 1937, p. 124.

[119] *Socialism and the Family* was critically reviewed in *Social Democrat*, April 1908 and in *Justice*, 12 January 1907 and more briefly on 17 November 1906. Other works by Wells were discussed in *Social Democrat*, October and November 1906.

[120] *Justice*, 12 January 1907.

[121] For example *Justice*, 21, 28 December 1907.

[122] For example, *Justice*, 3 August 1907; *Social Democrat*, August 1907, p. 451.

[123] Ibid., p. 461.

[124] Quoted in *Justice*, 7 December 1907. See also *Justice*, 19 March 1910 for an account of a similar attack in a Lancashire newspaper and the party's response to it.

in their own defence to undermine the purpose of these attacks. Public meetings were used by the SDF to confront this campaign of vilification,[125] but they failed to redress the balance. As often, meetings on other issues could be disrupted by 'the usual foolish questions on Atheism and Free Love'.[126] The incidence of these attacks dramatically increased at times of direct political competition, such as national and local elections. For instance, during the 1906 Altrincham by-election, Joynson-Hicks sought to link socialism and 'free love' by citing Wells' writings. Wells later wrote that this incident 'lured me into an excess of repudiation'.[127] The denials only added to the confusion which served the slanderer's interests more effectively than the victim's. Socialism continued to be linked with 'free love'.

This particular episode of the 'free love' debate saw the SDF at their most defensive, responding to overtly anti-socialist propaganda. The changing political climate, particularly the rise of the Labour Party, had extended the arena of political debate, from the street corner to the mass circulation newspapers. A silent socialist press no longer seemed appropriate, even on such a contentious subject as 'free love'. What the SDF had to achieve, if their defence was to be effective, was to counter anti-socialist slurs without making the issue appear that important. 'Free love' was not the SDF's chosen area of contest; their theoretical understanding of socialism meant that they felt much more secure on economic issues, and considerably less so when it came to any aspect of the woman question.

The SDF and 'free love'

How consistent were the SDF's responses to the issue of 'free love', and what dictated those responses? The party always assumed that 'free love' could only be politically embarrassing. Its experience of the Lanchester Case confirmed this, increasing its reluctance to engage in internal debate on the subject. Sometimes, indeed, the SDF could entirely ignore an 'opportunity' to comment on 'free love', such as during the Fabian Basis dispute. In other cases, when forced into public discussion, the party was able to present a 'free love' issue as something else such as a civil liberties matter. On yet other occasions, the debate on 'free love' seems to have welled up in response to the concerns of members; one instance was the apparently innocuous piece in *Justice* on Immorality in the Potteries. An emotive debate ensued because of members' strength

[125] *Justice*, 1 February 1908.
[126] *Justice*, 6 June 1908.
[127] Wells, *Experiment in Autobiography*, II, p. 479.

of feeling on 'free love'. However, individuals' views did little to shake the official party line: open debate on 'free love' was still viewed with some trepidation by the leadership of the SDF.

The SDF's theoretical understanding of socialism meant that issues such as marriage and 'free love' were peripheral to the central economic questions; they were therefore regarded as matters of personal conscience. As no party position was possible, when the matter was discussed any individual's view was apparently as acceptable as any other's, including the most extreme. In practice, therefore, to minimise the potential damage that such unresolvable debates might incur, the SDF evolved a view that, on the whole, silence was the best policy. This position was adopted on pragmatic grounds as any association with 'free love' was seen as a vote-loser which could endanger the propagation of socialism.

Essentially, this attitude to the discussion of 'free love' did not change over the lifetime of the SDF. However the earlier experience of the Lanchester Case coupled with an increase in anti-socialist agitation, did mean that later statements, such as Quelch's *Social Democrat* article, which was much quoted, gave a clearer SDF view. This view was that socialism only meant 'free love' in the sense that, in a future socialist society, love would be free from economic coercion but not that that would necessarily mean the end of marriage. No support was offered for those who practised 'free love' in capitalist society. The clarity of Quelch's statement stemmed from a determination that the party should, where possible, control the circumstances when 'free love' was debated, so that political embarrassment could be minimised.

The initial circumstances promoting discussion on marriage and 'free love' were often beyond the control of the party; such was the case with Edith Lanchester. But on most occasions, the terms on which the subsequent debate took place were those of the party leadership, and particularly the editor of *Justice*. Ultimately he could decide which articles and, in particular, which letters were printed. This is not to claim that direct censorship occurred; if so the evidence has been well hidden. But the editor still held great power, seen most clearly in the curtailment of debates.

More fundamentally the terms on which debates were held were those of the male membership which so eagerly leapt in to discuss 'free love'. The idiosyncratic influence of Belfort Bax was crucial here. For many of the men who debated the marriage question so vigorously, their primary interest seems to have been theoretical. The 'free love' debate was part of a more general discussion of the 'fads' or conscience issues, and the relationship they bore to the central tenets of socialism. For the majority of male writers, there was therefore no doubt that the woman question did not constitute part of this core of beliefs.

To what extent was 'free love' a debate in which women participated? Women were involved in discussions and decisions, as Edith Lanchester's experiences illustrate. Yet when it came to public discussions within the pages of *Justice*, fewer women than men participated. Of course, in general, far fewer women were ever published and one can only assume that, for all the obvious reasons, women seldom wrote to *Justice*. The individuals who dominated this particular debate were men such as Bax, who clearly intimidated others from writing. Margaretta Hicks confirmed this in her comment that *Justice* should not be just for men. One cannot conclude that women were not interested in debating 'free love', since the way in which it was presented in the columns of *Justice* did not obviously invite women's participation. The discussion tended towards the abstract with a strong flavour of misogyny, and may have seemed a fairly futile debate with little hope of resolution. Great concern was expressed within *Justice* that potential socialists should not be alienated through an apparent advocacy of 'free love', the abolition of marriage and the family; yet little concern was shown about the effect on potential, and actual, women SDFers of such a spectrum of sexist views.

Finally, what does the SDF's response to 'free love' as an issue say for its understanding of the split between the public and the private, so essential to its understanding of socialism? Although the 'free love' debate saw the concerns of the 'private' intruding into the public sphere, there was no real sense in which they had actually become public matters. Certainly, the party's reaction suggested otherwise. For the SDF the 'personal' did not, and could not, become political by design; for instance, by a decision of Party Conference or of the leadership. But 'personal' matters such as Edith Lanchester's did become 'political' for a time. The fact that 'free love' could fragment the party on unexpected lines was all the more dangerous for the SDF leadership, because it involved scrutiny of areas where they believed socialists had no business to be – that is, the 'private' sphere. It distracted attention from what they thought should be the real concerns of a socialist party – the public sphere, interpreted specifically as economic issues.

Once forced into the sphere of public debate, the 'private' was reinterpreted and simplified, so that it was no longer threatening. In this way, the party was able to seal itself off from the challenge posed to its socialism by the various aspects of the woman question, such as 'free love'.

5   Women and work

Work is a significant aspect of the woman question. As waged labour it represents an important element of the public sphere while as domestic labour it remains hidden within the private sphere. Labour is also a central concept of the Marxist analysis of society, providing the basis for the definition of classes, of class society and ultimately of human emancipation. Work, therefore, brings together the tension between sex and class which lies at the heart of the socialist construction of the woman question.

For the SDF and its contemporaries, women's work was an area of considerable debate. The most contentious issue was married women's participation in the labour market. Around this clustered concerns about the family wage and the sexual division of labour, as well as a variety of strategies to alleviate the conditions of women's labour, such as protective legislation, unionisation and the endowment of motherhood. Women's work was also one of the arenas in which feminists and socialists often clashed, and where women who were, in effect, feminist socialists found themselves torn. They attempted to voice their concern for the conditions of women's labour within socialist organisations steeped in conventional assumptions about woman's place and her capacities. In examining the way that the SDF tackled the issue of women's work, I want to ask whether the party produced greater homogeneity in its response to this issue, which was firmly embedded in the public sphere, than was possible over the matters deemed to be of private conscience.

Women's work as an issue for the SDF

In the theoretical underpinning of the woman question, paid work has a particular significance. For Engels, paid labour was a necessary precondition for women's emancipation.[1] Only then would women be

---

[1]   Engels, *Origin*, pp. 137–8.

full members of their class and be able to fight with their proletarian brothers to achieve a socialist society where women would be fully emancipated. Participation in the labour market also brought women clearly into the public sphere and the arena of economics, factors which were crucial for the SDF's socialism. Together this suggested that women's work would be an important issue for the party as a whole and central to their practice on the woman question.

What did the SDF understand by the term 'women's work'? Did it encompass unpaid as well as paid labour? This was never likely to be the case. The founding fathers' emphasis on paid labour meant that domestic labour was invisible labour. Hence it did not contribute to women's emancipation. Yet it was also assumed that domestic labour would and should continue, and that it would remain a female task. Most of the SDFers who dealt with domestic labour did so in these terms. They suggested that socialism would bring with it socialised housework and that it would once again be a 'public service'.[2] But there were exceptions. Herbert Burrows, for example, saw housework as the 'nightmare' of women's lives and he predicted that 'the woman of the future will [not] find her chief glory in the pan, the dishcloth and the scrubbing brush'.[3] Women SDFers also drew attention to the sexual division of labour and the effect of the double burden on women workers. Edith Lanchester pointed out that working women are 'compelled' to do domestic work in addition to their paid work but that men, even when they are unemployed, do not perform any domestic duties at all.[4] F. E. Powell added that much of women's social inequality stemmed from the fact that their domestic labour was 'unremunerative, unprofitable and therefore unpaid'. She therefore regarded it as essential to 'Appraise such work at its true value, recognise it as socially useful'.[5]

A few lone voices within the SDF raised the question of domestic labour as a pressing political issue. But domestic labour, although symbolic of women's oppressed condition, was scarcely addressed by the socialist strategy for woman's emancipation. Housework was a drudgery which might eventually be alleviated by technology and the state, but there was no suggestion that socialists should engage in domestic prefigurative practice. When *Justice*'s columnist 'Jill' was

---

[2] *Social Democrat*, December 1909, p. 544. See also Engels, *Origin*, p. 137.
[3] Burrows, *The Future of Woman*, pp. 8, 10. For contemporary ideas, practical proposals and activities around the socialisation of domestic labour see D. Hayden, *The Grand Domestic Revolution*, MIT Press, Cambridge, Mass., 1981, pp. 135–265; A. J. Lane, 'Charlotte Perkins Gilman: The Personal is Political', in D. Spender (ed.), *Feminist Theorists*, The Women's Press, 1983, pp. 203–17.
[4] *Justice*, 10, October 1896.
[5] *Justice*, 6 January 1897.

asked, 'How can people who profess to be Socialists allow other women. to wash, starch, iron, cook, and do all their dirty work for them?' She replied, 'I altogether fail to see how the Cause is injured. We cannot live the life of Socialism in capitalist surroundings.'[6] Changes in the organisation of domestic labour would be a consequence of socialism, not a means to it. That men should share in domestic labour, and thus challenge the sexual division of labour, was never seriously regarded as a political issue or even as a practical tactic to encourage female participation in the fight for socialism.

Few SDFers argued that domestic labour was as crucial a part of the labour process as women's and men's paid labour. It was women's paid labour which was the key to her emancipation and it was this which was understood by the term 'women's work'. Thus when the SDF discussed or described[7] women's work, it reflected many of the preoccupations of the labour movement and shared many of the assumptions of the wider society. The party did not produce an original or even particularly considered approach to the question. Nor was its practice as energetic as some policy statements might suggest.

A fundamental assumption of the labour movement was that the wage of a male worker should be a family wage; that is, sufficient to cover not only his needs as an individual but also those of his dependent wife and children.[8] This model was used to justify women's lower wages, which were merely to supplement the male breadwinner's family wage. Women's labour could therefore undercut male labour, and for many trade unionists this meant that women's work should be limited or even prohibited. Here was a direct contradiction of the founding fathers' view that labour itself was a prerequisite for emancipation.

Just as other aspects of woman's condition, such as her natural inferiority, were assumed by many SDFers and analysed by few, so the assumption of the family wage ran beneath much of the party's discussion of women's work. Hyndman, for example, saw the family

6   *Justice*, 5 October 1907.
7   *Justice* carried a series entitled 'A Few Facts about Women's Work and Wages in England, Scotland, Ireland and Wales' in the early months of 1894 which was written by Enid Stacy. These were descriptive pieces on particular industries, such as cotton, and areas of work, such as shop assistants, which drew heavily on the recently published Blue Book on Women's Labour.
8   For a broader discussion of the family wage, see M. Barrett and M. McIntosh, 'The "Family Wage": Some Problems for Socialists and Feminists', *Capital and Class*, 11, 1980, pp. 51–72. In contrast, see J. Humphries, 'The Working Class Family, Women's Liberation, and Class Struggle: The Case of Nineteenth Century British History', *The Review of Radical Political Economics*, 9, 3, 1977, pp. 25–41. See also W. Seccombe, 'Patriarchy Stabilized: The Construction of the Male Breadwinner Wage Norm in Nineteenth-Century Britain', *Social History*, 11, 1, 1986, pp. 53–76.

wage as the natural way to guarantee a future generation of workers by providing for their upbringing within a family maintained by the male breadwinner. He felt that the equilibrium within this system was compromised by the advent of women and children's labour which ensured that 'a man's foes are literally they of his own household'.[9]

Debate on women's work in *Justice* usually echoed the general discussion of the issue among contemporaries. Mention was made, for instance, of the deleterious effect of work on women workers themselves, and more particularly on that of their children.[10] But in keeping with their concern for economic issues it was the effect of women's low pay which received particular attention amongst SDFers hostile to women's work. They argued that women's wages undercut men's and dragged down everyone's standard of living.[11] It was in this context that women were called 'blacklegs' by the Tattler and others.[12] Most of these comments were particularly applicable to married women, and they were the principal targets of the implicit and explicit calls made by SDFers for the limitation of women's work.

John Brooke's call for the expulsion of married women from 'forges, workshops and places of manufacture'[13] was unusually explicit. But many others rehearsed the arguments for women's unsuitability for paid work and the danger it posed to male workers. The Tattler, in particular, kept up a persistent level of criticism of married women's labour in his weekly column.[14] This gave the impression that the party itself was hostile to women's work, reinforced when others reiterated his arguments in their own letters and pieces within *Justice*.[15]

The Tattler, in particular, distinguished between unmarried and married women workers, suggesting that the latter, in addition to harming their brother workers, undermined their unmarried sisters who had to earn a living. In most cases, he argued, women were only temporary entrants to the labour market as their real career was marriage

[9] H. M. Hyndman, *The Historical Basis of Socialism in England*, Garland, New York, 1984 (first published 1883), p. 152.
[10] *Justice*, 22 March 1884; see also 3 January 1885; 18 October 1902.
[11] *Justice*, 22 March 1884; see also 3 January 1885.
[12] *Justice*, 1 November 1902; 14 December 1907.
[13] *Justice*, 3 January 1885.
[14] For example *Justice*, 17 March 1894; 21 April 1894; 13 January 1900; 9 February 1907.
[15] See *Justice*, 13 July 1895; 27 July 1895. Socialists outside the SDF also opposed married women's work, for example, Katherine Bruce Glasier (*Woman Worker*, 3 February 1909), and Margaret MacDonald (E. F. Mappen, 'Strategists for Change: Social Feminists' Approaches to the Problems of Women's Work', in A. V. John, *Unequal Opportunities: Women's Employment in England, 1880–1914*, Basil Blackwell, Oxford, 1986, p. 253).

and thus their place was in the home. He laid the blame at the door of women themselves.[16]

The Tattler was not alone in speaking against married women's labour.[17] Yet other SDFers argued strongly for woman's right to work and the necessity for her economic independence. These members challenged the notion of a 'family wage'. Dora Montefiore pointed out that the Tattler's argument assumed that women entered the workforce voluntarily, whereas she argued they were driven into it by economic pressure.[18] Others pointed out that women were not selfishly engaging in waged work but that many were supporting their own dependants – old and invalid parents, children and unemployed husbands.[19] Elizabeth Wolstenholme Elmy argued in *Justice* that unless the maintenance of these women and their dependants, as well as those women whose husbands refused to support them, was to be provided by the state or municipality, then 'the exclusion of married women from the factory would be a mere piece of brutal and cruel tyranny'.[20]

Such critics also argued for a woman's right to work on the principled ground that there should be an 'absolute equality of rights of all men and women'.[21] Hyndman's reply to this proposition epitomised the SDF's whole approach to the woman question. He argued that 'it is absurd to strive for freedom under present economical conditions. Such false freedom could but lead to deeper degradation. She must work with the Socialists for a complete reconstruction of society.'[22] Such a perspective was in direct contradiction to the view of the founding fathers. As I. D. Pearce reiterated 'in no way could woman be freed from her sex dependence upon man except by being forced into the labour market'.[23]

The critics also occasionally took the offensive by questioning the motives of those who recommended the proscription of women's labour. Dora Montefiore queried whether it was 'really the question of the working woman's health, or the question of her working in the same employment, and sometimes in competition with men, which disturbs the mind of Socialists?'[24] Mrs Wolstenholme Elmy implied that men felt threatened by the idea of economically independent women no longer being the exception. She suggested that it was significant that there had

[16]   *Justice*, 23 February 1901; 9 February 1907; 17 March 1894; 21 April 1894.
[17]   For example, V. Fisher, *The Babies' Tribute to the Modern Moloch*, Twentieth Century Press, 1907, p. 10; Lady Warwick in *Justice*, 23 February 1901.
[18]   *Justice*, 13 September 1902.
[19]   *Justice*, 28 November 1896.
[20]   *Justice*, 25 October 1902.
[21]   *Justice*, 5 April 1884.
[22]   Ibid.
[23]   *Justice*, 4 October 1902.
[24]   *Justice*, 13 September 1902.

been no demand for the restriction of married women's labour until after the Married Women's Property Act – because only then had married women secured the ownership of their own earnings and thus the possibility of economic independence.[25] Thus the Tattler's comments amounted to little more than special pleading, for he 'does not complain of the lesser wage paid to women as an injustice to women, but as a wrong to men, whose displacement as workers may result'.[26]

Can any official SDF view be determined on the question of married women's labour? An 1891 article suggested that 'we have little inclination to discuss details of the wage slave system we are striving to end',[27] but increasingly readers of *Justice* expected a clear party position. By 1906, a front page article acknowledged 'the increasingly urgent question of women's work and wages'.[28] Yet editorial comment was not consistent. In 1902 the exclusion of married women from factories was included in a list of ameliorative measures which the party should advocate.[29] By contrast an article in 1903 insisted that 'we have always maintained that there should be no bar to the employment of women in any suitable occupation'.[30] Two years later there was another twist in the paper's position when the front page of *Justice* carried the clear statement: 'The place for the mothers of children is not at the factory or workshop, but at home; and we would like to see a clause inserted in the Factory Act prohibiting the employment of mothers'.[31]

In view of these statements and despite the persistent publication of the Tattler's personal views, it is not surprising that there remained doubt as to the party's official line. As late as 1908 Kathleen Kough was calling for a clear statement on the issue of married women's labour.[32] The SDF's Conference deliberations were of no help. The Executive did put a resolution to the 1896 International in London calling for women's labour to be prohibited six weeks before, and until one month after, confinement.[33] But this was a very specific issue which was considerably less contentious than any attempt to prohibit all married women's labour.

Comment in *Justice* tended to be prompted by specific aspects of the 'women and work' question, particularly strategies to improve women's

[25] *Justice*, 22 November 1902.
[26] *Justice*, 25 October 1902.
[27] *Justice*, 5 September 1891.
[28] *Justice*, 1 December 1906.
[29] *Justice*, 13 September 1902.
[30] *Justice*, 14 November 1903.
[31] *Justice*, 15 July 1905.
[32] *Justice*, 17 October 1908.
[33] *Agenda for International Socialist Workers and Trade Union Congress*, 1896, p. 17.

working conditions and on women's economic independence. A number of proposals were put forward within the labour movement to ameliorate women's working conditions including various forms of state intervention as well as collective organisation.[34] By examining the SDF's discussion of these issues and the extent of the party's involvement in contemporary campaigns, a more complete picture can be drawn of its attitude to women and work. Were these issues, like other elements of the woman question, those on which no consensus was deemed necessary? Or did their economic content override the SDF's reluctance to take a party position?

Protective legislation

The issue of protective legislation first arose in the 1830s and 1840s around the question of women working underground in coal mines.[35] This form of labour was outlawed by the 1842 Mines Regulation Act, thereby setting a precedent of state intervention in women's labour. The original debate cut across gender and class divisions, and produced some uncomfortable alliances of groups who had very different reasons for promoting or opposing legislation. Broadly speaking, the underground women workers were allied with middle-class feminists and the employers, who formed up against moral reformers and male trade unionists.

When about forty years later the SDF was formed, protective legislation remained a strategy advocated by many parts of the labour movement to regulate women's labour. It was still not an issue where arguments divided neatly along class or gender lines. Indeed, it was not clear what the socialist position on protective legislation should be. For example, Clara Zetkin changed her mind about the issue. In 1889 she

---

[34] For labour movement attitudes to women's labour in this period, see B. Drake, *Women in Trade Unions*, Virago, 1984 (first published 1920); S. Lewenhak, *Women and Trade Unions*, Ernest Benn, 1977, pp. 67–143; S. Boston, *Women Workers and the Trade Union Movement*, Davis Poynter, 1980, pp. 30–95; N. C. Soldon, *Women in British Trade Unions,1874–1976*, Gill and Macmillan, Dublin, 1978, pp. 27–77; S. O. Rose, 'Gender Antagonism and Class Conflict: Exclusionary Strategies of Male Trade Unionists in Nineteenth-Century Britain', *Social History*, 13, 2, 1988, pp. 191–208; Gordon, *Women and the Labour Movement in Scotland*, pp. 73–101.

[35] For an examination of the arguments surrounding protective legislation see A. V. John, *By the Sweat of Their Brow: Women Workers at Victorian Coal Mines*, Croom Helm, 1980; J. Humphries, 'Protective Legislation, the Capitalist State, and Working Class Men: The Case of the 1842 Mines Regulation Act', *Feminist Review*, 7, 1981, pp. 1–33; and Angela John's comments, *Feminist Review*, 9, 1981, pp. 106–9; J. Mark-Lawson and A. Witz, 'From "Family Labour" to "family wage"? The Case of Women's Labour in Nineteenth Century Coalmining', *Social History*, 13, 2, 1988, pp. 151–74.

argued against protective legislation on the grounds that wage labour was a precondition of women's emancipation. But by 1893, she was arguing in favour of legislation which would protect women workers, particularly those who were also mothers.[36]

The SDF never discussed protective legislation at its conferences, and in that sense there was no party position. As with so much of the woman question, a diversity of views became apparent in the party's press. As ever, certain views were unofficially endorsed and came to be seen as party policy.

This was clearly apparent in a discussion in 1902 in which the main protagonists were the Tattler and Dora Montefiore. The former took a labourist position, the latter a feminist one. This debate reveals the interplay of assumptions between SDFers on the issue of whether protective legislation was the most beneficial strategy for women workers. The little coverage given to protective legislation in the SDF press prior to 1902 had been generally approving.[37] But in August 1902, *Justice* carried a front page article on the increasing number of lower-middle-class women moving into the labour force, particularly into white collar work. The author questioned how much this contributed to the greater good, in so doing revealing his own hostility to women's work. A report from Saxony on the nervous illness to which women white-collar workers were said to be prone was used to suggest that existing restrictions on women's labour should be extended.[38] Dora Montefiore responded by pointing out that not all Social Democrats agreed with this and regretted that such an opinion had appeared in *Justice* as though it were official policy. This started the debate which continued throughout the autumn on protective legislation as a socialist demand.

The different arguments in favour of protective legislation can be categorised into two main groups: those advocating protective legislation principally as an instrument for restricting women's work; and those emphasising the protection of women workers.

Although the Tattler argued for the former position, he used arguments which appeared to be concerned with women's welfare. He wrote, for instance, that 'there is no reason why the health and lives of women and children should continue to be jeopardised while the revolution is in the making'.[39] His belief that protective legislation was a necessary reform of capitalism to be striven for by Social Democrats was

[36]   Thönnessen, *The Emancipation of Women*, pp. 39–43, 48.
[37]   For example, Burrows argued for protective legislation in the poisonous trades (*Justice*, 22 June 1895).
[38]   *Justice*, 23 August 1902.
[39]   *Justice*, 15 November 1902.

based on an appparent recognition of the greater exploitation suffered by women. But this was not a position that he usually voiced, and raises the suspicion that he adopted it for the purposes of this particular argument. Certainly *Justice* readers would have been aware of his longstanding ambivalence towards the fight for sexual equality. The Tattler's view of the woman question did not recognise woman's labour as essentially emancipatory for her principal role remained that of wife and mother. Even in this debate he made clear his own support for the restriction of married women's labour, although he put the demand in the mouths of women, many of whom, he said, were calling for the extension of the Factory Acts and the prohibition of married women's labour.[40] Indeed he argued that it was against the interests of 'the race' for mothers to work and affected surprise that 'even well-to-do women should be so enamoured of the factory hell as to think otherwise'.[41] This, then, was a rare opportunity where the Tattler's long-standing misogyny could be expressed in a manner which apparently supported many women's own definition of their emancipation.

The reality of the Tattler's position was as much about opposing feminist arguments as about positive support for reform. Feminism had been identified with opposition to protective legislation from the 1840s on the grounds of equal treatment for both sexes.[42] The Tattler therefore had a familiar 'enemy' whom he sought to paint as 'reactionary' and 'anti-Socialist'.[43] He suggested that the logic of Dora Montefiore and her supporters must mean that they favoured women working down coal-mines.

Nor was the Tattler alone in questioning the rights of 'well-to-do women' to consign their working-class sisters to continuing appalling working conditions which they themselves did not have to experience. Both Margaretta Hicks and Amie Hicks wrote as working-class women in support of protective legislation. Margaretta argued strongly against Dora Montefiore:

I have seen the workgirls (who had no votes) waltz around the room when they heard of the Bill to prevent work being taken home after shop hours, though

[40]   *Justice*, 18 October 1902.

[41]   *Justice*, 1 November 1902.

[42]   For a discussion of Victorian feminism and protective legislation, see Levine, *Victorian Feminism*, pp. 118–22; Banks, *Faces of Feminism*, pp. 103–9; R. Feurer, 'The Meaning of "Sisterhood": The British Women's Movement and Protective Labor Legislation, 1870–1900', *Victorian Studies*, 31, 2, 1988, pp. 233–60. For a critical account of feminist opposition to protective legislation made during the SDF's lifetime, see B. L. Hutchins and A. Harrison, *A History of Factory Legislation*, P. S. King and Son, 1911, pp. 183–99.

[43]   *Justice*, 27 September 1902; 18 October 1902.

afterwards when they thought of it they were a little doubtful whether it might not mean less money. Still I am glad to tell you it did not; in fact, indirectly the wages have been slightly raised through it.[44]

Moreover, Amie Hicks argued that as working women did not face equal economic conditions with men they needed legislation for their own protection, and that middle-class women should find out the truth before they spoke on the matter.[45] For these women, protective legislation was clearly a class question. Yet in all this debate it was of course assumed, as the Tattler indeed argued, that strategically the only options were protective legislation or unrestricted competition. The critics of protective legislation in *Justice* did not share this assumption.

Dora Montefiore, in particular, highlighted the Tattler's hidden agenda. If he was really interested in women's health then why was the focus purely on factories and not on nursing or dressmaking?[46] Surely the Tattler was more interested in areas where the sexes directly competed with one another, because there, as he himself argued, protective legislation benefited men's conditions of employment?[47] For Dora Montefiore, 'restrictive legislation' was no solution because the 'only way to decrease the competition between men and women is to raise the conditions of labour, and the wages of the latter by giving them equal political rights and equal possibilities of combination in trade unions'.[48] She believed that supporters of protective legislation failed to address many areas of women's work which were also detrimental to women's health and well-being. They also ignored the fact that equally unhealthy work was being done by men yet there was no argument that they should be 'protected'. Dora Montefiore therefore argued that if protective legislation was really needed it should apply irrespective of sex, as what was unhealthy or dangerous for women was surely also unhealthy and dangerous for men. Otherwise she feared that protective legislation would mean that women were forced out of certain 'protected' areas and would have 'to seek one of the rougher, and worse paid jobs, where "physiological and natural differences" are not so much considered'.[49]

Beatrice Browning felt that Dora Montefiore's position amounted to anarchism and was a recipe for unrestricted sweating. She argued, 'I as a Socialist and a woman, object to this shriek for women's right to work as

---

[44] *Justice*, 18 October 1902.
[45] *Justice*, 22 November 1902. See appendix 5 for a brief biography of Amie Hicks.
[46] *Justice*, 13 September 1902. For similar comments from ILP women, see Gordon, *Women and the Labour Movement in Scotland*, p. 278.
[47] *Justice*, 27 September 1902.
[48] *Justice*, 13 September 1902.
[49] *Justice*, 11 October 1902.

many hours a day, with as little pay, and under any conditions the capitalist class like to enforce without restrictions.' She felt that 'Such women as Dora Montefiore ought to know how difficult it is to organise women in any way, and therefore how necessary it is that the hours and conditions of labour should be regulated by law.'[50] This remained the nub of the dispute amongst those who genuinely wanted to see a real improvement in women's working conditions – what strategy would be most effective?

In that context, talk of protective legislation in isolation from other campaigns served to distinguish genuine reformers from those who were hostile or indifferent to women's emancipation. The Tattler, for instance, seemed to be more concerned to differentiate a socialist position from that of the feminists, and in so doing he managed to imply that the restrictive rather than the protective element was the more valued feature of legislation. Editorial comments also bore out the impression that the party supported protective legislation on these grounds.[51] But this was not an inflexible position. In reaction to the later campaign by Margaret MacDonald and others to prohibit women working as barmaids, the SDF's position was somewhat different. It was argued that although protective legislation was on the whole beneficial there seemed to be no argument for restriction in this particular case, which was being promoted by 'teetotal fanatics'.[52] In this case, the puritan element within the campaign against barmaids was one against which the SDF leadership instinctively reacted, overriding its more general prejudices against women's work.

Equal pay

The SDF was involved with another strategy to ameliorate one of the most criticised aspects of women's work, low rates of pay. If a single rate for the job, irrespective of the sex of the worker, could be established then this would, it was argued, end the problem of women's labour undercutting that of men. On occasions the SDF counterposed such a policy to that of protective legislation. For example, when the Postal Telegraph Clerks Association's Conference of 1893 was reported in *Justice*, a resolution to limit the employment of women staff was criticised as a 'most shortsighted and foolish policy'. Instead, the paper

[50] *Justice*, 25 October 1902.
[51] For example *Justice*, 13 September 1902.
[52] *Justice*, 11 April 1903; 14 November 1903. See also *Social Democrat*, February 1904, p. 68. For Margaret MacDonald's involvement in the debates on protective legislation, see J. R. MacDonald, *Margaret Ethel MacDonald*, Hodder and Stoughton, 1912, pp. 169–77; Mappen, 'Strategists for Change'.

recommended that the Association should agitate for equal payment for men and women in the telegraph service.[53]

There was a variety of different emphases amongst SDFers who espoused equal pay. Equal pay could be seen as a compatible demand with that of some protection for women workers. Herbert Burrows, for example, put forward equal pay as part of a package of measures to reform women's working conditions which also included the abolition of home work and protection from dangerous trades.[54] This combination of demands was pursued within the Second International.[55] But the two demands did not always go hand in hand. The editor of *Justice* endorsed equal pay in a list of proposed reforms to women's work set out in 1902,[56] but he also included the exclusion of married women from factory work. How equal pay was to fit into any overall strategy on women's work was therefore by no means clear.

Nor was there much debate on how to turn endorsement of equal pay as a demand into a practical campaign. This was partly because the party's commitment to the demand was less than total. The Tattler, in particular, superficially endorsed equal pay but undermined his own position by drawing attention to apparent objections. He maintained that it was women who objected to such a demand 'as another evidence of "sex bias", a sinister attempt on the part of men to get women shut out of employment altogether by demanding that they should have the same wages as men'. The Tattler further argued that men should have the right to combine to keep up their wages and resist undercutting by other workers.[57] In this manner, he contradicted his notional commitment to an equal pay campaign.

Some women SDFers took a more serious approach to the issue. Dora Montefiore suggested that 'wherever Socialists are working as administrators in municipal matters, we hope they will work strenuously for equal pay for equal work, and equal hours for men and women'.[58] Unfortunately there were not many SDFers in this position! Nevertheless this was the first, and only, suggestion that SDFers might be able to do something practical to further this campaign. It was not surprising that it was never taken any further, for despite the unanimous TUC vote in 1888 there was no real campaign in the labour movement for equal

[53] *Justice*, 6 May 1893.
[54] *Justice*, 29 December 1894.
[55] For example, see *Justice*, 8 August 1896.
[56] *Justice*, 13 September 1902.
[57] *Justice*, 1 November 1902. See also *Justice*, 27 January 1900. For the conflicting attitudes behind the first TUC equal pay resolution, see Soldon, *Women in British Trade Unions*, p. 34; S. Lewenhak, *Women and Trade Unions*, pp. 89–91.
[58] Ibid.

pay. Sarah Boston's study of women workers and the trade union movement concludes that low, not equal, pay was the central issue for most women workers of the late nineteenth century.[59] Campaigning for equal pay was not seen as a realistic means to improve women's wages in the short term. This concern was echoed in *Justice*'s women's column. 'Jill' foresaw the problems that equal pay for equal work might pose in the existing, sex-segregated labour market. She asked: 'But how much of that [equal work] would you get. It may very well be that the grievance, "a woman's work is anything too badly paid for men to do", will be accentuated and intensified.'[60] 'Jill' believed that equal pay must be demanded but added, presciently, that it must also be enforced.[61]

The SDF's discussion on equal pay therefore remained largely at a theoretical level. When the means to achieving equal pay were considered, it was assumed that collective bargaining rather than state intervention would be necessary. This showed how irrelevant much discussion was to the deep-seated problems of women's pay. Most women were unlikely to be organised and had little bargaining power, whilst the male-dominated unions were not yet convinced of the need for equal pay and were unlikely to act on behalf of low paid women workers.

Wages boards and minimum wage legislation

In the early 1900s, campaigners on women's work looked to state intervention to combat women's low pay. The focus of attention was on wages boards and minimum wage legislation. The issue was widely debated and divided the principal organisations which focused on women's work, the Women's Industrial Council and the Women's Trade Union League.[62] Yet this debate was rarely reflected in the SDF. Dora Montefiore, exceptionally, recognised the need for a minimum wage where women were unorganised. But she also argued against Fabian and much trade union thinking by emphasising that such a wage should be equal for both sexes.[63]

Although the SDF seem to have taken little notice of the contem-

[59] Boston, *Women Workers and the Trade Union Movement*, p. 57.
[60] *Justice*, 3 August 1907. See also B. Drake, *Women in Trade Unions*, pp. 227–37.
[61] For some of the problems of drafting and enforcing equal pay legislation, see E. M. Meehan, *Women's Rights at Work: Campaigns and Policy in Britain and the United States*, Macmillan, 1985; M. Snell, 'The Equal Pay and Sex Discrimination Acts: Their Impact in the Workplace', *Feminist Review*, 1, 1979, pp. 37–57.
[62] See Mappen, 'Strategists for Change' for the debate between the WTUL and WIC. See J. Morris, *Women Workers and the Sweated Trades: The origins of Minimum Wage Legislation*, Gower, Aldershot, Hants, 1986 for the wider context.
[63] Montefiore, *The Position of Women in the Socialist Movement*, pp. 11–12. Minimum wage

porary discussion on the merits of wages boards, they were reminded of the importance of the problem of sweated labour by the 1906 Daily News Sweated Industries Exhibition. This prompted the party to clarify its position on this area of women's work. *Justice*'s reviewer of the exhibition could do no better than recommend that the party 'awaken our class to class-consciousness. Sweating is inevitable under capitalism, and Socialism is the only remedy. Only an intelligent proletariat, organised into the Socialist Party, can beat down the sweating dens of capitalism.'[64] Other SDFers expressed scepticism about attempts to form a 'Consumers League' to combat sweating by boycotting goods produced in these conditions. They called instead for a complete prohibition of all home working as well as the restriction of all work of women and children which directly competed with that of adult males.[65] Indeed any discussion within *Justice* of the evil of sweating sooner or later came down to the problem of women working and to a demand for prohibition.[66]

Later in 1906, the SDF participated in a labour movement conference on the minimum wage. The party opposed the conference organisers' call for endorsement of a campaign to secure legislation for a minimum wage in the sweated industries. While arguing that sweating could only be fully abolished with the end of capitalism, the party put forward a series of measures to mitigate the worst aspects of sweating. These included the abolition of home working; the establishment of a minimum wage; the extension and more adequate application of the Factory Acts; the raising of the school leaving age; legislation for an eight-hour day and the state organisation of the unemployed.[67]

The strategy of using legislation to ameliorate the worst of women's working conditions was not one which the SDF could adopt whole-heartedly because of its ambivalence towards state action under capitalism. The party's political tactics did involve making demands on the state. But it was not concerned with the minutiae of single issue campaigns like that for wages boards, believing that no fundamental change was possible under capitalism. Hence the SDF put little energy into the campaigns for the reforms advocated by the 1906 Conference.[68]

campaigns in trade unions differentiated between the sexes (L. Holcombe, *Victorian Ladies at Work*, David and Charles, Newton Abbot, Devon, 1973, pp. 138–9).

[64] *Justice*, 12 May 1906.
[65] *Justice*, 2 June 1906.
[66] *Justice*, 30 June 1906.
[67] *Justice*, 3 November 1906.
[68] There are contrasting accounts of the SDF's role in the conference: G. M. Tuckwell, 'Women's Trade Unions and "Sweated Industries"', *The Socialist Annual*, 1907, pp. 63–6; S. Lewenhak, *Women and Trade Unions*, p. 121; *Justice*, 3 November 1906.

The party favoured campaigns which would make a mass of demands on the state. These were intended to stretch the system to its utmost if implemented. The real aim was not reform within the existing system but the exposure of its contradictions. The long list of demands put forward by the SDF at the 1906 Minimum Wage Conference should be seen in this light. Mere reformist measures were not of interest as an end in themselves. But they might be supported as part of a wider strategy of 'transitional demands' and as a means to promote the organisation and politicisation of the working class. Once again, the woman question was submerged within an understanding of political strategy which denied the complexities of the issue.

Trade unions

There were a number of reasons why the SDF might be expected to be ambivalent in advancing collective action in trade unions as a strategy for women workers. First, the SDF was seen by some contemporaries as generally hostile to trade unions. Despite the views of some labour historians, this is a misrepresentation of the party's attitude and the practice of many of its members.[69] It is, however, true that the SDF did not place trade unions at the heart of its political strategy, seeing them as just one potential arena for spreading socialist propaganda. Secondly, the party's ambivalence towards women's engagement in paid work suggests that it would see no need for women's trade unionism. Thirdly, the SDF's attitude to women as potential political activists meant that many SDFers, like many of their trade unionist brothers, did not view women as capable of sustained organisation.

Justice certainly gave space to reports of women's trade union activity, usually in its first, tentative stages. These were more likely to appear in times of increased union action, such as during the burst of New Unionism from 1889 to 1891,[70] rather than during quieter periods when SDFers could have chosen to take a more active role themselves. These reports, like those on women's working conditions, were descriptive pieces containing no comments on the broader questions of whether women ought to be encouraged to organise, or indeed to work at all. Nevertheless, the mere reporting of women's trade union activity without comment was in *Justice*'s terms almost a form of endorsement!

Local branches were occasionally involved in attempts to unionise

---

[69]   See the Introduction for a discussion of the SDF's attitude to trade unions, as part of the stereotype of the party employed by many contemporaries and historians.

[70]   For example, *Justice*, 14 July 1888; 12 October, 19 October, 26 October, 9 November 1889; 15 March, 29 March, 3 May, 10 May, 28 June 1890; 14 March 1891.

women workers. One example was the local SDF's role in helping to organise laundresses in Wandsworth in 1889.[71] Individual SDFers were also prominent in particular strikes such as the matchgirls', in which both Annie Besant and Herbert Burrows played a key part.[72] Amie Hicks was the main force behind the formation of the East London Ropemakers' Union, of which she became the first secretary.[73] More unusually given the SDF's general attitude to feminist organisations, individual SDFers, such as Burrows and Hicks, were involved in the Women's Trade Union League and the Women's Industrial Council.[74] Was this apparently favourable attitude to women's trade unions borne out in the comments made in the columns of *Justice*?

The general feeling within the labour movement was that women were notoriously difficult to organise.[75] The SDF's concurrence in this matter revealed its underlying attitudes to women. Yet SDF women who had experience of organising female workers admitted that they were hard to organise and highlighted specific obstacles which they had encountered. Margaretta Hicks emphasised the structure of women's participation in a labour market where more than half the women workers were under twenty-five and low wages prevented independent action. She stressed that for such vulnerable workers, gender was an additional factor in limiting unionisation for they also met the opposition of men; employers, fathers and male trade unionists.[76] She also highlighted the character of the work that many older women did. Home work particularly militated against organisation since these women often had to do their own housework as well, leaving them little time to think, let alone organise.[77] Her mother, Amie Hicks, also stressed another factor which inhibited women's unionisation. This was the absence of economic power to back up any protests that women tried to make.[78] Margaretta went further on another occasion and questioned the

---

[71] *Justice*, 24 August 1889. See also *Justice*, 21 April 1894; 4 November 1905; 11 January 1908.

[72] A. H. Nethercot, *The First Five Lives of Annie Besant*, Hart-Davis, 1961, pp. 263–75; D. Rubinstein, 'Annie Besant', in D. Rubinstein (ed.), *People for the People*, Ithaca, 1973, pp. 148–52; B. L. Hutchins, *Women in Modern Industry*, E. P. Publishing, East Ardsley, 1978 (first published 1915), pp. 127–8; A. Taylor, *Annie Besant*, Oxford University Press, Oxford, 1992, pp. 206–14; *Justice*, 9 August 1890.

[73] Hutchins, *Women in Modern Industry*, pp. 128–9.

[74] *Justice*, 22 February 1890; 13 April 1895; 7 July 1900; 27 April 1901; 8 April 1905.

[75] *Justice*, 8 April 1905; Drake, *Women in Trade Unions*, pp. 198–202.

[76] See also the comparable points made by Annie Besant in *Justice*, 12 October 1889. For a similar current analysis, see H. Hartmann, 'Capitalism, Patriarchy and Job Segregation by Sex', in Z. R. Eisenstein (ed.), *Capitalist Patriarchy and the Case for Socialist Feminism*, pp. 206–47.

[77] *Justice*, 6 April 1895.

[78] *Justice*, 22 November 1902.

appropriateness of trade unions as a form of organisation for women. She thought they compared unfavourably with such organisations as the Women's Cooperative Guild and the Working Girls Clubs. She speculated that in relation to trade unions, for women 'there is a feeling of shrinking from it, and I think the groundwork of that feeling is a consciousness that it is a fighting organisation, a perpetual antagonism between master and worker, with no hope of ceasing, no end or conclusion.'[79]

The strength of these women SDFers' analysis of their sex's relationship to trade unions was its basis in experience. They recognised the specificity of women's work. But SDFers also supported women's general right to work. To this end they saw unionisation as an important strategy for women, in improving pay and conditions. Nevertheless, recognition of the difficulties in organising women meant party members also looked to state intervention to protect women workers under capitalism.

There was no real consensus amongst SDFers on unionisation as a strategy to ameliorate women workers' conditions. Certainly not all SDFers' experience of organising women workers led them to the same conclusions. Will Thorne, one of the most experienced SDFer trade unionists, looking back in 1900 after a decade of trying to organise women in the National Union of Gasworkers and General Labourers, concluded that legislation was more appropriate for women workers than organisation. This was, he argued, because of the double workload of home and work which left women with little time or energy for organisation.[80] Later still, Thorne told B. L. Hutchins that he did not think women should be organised as 'they do not make good trade unionists'.[81] He felt that the energies of union organisers were better employed working with male workers. Although Thorne had long since ceased to be directly involved in workplace organisation, his views did reflect those of many senior male trade unionists.[82]

Other SDFers not so involved in organising women also commented

[79]   *Justice*, 29 October 1904. In a similar vein today, B. Campbell, *Wigan Pier Revisited*, Virago, 1984, pp. 129–52.

[80]   *Women's Trade Union Review*, January 1900 quoted in Boston, *Women Workers and Trade Union Movement*, p. 56.

[81]   Letter from Thorne to Hutchins, 30 March 1910, quoted in D. Thom, 'The Bundle of Sticks: Women, Trade Unionists and Collective Organisation before 1918', in John (ed.), *Unequal Opportunities*, p. 279.

[82]   See, for example, Joanna Bornat's interesting analysis of the General Union of Textile Workers, particularly her comments on the male leadership's paternalistic language and their emphasis on the problematic nature of women's union membership (J. Bornat, 'Lost Leaders: Women, Trade Unionism and the Case of the General Union of Textile Workers, 1875–1914', in John (ed.), *Unequal Opportunities*, pp. 207–233).

on the problem of women's unionisation. However, they contrived to concentrate on what they saw as the personal failings of women rather than structural problems inherent in the contemporary labour market. The Tattler, for example, thought he knew why women's wages were so low. It was because 'women as a rule are too narrow, too selfish and too much enamoured of their present position to combine to alter it'.[83] Neither did T. Relton have very high expectations of women as trade unionists. He reported that his own union had tried to organise women but 'they did not come in their thousands, at least not more than a dozen or so, the rest were busy looking at the bonnet shops'.[84] These negative images of women's capabilities were reinforced by the belief expressed by some SDFers that women 'are generally the cause of the breakdown of a strike'.[85]

The view that women were blacklegs was not uncommon. The Tattler argued:

There is a theory ... that women back men up, encourage them in every strike, in every struggle, in every enterprise ... So far as my own experience goes – and I have had more than most men – the theory is absurd and entirely wrong. For one woman who would strengthen a man's hands in a struggle against injustice, there are twenty who would strike them down ... 'Submit, submit', is always their cry to the men. 'What do you think you can do to alter it?' they ask, with a sneer, of any man who tries to rouse his fellows to revolt ... [Women] dominate the men and make blacklegs and cowards of them.[86]

There was therefore a strong image of women's relation to trade unions opposed to that put forward by women SDFers. It saw women as the cause of their own and men's problems. Although this view did not receive a particularly large amount of space within the SDF press, it was reinforced by the dominant, negative representation of women. This wider context must be considered when assessing the SDF's support for women's unionisation.

Various reasons were given for the necessity to unionise women. Many of these were more to do with protecting the male labour force, for example from being undercut by women workers,[87] than they were to benefit women themselves. It was even argued that women's unionisation should be encouraged in order to prevent women being driven into prostitution by low wages.[88] But Dora Montefiore saw trade unionism as being of direct benefit to women themselves: 'Women are

[83] *Justice*, 21 April 1894. See also *Social Democrat*, October 1909, p. 453.
[84] *Justice*, 8 November 1902.
[85] *Justice*, 17 March 1894; also, 31 March 1894; 14 December 1907.
[86] *Justice*, 12 May 1894.
[87] *Justice*, 19 October 1889.
[88] *Justice*, 22 August 1885.

newer to industrial life than are men; they need organisation and training, they need permeating, by those who are more evolved, with a sense of solidarity among workers'.[89] Zelda Kahan saw the positive effects of trade unionism for women as being directly linked to their whole experience of paid labour which, like the founding fathers, she recognised as a prerequisite for emancipation. She described the paradoxical effects of paid work:

If it forced her from her home it gave her independence or the germs of it; if it separated her from her children it gave her facilities for intercourse with her fellows; it gave her an opportunity of appreciating to some extent the social forces working around her, it slowly taught her the value of combination and co-operation.[90]

In many ways, the strategy of improving women's working conditions through collective organisation was, for the SDF, one of the least contentious of the solutions discussed by contemporaries. Yet the motives of particular SDFers for desiring women's unionisation, and their perceptions of the obstacles to the widespread organisation of women, were varied and even diametrically opposed. Despite the near unanimity on the necessity for women to be organised if they were to be workers, the party's underlying ambivalence towards women working meant that only a limited practical effort was put into this strategy. Even then, action occured only when the political climate was already conducive to a greater degree of militancy. There was, of course, nothing within the SDF's arguments to prevent individuals and branches aiding efforts to unionise women workers. But still, the underlying ambivalence towards women's work combined with the framework of their understanding of the woman question to discourage any systematic action in this area.

The SDF's theoretical ambivalence and practical sluggishness raises an important question. Were the various strategies, of protective legislation, equal pay, a minimum wage and unionisation regarded by the SDF as solely part of the 'labour question'? That is, were they theorised as essentially economic issues, or as aspects of the more contentious woman question? Such a dichotomy cannot be sustained. The SDF did not entirely separate any of these economic issues from the woman question. Assumptions about woman's role and her capacities were never far from the surface in any discussions about women, even when the content of that issue was essentially economic. Like the wider labour movement, the party showed considerable ambivalence about

[89] *Justice*, 13 September 1902.
[90] *Social Democrat*, December 1909, p. 541. See appendix 5 for a brief biography of Zelda Kahan.

women working, particularly when those women were married. There was no real consensus on how to deal with the poor working conditions and low pay of women workers. Restriction, organisation, and state intervention were all canvassed as possible solutions. The SDF did endorse equal pay, women's unionisation and protective legislation (although with dissent) and, less wholeheartedly, a minimum wage. But they were not clear how, or indeed whether, such commitments should become political campaigns, or what role a socialist party should have in achieving them. The mere fact that these proposals were part of the woman question seemed to inhibit party action. It was left to the individual, and even to branches, to take the action that they felt was most appropriate. This in turn simply reinforced the contradictory image of the SDF in relation to the issues surrounding women's paid work. Without a party position, the prejudices that powerful individual SDFers held could all too easily come to represent the party as a whole.

The endowment of motherhood: an alternative means to economic independence

The founding fathers had argued that woman's participation in the labour market was the key to her economic independence and thus to her emancipation. Yet for some of the SDF's contemporaries, the debate on women's economic independence was not limited to discussions of the labour market but also included women's unpaid labour as wives and mothers. This latter issue was crystallised in the demand for the endowment of motherhood: that is, payment from the state for mothers who stayed at home and looked after their children. As we have already seen, the SDF's discussion of paid work was permeated by an acceptance of the sexual division of labour. This was shared by large sections of the labour movement. All expressed concern at the involvement of married women and mothers in the labour market. Together, these factors meant that the endowment of motherhood could be seen as an alternative, desirable means to achieving women's economic independence, one which would not disturb the sexual division of labour. How then did the SDF view the endowment of motherhood? Was it a more acceptable demand than those which addressed the labour market directly, or was it merely another part of the woman question on which no consensus was possible?

For many socialist women the central issue of the woman question was women's economic independence.[91] This was particularly true for

---

[91] Women's economic independence was an important theme for many women who wrote on the woman question whether they placed themselves in the socialist and

the Fabian Women's Group, who defined what they called the theoretical side of their work as being 'to seek out and explain the conditions of economic independence for women under Socialism and the steps whereby it can be gained'.[92] Although Julia Dawson, of the *Clarion*, was also concerned to achieve women's economic independence, she felt that 'we have set about securing economic independence in the wrong way'. Women should not have to stand behind shop counters or work in mills to gain economic independence. Instead the payment of mothers by the state seemed to be a way to secure some degree of independence whilst also keeping women out of the workforce.[93] The sexual division of labour and even the future of the race would therefore be secured. In the years before the First World War, the principle of state endowment of motherhood was discussed within the Fabian Women's Group and the Women's Labour League (WLL), specifically in relation to the 'problem' of married women's work.[94] As with other aspects of women's relationship to work, there were major differences of opinion on endowment of motherhood as a strategy, particularly within the WLL. Indeed, Caroline Rowan has argued that women's economic independence was 'probably the most hotly debated issue in the League's history'.[95] Was it equally important and equally contentious for the SDF?

'Endowment of motherhood' was not a phrase which summarised a precise or detailed demand. A wide spectrum of individuals indicated support for it as a general principle without setting out what they hoped to achieve by such a strategy, or any detailed plan for its achievement. For the state to pay mothers might amount to full economic independence for such women.[96] Or it might also be understood as merely maternity benefit for a limited period: or one of various other steps in

labour movement or not. For example, in the SDF's lifetime the following were published: C. Perkins Gilman, *Women and Economics*, Harper and Row, New York, 1966 (first published 1898); C. Hamilton, *Marriage as a Trade*, The Women's Press, 1981 (first published 1909); O. Schreiner, *Women and Labour*, Virago, 1978 (first published 1911).

92 *Fabian News*, March 1909, p. 33.
93 *Clarion*, 25 September 1903.
94 For example *The League Leaflet*, April 1911. For the Fabian Women's Group discussion of economic independence and the endowment of motherhood, see P. Pugh, *Educate, Agitate, Organise: 100 Years of Fabian Socialism*, Methuen, 1984, pp. 107–9; S. Alexander, 'Introduction' to M. Pember Reeves, *Round About A Pound A Week*, Virago, 1979, pp. xv–xx. For the WLL, see Rowan, 'Mothers, Vote Labour!', pp. 59–84, particularly pp. 73–5.
95 Rowan, 'Mothers, Vote Labour!', p. 75.
96 This would be similar to the current campaign around Wages for Housework. See S. Fleming, 'Introduction', to E. Rathbone, *The Disinherited Family*, Falling Wall Press, 1986, pp. 9–120.

between. It was therefore possible to advocate endowment of motherhood without intending to demand women's economic independence.
The SDF contained just such a range of views.

Endowment of motherhood in its most limited form, of a maternity
benefit for women while bearing and suckling children, was supported
by a number of SDFers. In 1902, Dora Montefiore argued for such state
pensions for women when 'they are incapacitated by childbearing from
earning a living'.[97] This was therefore not a substitute for women
working in the labour market but a stop-gap, of maintenance for paid
workers temporarily unable to work. Dora Montefiore, at this stage,
assumed that woman's means to economic independence would remain
participation in the workforce. Later she was to develop her point of
view, when the idea of a full endowment of motherhood became more
widely discussed. Generally there was no agreement within the SDF on
the precise nature of a maternity pension. For example, Margaretta
Hicks in 1908 reported favourably on a scheme where payment was
made in kind rather than in cash. This was an experiment where the
council in St Pancras provided a meal a day to undernourished childbearing women.[98] Others, including the Second International, were
looking for full state maintenance for a period of pregnancy and
maternity[99] – but not full endowment of motherhood as a longer term
alternative to women being part of the workforce.

Much of the impetus for the debate within the SDF on the
endowment of motherhood came from books such as Dr Eder's
Endowment of Motherhood. Also influential was discussion in the Fabian
Women's Group, which directly touched the SDF through their mutual
participation in the national women's section of the Second International. But most significant of all was contemporary concern about the
health of the nation and the future of the race.[100] Some suggestions for
endowment of motherhood seemed to be wholly preoccupied with the
issue of health. One such was that made in *Justice* by a woman ILP
member. In order to improve the health of future generations she argued
that all women between the ages of twenty and thirty should be
responsible to the state for at least three children. In recompense they
would receive a state pension from their fiftieth birthday.[101] This was

[97] *Justice*, 1 November 1902.
[98] *Justice*, 28 March 1908. For the St Pancras scheme, see D. Dwork, *War is Good for
Babies and Other Young Children*, Tavistock, 1987, pp. 145–54.
[99] Montefiore, *The Position of Women in the Socialist Movement*, p. 12; *Justice*, 29
December 1906.
[100] See Anna Davin's influential article, 'Imperialism and Motherhood', *History Workshop
Journal*, 5, 1978, pp. 9–65; J. Lewis, *The Politics of Motherhood*, Croom Helm, 1980.
[101] *Justice*, 5 March 1904.

clearly not a recommendation which focused on women's need for economic independence, or even the perceived problem of the competition of married women with male workers in the workplace. Instead it saw some form of endowment as an inducement to women to take their responsibilities as mothers seriously. This was a similar proposal to that made later by H. G. Wells in his controversial book, *Socialism and the Family*. The reviewer of this in *Social Democrat* saw Wells' scheme as essentially being one of payment by results; the state would pay for legitimate children provided they remained healthy.[102] This was a purely eugenic recommendation designed to increase the birth rate.

Dora Montefiore's proposal of 1910 reflected many of these concerns but went much further in recognising motherhood as a valuable occupation in itself. She argued that 'mothers, in bringing healthy children into the world, and rearing them for useful citizens are fulfilling a State function; they must, therefore, inasmuch as they cannot during that period work industrially for the community, be maintained by the community, so that the health of the mother and the inviolability of the home be assured!'[103] This was much nearer to full state endowment of motherhood than earlier proposals. Dora Montefiore had been greatly influenced by Dr Eder's pamphlet and urged every Women's Socialist Circle to read and discuss it. In her account of his work to *Justice* readers she emphasised the fact that the experience of motherhood for her contemporaries was one of financial dependence on a man. She therefore called for motherhood to be made immediately a properly paid occupation. This was in anticipation of a socialism which would necessarily mean economic independence for women because all contributions to the community, including childbearing, would be recognised by state maintenance.[104] But although Dora Montefiore framed her argument in this way, she also used the language of eugenics, voicing her concern for the deterioration of the race. Generally, eugenic assumptions were almost always part of any argument made in this period for state endowment of motherhood.

Only when economic independence was included in discussion of the endowment of motherhood could the proposal be seen as a self-conscious demand to value woman's domestic labour and to provide her with an alternative waged occupation to participation in the industrial workforce. When endowment of motherhood was expressed in these terms, many

[102] *Social Democrat*, April 1908, p. 170.
[103] *Justice*, 5 March 1910.
[104] *Justice*, 17 October 1908. See also *Justice*, 30 March 1907. But other SDFers, such as Bax, could not accept this view of socialist society and argued that payment for mothers would neither be needed or possible in a future society (*Justice*, 17 November 1906).

male members of the labour movement found the concept deeply worrying. They foresaw their own wages being cut because they would no longer be able to claim that theirs was a family wage.[105] But such critics left unspoken the concern that probably lay behind their view; the impact on traditional marriage and the family of financially-independent wives. This question was never fully explored. When maternity benefit was introduced in 1911, it was granted for such a restricted period that it could hardly be called endowment of motherhood.

Did the SDF have a clear party position on endowment of motherhood as an alternative means to women's economic independence? Although there were those who argued for salaries for wives and mothers within the SDF press and even at SDF Conference, the issue never seems to have provoked much real discussion within the party.[106] This may have been because the term was understood so variously that there was no shared framework within which debate could occur. A more likely explanation was that because Bax and the Tattler were remarkably silent on the matter there was little need for supporters of endowment of motherhood to elaborate and defend their case. The dissensions amongst other socialist women, particularly the WLL, meant that the debate could not be easily caricatured by male SDFers as a feminist argument which therefore had to be attacked. Nevertheless, late in the SDF's lifetime there seems to have been an increasing interest among SDF women in endowment of motherhood. The Circles were encouraged to discuss the issue[107] and SDF delegates reported back to their sisters on the discussions on the same topic at the Socialist Women's Bureau (British).[108]

The SDF's treatment of endowment of motherhood was little different from that of the rest of the labour and socialist movement. No collective force was put behind any form of the demand. Caroline Rowan has argued that a key factor in the failure of endowment of motherhood to gain widespread support was the ambivalence of the labour movement to women's economic independence which she feels was 'clearly motivated by patriarchal interests'.[109] Certainly the subsequent history of the fight for family allowances bears this out, as women's economic independence was dropped from the campaign in order to maximise support for a much

---

[105] Rowan, 'Mothers, Vote Labour!', p. 75. Ramsay and Margaret MacDonald were two of the main proponents of this argument in the socialist movement.

[106] *Social Democrat*, January 1901, p. 73; May 1901, p. 142; *SDF Conference Report*, 1909, p. 20.

[107] *Justice*, 20 February, 20 March 1909.

[108] *Justice*, 28 March, 18 April 1908.

[109] Rowan, 'Mothers, Vote Labour!', p. 79.

more limited demand.[110] The SDF's own reluctance to arrive at any consensus on issues which were part of the woman question was in this case reinforced by the ambivalence of much of the labour movement to anything as apparently radical as full endowment of motherhood. There was a considerable irony here, for the demand was inherently conservative – it not only assumed the sexual division of labour but would have ossified it. However this was not generally recognised at the time. Instead, fear of women's economic independence seems to have blinded many to the likely nature of endowment of motherhood.

Women SDFers, like their sisters in other socialist organisations, seem to have toyed with endowment as part of the wider discussion on women, work and economic independence. But they did not place as much importance on it as a strategy as, for example, the Fabian Women's Group. This may have been merely to do with contingent factors, such as the timing of the general debate on the endowment of motherhood. For this came to a head in the years immediately before the Socialist Unity Conference in 1911, when the SDF dissolved to become the British Socialist Party. Not surprisingly, at this period the SDF concern with Socialist Unity came at the expense of that for other issues. In addition the lack of attention to endowment of motherhood was also exacerbated by the absence from the country during much of 1910 and 1911 of its principal advocate in the party, Dora Montefiore.

Endowment of motherhood was seen by the SDF as part of the woman question. But as an alternative means to women's economic independence, it never really became a coherent demand for SDF women, and hence it was never discussed in any depth by the party as a whole. The SDF's perspective on the woman question did not help this particular issue move from the margins to the mainstream of political discussion. Partly as a result, the party remained particularly ambivalent about this political goal.

Women and unemployment: a woman's right to work

Turning to the final aspect of the SDF's approach to the topic of women and work, I now want to examine the party's understanding of women's

[110] See S. Pedersen, 'The Failure of Feminism in the Making of the British Welfare State', *Radical History Review*, 43, 1989, pp. 86–110; H. Land, 'Eleanor Rathbone and the Economy of the Family', in Smith (ed.), *British Feminism in the Twentieth Century*, pp. 104–23; J. Lewis, 'In Search of a Real Equality: Women between the Wars', in F. Gloversmith (ed.), *Class, Culture and Social Change*, Harvester, Brighton, pp. 231–2; J. Lewis, 'Beyond Suffrage: English Feminism in the 1920s', *The Maryland Historian*, 1975, pp. 8–12; P. Graves, *Labour Women: Women in British Working Class Politics 1918–39*, Cambridge University Press, Cambridge, 1994, pp. 98–108.

relationship to unemployment. The specific nature of women's unemployment in this period and the campaigns around it have not been seriously addressed by historians.[111] Yet unemployment was a particularly important issue for the SDF, both in their theory and in their practice. Indeed the organisation of the unemployed in periods of recession was one of the SDF's major political activities throughout its lifetime. This in itself raises the question of the relationship between unemployment as a general campaigning issue for the SDF and the assumptions about women's nature and role that formed their understanding of the woman question. Was the party's approach to unemployment gender-specific? An analysis of whether the SDF conceptualised women's unemployment in the same way as that of men can clarify further the underlying assumptions about women and work. This issue therefore provides a double opportunity; to explore, first, the theorisation of women's unemployment, and secondly, the extent to which this affected the party's practice.

In the 1880s as unemployment increased, the SDF started to organise amongst the unemployed. The party saw them as a group whose disaffection from society might make them particularly open to socialist propaganda. This agitation focused on the demand for public work or public maintenance for the unemployed which was summarised in the slogan, 'the right to work'. Public meetings, protest marches and demonstrations were initiated by the SDF to bring the plight of the unemployed to public attention and to push the government to take action.[112] In November 1886 and November 1887 these demonstrations became riots and as a consequence unemployment was forcefully and effectively brought to public and political attention.[113] But the battle was hardly won for, as José Harris has commented, the government saw unemployment as a problem of public order rather than social distress[114] and they took action accordingly. The SDF continued to campaign for the right to work throughout its lifetime.[115]

---

[111] See B. B. Gilbert, *The Evolution of National Insurance in Great Britain: The Origins of the Welfare State*, Michael Joseph, 1966, ch. 5; J. Harris, *Unemployment and Politics: A Study in English and Social Policy 1886–1914*, Oxford University Press, 1972. Mary Langan does have one paragraph on the female unemployed in her article 'Reorganizing the Labour Market: Unemployment, the State and the Labour Market, 1880–1914' in M. Langan and B. Schwartz (eds.), *Crises in the British State 1880–1930*, pp. 120–1.

[112] Tsuzuki, *H. M. Hyndman*, pp. 73–9; Harris, *Unemployment and Politics*, pp. 55–7.

[113] Harris, *Unemployment and Politics*, pp. 56, 75–6; Pelling, *Origins of the Labour Party*, pp. 42–3.

[114] Harris, *Unemployment and Politics*, p. 56.

[115] A. J. Kidd, 'The Social Democratic Federation and popular agitation amongst the unemployed in Edwardian Manchester', *International Review of Social History*, 129, 1984, pp. 336–58. This article does not consider women's unemployment or the

Despite their limited long-term achievements, the tactics used by the
SDF in agitating among the unemployed set a precedent, even a model,
for later direct action. This was true not only for the unemployed
themselves but also for other groups who sought to change the political
agenda, such as the suffragettes.[116] In addition the images associated
with organised action by, or on behalf of, the unemployed had a
particular effect on the ways in which it was thought appropriate to bring
the question of unemployment to public notice. The degree to which
such forms of action were thought to be inappropriate for women to
pursue, and the extent to which this inhibited campaigns by, or on
behalf of, the female unemployed need to be explored. But first I want to
look at the SDF's argument concerning unemployment and specifically
the party's commitment to the right to work. Was this a right seen as
extending unproblematically to all people or did some groups in society
have less of a right, or indeed no right, to work?

In the SDF's writings on unemployment, and in particular in their
reports on agitational work, the assumed gender of the unemployed was
male. The language the SDF used made this assumption clear: its aim
was 'that every man who is willing to work shall be afforded the
opportunity to maintain himself and his family in decency and comfort
by productive labour'.[117] The references made to unemployed women
were rare and indicated that they were not part of the general term
'unemployed' but formed a separate category. Unemployed women
tended to be referred to in specific contexts which, again, emphasised
their difference. In addition, just as there was considerable vagueness in
the SDF's use of terms like 'women's work' so there was also a lack of
clarity when it came to considering 'women's unemployment'. There
was a tendency to see unemployment's effect on women as a composite
one. This allowed the SDF's theoreticians to unproblematically bring
together women who would usually be engaged in paid work with the
wives of unemployed men. Thus, for example, the unemployed
women's deputation to the Prime Minister, Arthur Balfour, which was
organised through the SDF-dominated Central Workers Committee,
consisted of both these groups of women.[118] The testimony of this
delegation shows that women were seen as representing the deleterious

SDF's involvement in agitation around it. See also K. D. Brown, *Labour and
Unemployment 1900–14*, Newton Abbot, Devon, 1971; P. Thompson, *Socialists,
Liberals and Labour*, pp. 122, 208.
[116] Pankhurst, *The Suffragette Movement*, pp. 184–5; D. Mitchell, *Queen Christabel*,
McDonald and Janes, 1977, p. 61.
[117] *Justice*, 21 February 1903.
[118] *Deputation of Unemployed to the Rt. Hon A. J. Balfour MP*, Twentieth Century Press,
1905. See also *Justice*, 11 November 1905, 22 July 1905.

effect of unemployment on the family rather than on women as individuals. It was hard to hear in the general campaign for the right to work the voices of those who spoke up for the particular experience of the women unemployed and who offered solutions which might relieve their distress. But this was not in itself surprising given general attitudes which simply reinforced the SDF's assumptions.

The Poor Law, as Pat Thane has shown, 'reinforced the notion of women as non-wage-earning dependants'.[119] This was particularly important to the way in which women's unemployment, specifically that of married women, was more generally understood. For it was to the Poor Law that the unemployed would ultimately have recourse, if they became destitute, yet women as wage-earners, and thus as potentially unemployed women, were not recognised as such within it. In terms of official policy (from which there were some deviations at a local level) the Poor Law Board had made explicit their expectation that single women had a duty to work and were therefore ineligible for outdoor relief; that is minimal cash relief in return for a labour 'test' such as breaking stones for men and cleaning in the workhouse for women. In that sense, single people were similarly treated within the Poor Law irrespective of gender.

For those who were married, gender differentiation remained. For once a married woman disappeared into the family unit with its male breadwinner, she did not exist in the Guardians' eyes as an individual. Even if deserted, widowed, or with a husband in prison, there was considerable reluctance to support such women from the rates. The idea that married women still living with their husbands could be unemployed was therefore not countenanced by the Poor Law. Women's unemployment could only be recognised officially when it concerned single women, when the responsible male had died, or had reneged on those responsibilities. Even in these last two instances, women's unemployment was hidden within the more general term of destitution. Under the Unemployed Workmen's Act (1905) no married woman whose husband was registered at the Distress Committee could also register herself, and thus her unemployment was rendered invisible. This prohibition was later reinforced by the 1911 National Insurance Act, where the arrangements for casual workers specifically excluded married women workers on the assumption that their earnings were supplementary to those of their husbands. Lack of work for such women was not officially defined as unemployment.[120] Clearly these official attitudes, coupled with the SDF's own ambivalence about women's

---

[119] P. Thane, 'Women and the Poor Law in Victorian and Edwardian England', *History Workshop Journal*, 6, 1978, p. 31.
[120] Ibid., pp. 33, 38–40, 48.

work – particularly married women's work – made it much easier for the party to overlook women's unemployment and to concentrate on the more emotive subject of the effect of unemployment on the family.

Gender differentiation in relation to unemployment was also reinforced by the tactics used by the SDF in unemployed agitation. The form of the 1880s unemployed protests, particularly when organised by socialists, had been seen as threatening. There had been a potential for violence even if it was not often realised. Therefore although these tactics were thought by the party to be successful, the SDF did not think that they were appropriate for women's direct involvement. Thus most of the marches and demonstrations organised by the SDF or by groups in which they played a leading part, such as the London and District Right to Work Council, were for the male unemployed.[121] Women's events were organised separately. This difference is underlined by the comments made in *Justice* after the women's delegation to Balfour in 1905:

On Monday, had only the word been given, when the women were safely settled indoors, the scenes of 1886 might have been repeated. Whether it is necessary to repeat that history remains to be seen, but the workers should organise, should prepare for the next great march – this time not of weak though brave women, but of men who, with what strength semi-starvation has left in them, will demonstrate in such fashion that neither Balfour nor any other shall say them nay.[122]

Although women SDFers spoke at meetings of the unemployed and took part in the general campaign, for example through sitting on Distress Committees, unemployed women were not encouraged to attend public marches. As Agnes Bain, who had helped to collect funds to feed unemployed men, complained, 'I venture to enquire why unemployed women were not invited to join in the march to Hyde Park? Do none of those 999 disappointed woman typists, among the 1,000 applicants to a Lambeth firm, need a good square meal – I wonder?'[123] This party attitude made women's experience of unemployment seem marginal to the SDF's unemployed agitation. It seemed that once again women were being called upon to support an essentially male campaign by working quietly in the background. Women's activities were to be confined to reinforcing the overall campaign by demonstrating the effect of male unemployment on wives and children. Did SDF women acquiesce in this? Were women not to make their own demand for the right to work?

SDF women did use the language of rights and extended the concept

[121] See Brown, *Labour and Unemployment.*
[122] *Justice,* 11 November 1905.
[123] *Justice,* 9 May 1908.

of a right to work beyond a purely male right to include women as well. Thus although the 1905 March of the Women included banners demanding 'Work for our men', there were also banners which read 'We demand the right to labour in order that we and ours might live'.[124] At a Right to Work meeting in 1906 Margaret Bondfield, at that time an SDFer, made a strong demand for 'woman's right to work – not to drudgery'.[125] Margaretta Hicks was driven to ask, during the 1907 SDF Conference's debate on unemployment, 'This resolution speaks of 'men'. I take it that it refers to women also. I should like women to be put in.'[126] But this was one of only two references to women in Conference debates on unemployment.[127] By contrast, the SDF Women's Annual Conference in 1911 discussed a much clearer resolution which recognised that 'unemployment affects women, both as wage earners and housekeepers'.[128] Clearly, therefore, SDF women did make an explicit commitment to women's right to work. But this demand was also implicit in the practical action for which they argued and, indeed, took.

SDF women were particularly concerned that public works should be started for the female unemployed and not just for unemployed men. They therefore made a number of suggestions which included the provision in every London borough of workrooms specifically for unemployed women. In particular they suggested that municipal dairy farms should be started so that women could be employed on the land, an initiative which was designed to mirror the men's colony at Hollesley Bay. These were very similar to the demands being made by the Women's Industrial Council.[129] Most of the SDF women's energy went into the women's workrooms: calling for them to be set up; stopping them being closed; assisting in running them; and trying to ensure that the women who attended the workrooms had useful work to do which would help them get a job.[130] The three women's workrooms set up in London had a very precarious existence and their funding was constantly under threat from John Burns at the Local Government Board.[131]

Justice readers could follow the fate of the workrooms through the

---

[124] *Justice*, 11 November 1905.

[125] *Justice*, 3 March 1906. See appendix 5 for a brief biography of Margaret Bondfield.

[126] *SDF Conference Report*, 1907, p. 19.

[127] The other was in the *SDF Conference Report*, 1905, p. 25.

[128] *Justice*, 1 April 1911.

[129] *Justice*, 26 October 1907; 23 December 1905; E. Mappen, *Helping Women at Work: the Women's Industrial Council, 1889–1914*, Hutchinson, 1985, pp. 121–2.

[130] *Justice*, 30 September 1905; 26 September 1908; 12 December 1908.

[131] See Keir Hardie's protest in the House of Commons when Burns refused to give more financial support to the London workrooms for unemployed women (Brown, *Labour and Unemployment*, pp. 81–2; *Justice*, 6 April 1907).

reporting of Margaretta Hicks who was closely involved in their development as the Honorary Superintendent of the St Pancras Women's Workroom.[132] She had campaigned for the workrooms with other SDF women such as Mrs Jefferson and Mrs Wilson and stressed that they had always had to 'work under sufferance'.[133] Although SDFers had managed to get on to the Distress Committees set up by the Unemployed Workmen's Act they had little influence over the workrooms which were controlled through a sub-committee of the Central (Unemployed) Body.[134] They were critical about the lack of central commitment to these workrooms and the work that the women were asked to do.[135] They therefore formed deputations to persuade the Central (Unemployed) Body to continue, and to expand, the workrooms and to make additional provision for unemployed women. For example, in November 1908 one such women's delegation made a strong case for crèches to be provided so that widows with dependent children could attend the workrooms. They also emphasised the 'trifling proportion of women actually provided with work'.[136] These experiences made some women, such as Dora Montefiore, cynical about urging unemployed women to register with the Distress Committee as so few got any work as a result.[137] But other SDF women urged unemployed women to register as only then would the scope of the problem be revealed.[138] All this activity emphasised the practical commitment of many SDF women to the fight for a woman's right to work.

SDF women were involved in many different aspects of the SDF's agitation concerning the unemployed, setting their own priorities within this. It is not so clear how much they were able to affect the overall SDF view of the issue. The SDF had recognised the importance of getting its own members onto the Distress Committees and several women SDFers were successful, including Margaretta Hicks, Mary Gray, Lena Wilson, Margaret Bondfield, Mrs Layton and Dora Montefiore.[139] Leading women SDFers also spoke at many of the meetings organised by the party for the unemployed. They therefore could not be accused of opting out from the general agitation. But they also were involved in particular campaigns which women organised around unemployment.

---

[132] *Justice*, 25 May 1907.
[133] *Justice*, 6 October 1906; 25 May 1907. See also *Justice*, 1 June 1907.
[134] See Harris, *Unemployment and Politics*, pp. 168–76.
[135] *Justice*, 26 October 1907.
[136] *Justice*, 28 November 1908.
[137] *Justice*, 26 October 1907.
[138] *Justice*, 6 October 1906; 26 September 1908.
[139] *Justice*, 30 September 1905; 21 October 1905. See appendix 5 for a brief biography of Lena Wilson.

The Circles and the Women's Education Committee campaigned around unemployment, organising deputations and affiliating to the Right to Work Council as a Committee and at the Circle level.[140] SDF women were also more than willing to work with other women who were campaigning on women's unemployment. They took part in events organised by groups such as the Women's Industrial Council and the WLL.[141] Theirs was therefore not an insular approach although, as with any members of the SDF, it seems that these interventions were not always welcome to the other organisations.

Thus it was women SDFers who recognised and promoted women's right to work within their own party. But despite making interventions within the SDF and publicising their own work they had little impact on the primary campaign for the right to work. This was stubbornly focused almost exclusively on the male unemployed. SDF women were able to argue for women's right to work and engage in practical campaigns to help unemployed women without meeting criticism from the party. Yet they were unable to change the fundamental assumptions on women and work to which many party members clung. This is further evidence of the practical implications of the SDF's theoretical formulation of the woman question. There was space for women to set their own priorities provided they did not threaten the party itself. Anything which smacked of feminism was thought to do just this. The price that women paid for even this limited freedom was that no party decision was ever made on subjects that were deemed part of the woman question. It was also very hard to change the terms of the debate on issues already regarded as important, such as unemployment. This was particularly the case when both the general context and assumptions within the party were unsympathetic to the principle of a woman's right to work.

To sum up, despite being part of the public sphere, women's work was as much a part of the woman question for the SDF as the family and marriage. Although much of the content of the debate which surrounded women's work concerned, for example, working conditions, pay and unionisation, which were part of the broader 'labour question', it was the fact that it was women's experience of these that was crucial to the SDF. In the end any discussion which touched upon women always reflected assumptions about woman's proper role, her capacities and her potential. Thus despite the founding fathers' commitment to woman's labour as a prerequisite for her emancipation, the SDF was unable to transcend its own ambivalence about women working, particularly married women. Within the party's general understanding of the woman

---

[140] *Justice*, 14 November 1908; 6 March 1909; 1 April 1911.
[141] For example *Justice*, 4 July 1908; 16 January, 30 January 1909.

question there was no mechanism to overcome these assumptions. The SDF simply maintained that consensus was neither necessary nor desirable. In practice, this meant that the party's underlying commitment to the family wage was protected from any real scrutiny. As a result, the question of women's economic independence was projected into some distant socialist future.

This does not, of course, mean that no discussion took place on the constellation of issues which surounded women's work. As we have seen, this was clearly not the case. But the understanding that no party position was possible led to a much more insidious method of achieving unofficial party policy. All debate was loaded in favour of the powerful within the party and those with access to the SDF press. In practice this meant that few women were ever able to influence the party in the way that, for example, Harry Quelch was able to do through his editorship of *Justice*. Thus, although many of the contemporary strategies to ameliorate women's working conditions appeared to be endorsed within *Justice*, they never became party policy. Indeed, they sat rather awkwardly beside other assumptions about women which were much more ambivalent about women's right to work. This made it difficult to move the party beyond discussion to action. In particular, this was the case when it came to reformist demands to improve women's pay and conditions which were being more generally discussed within the labour movement. The SDF was reluctant to put energy into such short-term demands. Even with its own campaigns, such as that around unemployment, there remained an inability to recognise women as an inherent part of the workforce and thus of the unemployed. Women were marginal even to this SDF dominated campaign.

Yet SDF women did have views on women's work and economic independence which they not only discussed publicly but also put into practice. The irony of the SDF's understanding of the woman question was that the party was able to tolerate this, provided that the women did not stray too far into what could be deemed to be feminism. But this was at a price. The price was that SDF women's concerns would remain marginal to the party as a whole and could be interfered with at any time by the leadership. There was no official party position to shield women SDFers and their practice.

Women within the party were not united around all of these issues, as the debate around protective legislation shows. But then there were also differences between women in the wider socialist and labour movement on the strategies to improve women's working conditions. Such differences were nothing compared to the widespread ambivalence and even hostility to women engaging in paid work which were to be found in the predominately male socialist and labour movement. In this sense the SDF's own ambivalences over women's work and their economic independence only reflected those of the wider society. With no strong or agreed party position on the woman question, the membership of the SDF allowed deep-set assumptions to go unchallenged so that the party often seemed to present a contradictory position on issues surrounding women's work. There could be no real homogeneity of theory or practice on women's work whilst such fundamental assumptions on woman's right to work remained unchallenged and unresolved. Thus although women's work might seem a more likely area for consensus, it remained as much a part of the woman question as anything in the private sphere.

6   The suffrage

The enfranchisement of women and their admission to citizenship is an aspect of the woman question which is, by definition, part of the public sphere. The suffrage became an increasingly prominent item on the agenda of all political parties during the lifetime of the SDF and was a subject which much exercised socialists, in Britain and internationally. For the SDF the suffrage, at least in theory, produced a greater degree of unanimity than other aspects of the woman question. But as a practical campaigning issue it exposed fissures in the party and brought into question the credibility of the SDF in the eyes of many women.

From its earliest days the SDF had included in its political programme the demand for universal suffrage.[1] But from the beginning the terms universal or adult suffrage were contested. Although generally defined as the enfranchisement of all male and female adults without property qualification, adult suffrage was taken by some to be synonymous with manhood suffrage. For instance, in the first edition of *Justice*, Stewart Headlam questioned whether the party programme made it clear that women were included within the demand for universal suffrage.[2] Although it might seem obvious that a demand for adult suffrage necessarily included limited women's suffrage, as contemporary suffragists demanded, yet strategically the two positions came to be seen as counterposed. It is the process whereby the democratic demand for adult suffrage came to be seen by many as the least progressive position which is of interest, because the SDF's strategic thinking on the suffrage reflects many of the same ambivalences that are enshrined in the larger woman question.

Within the SDF a full range of positions can be found on the suffrage question, yet the organisation is usually portrayed as anti-women's suffrage. For example, Jill Liddington and Jill Norris have described the

---

[1]   *SDF Programme and Rules*, 1888, 1894; H. Quelch *The SDF: Its Objects, Its Principles and Its Work*, Twentieth-Century Press, 1907; *Justice*, 30 June 1906; 9 August 1890.

[2]   *Justice*, 19 January 1884. Reverend Stewart Headlam was a Christian Socialist, founder of the Guild of St Matthew and a member of the Fabian Society.

SDF as having 'no brief for women's suffrage' and Marion Ramelson thought it was 'not enthusiastic about women gaining the vote'. Constance Rover implied that the SDF was a reluctant supporter of women's suffrage, only including it within adult suffrage because of the vigour of the women's suffrage campaign. These historians' judgements and the assumptions of many others are drawn from the views of women suffragists, particularly suffragettes, such as Hannah Mitchell, who wrote of SDFers 'who were for some reason opposed to us' while Evelyn Sharp thought SDFers 'were definitely hostile'.[3] Certainly Belfort Bax was an anti-suffragist but, equally, Mary Gray, Amie Hicks and Dora Montefiore, for example, were suffragists; that is, they supported the extension of the franchise to women.

The rich variety of views on the suffrage was, of course, a consequence of the SDF's understanding of the woman question. Yet there are reasons for thinking that perhaps the suffrage was not merely another aspect of the woman question. Did its position in the public sphere put political pressures on the SDF to acquire a firm party position, despite the issue being part of the woman question? And did the public prominence of the suffrage in turn affect the SDF's conception of the woman question, limiting its diversity and making it effectively into a single-issue campaign? These are the key themes in the following discussion of the SDF's changing perception of the suffrage as an issue for the party.

The years before the militants (1884–1905)

The SDF discussed and campaigned around the suffrage in the years before the women's suffrage campaign became a major public political issue; that is, before October 1905, when, Christabel Pankhurst and Annie Kenney were arrested at the Free Trade Hall. The SDF therefore cannot be accused of ignoring the issue until it was forced upon it, although this, of course, is very different from arguing that the party gave priority to the suffrage. From the earliest days of the party, opposition to limited suffrage and advocacy of universal adult suffrage seemed to be clear. In 1884 *Justice* stated, 'We are not in favour of mere fine-lady suffrage ... We want the enfranchisement of all women.'[4] In the 1880s and 1890s the SDF responded in this vein to various parliamentary

---

[3] J. Liddington and J. Norris, *One Hand Tied Behind Us*, p. 199; M. Ramelson, *The Petticoat Rebellion*, Lawrence and Wishart, 1972, p. 81; C. Rover, *Women's Suffrage and Party Politics in Britain, 1866–1914*, Routledge and Kegan Paul, 1967, pp. 159–60; H. Mitchell, *The Hard Way Up*, Virago, 1977, p. 156; E. Sharp, *Unfinished Adventure*, Bodley Head, 1933, p. 131.

[4] *Justice*, 21 June 1884.

attempts to extend the franchise. Mary Gray pronounced on a limited women's franchise bill in 1892 that it was 'a fraud and a snare for the working women of England'. Instead of putting their faith in bills such as these, she urged working women to 'fight under the Red Flag of Social Democracy, for that alone will give us women freedom'.[5] This was not untypical of a general SDF sentiment, although it was expressed in a more woman-centred manner than usual. It was generally argued within the SDF that a limited women's franchise would be a class measure, giving votes to bourgeois rather than working class women. Indeed a *Justice* leader in 1897, warned SDFers of another limited women's suffrage bill which 'is not a measure to give political freedom to women but to extend it to the propertied fossils and failures of their sex'.[6] The different tone in which these two writers expressed their opposition to limited women's suffrage suggests that the manner in which the argument was made might be as important as its content in persuading others of the SDF's genuine commitment to reform.

Although the SDF explicitly supported adult suffrage, some members managed to sow the seeds of doubt in the minds of suffragists over the SDF's commitment to this goal. In 1887, Amie Hicks wrote in *Justice*:

I have noticed some of our speakers, either from want of knowledge, or from a desire to catch the popular breeze, lower our standard and speak of manhood suffrage as a thing to be striven for, setting aside our grand idea of 'equal justice, equal rights, equal duties for all'. And when taxed on the subject, bring out the old fallacy of 'women not being educated enough'.[7]

There is little evidence that SDFers were actively campaigning for manhood suffrage or indeed that anyone was.[8] Yet the way that some presented the suffrage question appeared to undermine the SDF's stated belief that adult must include women's suffrage. This image was reinforced by the presence in the SDF of some who did explicitly oppose women's suffrage, and a further number who, whilst not opposed, were clearly indifferent to the women's case. Yet we must be careful in our assessment of the influence of these individuals. Generally, historians of the suffrage have misconstrued the SDF.[9] Paradoxically, those party members who argued against a limited franchise and for full adult suffrage have come to be represented as being anti-woman, rather than as against property qualifications and for the full enfranchisement of all

---

5   *Justice*, 14 May 1892.
6   *Justice*, 13 February 1897.
7   *Justice*, 24 September 1887.
8   M. Pugh, *Electoral Reform in War and Peace, 1906–18*, Routledge and Kegan Paul, 1978, pp. 3–4.
9   See, for example, S. Pankhurst, *The Suffragette Movement*, p. 111.

women. The roots of this misrepresentation of adult suffrage as a legitimate demand can be seen in the 1890s; it later came to fruition in the years of the Women's Social and Political Union (WSPU).

Nevertheless, there was a degree of ambivalence in some SDFers' support for adult suffrage. For example, the Tattler wrote, 'Personally I am in favour of universal adult suffrage, but I do not wonder that women show so little enthusiasm for the franchise while they enjoy such privileges under 'man-made' law.'[10] The language of the anti-suffragist employed here successfully undermined the Tattler's nominal support for adult suffrage. A similar effect was achieved by giving a disproportionate amount of space to arguments that were supposedly being refuted; the eccentric or reactionary position was given a degree of legitimacy by the space given to it and by its continued repetition. The arguments used by anti-suffragists were given considerable exposure in this manner in the SDF press. They included the contention that women were reactionary and therefore their votes would be used against progressive causes; and that as women were a majority in the population, the enfranchisement of women would lead to domination by the female sex.[11] The use of this form of argument had particular resonances within the SDF as they referred directly to the ideas of Belfort Bax.

Bax's misogyny affected the party's presentation of the adult suffrage case. As we have seen, Bax's views were not those of the party as a whole, and yet he appears to have had complete access to official party publications. Here he was able to argue that because women were organically inferior yet also privileged, there was no reason to further privilege them by granting them the vote. In particular Bax warned that women's suffrage would mean domination by the female sex and the political subjugation of men. Despite the changes in women's social position and in the suffrage campaign itself, the form of Bax's argument did not alter over the whole of the SDF's lifetime.[12]

Few SDFers accepted all of Bax's views. Yet the prominence given to his and his supporters' arguments within the SDF press made it all too easy for the party's critics to assume that these were SDF views, even when particular correspondents were revealed as non-party members. For example, in October 1909 H. B. Samuels, a trenchant critic of women's suffrage, published a long critical article in *Social Democrat*. However, Samuels was not even a member of the SDF, having been

---

[10]   *Justice*, 15 January 1898.
[11]   See, for example, *Justice*, 13 February 1897, 25 June 1904.
[12]   Compare, for example, Bax's *The Fraud of Feminism*, Grant Richards, 1913, with his journalism in the 1890s and 1900s.

refused membership by Paddington SDP.[13] Certainly, the continual appearance over the years of unchanging Baxian arguments enhanced the impression that his view was not merely a view but *the* view of the SDF.

Bax provides a test of the difference between the SDF's approach to the woman question as a whole and the specific issue of the suffrage. Bax saw the two as integrally linked and therefore expected the same freedom of expression for his atypical views. Unlike the woman question, the party did take a position on the suffrage, and so Bax's insistence on freedom of expression in both spheres challenged the SDF's commitment to the suffrage cause. But it was not until 1909 that any attempt was made to censor him over the suffrage.

We must also consider those SDF members who were indifferent to the whole suffrage question. For example, Annie Sleat argued, 'I am not keen on my sex getting into Parliament. As for female suffrage, I am sick of it: it spells to me delusion, snare, cant and hypocrisy. What I want is Social Democracy.'[14] The political problem with indifference was that it could easily slide into apparent opposition. Thus, for example, 'That every man and woman should have a vote I, for one, am perfectly agreed, but I am not going to bother about giving votes to those who haven't got them while I see those workmen who have got them making such unmentionable asses of themselves and voting for their enemies every time.'[15] This kind of remark anticipated what became a more coherent position for the SDF once the suffragette campaign was under way. Whilst support for the enfranchisement of all women through adult suffrage was acceptable, there were other issues which had a greater priority for the party as a whole.

The mere fact that the SDF had a party line on the suffrage could not hide the internal divisions. This was made most apparent by the supporters of women's suffrage within the party. There were those, like Herbert Burrows who consistently argued against the anti-suffragists within his own party and emphasised women's suffrage.[16] But these divisions did not develop into anything more serious because the suffrage was not a major political issue in the 1890s.[17] Burrows was a member in the early 1890s of the Women's Franchise League, a small group who campaigned for the enfranchisement of married women, but

13   *Justice*, 16 January 1909, 23 January 1909; *Social Democrat*, October 1909, pp. 450–8. See also P. Thompson, *Socialists, Liberals and Labour*, p. 160.
14   *Justice*, 2 November 1895.
15   *Justice*, 20 April 1901.
16   For example, see *Justice*, 29 December 1894, 22 February 1896.
17   For an account of the women's suffrage campaign of the 1890s, see D. Rubinstein, *Before the Suffragettes*, ch. 9.

he never announced this to the readers of *Justice*.[18] Other SDF suffragists, such as Amie Hicks and Mary Gray, did not place suffrage at the top of their political agenda. Matters might have been more serious if either of these women had held dual membership with one of the suffrage pressure groups. But they did not; there was little room within the suffrage societies for socialists who took an adult suffrage position.

Nevertheless it would be incorrect to conclude that the party, or individual SDFers, were inactive over the suffrage between 1884 and 1905. However, there is little evidence of any systematic campaigning. What is interesting is that when the SDF did hold a series of demonstrations for universal suffrage throughout England on 22 October 1893,[19] it was in response to pressure from the International. Domestically, there was no obvious reason for holding a demonstration; it was a direct response to the pledge on universal suffrage given by all delegates to the 1893 International.[20] The importance of the International in determining the SDF's practice on suffrage was to increase in the 1900s.

Unexpectedly, even this limited action drew criticism of the SDF from those from whom the party had expected support. Central to the opposition was the charge that this revolutionary party was engaging in reformism. Quelch went to some lengths in *Justice* to deny this, going so far as to state that 'while we agitate for the suffrage, we should learn the use of arms and the arts of warfare'.[21] *Justice* saw the 1893 demonstration as the beginning of an SDF campaign for the suffrage,[22] less surprisingly other suffrage and socialist organisations kept their distance.

Very little happened subsequently, certainly nothing which deserves the title of campaign. A further demonstration was held a year later in August, with Mary Gray, Rose Jarvis and Edith Lanchester among the 24 announced speakers.[23] Unfortunately the day was not seen as a success by the SDF, as fewer people attended than the year before. In terms of publicising the demand for universal suffrage, the demonstrations failed; their existence was not even noted by the major daily newspapers of the day. After 1894, no further attempt was made until after 1905 to take party action on the issue.

The lack of a sustained campaign by the party permitted individual

[18]   D. Rubinstein, *Before the Suffragettes*, pp. 143–5; S. Pankhurst, *The Suffragette Movement*, pp. 95–6.
[19]   *Justice*, 28 October 1893; *SDF Conference Report*, 1894, p. 11.
[20]   There was no suffrage bill before parliament at this time (C. Rover, *Women's Suffrage and Party Politics*, p. 220). *SDF Conference Report*, 1894, p. 11.
[21]   *Justice*, 21 October 1893.
[22]   *Justice*, 28 October 1893.
[23]   *Justice*, 4 August 1894.

SDFers to take personal action. In particular, several leading members adopted the tactic of intervention at women's suffrage meetings in order to promote the alternative of adult suffrage. Mary Gray, for example, moved an amendment at a 'fine lady' suffrage meeting in November 1893 which was seconded by Eleanor Marx. This was in favour of 'women's suffrage', that is the vote for all, rather than some, women. The amendment was lost by an 'overwhelming majority'.[24] This kind of tactic was widely supported within the SDF; for example, it gained the approval of the Tattler, who called on comrades, 'their sweethearts, husbands, cousins and uncles' to attend the meeting.[25] Unfortunately, few SDFers and their families appear to have heeded the call. In contrast, *Justice* did not support the more violent intervention by Burrows at a women's suffrage meeting which had been held in 1892 in support of Rollit's limited suffrage bill. Burrows led an attack on the platform, which caused the collapse of the reporters' table, hand to hand fighting, and the tearing down of the brass railings protecting the platform.[26]

Overall, however, individual action on the suffrage remained a personal choice for SDFers, and few chose to take it; it was one of many issues to which no particular priority need be given. Unusually for a socialist party, it was the advent of a new member of the SDF which helped to change the way in which the party discussed, and even acted upon, its nominal commitment to adult suffrage.

Dora Montefiore came to the SDF as an active suffragist, having been involved in campaigns in Australia[27] and Britain. She was the author of a suffrage pamphlet, *Women Uitlanders* in which she pointed out the double standard of a British government willing to fight a war in South Africa over the Uitlanders' disenfranchisement whilst refusing to act on a similar case much nearer to home, that of voteless British women.[28] Through the League of Practical Suffragists and the Women's Liberal Association, she had in the first years of the century sought to make the suffrage the priority for a major political party. She was clearly more interested in the vote than in Liberalism, for at the same time she was increasingly active in socialist politics. This can be seen by her letters

[24]   *Justice*, 18 November 1893. See also *The Times*, 11 November 1893.
[25]   *Justice*, 4 November 1893.
[26]   *The Times*, 27 April 1892; D. Rubinstein, *Before the Suffragettes*, p.144.
[27]   Dora Montefiore was a founding member of the Womanhood Suffrage League of New South Wales in 1891 which campaigned for full women's suffrage rather than the limited franchise (D. B. Montefiore, *From a Victorian to a Modern*, pp. 32–9). See also A. Oldfield, *Woman Suffrage in Australia*, Cambridge University Press, Cambridge, 1992, esp. ch. 5.
[28]   D. B. Montefiore, *Women Uitlanders*, Leaflet XIV, Union of Practical Suffragists, October 1899.

published in *Clarion* from 1897; the week she spent working on the *Clarion* van in 1898; and her attendance at the ILP Conference in 1899. From 1900 she wrote a column for *New Age*. In her autobiography she remembered, 'my mind was slowly maturing and my heart opening out on the subject of many social questions, besides that of the political vote'.[29] We have no date for Dora Montefiore's joining the SDF, but from 1901 she was writing for *Justice* and for *Social Democrat*, and in 1903 she was elected to the Executive. Yet she was also an early member of the WSPU and only broke with them in January 1907.[30] Membership of several key political organisations was unusual for SDFers.[31] What was even more unusual was for such a vocal and leading SDFer to be also a prominent suffragist. Her presence directly affected the development of the SDF's presentation of the suffrage question as the issue moved into a different era, one characterised by the advent of the WSPU.

The polarisation of positions: limited women's suffrage versus adult suffrage (1905–1907)

The period 1905 to early 1907 is marked at one end by the advent of the WSPU onto the national stage as the militant proponents of limited woman suffrage, and at the other both by the Stuttgart resolution of the Second International on adult suffrage, and Dora Montefiore's change of allegiance from the WSPU to the Adult Suffrage Society (ASS). The much higher profile of the suffrage campaign during this short period, the changing arguments around the suffrage demand, the shifts in tactics needed to realise such a demand, all had important repercussions for the SDF.

The advent of the WSPU marked a growth in suffrage activity, and a change, from 1905, to more militant tactics.[32] But even before this a different emphasis had entered suffrage politics with the activities of the

---

[29] Montefiore, *From a Victorian to a Modern*, p. 56.
[30] Ibid., p. 108.
[31] There were always some SDFers who had joint membership with the ILP. There were even rare members like Charlotte Despard who was, for a time, a member of the SDF, ILP and WSPU (*Clarion*, 27 April 1906; *The Reformers' Year Book*, 1907, p. 153; A. Linklater, *An Unhusbanded Life*, Hutchinson, 1980, pp. 88–9).
[32] See, S. Pankhurst, *The Suffragette Movement*; A. Rosen, *Rise Up Women*, Routledge and Kegan Paul, 1975; C. Pankhurst, *Unshackled*, Hutchinson,1959; B. Harrison, 'The Act of Militancy: Violence and the Suffragettes 1904–1914', in his *Peaceable Kingdom*, Clarendon, Oxford, 1982; M. Vicinus, *Independent Women: Work and Community for Single Women, 1850–1920*, Virago, 1985, ch. 7; S. S. Holton, 'In Sorrowful Wrath: Suffrage Militancy and the Romantic Feminism of Emmeline Pankhurst', in H. L. Smith (ed.), *British Feminism in the Twentieth Century*; introduction to J. Marcus (ed.), *Suffrage and the Pankhursts*, Routledge and Kegan Paul, 1987.

largely working-class radical suffragists of Lancashire.[33] These developments did not go entirely unremarked within the SDF. *Justice* gave publicity to the Lancashire and Cheshire Women Textile and other Workers' Representation Committee, the WSPU and the Women's Freedom League (WFL).[34] But the acknowledgment of other organisations and the publication of their material does not indicate how the party responded to the reviving fortunes and the shifting character of the suffrage campaign.

Although the SDF was not particularly prompt in its coverage and discussion of the suffrage, the campaign did become a significant item in the party's deliberations from 1905. The number of issues of *Justice* in 1905 with relevant pieces quadrupled over that in 1904. Coverage continued to increase, taking a significant leap in 1907, when over two thirds of that year's editions contained suffrage items. A decline occurred in 1909, but the issue was then taken up by the party's monthly journal, *Social Democrat*. In 1909, ten out of the twelve editions contained pieces on the suffrage. *Justice* continued to include a significant number of suffrage items during the rest of the SDF's lifetime, and coverage of this aspect of the woman question never returned to its low, pre-1905 levels.[35]

To begin with, the SDF's position was reactive, depending on outside events to force suffrage onto the party's agenda. The SDF quickly developed a view of the new factor in the campaign, the suffragettes. The WSPU, and the Pankhursts in particular, were increasingly attacked in *Justice*. This in turn affected the way in which the SDF's own position on the suffrage was regarded by some of its own members and, indeed, potential members.

With increased activity around the limited suffrage demand, the SDF reviewed and developed its own arguments. It had always viewed limited

---

[33] See J. Liddington and J. Norris, *One Hand Tied Behind Us*.
[34] See *Justice*, 14 January 1905; 19 May 1906; 24 March 1906; 23 November 1907.
[35] The figures below represent the number of editions per year of the SDF press which contained pieces on the suffrage. *Justice* was a weekly newspaper which was published from 1884 and *Social Democrat*, a monthly journal, was first published in 1897. Since 1911 was the year that the SDP became the British Socialist Party, it is not included here.

Year	J	SD	Year	J	SD	Year	J	SD
1884	3		1893	7		1902	5	0
1885	3		1894	4		1903	1	0
1886	0		1895	4		1904	4	2
1887	1		1896	2		1905	12	0
1888	0		1897	1	0	1906	16	2
1889	0		1898	1	0	1907	36	4
1890	1		1899	2	1	1908	33	1
1891	0		1900	1	0	1909	16	10
1892	3		1901	3	3	1910	14	3

women's suffrage as an anti-working-class demand, but the practice of
the WSPU reinforced this conviction. Thus in articles on the suffragettes
the term 'class measure' was used to describe what the SDF called 'fine-
lady suffrage'.[36]

As the slogans and militant activity of the WSPU gained more
publicity for the limited suffrage cause, the SDF refined its arguments.
The main point was that the limited demand, as encapsulated in a series
of unsuccessful Women's Enfranchisement Bills, gave the impression
that many more women would be enfranchised than was actually the
case. The SDF increasingly talked of fraud in this context. Herbert
Burrows described the campaign for limited women's suffrage as 'a
crooked, misleading and disingenuous fight'; women who were promoting a bill for limited women's suffrage 'at the same time, daily, by
meetings, speech and pen, purposely delude the women, especially the
working women, to whom they address themselves into the belief that
under that Bill they will all be enfranchised'.[37] All agreed, across the
suffrage divide, that by definition limited suffrage would not give the
vote to all women; but the numbers and class of the women who would
be enfranchised was disputed particularly within the broader labour
movement, as suffragists attempted to win the support of the Labour
Party. There were two aspects of this calculation which the SDF
emphasised. One was the fact that all married women would be excluded
from the vote under the Bill supported by the WSPU. Burrows pointed
out how some of the anomalies would affect SDF members, and also
managed to imply that the suffragists were self-seeking. He noted that
the Bill would enfranchise Mrs Despard, Mrs Montefiore and Mrs
Pankhurst and her daughters, but that it would not give the vote to
Annie Besant or Mrs Hyndman and Rose Scott.[38] As other SDFers were
to point out, such limitations made a nonsense of the claim that the
demand was for an equal franchise to that of the men.[39]

Discrepancies such as these permitted the expression of certain
misogynist views. The anti-spinster tone of much anti-suffragism was
evident in the apparent defence of 'normal' mothers against the
embittered self-serving spinsters and widows, who were to get the
vote.[40] Some SDFers adopted this tactic in their own propaganda, as
can be seen in this report of a South Salford meeting in January 1907:

---

[36] *Justice*, 1 December 1906.
[37] Ibid.
[38] Ibid.
[39] See, for example, *Justice*, 24 November 1906.
[40] For an analysis of the issues surrounding spinsterism and their mobilisation before the
First World War, see S. Jeffreys, *The Spinster and Her Enemies*.

The present agitation had been largely carried on by spinsters and widows, for giving them votes, because they happen to rent a house or pay taxes, and they altogether ignore the fact that their Bill will only enfranchise one tenth of the women in this country, and will not admit the married women, who are the first women who should be given the vote. The married women – the mothers of their country – are not recognised as citizens, but are placed upon the same plane as lunatics and criminals, which was an insult to the glorious institution of motherhood.[41]

This argument exploited pro-motherhood sentiments, by turning against the suffragettes their own cry of the injustice of the existing franchise, which equated the unenfranchised woman with the unenfranchised criminal and lunatic.

Suffragists did not take such criticism lightly and this affected the public expression of the SDF's arguments. A number of surveys were conducted by suffragists which sought to demonstrate that a significant number of working-class women would be enfranchised by a limited Bill. Selina Cooper's survey of a Nelson ward in 1904 concluded that 95 per cent of those who would be enfranchised under an equal suffrage Bill would be working class women. Although this information, published in the *Co-operative News*, was much quoted, it did not in fact produce data that was relevant to the limited Bill for married women were not excluded from it although they were from the Bill. Nelson was also a fairly untypical example from which to generalise for the whole country, as such a large proportion of women, particularly married women, worked. The ILP conducted their own survey through their branches which concluded that at least 80 per cent of the women who would be enfranchised under a limited Bill would be working women. Both surveys could not be described as scientific and relied on a subjective and assumed definition of working class.[42] Nevertheless, Keir Hardie drew on these to claim at the 1907 Labour Party Conference that the limited Bill would enfranchise 2 million women, of which 1.75 million would be working class.[43] The SDF, on the other hand, was vehement that the Bill would only benefit the propertied. Burrows estimated that only 10 per cent of women would be enfranchised under the limited Bill.[44] Neither side produced conclusive evidence acceptable to their opponents and quickly the argument slid into caricature, polarising the two positions.

[41] *Justice*, 26 January 1907.
[42] J. Liddington, *The Life and Times of a Respectable Rebel*, p. 144–5. For a discussion of these and other surveys of the numbers of women who would be enfranchised, see D. Tanner, *Political Change and the Labour Party 1900–18*, Cambridge University Press, Cambridge, 1990, p. 126.
[43] *Labour Party Conference Report*, 1907, p. 61.
[44] *Justice*, 26 January 1907.

The second aspect of the dispute emphasised by the SDF was whether limited suffrage would be the first stage on the way to adult suffrage; more specifically, whether the women who would gain the vote under a limited Bill would use this to enfranchise the remaining voteless women and men. Initially, many WSPU members claimed that their goal was adult suffrage and that limited suffrage was tactically the best step in this direction, as it would establish the principle of women's right to vote. This was Charlotte Despard's argument when a member of the SDF and the WSPU[45] as well as Dora Montefiore's in this period. But many SDFers were not convinced. Rose Scott, for instance, argued that propertied women were unlikely to agitate for adult suffrage once they were enfranchised because they would 'look after their class interests'.[46] As the adult suffrage and limited suffrage positions became more polarised, it was harder to keep a foot in each camp. After 1907 the argument that limited suffrage was a tactical demand was no longer seriously advanced within the SDF.

The effect of these criticisms, articulated by a range of SDFers, was to narrow the debate within the party from a general discussion of women's suffrage to the merits of limited suffrage as a tactical political demand. Women's suffrage became the 'fine-lady suffrage' advocated by the WSPU, and adult suffrage was emphasised within the SDF as the only demand which could enfranchise all working-class women. Yet despite the party's long standing commitment to adult suffrage, there remained space within SDF publications for the views of dissenters. There was certainly no desire, as yet, even to attempt to make adult suffrage an enforceable party line.

With some semblance of unity, the SDF increasingly concentrated their attention on the WSPU. The ideological distance between the demand for limited women's suffrage and that for adult suffrage developed into an ever-increasing gulf over tactics and organisation. To begin with, in the first stages of WSPU militancy, some admiration was expressed within the SDF for their tactics. Thus, after Christabel Pankhurst and Annie Kenney's arrest at the Free Trade Hall, the Tattler expressed his 'admiration for the zeal, courage and determination' with which the limited suffragists had been carrying out their propaganda.[47] He suggested that lessons could be drawn by the SDF from such tactics which could then be used to promote what he saw as more important political questions.

---

[45]   See C. Despard, 'The Next Step to Adult Suffrage', *Reformers' Year Book*, 1907, p. 153. See also *Justice*, 8 December 1906.

[46]   *Justice*, 8 December 1906.

[47]   *Justice*, 30 December 1905.

But only a year later, correspondents to *Justice* were using pejorative terms, such as 'wild cats', to describe suffragettes.[48]

As WSPU militancy increased, there was initially an air of bewilderment in *Justice* that women would actually choose prison when they could pay their fines, and that they apparently courted police violence as a tactic. There was a tinge of misogyny in the comments of some: 'These women presume on the consideration which they know will be shown to them as women to act in a way in which it would be impossible for men to act. This is not revolutionary, it is simply taking advantage of sex privilege.'[49] In 1907 the SDF's women's column did not accept that there was police brutality against the suffragettes, believing that the policemen were only doing their duty.[50] As the distance grew between the two organisations, the SDF became more concerned about the effect that suffragette militancy might have on other political activity, in particular the general principle of freedom of speech and public meeting. In a *Justice* leader the tactics of the suffragettes were condemned because they endangered the right of public meeting by 'the tactics of the hooligan'.[51] Increasingly the issue was presented as one of freedom of speech. The behaviour of the suffragettes and the police was equally condemned. Protests were entered when suffragette meetings were broken up. Yet 'the suppression of free speech by hysterical women is no less reprehensible than its suppression by the capitalist forces of "law and order"'.[52] Despite some criticism of *Justice* for this stand,[53] the increasing polarisation of suffrage demands meant that the suffragettes and their tactics were not viewed sympathetically by the SDF. The party did not believe that the cause merited such sacrifice. Further, it was suggested that if the working class were to adopt such tactics, a much harsher response could be expected from the state.

It was not just militant action which brought an increasingly hostile response from the official voice of the SDF. Other aspects of the WSPU got an increasingly critical press. Their methods were presented as generally 'unscrupulous', and they were described as 'very artful and disingenuous'.[54] Much was made of the 'lavish' amounts of money at the disposal of the suffragettes. The WSPU's money confirmed to the SDF the class basis of limited suffrage, and also provided a contrast with

48 *Justice*, 7 July 1906.
49 *Justice*, 24 November 1906.
50 *Justice*, 23 February 1907.
51 *Justice*, 23 November 1907.
52 *Justice*, 4 January 1908. See also *Justice*, 17 October 1908.
53 For example, *Justice*, 18 March 1911.
54 *Social Democrat*, December 1907, p. 709; *Justice*, 18 March 1905.

the party's own poverty which was used to excuse its own inactivity.[55] The development of the WSPU as an organisation also made it easier for the SDF to claim, with some justice, that it was anti-democratic,[56] both internally and in terms of its central demand. After 1907, the language used in the representation of the suffragettes within SDF publications was mostly that of caricature, with little dialogue between the two organisations to alleviate the situation.

Although the suffrage question became increasingly polarised, this was not due entirely to the SDF's characterisation of limited suffrage. The party was particularly conscious of the criticism levelled at it as an organisation. This aimed to undermine the SDF's advocacy of adult suffrage by suggesting that its demand was merely a cloak to hide the real demand of manhood suffrage. This argument has found favour with some historians. David Morgan suggests that Christabel Pankhurst believed that the true goal of adult suffrage would eventually emerge; this was universal male suffrage and an anti-feminist majority. Undoubtedly Christabel was not alone in this view, but other historians have taken this to be an accurate summary of the nature of adult suffrage. Thus Andro Linklater claims that 'the SDF differed only in being honest enough to state frankly its hostility to the enfranchisement of any woman until every man had the vote'.[57] Such judgements gain support from statements such as that from Sam Robinson, of the ILP, who wrote to *Justice* in 1906 asserting that within the last year Hyndman had 'declared openly for manhood suffrage'.[58] But we need to be very careful in assessing the reliability of such observations by contemporaries. In fact, Hyndman was not an advocate of any particular form of suffrage but was indifferent to the whole debate. He admitted the justice of women's suffrage but could not get up much enthusiasm for it. For him suffrage was a means to an end and not an end in itself.[59] Yet the party was certainly not beyond all criticism. Hyndman's indifference did not equal support for manhood suffrage, but neither did it mean support for women's suffrage, and this rankled with suffragists. Certainly the insensitivity of some *Justice* reporting fuelled this view of the SDF, as Dora Montefiore pointed out in her criticism of an article on the Transvaal Constitution. The report described the constitution as 'quite democratic – manhood suffrage, and one man one vote'. As she commented, 'why bother to form adult suffrage leagues when the

[55] *Justice*, 1 December 1906; 20 June 1908.
[56] *Justice*, 26 January 1907; *Social Democrat*, July 1910, p. 293.
[57] D. Morgan, *Suffragists and Liberals*, Blackwell, Oxford, 1975, p. 47. See also A. Linklater, *An Unhusbanded Life*, p. 94.
[58] *Justice*, 8 December 1906.
[59] H. M. Hyndman, *Further Reminiscences*, pp. 285–6.

principle of manhood suffrage seems to be so entirely satisfactory, and so "quite democratic" to the SDF male leader writer?'[60]

Another major criticism of the SDF made by suffragettes and suffragists was that adult suffrage was not a realisable demand.[61] G. Wilson, a WSPU member, argued in *Justice* in early 1907 that if unenfranchised men wanted the vote then men as a sex had the power to get it: 'I don't think it reasonable to expect women to give up agitation for a measure of great importance to them, in order to help another reform that men can get whenever they want it.'[62] This illustrates the degree to which the two positions had become polarised; the two demands were no longer part of one another, but were being posed as alternatives.

The motives of the adult suffragists were also questioned. For example, Teresa Billington Greig took the view that the WSPU's task had been made more difficult because they had had to fight the adult suffrage demand to which in principle they were not opposed 'but which was obviously raised to postpone our equality measure'.[63] Similarly, Keir Hardie could not understand why any woman should be an adult suffragist since, as he saw it, this meant having 'to wait for the first recognition of her sex until the whole of the other sex has had its full rights conceded'.[64] This, of course, was not the basis on which adult suffragists presented their own case. Once again, each side in the dispute polarised it further by caricaturing the other's argument and motives.

The SDF's practice from 1905 to 1907 left the party particularly vulnerable to criticism. Little systematic action resulted from the increasing amount of space devoted to the suffrage within *Justice*. Dora Montefiore criticised the gap between the SDF's programme and practice.[65] Hers was not the only criticism, as was acknowledged in a front page article in December 1906:

The SDF has been reproached by some of the Suffragettes for not having undertaken a vigorous campaign in favour of Adult Suffrage ... But the efforts of the SDF are limited by its means ... The SDF is constantly exhausting its

[60]   *Justice*, 6 May 1905.
[61]   For example, *Justice*, 8 December 1906. See also S. S. Holton, *Feminism and Democracy: Women's Suffrage and Reform Politics 1900–18*, Cambridge University Press, New York, 1986, ch. 3, esp. p. 54; D. Rubinstein, *A Different World for Women, The Life of Millicent Garrett Fawcett*, Harvester Wheatsheaf, 1991, pp. 157–8.
[62]   *Justice*, 5 January 1907.
[63]   T. B. Greig, *The Militant Suffrage Movement*, Frank Palmer, 1911, p. 23.
[64]   K. Hardie, *The Labour Party and Women's Suffrage*, nd, quoted in C. Rover, *Women's Suffrage and Party Politics*, p. 151.
[65]   *Justice*, 6 May 1905.

resources in agitating questions of even more urgent importance than any extension of the franchise.[66]

Despite such a public acknowledgement of its failure to actively campaign, the SDF did not as a consequence do anything. Indeed, what activity there was, in particular the meetings of the newly formed Adult Suffrage Society (ASS), received little systematic coverage within *Justice* and, therefore, apparently little party support. The ASS was formed in 1904 and held its first meeting in January 1905. It was open to all men and women prepared to fight for adult suffrage but it remained a fairly small pressure group during its early years. Although SDFers were involved in it, and were to be increasingly so, initially the Society was not identified with the SDF as an organisation.[67]

Burrows, the voice of the SDF on the suffrage at this period, was concerned with the lack of practical opposition to the limited suffrage demand. He felt that adult suffragists should adopt a more aggressive attitude towards the supporters of limited suffrage. He suggested 'a band of Adultists – women and men – being formed to go round to all Limited meetings and show the truth of the matter.'[68] Interestingly, he did not advocate joining the ASS, and indeed his comments appear to be as much a criticism of this organisation as of the SDF. Some limited action was taken to this end. In early 1907, SDFers attended a Bradford suffrage meeting held under the auspices of the ILP, where Mrs Pankhurst and Teresa Billington were speaking. At the meeting they sold SDF and ASS literature. Although this seems to have been a successful propaganda drive, it was, perhaps, not the aggressive approach advocated by Burrows. In contrast, another meeting reported in the same edition of *Justice* featured direct intervention by the SDFer Kathleen Kough. At a Reading suffragette meeting she had attempted to move an amendment and, after initially being denied, persuaded the chair to change his mind by threatening, 'I think I can guarantee, Mr Mayor, that there will be no further meetings unless I am allowed to move it'. Her adult suffrage amendment, seconded by another SDFer, was carried by a substantial majority.[69] But these remained particular instances, rather than elements of a systematic SDF campaign.

Burrows did not look favourably on the tactics of other SDFers engaged in suffrage work. He poured scorn on Dora Montefiore's

[66]   *Justice*, 1 December 1906.
[67]   *The Reformers Year Book*, 1906, p. 159; *Justice*, 4 February 1905.
[68]   *Justice*, 8 December 1906.
[69]   *Justice*, 2 February 1907.

famous tax resistance stand.[70] Dora Montefiore, having been a tax-resister since the Boer War, decided in 1906 to publicise her position of no taxation without representation by refusing to cooperate with the bailiffs sent to distrain her goods. As a result, her home in Upper Mall, Hammersmith was beseiged for six weeks by the bailiffs while the WSPU and others demonstrated outside. Her home with its walled garden was christened 'Fort Montefiore' by the press. Despite Burrows' desire for more assertive SDF action over the suffrage, he could not support Dora Montefiore, believing that she only 'tends to make the agitation ridiculous'.[71] This was not the only occasion when he singled out Dora Montefiore for criticism.[72] Her involvement in the WSPU and in suffragette action, including being arrested and going to prison, was seen by Burrows, at least, as a challenge to his role as the party's suffrage expert. It also seemed that Dora Montefiore's activism in pursuit of the limited suffrage demand, which she claimed was a tactic towards adult suffrage,[73] exposed the party's own lack of action and undermined the assumed consensus on the matter.

The SDF's sense of rivalry with the suffragists was fuelled by anxiety that the party might lose members to the suffrage organisations.[74] There was also a fear that they might lose potential recruits such as 'Yorkshire Woman', who identified the SDF's attitude to women's suffrage as the one thing that prevented her from joining the party.[75] It is hard to gauge how many women shared this view of the SDF. Clearly some did, such as Kate Cording[76] and Dora Montefiore, who until 1907 voiced the same doubts from within the party. The energy that the SDF put into justifying their own position does at least indicate a real sense of rivalry with the suffragettes in particular and that, initially at least, they addressed a shared audience.

Rivalry for potential supporters was also one reason for the polarisation of debate between the organisations. The Tattler argued in early 1907 that he was not asking the suffragettes to give up their agitation, but he attacked 'those who are trying to bluff us Socialists into helping them, as if it were our affair'.[77] Socialism and limited suffrage were

[70] D. B. Montefiore, *From a Victorian to a Modern*, pp. 72–9; S. Pankhurst, *The Suffragette Movement*, p. 214. For other suffragist tax resistance, see M. Kineton Parkes, *The Tax Resistance Movement in Great Britain*, Women's Tax Resistance League, nd.
[71] *Justice*, 30 June 1906.
[72] *Justice*, 27 May 1905; also 1 September 1906.
[73] See *Justice*, 15 September 1906.
[74] *Justice*, 1 December 1906.
[75] *Justice*, 5 October 1907.
[76] *Justice*, 5 January 1907.
[77] *Justice*, 12 January 1907.

incompatible, so it was argued. Finally, in December 1907, this was formalised in the party's Manifesto on the Question of Universal Suffrage, which called on all loyal socialist men and women 'to cease to associate themselves with the middle class propaganda of "Votes for Some Women" and join in an active and militant propaganda for Adult Suffrage and Votes for All Women'.[78]

There was, of course, much more to the polarity than competition for members. With the increasing publicity for an active and even militant campaign, the SDF was forced to consider the theoretical arguments that underpinned its opposition to limited suffrage. The SDF's identification of an irreconcilable theoretical divide between the women's suffrage and adult suffrage positions reached the heart of its understanding of the woman question. Crudely, what was at issue was the primacy of sex or class. Many SDFers were concerned to distance themselves from what they saw as the 'sex-antagonism' inherent in the women's suffrage position.[79] The raising of sex-antagonism by woman suffragists was variously seen as 'mischievous' and 'a mistake'[80] because it endangered class solidarity. As Harry Quelch argued:

We, as Social Democrats, are concerned in maintaining and perfecting the solidarity of the working class. The suffragette agitation is wholly mischievous in its attempt to create a division in that solidarity, by endeavouring to establish in its stead a sex solidarity, and to set up an analogy between woman as a sex, and the proletariat as a class. They may be assured that, if they persevere in this, it will be found necessary to raise the whole question of . . . sex privilege.[81]

Quelch was one of a group of SDFers who, as soon as any aspect of the woman question was raised, suggested that women were in fact a privileged sex, with the implication that socialists therefore had no business fighting for them. But it was not necessary to hold to this very particular view to be opposed to sex antagonism. Zelda Kahan, for instance, argued that 'working women need the vote not for purposes arising out of any sex antagonism, which has no existence except in the imagination of a few individuals, but in order to be able to fight the more effectively side by side with men for the emancipation of both sexes from the fetters of capitalism'.[82]

Not every SDFer felt the suffrage question fitted easily into the sex-versus-class debate. Margaretta Hicks, ever watchful for working-class

[78] *Justice*, 14 December 1907.
[79] *Justice*, 21 January 1905; also 9 February 1907; M. Bondfield, *The Women's Suffrage Controversy*, Leaflet 1, ASS, nd (?1905).
[80] *Justice*, 16 March 1907; 9 February 1907.
[81] *Social Democrat*, December 1906, p. 716.
[82] *Social Democrat*, December 1909, p. 542.

women's interests, took a rather different view, suggesting that 'when working women know that they are not disenfranchised by reason of their belonging to the working class, but because they are women, it is no wonder that they fall into the slightly logical error of asking for votes because they are women'.[83] But, as one has come to expect, women SDFers, like SDFers generally, did not agree on this matter. For example, the woman columnist of *Justice* argued 'That a woman should not be allowed to vote because she is a woman does not appear to me to be so insulting, so tyrannical or so unjust as that she should not be allowed to vote because she is poor'.[84]

By early 1907, therefore, the two positions, of limited women's suffrage and adult suffrage, were thoroughly polarised. Staged debates such as that between Margaret Bondfield and Teresa Billington Greig, M. M. A. Ward and Mrs Tanner, and Dora Montefiore and Annie Kenney[85] did occur, but these were aimed at the undecided, not the main protagonists themselves. From 1907 on, particularly once Dora Montefiore severed her links with the WSPU, there was no longer any space for the limited suffrage position within SDF publications. Yet the debate from 1905 to 1907, had made explicit the links between the suffrage and the woman question, although the party view of the relationship between the two issues was still unclear. From 1907, the issue of translating assumed support for adult suffrage into a party line became paramount for the SDF. This necessarily had ramifications for campaigning, and for the difficult question of disciplining anti-suffragists.

Adult suffrage as a socialist demand (1907–1911)

1907 was a year of transition in the SDF's approach to the suffrage question. By the end of that year, the party produced its own manifesto on adult suffrage and, in so doing, went much further than it was to go on any other aspect of the woman question. But why did the SDF make this statement, and what was its significance for the adult suffrage campaign and for dissenters from it?

One of the most influential events for the SDF's suffrage position was the 1907 meeting of the Second International at Stuttgart, where the first Socialist Women's International was also held. Both meetings had the suffrage as a key agenda item, and both came out very strongly against limited women's suffrage and for an adult suffrage agitation. At

---

[83] *Justice*, 19 January 1907.
[84] *Justice*, 8 February 1908; also 25 June 1910.
[85] *Justice*, 7 December 1907; 16 May 1908; 12 December 1908.

the full Congress an elected Women's Franchise Commission, which included Kathleen Kough of the SDF and ASS, drew up the resolution for debate. This repudiated limited women's suffrage 'as an adulteration of, and a caricature upon, the principle of political equality of the female sex'. Instead, it called for 'universal womanhood suffrage'[86] and sought to sever any links between socialists and bourgeois women suffragists. This was an issue which underlined the divisions within the British delegation.[87] In the debate, the ILP objected to prohibiting cooperation with middle-class women suffragists[88] whilst Burrows, for the SDF, spoke in favour of the resolution. The Social Democrat position prevailed, and in the Congress report the SDF's contribution contained a strong sense that, despite being maligned and misunderstood at home by 'so-called Socialist English women', their position had been vindicated.[89]

Members of the International therefore appeared to be bound to campaign for adult suffrage. None the less, an amendment was accepted at the Congress from Victor Adler, leader of the Austrian Social Democratic Party, which acknowledged the impractability of fixing a definite date for the beginning of a general campaign for franchise reform.[90] The SDF therefore had the strongest moral imperative from Stuttgart to organise a systematic campaign for adult suffrage, particularly as it knew the ILP would not take this issue up. What it did not have was any deadline. The test of the party's commitment to adult suffrage was, therefore, how long it would be before the Stuttgart resolution affected SDF practice.

It was not long before the International's decision was cited in calls for an SDF campaign. For instance, Kathleen Kough, in her Congress report in *Justice* made it clear that the International's 'mandate' had strengthened the SDF's hand. She felt 'convinced that concerted action on our part would soon settle this question, once and for all, and leave us free to work for what may be more important measures'. To reinforce

---

[86] *Justice*, 31 August 1907.

[87] Unlike most of the other member countries of the Second International, Britain did not have a united socialist party and it was therefore represented by delegates from a variety of organisations including the SDF, ILP, Fabian Society, Labour Party and even the TUC (G. D. H. Cole, *The Second International*, p. xiii; J. Joll, *The Second International*, Routledge, 1974, pp. 123–4).

[88] See a similar Austrian Social Democratic Party position (R. J. Evans, *The Feminists*, pp. 166–7).

[89] K. B. Kough 'Report of the Women's Committee of the Social Democratic Federation of England', in *Report of the First International Conference of Socialist Women*, p. 31, in Gertrude Tuckwell Papers, File 353; also *Justice*, 7 September 1907.

[90] G. D. H. Cole, *The Second International*, p. 74.

this, she added, 'Seething dissatisfaction among our women workers will always obtain until their citizenship is secured'.[91]

Another event made 1907 an important year for the SDF's approach to the suffrage question. Surprisingly, this was the decision of an individual to leave one organisation and join another. Dora Montefiore's leaving the WSPU was bound to have a considerable impact on the presentation of the suffrage argument within the SDF, for she was the most significant critic of the party's suffrage debate. Her energy and persistence were apparent even when she took a position which was disturbing to others, and with her considerable charisma, few found it possible to be indifferent to her or her politics. What is most striking about this woman is the extent to which her support for a cause found expression in action. Dora Montefiore had quickly become an Executive member of the SDF on joining the organisation, although she resigned on a matter of principle only three months after being elected for a second term. Such political rectitude and energy did not make her an easy person to work with. Nevertheless, she was very strongly enmeshed in various women's networks, such as the suffragist correspondence circle which centred on Elizabeth Wolstenholme Elmy.[92] Dora Montefiore was one of the very few women who had anything approaching the authority of the male leadership of the party. What she said and did mattered in the SDF, whether she caused annoyance, took on Bax when others flinched, or persistently argued for the importance of a socialist understanding of the woman question.

Dora Montefiore had always argued that she was an adult suffragist but that during her membership of various English women's suffrage organisations she regarded the limited women's demand as a necessary tactic in moving towards full female enfranchisement.[93] She was an early member of the WSPU and organised in London, particularly the East End, while the Pankhursts were still based in Manchester.[94] Her focus was working-class women rather than the bourgeois women who were latterly the centre of WSPU attention. This caused an increasing tension between her and the Pankhursts, once they moved their headquarters to London in 1906 and took direct control of the organisation there. During that year Montefiore had an extraordinarily demanding speaking

[91] *Justice*, 7 September 1907. See also *Social Democrat*, October 1907, p. 605.
[92] Dora Montefiore was part of Elizabeth Wolstenholme Elmy's correspondence circle from 1897 until 1907. See Mrs Wolstenholme Elmy to Mrs McIlquham, BL Add Mss. 47,454, f.175, 3 December 1905; also L. Stanley, 'Feminism and Friendship in England from 1825 to 1938: The Case of Olive Schreiner', *Studies in Sexual Politics*, 8, 1985, pp. 10–46.
[93] D. B. Montefiore, *From a Victorian to a Modern*, p. 75.
[94] Ibid., pp. 51–2.

programme both in Britain and also in Europe.[95] She was also imprisoned as a consequence of a lobby of the Houses of Parliament on 23 October 1906. Imprisonment seriously affected her health and disturbed her so deeply that her daughter arranged for an early release. Sylvia Pankhurst paints an unkinder picture of Dora Montefiore's prison experiences, including the story that she was released because she was horrified to discover her head was infested with lice and she therefore 'precipitatively' arranged her release.[96] But Dora Montefiore's differences with the WSPU ran deeper than this.[97] After her period in prison, she left the WSPU, critical of the new militancy, particularly the tactic of resisting the police. She was also concerned about the increasing secrecy and high-handedness of the Pankhursts.[98]

Montefiore's commitment to the suffrage was such that she could not remain inactive for long, despite the harrowing cost of severing her links with the WSPU, which included losing the friendship of Elizabeth Wolstenholme Elmy among others. In 1907 Montefiore joined the ASS and was soon speaking as enthusiastically and as often for it as she had done for the WSPU. The ASS gained a tireless speaker, advocate and committee member. She became Honorary Secretary in January 1909,[99] giving it an undoubted boost when so many of its key supporters, such as Margaret Bondfield who was President of the ASS until 1909, were already committed elsewhere. This move meant that all the key advocates of the suffrage within the SDF were now pulling in the same direction. Dora Montefiore moved quickly into print and maintained a steady number of articles and pieces on adult suffrage within *Justice*.[100] She also represented the ASS at the 1907 Socialist Women's International Congress.[101]

Montefiore's role as an ASS activist, coupled with the Stuttgart resolution, heightened the existing debate over priorities both within the SDF and between it and the suffragists. Woman suffragists were asking all political parties to make the vote their principal priority. Yet Burrows, for example, despite being an advocate of all women's suffrage, responded that 'there are two things for which we are working, which are infinitely more important – the unemployed and the feeding of the

[95] Ibid., pp. 84–91.
[96] Ibid., pp. 92–107; S. Pankhurst, *The Suffragette Movement*, pp. 228–38.
[97] Mrs Wolstenholme Elmy to Mrs McIlquham, BL Add.Mss.47,454, f.192, 6 January 1906.
[98] D. B. Montefiore, *From a Victorian to a Modern*, p. 108; D. Mitchell, *Queen Christabel*, p. 102.
[99] *Justice*, 16 January 1909.
[100] For example, *Justice*, 9 February 1907; 30 March 1907. See also comments in *Clarion*, 22 February 1907; C. Zetkin, *Woman Suffrage*, p. 8.
[101] See *Clarion*, 23 August 1907; D. B. Montefiore, *From a Victorian to a Modern*, p. 120.

school children'.[102] Many SDFers presented their political agenda in a similar way to Burrows, as one which might include the suffrage, but only behind a range of other issues. This in turn left the party open to criticism for apparently ignoring the suffrage altogether, drawing a vigorous response from the party:

> We have not ... been willing to sacrifice more important matters to any mere political agitation; and to our view, the safeguarding of the physical well-being of the children is of infinitely more importance than any extension of the franchise whatsoever. At best the possession of a vote is only a means to an end, and the means must always be subordinate to the end, rather than the end to the means.[103]

This argument over political priorities was not restricted to the party leadership. It was also to be found amongst a range of woman SDFers. Here it is easier to see that the argument for giving a higher priority to issues other than the suffrage was not just an evasion. Thus, for example, M. A. Jackson argued as a revolutionary socialist and strong supporter of adult suffrage that 'there are items on our programme far more important, such as feeding little children and the unemployed question'.[104] Similarly, Margaretta Hicks, who was keen that working-class women be enfranchised, nevertheless recognised that there needed to be priorities. She placed 'the right to live' above all others, particularly over the 'question of how we shall govern our lives, or who shall make the rules'.[105] Kathleen Kough, an active member of the ASS who gave a considerable amount of her time to campaigning for franchise reform, nevertheless argued at the 1907 SDF Conference, 'I am not for a moment suggesting that our economic propaganda should be put on one side, or that SDF energy should be exclusively devoted to any franchise agitation'. She listed other issues which appealed to the party more strongly than the franchise, such as state maintenance of children, unemployment, old age pensions and working-class housing. But she felt that, without neglecting these, 'we may still take advantage of every opportunity offered by the discussion of this franchise question to vigorously press forward its adult side, and strenuously oppose any limited and propertied measure'.[106] Another leading SDFer who took anti-suffragists like Bax and H. B. Samuels to task was Zelda Kahan. She, like Kathleen Kough, had a much more positive interpretation of the argument regarding priorities

---

[102] *Justice*, 30 June 1906.
[103] *Justice*, 23 November 1907; see also *Justice*, 12 October 1907.
[104] *Justice*, 12 January 1907.
[105] *Justice*, 19 January 1907.
[106] *Social Democrat*, October 1907, pp. 600–1.

which did not lead her audience to the conclusion that she was indifferent to the suffrage question. Kahan accepted the traditional Social Democrat priorities, but argued: 'I do not mean that we ought to sink the rest of our programme and simply agitate for adult suffrage. On the contrary, there are many far more urgent questions, but in all our meetings reference should be made to the necessity of votes for all women as well as for all men.'[107]

As pressure mounted within the party for the SDF to clarify its position by taking action, it became possible to admit that the schema of priorities could be amended so that suffrage might find a place. In early 1907, a front-page article in *Justice* noted that the party could not be pledged to any course of action without consulting the membership. Yet it also reminded readers that the party had always been committed to adult suffrage as part of its programme. It was suggested that there is 'no reason why we should not, as the occasion offers, concentrate all our efforts upon, and throw ourselves vigorously, into an agitation for Universal Adult Suffrage'.[108] The most obvious way to pledge the party to action would be through its own conference, and, indeed, the suffrage was discussed at the SDF Conference of that year. Although the reported discussion was unanimously, if somewhat rhetorically, in favour of adult suffrage, the conference could not manage a united vote on the matter.[109] The suffrage had been debated at past conferences and was to continue to be an item at subsequent ones.[110] Yet by the end of 1907, the SDF produced a manifesto on the suffrage which included a 'call upon all branches of the party to give the question of adult suffrage special prominence in their educational and revolutionary propaganda'.[111]

Why was the SDF Executive at last calling for priority to be given to this question? The answer lies with the resolutions of the International Socialist Congresses. The manifesto was intended to bring the SDF into line with the International's suffrage propaganda, and enable 'Socialist women comrades [to] keep in democratic touch with their continental Socialist sisters'.[112] Apart from the international mandate, other reasons cited for a campaign at this time were the facts that the Newcastle Programme of the Liberal Party included adult suffrage, and Bannerman had indicated his sympathy for adult suffrage in the House of Commons. The time, in short, appeared to be right.

[107] *Social Democrat*, December 1909, p. 542.
[108] *Justice*, 9 February 1907.
[109] *SDF Conference Report*, 1907, pp. 25–6.
[110] The following SDF Conferences had debates on the suffrage: 1894, 1904, 1905, 1907, 1908, 1909.
[111] *Justice*, 14 December 1907.
[112] Ibid.

What effect did this new clarity of commitment and exhortation to action have on the SDF's contribution to the adult suffrage campaign? The party's most obvious ally was the ASS. This might appear a strange judgement. This organisation has not fared well in the hands of suffrage historians. It is one of the most invisible of the suffrage organisations, entirely absent from many accounts, misnamed or caricatured.[113] Undue reliance has been placed on Keir Hardie's assessment of the society: 'It holds no meetings, issues no literature, carries on no agitation on behalf of Adult Suffrage ... Its policy is that of dog in the manger.'[114] Hardie, of course, was one of the leading male supporters of limited suffrage and was hardly an unbiased commentator. More telling, perhaps, were the comments of Charlotte Despard on leaving the ASS for the WSPU. Although she felt that some of its members had done good work she thought that the ASS was not 'an honest movement', 'it had little enthusiasm and no hope'. In particular, she identified socialists as not being earnest in their support for adult suffrage, identifying the poor response of SDF branches to ASS circulars. She suggested that male socialists were holding back socialist women from the suffrage campaign because adult suffrage would inevitably mean greater political power in the hands of women rather than men.[115] Certainly, the ASS did not have the high profile of the WSPU nor the numbers of the National Union of Women's Suffrage Societies (NUWSS) and failed to make any significant impact in its early years. Although the society claimed that it had been mainly instrumental in securing the steady vote during these years of the TUC and the Labour Party Conferences in favour of adult suffrage, this is to overestimate its influence.[116]

Yet the picture was not one of unrelieved gloom. Charlotte Despard's parting shots at the ASS were swiftly answered in a letter to *Clarion* signed by a number of key SDFers.[117] Margaret Bondfield, as President of the ASS, also replied, acknowledging that at the end of 1906 the policy of the society had been one of temporary inaction. This had been

---

[113] Sylvia Pankhurst briefly mentions the organisation but misnames it the Adult Suffrage League (S. Pankhurst, *The Suffragette Movement*, p. 245); neither Ray Strachey (*The Cause*, Virago, 1979) nor Constance Rover (*Women's Suffrage and Party Politics*) mention it; and Marion Ramelson has one adverse remark (*The Petticoat Rebellion*, p. 154). Liddington and Norris, (*One Hand Tied Behind Us*), give the ASS some space as does Sandra Holton's *Feminism and Democracy*.

[114] Keir Hardie in *Labour Leader* quoted in M. Ramelson, *The Petticoat Rebellion*, p. 154: S. Pankhurst, *The Suffragette Movement*, p. 245.

[115] *Clarion*, 23 November 1906; see also C. Despard, 'The Next Step to Adult Suffrage' in *The Reformers' Year Book*, 1907, p. 153.

[116] *Reformers' Year Book*, 1909, p. 199. See also C. Rover, *Women's Suffrage and Party Politics*, pp. 146–56.

[117] *Clarion*, 7 December 1906. The SDF signatories included Harry Quelch, Fred Knee, A. P. Hazell, A. A. Watts, C. T. and Clara Hendin.

because the ASS could not identify with the Limited Bill and had chosen not to accentuate the difference of opinion which existed among socialist women on the best way of achieving full suffrage. She also clarified the criticism made by Charlotte Despard of the SDF's lack of support for the ASS. She argued that most SDF branches had reasoned that adult suffrage was to the forefront of their party programme and that therefore it would be a duplication of expense to affiliate with the ASS.[118]

Was there, then, any evidence that the ASS received much support from the SDF as a party, or through individuals, before the 1907 SDF Manifesto? Affiliation of branches did not, of course, necessarily mean that these branches were assiduously campaigning for adult suffrage. Moreover, although some meetings of the ASS were advertised and reported in *Justice*,[119] there was never systematic coverage from the SDF. In fact, *Clarion* consistently gave a better coverage of ASS activities. By 1907 the organisation was short of funds and speakers, and had to postpone a projected demonstration in August because many of its main speakers were going to be out of London.[120] Yet leading socialists, including SDFers, were numbered among its membership. Members included Pete Curran, W. C. Anderson, Gertrude Tuckwell and H. Jennie Baker, as well as SDFers Hyndman, Burrows, Quelch, Knee, Hazell, Watts, Charlotte Despard, Kathleen Kough, Dora Montefiore, Clara Hendin and M. M. A. Ward.[121] Only a few of these were active in the Society and this perhaps accounts for some of the criticisms of inertia made against the ASS in the early years. SDFers were occasionally encouraged to attend adult suffrage meetings which included SDF/ASS speakers.[122] In 1907, *Justice* was willing to admit that the ASS had 'not yet received the support it deserved' and noted that the Society was going to start a vigorous campaign and that this should have the hearty co-operation and support of every Social Democrat.[123] Despite the assumption of some that the ASS was essentially an SDF organisation,[124] the party did not put its full weight behind the society. It was just that some of the most active ASSers happened also to be SDFers. None the less, the ASS might have hoped for greater support in active campaigning from the SDF as a party once the Executive produced its Manifesto at the end of 1907.

[118] Ibid.
[119] For example *Justice*, 4 February 1905; 18 May 1907.
[120] *Clarion*, 12 April, 5 July, 2 August 1907.
[121] *Clarion*, 20 January 1905; 31 August, 7 December 1906. See appendix 5 for a brief biography of Clara Hendin.
[122] *Justice*, 6 May 1905.
[123] *Justice*, 9 January 1907.
[124] For example, C. Zetkin, *Woman Suffrage*, p. 9; C. Porter, *Alexandra Kollontai*, p. 165.

There certainly was some action following the manifesto. This was scarcely surprising, since it linked the SDF and the ASS more explicitly. There was, for instance, evidence of local SDF endorsement when women in Canning Town enthusiastically formed their own branch of the ASS.[125] At the opening of Parliament in 1908, members of the S. W. Ham branch of the ASS joined with women SDFers and other adult suffragists to hold an adult suffrage demonstration. This was fully reported in *Justice*, although it was not even mentioned in the mainstream press.[126] Ironically, the event was overshadowed by suffragette action. Clearly, adult suffragists had real difficulties in capturing the public's attention in a period of increasing suffragette militancy.

Despite these events, at the SDF Conference in April 1908 Dora Montefiore was still having to ask that the party implement the mandate of the Stuttgart Congress. She warned that if they did not make adult suffrage a prominent part of their propaganda all over the country 'they would be alienating some of the best women comrades in the Party. The women were looking for a lead on this question'. She said she was 'voicing the wishes and desires of thousands of working women who would come along and help them if they knew they were working for adult suffrage'.[127] The resolution to which she was speaking instructed the Executive to begin a national campaign for adult suffrage as well as for a list of other political reforms, such as payment of MPs. Hyndman, showing his lack of interest in the suffrage issue, only spoke to the latter part of the resolution. Although the proposal was carried by 91 to 28 votes,[128] the number of objectors was not insignificant. Attempts to build on this vote met with the usual problems of inter-factional disputes. A national conference of the socialist and labour movement, covering all the elements of electoral reform, and organised by the party was boycotted by most of the labour movement. The ILP objected to the centrality of adult suffrage to the conference and to the refusal of the SDF to take any amendments to the stated aims.[129] Consequently, of the 150 delegates, most were SDFers from branches or Circles, although there were also representatives from trade unions, trades councils, four ILP branches and, of course, the ASS.

Later that year questions were being asked in *Justice* about the tactics of the ASS in response to suffragette militancy.[130] At the ASS annual

---

[125] *Justice*, 28 December 1907.
[126] See, for example, *The Times* and *The Daily Express*, 30 January 1908. Apart from *Justice*, only *Clarion* had a report (7 February 1908).
[127] *SDF Conference Report*, 1908, p. 27.
[128] *Justice*, 25 April 1908.
[129] *Labour Leader*, 10 July 1908.
[130] *Justice*, 14 November 1908.

meeting, held in January 1909, the Society decided to stick to constitutional methods, concentrating on 'steady educational work' and making 'strong and active propaganda' throughout the country for a Bill for democratic franchise reform.[131] At this meeting, Dora Montefiore was elected as Honorary Secretary and this brought the SDF and ASS more closely in contact. She announced that there would be regular reports in *Justice* on the ASS and that adult suffrage would form a regular part of the new 'Our Women's Circle' column, which she was to edit.[132] Yet what initiative the ASS had was slipping away. By August 1909 and the favourable vote of the Women's Co-operative Guild, every labour and socialist organisation, with the exception of the ILP, had declared for adult suffrage, yet the ASS still appeared to be marginal to the debate. In October 1909, the People's Suffrage Federation (PSF) was formed to re-invigorate the campaign and, possibly, to distance it from the SDF. Within weeks they were claiming a membership of nearly 1,000 and the affiliation of Women's Labour Leagues, Women's Co-operative Guilds, Railway Women's Guilds, ILP branches, Women's Liberal Associations, trade unions and trades councils.[133] Yet the ASS decided by a large majority not to affiliate because the PSF was not explicit enough about limited suffrage.[134] SDF individuals and branches did not involve themselves with the PSF. The ASS campaign, such as it was, was therefore carried out in increasing isolation. Indeed, the ASS decided in 1910 that because of the overwhelming public interest in the constitutional issue of the Lords and the Budget, 'it was better to go on quietly with educational work until interest in franchise reform revived throughout the country'.[135]

The extent to which the SDF (by now the SDP) would ever actively campaign for adult suffrage, and make it a priority, remained in doubt. During 1909 there were several reports in *Justice* which revealed the ASS's dissatisfaction with the SDP. For example, Dora Montefiore protested that the ASS had been refused a platform at the SDP's May Day Demonstration because no sectional platforms were allowed. She concluded 'that where there is not apathy on the part of the rank and file of the SDP, there is too often hostility to the agitation for adult suffrage as a political reform here and now'.[136]

Despite the 1907 manifesto and the Stuttgart resolution, the SDP

[131] *Justice*, 16 January 1909.
[132] *Justice*, 27 February 1909; 20 March 1909.
[133] *Woman Worker* 25 August, 27 October, 10 November 1909.
[134] *Justice*, 27 November 1909; 16 July 1910.
[135] *Justice*, 26 March 1910.
[136] *Justice*, 8 May, 15 May 1909; also 24 April 1909.

remained ambivalent when called upon to take action rather than merely to debate or argue from the sidelines. Although all the Women's Socialist Circles were called upon to affiliate to the ASS,[137] there was never an equivalent drive to affiliate all the branches of the party. The excuse that affiliation was unnecessary as the SDF had always included adult suffrage in its programme simply reinforced criticism from outside the party of the sincerity with which adult suffrage was espoused. It also caused the SDP's own adult suffragist members to grow increasingly cynical about ever mobilising the organisation as a whole in a campaign. Adult suffragists persisted in trying to keep the issue before the party but, with Dora Montefiore travelling abroad for most of 1910 and 1911,[138] one of the most vocal advocates fell silent.

A further, crucial test of the SDF's credibility was its response to dissenters such as Bax, who argued as assiduously against, as Dora Montefiore did for, the suffrage. Although the issue had simmered for years, it came to the boil in 1909. That Bax's views damaged the SDP and the campaign for adult suffrage was obvious from a letter, originally published in *Women's Franchise*, that Dora Montefiore published in *Justice*. Frances Swiney had written:

The mask has fallen and also the cloven foot has appeared. What many shrewd minds have long suspected is proved by the most potent of arguments – action. Mr E. B. Bax is one of the signatories to an invitation widely issued to form a Man's Committee for Opposing Woman Suffrage.

Thus one of the leaders of Social Democracy would, in his ideal state, still deny women citizenship, and keep her the irresponsible dupe, tool, toy and slave of the brotherhood.

She continued in this vein, linking 'the low aspirations of a sensualist and a degenerate' Bax with the party as a whole.[139] Dora Montefiore felt that Bax had gone too far, and called on the party to deal with him; her view was shared by other SDPers, and branch resolutions were passed calling for him to be censured.[140]

At the 1909 SDP Conference, Bax was openly criticised in the suffrage debate for his undemocratic attitude and it was reported that the Executive had pointed out that Bax's membership of the Men's Anti-Suffrage League 'was not in harmony with the objects and principles of the Party'. Although no one defended Bax's anti-suffragism at the Conference, one delegate argued that 'every member had the right to express his personal opinions upon any item in the programme so long

---

[137] *Justice*, 18 April 1908; *Clarion*, 7 August 1908.
[138] D. B. Montefiore, *From a Victorian to a Modern*, pp. 124–52.
[139] *Justice*, 23 January 1909.
[140] For example *Justice*, 23 January 1909.

as he subscribed to the aims and objects of the party'. Here was a reminder, if one was needed, that the suffrage was part of the woman question; and, as such, merely a matter of conscience! The same kind of argument was now being used to marginalise the suffrage from the essential features of socialism as had previously been mobilised against the woman question. But as if to illustrate that the suffrage could be regarded as a special case within the woman question, Burrows argued that as adult suffrage had been part of the party programme since 1881 there could be no argument about it. He admitted that there were possibly many men in the organisation who were opposed to women's suffrage; but they, at least, did not use the same contemptible methods as Bax. He then moved a resolution which called upon the Executive to 'require' Bax to withdraw from membership of the Anti-Suffrage League. Burrows also protested at the SDF's Twentieth Century Press announcing Bax's *Legal Subjection of Men* in their list of socialist publications. The resolution was carried 92 to 1.[141]

There never seemed to be any question of expelling Bax from the party; he was merely to be, as he saw it, 'muzzled'[142] over this particular issue. Yet SDP publications continued to carry Bax's misogynist, undemocratic and now officially censured views. *Social Democrat* carried three major articles by Bax, and another one supporting him[143] during 1909, as well as articles commenting on or disputing his contributions. He and his views effectively dominated the SDP's journal for a whole year. There is no evidence that any effective action was taken against him. As Zelda Kahan wrote, 'We have learnt, if not to forgive, at all events to tolerate Belfort Bax's little eccentricities on this matter, and to dismiss his outbursts with a mere shrug of the shoulders.'[144] But she was worried that tolerating Bax as an eccentric member of the SDP family could entirely mislead others as to Social Democracy's attitude to the suffrage. This remained the nettle the party leadership refused to grasp.

This reluctance effectively to censor Bax, and therefore to sustain party policy on the suffrage, takes us right back to the central ambiguities of the woman question. The years from 1907 amply illustrate the SDF's ambivalence about the suffrage, treating it sometimes as a matter of

---

[141] *SDP Conference Report*, 1909, pp. 25–6.
[142] *Social Democrat*, September 1909, p. 390.
[143] E. B. Bax 'A Study in Socialist Heresy Hunting: Why I am Opposed to Female Suffrage', *Social Democrat*, March 1909: 'Why I am an Anti-Suffragist', *Social Democrat*, May 1909; 'Women's Privileges and "Rights"', *Social Democrat*, September 1909: H. B. Samuels, 'Women's Rights and the State', *Social Democrat*, October 1909. For a context to these arguments, see B. Harrison, *Separate Spheres: The Opposition to Women's Suffrage in Britain*, Croom Helm, 1978.
[144] *Social Democrat*, December 1909, p. 337.

fixed policy and on other crucial occasions as merely another element in the woman question, to be ignored or supported as the individual saw fit.

The suffrage and the woman question

That the suffrage was part of the woman question was generally understood within the SDF. But was the suffrage like all the other component parts of the woman question? If not, how and why was the suffrage different, and what ramifications did this have for the woman question itself?

One obvious difference was that for no aspect of the woman question other than that of the suffrage did the party issue a manifesto. This ran against the predominant current of the party's understanding of the woman question. A virtual consensus on the suffrage was reached and acknowledged in SDF publications; it was not a matter of private conscience, as the party had from the outset written into its programme the demand for adult suffrage. This kind of commitment did not characterise any other aspect of the woman question.

Nevertheless, the difference in practice was not as great as might be supposed. SDFers were never asked very emphatically to take action to realise the demand of adult suffrage. Campaigns were mooted, but rarely organised. It was left to individuals to take action if they chose. To justify this, the party cited reasons which were more commonly associated with the woman question as a whole. Adult suffrage was enshrined within socialism, and specifically within the party programme, and therefore those who desired suffrage reform should give their commitment in the first instance to the struggle for socialism. Nor was this simply the response of the leadership; the majority of SDF branches replied in a similar vein when they were canvassed for support by the ASS. Theoretical commitment faded into practical quietude.

Ironically, this ambivalence helped foster the misrepresentation of the party's theoretical position on adult suffrage and, indeed, its campaigning in this sphere. As it was formulated and argued for within the SDF, adult suffrage was essentially a socialist demand and *not* an anti-woman demand. It was not deliberately conceived of as a smokescreen for a manhood suffrage campaign. Nonetheless, the party's lack of action came to look more and more like indifference. This impression was reinforced by the unwillingness of the party leadership to see the suffrage as a crucial matter over which party discipline might be enforced. As a result, Bax and his supporters could continue to promulgate their misogynist anti-suffragism. The party was thus never really able to salve its collective reputation, although the commitment of individuals to the suffrage cause could not, of course, so easily be called into question.

Why was the suffrage different to a degree from other aspects of the woman question? The external pressure on the SDF of the campaign for women's suffrage was crucial. Domestically, the WSPU, in particular, was seen as a rival for women's allegiance, while internationally the 'bourgeois women's movement' had a significant effect on European socialists, who in turn greatly influenced the SDF through the Second International. These factors moved the suffrage from being merely an aspect of the woman question to an issue discussed in its own right. From 1905, it increasingly overshadowed other aspects of the woman question. Yet the link between the two was never broken. As suffrage was seen as part of the woman question, the SDF took a re-active rather than pro-active stance. The party's understanding of the woman question meant it was very difficult to take a united, pro-active stand on the suffrage, and consequently the SDF's policy was particularly susceptible to external events.

These external pressures did not exert themselves on an unchanging, unreflective membership. Individuals, both SDF members and potential members, changed in their political concerns and emphases, and were genuinely affected by the 'Socialism versus Suffragism' debate. The fact that someone as influential within the party as Dora Montefiore could apparently change her mind and her allegiances showed that others might do the same. Those outside the SDF who were contemplating a suffragist or suffragette stand might also be open to socialist ideas, and hence, as some recognised, it was important for the SDF to have a clear and credible position on the suffrage. The urgency was all the greater because a group who were regarded as a significant part of the SDF constituency – working-class women – were being fought over by both sides of the suffrage debate.

By 1907, suffrage had become the prism through which the SDF's stance on the woman question was seen. The woman question had not become a single-issue campaign. Other elements were still being discussed, developed and acted upon by women SDFers. But the suffrage was at centre stage, both ideologicaly, in focusing theoretical arguments central to the woman question, and, more practically, when it took the form of political warfare, name-calling, disputing opponents' statistics and competing for audiences.

In the period before World War I, the possibilities for women's political action were widening outside the SDF. This alerted some of the male membership to what many women SDFers had been saying for some time. Women were necessary for a socialist victory, and they too had to be won for the cause. Yet the SDF's behaviour over the suffrage and its representation by others had clearly affected general perceptions of the party. The SDF's inability to move as an organisation from rhetorical to practical commitment had contributed to the negative stereotype of the party. It had also affected women's perception of the party's approach to the wider woman question. If the SDF could not take concerted action over what seemed to be one of the least contentious aspects of the woman question, what hope was there for the question as a whole, and thus what hope for a socialist future?

Part 3

Women and the SDF: the practical
implications of the SDF's understanding
of the woman question

7   The SDF's attitude to women as potential socialists

The SDF's understanding of the woman question made a virtue out of the political vacuum it created around women. In particular, the notion that issues associated with the woman question were matters of conscience allowed all sorts of assumptions about women to gain credibility within the SDF. Views which stereotyped and denigrated women appeared alongside pleas for toleration and positive images of women's capabilities. To say the least, this gave a contradictory and confusing picture of the party to existing and potential women members.

Women as a problem for socialism

Within the SDF, just as outside it, women as a sex were generalised about in a way which was never done for men. The male sex was not dealt with as an undifferentiated mass; it was distinguished through a variety of categories such as class, trade and political conviction. The same rarely applied to women. As a sex, they were seen by SDFers as a reactionary force in society.[1] There was disagreement as to whether women were naturally or socially conditioned to be conservative, but there was a general fear that they constituted a threat to socialism. This was sometimes voiced in terms of women's presumed reactionary influence in municipal elections, but it was more commonly expressed as a general belief in women's 'indifference, ignorance and apathy'.[2]

The assumed conservatism of women took two forms: one based on apathy with conservatism as its result and another rather more active conservatism where women's influence prohibited or limited the participation of others in socialist politics. Women's lack of direct political power, particularly the parliamentary vote, was meant to

[1]   See M. Goot and E. Reid, *Women and Voting Studies: Mindless Matrons or Sexist Scientism*, Sage, Beverly Hills, 1975; V. Randall, *Women and Politics*, Macmillan, 1982, pp. 49–53.

[2]   *Justice*, 18 August 1894. The defeat of SDF candidates in municipal elections was often blamed on women and their 'anti-socialist' vote. For example, *Justice*, 1 December 1894, 14 November 1903; H. M. Hyndman, *Further Reminiscences*, p. 289.

explain their indirect, but insidious, influence over others. Such ideas could be expressed with considerable venom which betrayed an underlying contempt for women, thus:

For one woman who would strengthen a man's hands in a struggle against injustice, there are twenty who would strike them down. If the women are the greatest sufferers by the present system – which I do not deny – it is but just for they are the greatest sinners. 'Submit, submit', is always their cry to the men. 'What do you think you can do to alter it?', they ask, with a sneer, of any man who tries to rouse his fellows to revolt ... They dominate the men, and make blacklegs and cowards of them.[3]

This image sat awkwardly beside the other form of conservatism attributed to women, which while passive was often held equally in contempt. Women were thought almost incapable of understanding socialism, and much too foolish to do anything about it. According to this stereotype, 'The vast mass of women would consider a man a terrible bore who spoke to them on politics. The delight of women is to gossip about other people, and a thousand other frivolous things.'[4] Only male members used such belittling language, which in some cases verged on the misogynic.

SDF women were less contemptuous but they too regarded their sex as essentially conservative. The explanations were, however, very different. While many male SDFers implied that women's conservatism was innate, women correspondents to *Justice* preferred a social explanation for a condition they could not deny. For example, Ellen Batten wrote: 'Most women are intensely conservative. How can they be otherwise, when their whole training is opposed to free thought? Centuries of subjection and repression have forced women to centre their minds on trivialities, and long habit is hard to break.'[5]

Whatever the explanation, women's conservatism was seen as a problem for the party. Members accepted that 'without women a movement lacks half its vitality'.[6] They therefore wanted women's support for the SDF whilst viewing the whole sex as deeply resistant to socialism. In order to cope with this problem, SDFers focused their discussion of women's potential for politicisation around what they perceived as the most immediate issue for the party. It was women's influence as wives of socialist men which most concerned them to the extent that, in the 1890s, the relationship between women and socialism was predominately discussed in these terms.

[3]   *Justice*, 12 May 1894.
[4]   *Justice*, 7 October 1893.
[5]   *Justice*, 30 September 1893; also 10 October 1896, 16 January 1909.
[6]   *Justice*, 4 July 1891.

The whole conception of 'the problem of socialists' wives' was, of course, redolent with assumptions. Socialists were generally assumed to be men; women SDFers were noted in terms that suggested they were exceptions.[7] Moreover, although there were criticisms of socialist men, there was no discussion of the 'socialist's husband'. By focusing on woman the wife, and indeed woman the mother of a potential socialist generation, the project became less one of recruiting women as activists and more one of neutralising their unfortunate influence. The priority was to prevent wives and mothers acting as a brake on male socialists' activism.[8] In that sense, women's politicisation was conceived of as significantly different from that of men for the goal was, at minimum, to win women's acquiescence and even support for socialist politics rather than primarily looking for female recruits to full and active party membership. This was reflected in the strategies adopted by the SDF in relation to women's politicisation.

The SDF, like other parties of the Second International, sought to mobilise the family as an area of support and reinforcement for its membership. Female members of the (presumed male) SDFer's family were expected to extend their caring and supportive role to sustain practically and psychologically the party member against a hostile world. On this assumption, the 'want of sympathy shown by the wives of socialists for the work we have in hand'[9] presented a pressing practical problem to the SDF. It was concerned that 'members are often lost because their wives are prejudiced'.[10] Maud Ward presented the issue more sympathetically in 1908:

One hears even today the complaint that 'I could do much more for the movement if my wife were not so much opposed'; the process of converting the wife was probably never very seriously undertaken. It is not difficult to foresee that prejudices against a movement which has too often led to persecution and loss of employment are somewhat difficult to remove, but when women do grasp the meaning of the sacrifice, they are generally willing to bear their share of the burdens.[11]

The Tattler saw women's indifference as the root of the problem, insisting that there were 'plenty of men in the movement today who

---

[7] The most obvious way in which women were noted as exceptions to the male membership was the self-congratulatory branch reports which announced the branch's first woman secretary (*Justice*, 18 April 1896); a woman 'very pluckily taking the chair' (*Justice*, 16 July 1898); or even their first women members (*Justice*, 16 December 1905; 23 January 1909).
[8] See, for example, *Justice*, 2 April 1904.
[9] *Justice*, 15 May 1886.
[10] *Justice*, 28 September 1907.
[11] *Justice*, 25 April 1908.

would give anything to get their wives or sweethearts, or mothers and sisters, to take some little interest in the cause'.[12] However, the party's discussion on the problem of socialists' wives revealed a different picture. It was by no means clear that men would give, or do, anything in order to involve their womenfolk in the SDF.[13]

Women responded in a number of ways to their characterisation as the unsympathetic wife of the socialist. Although a few women actively endorsed the stereotype,[14] others turned the argument around on their accusers and highlighted the difficulties of living with a socialist husband. One socialist wife complained that her husband came home only to bolt a meal down before rushing off to a meeting. She said, 'I kept a count once for a month how many hours he spent at home, and when I showed him and he could not deny it, he lost his temper and said he was a revolutionist and wasn't going to be henpecked'.[15] She emphasised that this level of activity took a toll not only on her marriage but on her husband too. It was as if a household could only bear one active socialist, and then with a strain on all concerned.

In such a model not only was the socialist unlikely to be female but also there was every reason for her to be less than sympathetic to the cause which disrupted the household. A male SDFer argued in response that it was not 'any part of true socialism to neglect any duty at home for anything that is to come in the future'.[16] This comment was directed at the 'unreasonable' socialist husband but could, as easily, have been an exhortation to the socialist's wife.

Another description of the reality of a Social Democrat marriage has a timeless quality to it:

Social Democrats as a rule are not domesticated ... I know good Socialists but they are not good husbands, you know. He is out every night in the week, Sundays never home to dinner ... Even if one should have company ... he must go to see how the meetings are getting on, everything would go wrong were it not for this man, so he thinks, and the company thinks how unsociable the Socialists are ... yet we want more men like this for the good of the cause.[17]

Here the paradox was recognised: what made a good socialist might not necessarily make a good marriage. This made for a particularly ironic difficulty; socialists complained about the traditional socialist's wife

---

[12]   *Justice*, 9 September 1893.
[13]   This ambivalence was also to be found in the SPD. See J. H. Quataert, *Reluctant Feminists*, p. 148.
[14]   *Justice*, 9 September 1893.
[15]   *Justice*, 5 June 1886.
[16]   *Justice*, 19 June 1886.
[17]   *Justice*, 21 October 1893.

when it seemed that the traditional family would have been unable to cope with a socialist wife in its midst!

The challenge to the sexual division of labour, which might have enabled women's participation in political life, was not generally forthcoming. The problem was not exclusive to the SDF, for Julia Dawson highlighted a similar situation in the woman's column of *Clarion*.[18] Her support for the socialist's wife and criticism of socialist husbands was similar to that made by women in *Justice*. She reported that, as a result, some husbands had unsuccessfully tried to keep that particular edition of *Clarion* from their wives, while others complained that if they did as she had asked, they would be tied to their wife's apron strings and there would be no work done for socialism at all. However, some of *Clarion*'s correspondents resolved to turn over a new leaf and look upon their wives as women instead of household chattels.[19] Whether recognised or not, the problem of the socialist husband was clearly as widespread as that of the socialist's wife.

Nevertheless, it was, of course, women who were perceived as *the* problem for the SDF. This was a problem which focused particularly on the familial; the wives, mothers, sisters and daughters of existing members. Its focus was also domestic,[20] for the discussion was based on an acceptance of the sexual division of labour, and concentrated on women within the home rather than the workplace. The SDF's concern about the problem of socialists' wives reflected the party's perception of them as a threat to the activity of members. What the party did not address was the way in which this emphasis on women as a problem for socialism could turn socialism into a problem for women.

Socialism as a problem for women: barriers to participation

Many women writing in *Justice* echoed the view that 'There are many wives who would only be too glad to join the Socialist movement if they had the chance'.[21] However, it was the barriers to women's participation which these women continually highlighted and which the party as a whole found so difficult to acknowledge.

---

[18] *Clarion*, 27 March 1897.

[19] *Clarion*, 17 April 1897.

[20] The German socialist women's movement was most successful when it emphasised the domestic aspect of women's lives. Mass recruitment of women to the SPD began when campaigns and propaganda were directed towards their interests as housewives and mothers rather than their interests as workers (R. J. Evans, 'Politics and the Family', p. 265).

[21] *Justice*, 30 September 1893.

Practical help from SDFers was never forthcoming on anything other than an individual basis, and there is little evidence even of this.[22] It certainly did not seem that socialist men 'would give anything' to get their womenfolk involved, as the Tattler had claimed. For example, Sarah Lay, a member of Reading SDF, explained that in the eighteen months of her membership she had been able to attend only two branch meetings and about half a dozen lectures because 'my whole time is occupied in attending to the wants of my husband and bairns, and in my home'. She suggested that comrades could give practical support to their wives: 'now and again stay at home and mind the babies, so that she can attend a lecture or a branch meeting'.[23] But childcare seemed to be beyond the practical support that male SDFers were willing to give, and other complaints from women showed the extent to which the family and its domestic servicing were taken for granted within the SDF.

One apparently trivial matter became symbolic of women's general complaint. This was the spoilt Sunday dinner. Sunday, as the one day free from work, was a time the family could spend together or when the husband could free his wife for an hour or two by childminding. But Sunday was also the main focus in the week for socialist propaganda, and many branches held three, usually open-air, public meetings during the day.[24] This produced some conflict, as Rose Jarvis reported:

women are in some cases being kept out of sympathy with the organisation by the fact that their husbands occasionally go into the pub after a Sunday morning meeting and keep dinner waiting for an hour or so, this making it almost impossible for the women who have been at home cooking all the morning to get out in the afternoon.[25]

In contrast, the Tattler thought that the fault lay in keeping the dinner waiting, not in the men going into the pub![26]

Although the focus of the SDF's discussion on women's potential to become socialists was essentially domestic, the solution sought was not. Not only was the sexual division of labour to be left unscathed, even the

---

[22]   There are few surviving accounts of socialist women's domestic arrangements but see Hannah Mitchell's *The Hard Way Up*, pp. 95–132. She was a socialist before her marriage and was able to shape her family responsibilities to some extent by deliberately having only one child. Although her husband was also a socialist she got other women to substitute for her in the home rather than encourage her husband to take on domestic responsibilities, something which she regretted in later life. She highlighted not only the organisational but also the emotional difficulties for married women engaged in socialist activity.

[23]   *Justice*, 23 September 1893.

[24]   For example, Burnley SDF usually held open-air public meetings at 11 am, 3 pm and 6.30 pm on Sundays (*Burnley Gazette*, 15 April 1893).

[25]   *Justice*, 30 September 1905.

[26]   *Justice*, 7 October 1905.

amelioration of women's condition by occasional childcare, and the appreciation of the work that went into Sunday dinner were requests ignored by the party. Women's contribution to socialism had to fit the prevailing notion of the family and the sexual division of labour.

It is in this context that the notion of socialist motherhood as women's contribution to the socialist struggle can best be understood. The bringing up of children as socialists was an activity which reinforced women's place in the traditional sexual division of labour while giving them some sense of involvement in the socialist project. Many women SDFers supported this view of 'woman the mother' as an insurance policy for socialism. For example Rose Jarvis argued that 'we are anxious to draw women into the movement, as they will influence the children, and so we hope to gain the future generations'.[27] In general, motherhood was venerated as women's contribution to socialism and was backed by the whole of the socialist movement's commitment to Socialist Sunday Schools.[28] In keeping with this, it was often women who specialised in children's work within the SDF.[29]

Some women recognised the strain that the competing images of the socialist woman put on female socialists. Socialist motherhood might be the pragmatic recommendation of the party for the socialist wife but its responsibilities limited women themselves reaching out to socialist ideas. One socialist's wife wrote to Justice with her dilemma: 'my husband and myself have talked this over, and in order for us both to work for Social Democracy we have made up our minds to have no more children, and yet it would appear that socialists should have large families that we could bring up our children to be enthusiasts like ourselves'.[30] S. Gardiner suggested birth control as a means to free woman to take her part in socialist politics,[31] but it was unusual to take such a radical position. If women were already mothers, they were likely to get a rather jaundiced view of socialism, according to many socialists' wives, whereas if they were already active socialists it was difficult to combine the responsiblities of childcare with continuing activism.

Although the focus on women as a problem for socialists was principally domestic, women identified the practice of the SDF as a

---

[27] Justice, 23 April 1904. For a broader discussion of contemporary maternalism, see S. Koven and S. Michel (eds.), Mothers of a New World.

[28] See F Reid, 'Socialist Sunday Schools in Britain, 1892–1939', International Review of Social History, 11, 1966, pp. 18–47.

[29] For example, Mary Gray of Battersea SDF (F. Reid, 'Socialist Sunday Schools', p. 21) and Mrs Spinks of Edmonton SDF (Justice, 16 November 1912).

[30] Justice, 21 October 1893.

[31] Justice, 23 June 1894. For a not entirely sympathetic account of the SDF and birth control, see A. McLaren, Birth Control in Nineteenth Century England, Croom Helm, 1978, ch. 9.

barrier to participation. Women complained that the party seemed to have a particularly male feel to it, both in its membership and its practices, which meant that women did not feel welcome. Annie Oldacre suggested that women did not attend socialist meetings 'for fear that they should be considered not modest – a few, or perhaps one woman – among a number of men. Or worse still they might be suspected of having an ulterior object in view.'[32]

Women's complaints about the male atmosphere of SDF branches were not on the whole acknowledged or understood within the party. Ellen Batten felt that women socialists were regarded as a nuisance or as mild enthusiasts who must be tolerated but who would be better off at home engaged in gossip, tea drinking and other feminine frivolities.[33] Complaints were made in *Clarion* that ILP and SDF branches gave a cold reception to those women who ventured to attend them and that neither gave any indication that they actually welcomed women.[34] Although all women's experience was not the same, some women spoke of being 'like a fish out of water, or a stranger listening to a foreign tongue'[35] when attending an SDF meeting. On the other hand, Nellie Bloodworth, a long time member of the SDF, disagreed that women were contemptuously brushed aside in meetings or treated as camp followers.[36] Nevertheless, other SDFers felt that in order to attract women the way in which meetings were conducted had to be changed. Meetings were felt to be too dull and uninteresting and that in order to 'capture the women', socialist songs and music should become part of these gatherings.[37] The conduct of meetings, which one woman described as 'stiff, formal and gloomy',[38] could have a crucial impact on women who were isolated within and outside the party. Tentative political commitment could be crushed in a hostile environment, particularly when women's political activity was vulnerable to social pressures beyond those experienced by men.[39]

Probably the most important barrier to women's participation in the SDF was the manner in which they were represented within the party press. There were objections to the way in which women were

32   *Justice*, 10 October 1896.
33   *Justice*, 2 September 1893; also 22 May 1909.
34   *Clarion*, 25 January 1896; 24 July 1897.
35   *Justice*, 22 May 1909.
36   *Justice*, 8 May 1909.
37   *Justice*, 27 February 1892.
38   *Justice*, 9 September 1893.
39   See, for example, M. McCarthy, *Generation in Revolt*, p. 37. By this period there was no sense of a tradition of public political activity by working class women (D. Thompson, 'Women and Nineteenth Century Radical Politics', particularly pp. 137–8).

stereotyped. Marion Coates demanded of *Justice* that they 'Stop putting flippant silly pictures in front of us women. Treat us with the reverence and respect that you wish for yourself.'[40] But the stereotypes continued with the Tattler being a particular offender. He would make flippant remarks in response to women's criticisms, such as: 'to return to our sheep – I beg their pardon, the ladies and their woes'.[41] Mary Boyd was one of the women who warned against the 'vulgar abuse' and 'insidious innuendoes' which appeared in *Justice*: 'It is not calculated to induce women to join the organisation and may alienate some who belong to it already.'[42]

There was a particularly strong reaction when blatant misogynism was printed within *Justice* and *Social Democrat*. Critics suggested that not only was this unacceptable in itself but also that it would damage the SDF in the eyes of actual and potential women members. After a particularly virulent piece by Bax, Catherine Davidson asked angrily whether the party would castigate Bax or would choose to remain silent and, in effect, endorse his views. She argued:

If this view be upheld by the SDP then women's place is outside; let our members take their courage in both hands if they believe it and say so. Self-respecting women members will then resign. If this view be not upheld, then the columns of *Justice* ought to be closed to anyone who wishes to insult either sex.[43]

Arguments like this were repeatedly made against Bax and others, yet the way in which the woman question had come to be understood ensured that the leadership's complacency remained unshaken. This was despite the pragmatic case that was being made by both female and male SDFers that women would neither join nor stay in a party which appeared to condone abuse of them.

Women SDFers commented on the male image of the party and since there was little belief that other socialist organisations differed, this easily became criticism of socialism itself. 'Hopeful', a correspondent to *Justice*, pointed out that the language used by most socialists reflected the assumption that socialists were necessarily male. She warned, 'all speakers must be very careful to avoid speaking of "working men" and omitting the women. We women feel repelled at the continual sole use of the masculine nouns and pronouns'.[44] Women's absence from the collective language of socialism was reinforced by the use of phraseology

[40] *Justice*, 30 June 1894.
[41] *Justice*, 12 May 1894.
[42] *Justice*, 18 April 1896. Also see her letter in *Justice*, 9 May 1896.
[43] *Justice*, 9 April 1910.
[44] *Justice*, 23 September 1893. See also *Clarion*, 14 September 1906.

that stereotyped women as a problem for socialists.[45] As she said, 'the chief thing is to awaken interest. Now this will never be done if men call us frivolous'.[46] Ellen Batten shared this concern and commented on male socialists' behaviour towards women: 'When one sees the half-contemptuous smile, or hears the slighting remark when women are mentioned as workers or speakers one cannot help feeling that those socialists are not as advanced or as true to their principles as they ought to be.' She warned that such behaviour would repulse potential women socialists and would eventually drive existing women members to abandon socialism.[47] It seemed that the gulf between socialist men's theory and practice was the final barrier to women's participation in the party.

Women's expectations of socialist men's practice were based on the identification of socialism with a commitment to sexual equality. Some were disillusioned when their own experiences of socialist parties failed to include any measure of prefigurative practice and little respect for women. Dora Montefiore quoted from one woman who had been an active socialist:

Honestly I have little hope of making any impression on the mind of the ordinary male Socialist, who I believe, notwithstanding all his professed theories of equality,etc, has little or no sympathy with the women's movement. That fact chiefly led to my complete withdrawal from the Socialist movement. I would rather be associated with the ordinary 'mere male man', whose ignorance and inherited prejudices are not so closely bound up with exalted notions of theories.[48]

Disappointment could turn to cynicism, when socialist men turned out to be little different from their non-socialist brothers.

This complaint was one made against socialism generally rather than merely against the SDF.[49] For example, Elizabeth Wolstenholme Elmy argued in *Justice* that a large number of women were sympathetic to socialism but were driven away from socialist parties 'by the all but universal failure of male Socialists to recognise *practically* in women the other half of humanity, with rights absolutely equal to those of the male half.'[50] Hannah Mitchell, as a member of the ILP, had been similarly disappointed by the gap between the anticipated and actual behaviour of

---

[45] For example, Dora Montefiore objected to socialists marginalising women by classifying them with children (*Justice*, 11 October 1902).
[46] *Justice*, 23 September 1893.
[47] *Justice*, 2 September 1893; 30 September 1893.
[48] *Justice*, 11 October 1902; also 4 October 1902, 18 October 1902.
[49] This was a complaint made by socialist women throughout the Second International. For example, in the Socialist Party of America (B. Dancis, 'Socialism and Women in the United States, 1900–17', *Socialist Revolution*, 27, 1976, p. 86) and in the SPD (K. Honeycutt, 'Clara Zetkin', p. 338).
[50] *Justice*, 25 October 1902.

socialist men, which was generally undifferentiated from male attitudes within the wider society. She remembered that 'A lot of the Socialist talk about freedom was only talk and these Socialist young men expected Sunday dinners and huge teas with home made cakes, potted meats and pies, exactly like their reactionary fellows'.[51]

The SDF did not escape criticism. Hannah Taylor pointed out that the rules of the SDF included working for equality between the sexes, yet 'We do not see the spirit of this object carried out in our branches to any great extent'.[52] John Spargo, an ex-member of the SDF who had emigrated to the United States, was willing to acknowledge 'that we have consistently and deliberately ignored the women's side of our programme'. This had blinded socialists to 'the fact that "Workers of the World Unite!" means the woman in the factory as well as the man who works by her side; the woman toiling at home with the babies as well as her husband in the workshop or mine'.[53] This was a statement which many male socialists seemed unwilling to endorse. However, even this was an impersonal acknowledgement of the particular experiences that women faced within the SDF and other socialist parties. For them the gulf between the theory and practice of the woman question was not an abstract or a rhetorical issue but one that affected their daily lives and their choices of becoming or remaining socialists. The SDF's understanding of the woman question permitted the voicing of such criticisms, doubts and disillusionment but it provided no impetus for action at an organisational level. This reinforced the isolation of individual women socialists, and indeed socialists' wives, and made it all too easy to dismiss their experiences as either unfortunate but not typical, or as demonstrating the problem that women posed for socialism.

The SDF's understanding of women's politicisation

Although there appeared to be considerable ambivalence in the SDF's message to women, the party maintained throughout its lifetime that it wanted women members.[54] The practice of male members of the SDF showed that there was a considerable difference between this nominal commitment and actually putting energy into their recruitment. So, how did the SDF believe women would become socialists? Was this process assumed to be any different than that for 'making' male socialists?[55]

---

[51] H. Mitchell, *The Hard Way Up*, p. 96.
[52] *Social Democrat*, December 1901, p. 369.
[53] *Justice*, 25 April 1908.
[54] For example *Justice*, 4 July 1891; 18 January 1896; 11 October 1902; 26 March 1904; 28 September 1907.
[55] The notion of 'making' socialists to describe the process of politicising non-socialists

The purpose of the SDF as a political party was essentially evangelical: that is, to make socialists in the broadest sense and SDFers in particular. Yet the theory of the process of politicisation and the creation of class-conscious socialists was not something to which the SDF and its British contemporaries gave much thought.[56] Nevertheless, there was an implicit SDF model of politicisation. It focused on the crucial effect of political propaganda on an already discontented individual when combined with the experience of collective action in a strike or a political campaign. This model was highly gendered and deeply affected the party's ability to 'make' socialist women.

The political purpose of the party was to educate the working class in socialism through propaganda and practice. Education was therefore at the heart of the SDF as an organisation, not as an end in itself but as the basis of the party's political strategy. William Morris, while still in the SDF, described the means to achieving socialism as 'First, educating people into desiring it, next organizing them into claiming it effectually'.[57] Although the party as a whole recognised the need for education and organisation, it did not see them clearly as the separate stages which Morris had implied. For the SDF, education towards becoming a socialist was as likely to occur after joining the party; thus education and organisation were entwined, for the process of organising could also educate.[58]

Socialist education, as understood by the SDF, encompassed both initial politicisation and the creation of class-conscious socialists.[59] It was therefore more than conversion and implied a progression towards class-consciousness. The essential tool for 'making' socialists was propaganda – both written and spoken. The assumption was that if the working class were told the truth about the society in which they lived, they would soon see the virtue of socialism and the need to organise as socialists. This was thought to be an unproblematic process: one member of South Salford SDF remembered that 'we had convinced ourselves that two years propaganda with meetings three times every week, would convert everybody, that poverty and insecurity would be

and winning them to the Cause was a contemporary one used particularly by William Morris. See, for example, *Commonweal*, July 1885 quoted in E. P. Thompson, *William Morris*, p. 382. For a development of the argument in this section, see K. Hunt, 'Making Socialist Woman: Politicisation, Gender and the SDF, 1884–1911', paper given at Ninth Berkshire Conference on the History of Women, Vassar College, 1993.

[56] As for example Lenin attempted to do in 1902 with *What Is To Be Done?*, Oxford University Press, 1963, pp. 82–118.

[57] Quoted in E. P. Thompson, *William Morris*, p. 325.

[58] See, for example, J. Hunter Watts' memories in *How I Became A Socialist*, p. 30.

[59] See *Social Democrat*, August 1897, pp. 229–30.

abolished'.[60] With no analysis or strategy to combat working-class resistance to socialist ideas, the SDF found it hard to understand the kind of reaction to its propaganda which Robert Roberts described amongst the working people of Salford:

Marxist 'ranters' . . . paid fleeting visits to our street and insisted that we, the proletariat, stood locked in a titanic struggle with some wicked master class. We were battling, they told us . . . to cast off our chains and win a whole world. Most people passed by; a few stood to listen, but not for long: the problems of the 'proletariat', they felt, had little to do with them.[61]

In order to explain the limited results of its propaganda, the SDF assumed that receptivity to socialist education was linked to a certain level of general education. When, in 1901, Hyndman resigned for a few years from the SDF Executive his disillusionment focused on the working-class's lack of education, which he blamed for the relative failure of SDF propaganda.[62] Yet this concern did not prompt a thoroughgoing review of the SDF's political strategy and the effectiveness of their propaganda methods.[63] Instead, attention was focused on what were seen as the inadequacies of those who failed to be 'made' into socialists. This was remarkably similar to the party's attitude to women and their politicisation. Women were thought to lack a general education, which apparently explained the absence of mass conversions, and even the failure to neutralise the residual conservatism of their sex.

Education and politicisation were thus closely bound together for the SDF. In order for its propaganda to have the desired effect not only did the party need a platform,[64] but it also needed individuals to stop and listen to a speaker, or to pick up and read *Justice* or a pamphlet. Experience showed that those who had begun to be educated, particularly those who were educating themselves, were most open to socialist ideas.[65] Thus in the tradition of working-class radicals, many

---

[60] J. Toole, *Fighting Through Life*, Rich and Cowan, 1935, p. 87. See also H. Snell, *Men, Movements and Myself*, J. M. Dent & Sons, 1936, p. 59; H. W. Lee and E. Archbold, *Social Democracy in Britain*, p. 98.

[61] R. Roberts, *The Classic Slum*, Pelican, 1973, p. 28.

[62] *Justice*, 10 August 1901. See also H. M. Hyndman, *Further Reminiscences*, p. 73.

[63] As H. W. Lee, longtime secretary of the SDF, remembered 'what was equally needed, if not equally recognised, was organised effort to gather into our ranks and keep with us the converts made and people influenced by Socialist propaganda' (H. W. Lee and E. Archbold, *Social Democracy in Britain*, p. 29).

[64] Hence the SDF's involvement in campaigns for free speech, specifically the right to hold street meetings, such as that at Dodd Street, Limehouse in 1885 and at World's End, Chelsea in 1892.

[65] For one account of the process of becoming a socialist, see J. Toole, *Fighting Through Life*, pp. 48–83.

SDFers were autodidacts.[66] Once in the party, the educative process continued with branches offering a variety of general educational subjects which ranged from botany to economics.[67]

This conception of the socialist as an autodidact was in effect a gender-specific model, for few working-class women had the opportunities for self-education. The pressure of domestic responsibilities did not create ideal conditions for study, as Sarah Lay explained in *Justice*: 'I should like to know how a woman is to learn anything at all about Socialism under like conditions? Read! Why we scarcely dare look at a book. By the time I have scrambled through *Justice* and glanced at the births and marriages in our local paper I have spent all the time I can possibly spare for reading.'[68] The same conditions severely limited many women's access to public meetings and thus to hearing socialist propagandists.

Propaganda and education were only part of the SDF's model of politicisation. It also relied on the experience of collective action.[69] The SDF was particularly interested in campaigns and industrial activity as vehicles for socialist propaganda. While the party has often been criticised for this, it recognised the part that collective action played in the making of socialists. Yet it was this collective experience which women so often lacked.

The SDF's understanding of the process of politicisation assumed a very public definition of politics; it used methods which depended upon access to public meetings, to demonstrations, and to campaigns. Although this strategy could, and did, reach some women, it was not designed to meet their special needs, or to overcome the practical barriers that prevented most women's participation in the public world of politics. The mechanisms adopted by the party might reach some women who could stop and listen, join campaigns, become propagandists or organisers. Yet this seems to have been an incidental benefit in a process principally conceived of as reaching potential male socialists. Despite the SDF's stated view that they needed women if socialism were

---

[66] The achievements of SDF autodidacts were various: Harry Quelch taught himself French so that he could read *Capital*; Fred Knee taught himself Greek, Latin, Music and shorthand while Joseph Toole also taught himself shorthand and read widely in the Free Library on economics and philosophy.

[67] For example, see *Justice*, 21 March 1896; T. Mann, *Tom Mann's Memoirs*, MacGibbon and Kee, 1967, p. 50; H. McShane and J. Smith, *Harry McShane: No Mean Fighter*, p. 54.

[68] *Justice*, 23 September 1893.

[69] See, for example, H. M. Hyndman, *Further Reminiscences*, p. 59. For debate on the balance between education and collective action in the SDF's model of politicisation, see T. Rothstein, 'Our Policy', *Social Democrat*, June 1900 and H. Quelch's reply in *Social Democrat*, July 1900.

to ever succeed, the party's conception of the woman question led it to see general politicisation only in terms of class, rather than as a problem permeated by class and gender difference.

How, then, were women socialists to be 'made'? By conceptualising women principally as a problem and then failing to recruit them to any significant degree through the traditional model, the SDF was left in a state of bewilderment. The combination of the party's understanding of the woman question with its recognition of the need for female support for socialism created the space within the party for the continuing theme of Women and Socialism. Yet the failure to forge a clear party position from the various views expressed meant that men's bewilderment was matched by women's frustration.

Women's politicisation was dealt with in a number of ways by the SDF. In contrast the methods of rational persuasion to be applied to men, it was thought necessary to discuss how socialism could be 'sweetened' for women's consumption.[70] It was suggested that women's support could be won by playing to their supposed trivial, parochial, individualistic natures. So one writer, in a bid to win women over, painted a picture of the future socialist society as a shoppers' paradise. He felt that the point was to 'captivate and charm the women with the beauties and possibilities of socialism'.[71] This approach to women's politicisation was condemned by Marion Coates, who said, 'We women are not going to be bought like goodies ... We are coming as comrades, friends, warriors to a state worthy of us, not to dolldom'.[72] This highlights two unreconciled visions of women within SDF discourse. On the one hand, the socialist's wife was to be won from apathy and reaction to a supportive role for her socialist husband and brothers. On the other, the SDF's desire for women activists was more likely to be met from the few women open to the traditional model of politicisation.

Another extraordinarily patronising approach was, in a sense, to deceive women as to the nature of socialism by attracting them to its social side with the 'boring' politics removed. Thus, for example: 'The only opportunity that a Socialist has of getting women to attend a Socialist gathering is to paint a glowing picture of a tea fight, of a concert where certain celebrity artists will appear, of a soirée and dance where there will be a possibility of witnessing new fashions'.[73] Such a view reflected little understanding of the reality of a working-class woman's life and, in

---

[70] See the correspondence under the heading 'How to Induce Women to Become Socialists' in *Justice*, 16 June, 30 June, 7 July, 28 July 1894.
[71] *Justice*, 16 June 1894.
[72] *Justice*, 30 June 1894.
[73] *Justice*, 18 August 1894.

particular, her domestic burden. It also never made clear how any woman so recruited was to make the transition to the reality of socialist politics – the branch meetings, outdoor propaganda and campaigning.

Women themselves made much more practical suggestions in their consideration of how women might become socialists. They sought practical changes which would address women's experiences and the barriers which prevented their participation; examples in the 1890s included a page of *Justice* given over to women; a good socialist story that would make *Justice* more accessible to women; and a penny pamphlet designed specifically for women.[74] It was suggested that propaganda would be more effective if it were targeted on the everyday concerns of working-class women. Yet despite these and other suggestions, no such practical steps were taken by the party leadership at the time. It was not until after the inception of the Women's Socialist Circles in 1904 that any consistent attempt was made to propagandise among women; and the impetus for that came largely from the efforts of SDF women themselves.

Women also made specific requests of SDF men which they thought would greatly increase women's participation in the party. Socialist men, it was argued, should 'begin in their own homes', relieve women of some of 'their household cares' and give them 'a little leisure'. This would allow socialist men to talk about socialism to their wives 'quietly and sympathetically'. Sarah Lay suggested to her male comrades that 'instead of reading their pamphlets ... all to themselves read a little to the "missus" of an evening'.[75] Although these suggestions arose from a recognition of woman's condition, specifically her domestic responsibilities, not all the recommendations were based on the home. Sarah Lay also thought that if male SDFers helped by minding their own children sometimes then that would enable their wives to attend lectures or branch meetings. There was certainly a feeling that men should take some responsibility, for example: 'If our comrades really wish to interest the women, and enlist their services, they must first teach them that they can trust them. So far women have been treated to a good share of ridicule, and very little respect'.[76] M. A. Jackson also urged men 'to awake and help the women to understand Socialism'.[77] In this approach to women's politicisation the problem was seen as one which all socialists, male and female, should tackle together, and which would involve changes in behaviour and attitudes by male SDFers.

---

[74] *Justice*, 21 October 1893.
[75] *Justice*, 23 September 1893; also 15 May 1886.
[76] *Justice*, 7 October 1893.
[77] *Justice*, 9 September 1905.

Yet the parent party's attitudes were not, in the end, the focus for change. The SDF's understanding of the woman question meant that anything which related to women – including their own practice within the party – was a matter of individual conscience. It was therefore, by definition, impossible to take a party position to reform these practices. Hence, it was women's attitudes which would have to be changed to bring them into the party and socialism.

Thus education was central to the process of politicisation for women, just as it was for socialists generally. Yet because women were recognised as being disadvantaged educationally, both in a general sense and in terms of any openness to socialist ideas, their education was conceived of differently from that of men. Women were seen as starting back beyond the baseline where men entered the process of politicisation. Eventually it was recognised that women needed their own 'remedial' education before they reached the stage at which men automatically entered, that is party membership. Thus, for example, the Women's Circles were seen as a 'preparatory school' for women.[78] In the eyes of the parent party their role was clear: 'we are only desirous of interesting and educating women and are endeavouring to lead them into the organisation'.[79] Of course, this solution reinforced the idea that women were the problem, rather than socialism and its model of politicisation.

The attitudes expressed by SDFers on women reflected deep-seated assumptions about their potential and their role in society. These became particularly apparent when the SDF considered why women were not involved in the party in great numbers. Unresolved, these debates bubbled up at different points in the SDF's history. Despite a stated commitment to women's participation in socialism, the party gave an ambivalent impression to potential women socialists and provoked some resentment from its own female members. Despite practical suggestions from its own membership the party made little attempt, at an organisational level, to encourage women's participation. Women, whether specifically as the socialist's wife or as a sex as a whole, remained a problem which bewildered most male SDF members. They could not conceive of the need to refine their own model of politicisation to encompass women's particular experiences and needs. The nature of women's role within the party and their attempts to organise reflect many of these assumptions about women and their potential. The lack of any significant questioning of the sexual division of labour and the party's consuming priority of propaganda and education are themes which bridge these areas.

[78] *Justice*, 28 October 1907.
[79] *Justice*, 25 June 1904.

8   Women SDFers and their role in the party

This chapter focuses on the influence of the SDF's assumptions about women and their potential on women's roles within the party. It also considers whether the female membership was more diverse than the stereotype of the problematic socialist's wife found in the SDF press. Women's actual role in the party was of importance whether a woman was looking for some commitment from the membership to prefigurative practice, or whether her concern was to find a means of participation which was compatible with domestic responsibilities. The roles women were expected to play within the party may well have been a factor in their assessment of the SDF.

Although the SDF claimed to be much larger, its membership seems to have been no more than 4,500 at any one time.[1] The number of women in it could probably only be measured in hundreds. But as there are no accurate official figures for SDF membership, the numbers have to be estimated from branch dues which give no clue to the sex of the party member. There is therefore no accurate way to determine the number of SDF women members. Occasionally there are branch reports which contain figures for female membership, such as that in December 1895 when Nelson SDF claimed to have nearly forty women comrades.[2] But these figures were never consistently reported and women's membership continued throughout to be sufficiently novel to be worthy of comment. This alone suggests that they constituted only a fraction of

---

[1]   On occasions the SDF claimed an inflated financial membership, for example, 17,000 in 1909 (*Report to the Socialist International Conference*, 1910, p. 5). But P. A. Watmough ('The Membership of the Social Democratic Federation') has challenged the SDF's claims and the figures calculated by historians such as P. Thompson, H. Pelling, C. Tsuzuki and W. Kendall. He recalculated party membership for the period 1885–1902 by using the acknowledgements of branch dues printed in *Justice*. This suggested a membership peaking in 1897 at over 3,000 with an average over the 1890s of nearly 2,000. But he warns that his figures are likely to be conservative. Therefore the SDF's claim at their 1894 Conference of a membership of 4,500, which was based on the party's return sheets, seems fairly accurate (*SDF Conference Report*, 1894, p. 16).

[2]   *Justice*, 14 December 1895.

the total. The dearth of women members and their random geographical distribution meant that even as late as 1909 a branch could report its first woman recruit.[3]

There was always the suspicion that women were working for socialism but that their activities were almost invisible amongst those of the socialist brotherhood. Thus Sandy Macfarlane commented in 1894: 'I believe there are far more women engaged in active work on behalf of Socialism than we are aware of. I think we ought to hear something about these women and the work they are doing.'[4] Yet when Enid Stacy reported on women in the following week's *Justice* she noted, as a preface to her description of two very active socialist women's groups, that 'In many towns unfortunately women are very quiescent, attend meetings in small numbers, and are extremely apathetic'.[5] This remained the dominant image of women in socialist groups. It seemed only to be confirmed by the infrequency of women's names in *Justice* reports and the emphasis given to what, in consequence, appeared to be the occasional participation of women in local branch work. Was this an accurate impression of the extent and nature of women's participation in the SDF or were women, in fact, invisibly participating in many different ways, as Sandy Macfarlane suspected?

Like any attempt to calculate the numbers of SDF women, it is difficult to build up a systematic profile of the typical SDF woman. The SDF's ignorance of the extent and nature of women's work for socialism is compounded by the lack of systematic information on the party's rank and file. There only remains a partial record of this semi-visible group. What follows, therefore, has to be impressionistic.

Historians of women in other parties in the Second International have noted the extent to which their women members were related to male party members; daughters and sisters, but particularly the wives of party men.[6] In the SDF this was much more likely to be true of rank and file members; for example, Sarah Lay, who complained how difficult it was for her to attend meetings, was married to the secretary of her branch. Miss Emmeline Powell was the lecture secretary of Brixton SDF, whilst J. E. Powell was its financial secretary – although it is not clear if he was her father or brother.[7] The family could also sustain more well-known SDF women. One example is the Hicks family where Amie, her

---

3   *Justice*, 23 January 1909.
4   *Justice*, 11 August 1894.
5   *Justice*, 18 August 1894.
6   C. Sowerwine, *Sisters or Citizens?: Women and Socialism in France since 1876*, Cambridge University Press, Cambridge, 1982, p. 198; R. J. Evans, 'Politics and the Family', pp. 264–5.
7   *Justice*, 10 October 1896.

husband William and their daughter Margaretta all joined the SDF in the spring of 1883.[8] Margaretta, in particular, was involved in the SDF throughout its lifetime and into the BSP, where she became the main force in its Women's Council and started the women's paper, *The Link*. But for other women SDFers, family relations were less important. Although, for instance, Mary Gray's husband was probably in the SDF, as he agreed to spend his holiday in 1891 helping to organise Reading SDF,[9] there is no record of his activity. Dora Montefiore had no familial connection with socialism.

The most active of SDF women did not fit the party's stereotype of socialists' wives, who sustained their male relatives. Nor were many of the wives of leading male SDFers, activists themselves. For the active women SDFers some measure of independence was clearly important. Dora Montefiore and Charlotte Despard both had independent means. Although Dora Montefiore had two children to support, other women were childless, such as Margaretta Hicks, who was single, and Rose Jarvis, who married SDFer Charles Scott after the death of her first SDFer husband Tom Jarvis. Mary Gray seems to have had one child who was an 'imbecile' and was sent to an asylum.[10] For these women, domestic responsibilities were probably considerably less than for many others. But there is no one clear model of the activist SDF woman: for they were married, single or widowed; some had children but generally not very many; some were of a middle-class background, while others were working class; and some were in their twenties whilst Dora Montefiore and Charlotte Despard were of an older generation. We simply do not know enough about these women, let alone their less visible sisters, to discern any detailed picture of an archetypal SDF woman. None the less, it is easier to see how Dora Montefiore's circumstances gave her more choices in the form that her party membership took than, say, Sarah Lay, let alone the women whose names we do not even know.

In searching for women within the SDF, the most obvious place to start is where they would be most visible: that is, in elected positions. Apart from the initial period of 1884–5, the SDF Executive Committee never contained more than two women and for a significant part of its lifetime, none at all.[11] There were two slates for the Executive, which was elected at the Party Conference. One was for London while the

8   For the Hicks family, see the entry for Amie Hicks in J. Bellamy and J. Saville (eds.), *Dictionary of Labour Biography*, vol. 4, pp. 89–92.
9   *Social Democrat*, November 1899, p. 325.
10   Ibid, p. 324.
11   See appendix 1.

other was for the Provinces, that is the rest of Britain. Until 1905 there were twelve seats in each division. This number was then reduced by half. It was the London group which effectively formed the Executive during the year, as logistics prevented the other half of the Committee attending the Executive's fortnightly meetings.[12] It seems to have been harder for women to build up a national profile from a provincial base and be elected to the Provinces' division of the Executive. Indeed the only woman who ever stood on that slate, Rose Jarvis, was elected in 1905 and 1906. She was already well-known in the national party. Not only a member of one of the party's largest branches, Northampton, Rose Jarvis had earlier been active in the Croydon branch and was a well-known speaker. In 1895 she had even stood, unsuccessfully, for the Executive on the London slate. All the other women who stood were from the London division; the successful candidates were Edith Lanchester (twice), Mary Gray (seven times), Clara Hendin (twice) and Dora Montefiore (four times).[13] Women as a group were therefore marginal to the SDF's leadership. Although a few women had access to the deliberations of this powerful body, their isolation made it hard for them to act as anything other than individuals. Indeed it was as exceptional women that they had come to be elected in the first place.

Most of the leading SDF women were public speakers; that is how they became well-known throughout the party. Being a socialist propagandist was a demanding life. It meant often being away from home, as well as arduous travelling and speaking in all conditions. Enid Stacy told *Justice* in 1894 that she lectured about 229 times a year, averaging about twenty-five a month. Between April and October five sixths of these lectures were in the open air.[14] Such work took its toll on several of the leading women socialist speakers who died young; for example, Caroline Martyn died in 1896 and Enid Stacy died in 1903 aged thirty-five.

Women who chose to be socialist propagandists made a double break with society, first by becoming a socialist and secondly by stepping outside their expected gender role.[15] In the 1880s and 1890s it was particularly unusual for women to speak on public platforms and at street meetings and even with the upsurge in the suffrage campaign after 1900, when more women took part in public speaking, such behaviour was still at some cost to the woman concerned. Male SDFers seem to

---

[12] *SDF Conference Report*, 1901, p. 7; *Justice*, 19 January 1884.
[13] The ILP's record was certainly no better than the SDF's. They elected few women of whom most were already well-known activists. See appendix 1.
[14] *Justice*, 13 October 1894.
[15] See similar comments in relation to the SPD (R. J. Evans, 'Politics and the Family', p. 275).

have been in a dilemma over socialist women propagandists. They recognised women's high publicity value in socialist propaganda but were unwilling to address the reasons for the failure to recruit their own women members into this role in any great numbers.

The ambiguous feelings that socialist women activists brought out in their male comrades were reflected in this 1893 report from Salford:

Do we want the women? Cease your silly tattle. Don't you know we have got the women – in Lancashire. In some of the branches the men are at home mending the stockings and nursing the baby – the best place for them – whilst the women are out in the squares and at the street corners. The lady members are taking the chair so often now that our speakers are finding some difficulty in beginning their addresses. 'Mrs Chairman' won't do; 'Comradess' won't do; and one of the dear, darling creatures was offended the other Sunday because the speaker addressed her as 'Madam'![16]

Here was a warning to other men of the danger of reversed sexual roles which could be associated with women taking a more assertive role, although not so assertive as to be the speakers themselves. The quibble about nomenclature suggested that there was no name, and therefore no acknowledged tradition, for this form of women's activism. The writer also engaged with the dominant stereotype of woman by suggesting that women have no sense of humour. Altogether a piece such as this reflects the dilemma of many SDFers, and other socialists. They wanted women to be more involved as activists in the Cause but were unwilling to address the conditions of women's lives which formed a real barrier to their participation. Any suggestion of bending gender roles clearly made male activists very uncomfortable.

The dearth of women speakers continued to be commented on throughout the SDF's lifetime,[17] as did the effect that a woman speaker could have. As late as 1905 it was noted in a report in *Justice* that 'a lady socialist lecturer in town created some stir, and was quite a novelty to most folks'.[18] Sometimes that novelty could be put to good effect, as when Amie Hicks offered to speak at Dodd Street as part of the campaign for freedom of speech. Comrades were being arrested for public speaking and Jack Williams of the SDF got two months hard labour. Amie Hicks offered to speak 'feeling that a woman's arrest would make the matter still more notable and freely discussed'. The police were surprised at first but she was eventually arrested and bound over, gaining the desired publicity.[19] Certainly then, there were few women

16   *Justice*, 23 September 1893.
17   *Justice*, 9 September 1905; 9 February 1907.
18   *Justice*, 26 August 1905.
19   *Woman Worker*, 30 June 1909.

speakers to act as role models for women SDFers. 'Hopeful' suggested that one way to get more women involved was to get more women to address meetings.[20] Yet how were women to be encouraged to take on this role?

One way that the party could have encouraged its women members was to provide them with some experience in a more protected environment, like the branches and party conferences. Yet when the numbers of delegates to the Annual Conference are analysed it is clear that women never constituted as much as 10 per cent of the delegates. The same was true of the ILP Conference.[21] At the SDF Conference it was a rarity for a woman to speak and many women delegates stayed silent. There is no evidence that women were positively encouraged to participate, and even in debates that were specifically on women's issues or organisation it was mainly men who spoke.[22] Although ILP Conferences were much larger than those of the SDF – which could have proved intimidating – it did mean that women were present in larger numbers, albeit still below 10 per cent. They seem to have been less reluctant to speak, but then many of them were already experienced propagandists.[23]

It may be that rather than putting the time into encouraging new women to come forward, SDF men took the easier option and put increasing demands on existing women propagandists.[24] Certainly Margaretta Hicks complained of this:

The woman speakers are so few yet, and the work to be done in our organisation is so large, that it is not fair to say publicly they are indifferent because they do not take part in every good work that is being done ... I remember being grumbled at because I did not help in the Sunday Schools more, and now the few of us, because we do not help the Circles more. It is not unwillingness, but further work cannot often be undertaken except at the sacrifice of present duties.[25]

What action there was to encourage women to become public speakers was taken by women. Clara Hendin and Kathleen Kough set up a Socialist Dramatic Club in 1908 which offered to train speakers in

---

[20] *Justice*, 23 September 1893.
[21] See appendix 2 for a comparison between women delegates to SDF and ILP Conferences.
[22] *SDF Conference Report*, 1905, p. 20; 1907, pp. 25–6; 1909, pp. 18–19.
[23] Julia Dawson commented that women did not 'loom very large' in the proceedings of the socialist Annual Conferences (*Clarion*, 27 April 1906). In comparison, women delegates to SPD Conferences in the 1890s averaged only 3.3 per cent of delegates which rose to 5.4 per cent in 1900–08 (K. Honeycutt, 'Clara Zetkin', p. 291).
[24] See A. A. Watts' comments in *Justice*, 1 May 1897.
[25] *Justice*, 12 October 1907.

elocution, voice production, and to face audiences.[26] It is not clear how successful this venture was, but it was unlikely that it alone would have been sufficient to address the national problem. The Women's Socialist Circles were also partly intended to give women more confidence. But this aspect of their work was not undertaken systematically and with their uneven distribution throughout the country, they could not radically alter the ethos within the party as a whole.

Nevertheless, women speakers were much in demand within the party as their presence ensured good collections and sales of literature as well as larger audiences.[27] The visit of a woman speaker could provide the necessary stimulation for women to organise, as in the case of the visit of Mrs Saunderson to the Nelson branch in May 1894. After her lecture, twenty-six women formed a women's section of the branch of whom only six were formerly members.[28] Local, as opposed to national, speakers could develop their own following; for example, Isabel Tiplady of Blackburn SDF, whose 'name was almost a household word amongst working girls in Liverpool, Blackburn and other manufacturing towns in Lancashire'.[29] The débuts of local women speakers were still being noted in branch reports as late as 1909 as something out of the ordinary.[30] If the party had had women's platforms at their demonstrations, as the Lancashire district did at the May Day demonstrations of 1894 and 1895, this might have encouraged more women to speak and forced the party to look beyond its established women propagandists.

Although many SDF women were involved in Socialist Sunday Schools, there were also some SDF women who ran classes for the adult members of the branch. These would have given the women themselves greater confidence and provided a role model for other women members. Zelda Kahan gave a class in industrial history while Bertha Morley and Maud Ward offered economics.[31] Comment was made in the Tunbridge Wells SDF report on Miss Ward's class, 'the splendid grasp that our lady comrade has of the teachings of Marx is gaining the admiration of all those who are fortunate enough to be able to attend'.[32] Women teaching their male comrades in such areas of study must have done something to shake the stereotype in the party of the trivial, silly woman.

[26]   *Justice*, 16 May 1908; *Northampton Pioneer*, August 1908. It was only in the BSP period that a class was set up specifically for women speakers (*Justice*, 23 August 1913).
[27]   For example *Justice*, 18 May 1895.
[28]   *Justice*, 2 June 1894.
[29]   *Clarion*, 25 July 1896.
[30]   *Justice*, 9 January 1909.
[31]   *Justice*, 31 October 1908; 16 January 1909; 20 February 1904.
[32]   *Justice*, 20 February 1904.

It was more common to find women in the less visible work of administration, including being a secretary of a branch. This description of Isabella Ross, in her obituary, would fit many of the women activists: 'one of the most energetic of our few active members ... Her Socialism was not of the passive sentimental kind, for she was enthusiastic and deeply sincere, accepting the truths of Social Democracy from conviction. Whilst she took no prominent part in our propaganda meetings, yet for a lengthy period she acted as our secretary.'[33] Although a few women were appointed treasurer of their branch, such as Miss Riley of Ilkeston SDF, or even of a district committee, such as Isabel Leatham for the London Committee of the SDF,[34] the more common office for women members was that of lecture secretary or full secretary to the branch. Obviously this kind of work was compatible with women's domestic responsibilities and men's preconceptions of the part that women, and in particular their wives, could play. But when the branch was large and could pay a full-timer to be secretary, as in Burnley, the job was held by a man – in this case Dan Irving. There were few paid jobs in the SDF and these went to men.

Women were particularly encouraged to take on the less demanding aspects of routine branch work. It was suggested in *Justice* that some of the energy that women put into collecting for charity hospitals should be put into collecting for the SDF: 'Half-a-dozen good looking girls would treble and quadruple the usual collection made at any open air meeting.'[35] Clearly parts of the SDF were more than willing to mobilise the traditional stereotype of women to their own ends. But women members seem to have been more concerned that their sister SDFers take as active a role as possible in the party. Annie Oldacre wanted women to be more than financial members of the party and to take a share in the work of the organisation, for 'if we do not ... we are practically Anarchists'. In particular, she urged women members to attend the business meetings of their branch where possible, 'For even when this despotic capitalist system has ceased to exist another despotic system will arise in its place, if a part of the people neither know nor care what is being done'.[36]

There was a sense that women should take responsibility where possible, for that would give them the experience and confidence to play an even greater part in the organisation. Kathleen Kough urged women

---

[33] *Justice*, 30 September 1899. See also the obituary of Annie Young of Battersea SDF (*Justice*, 15 November 1902).
[34] *Justice*, 16 February 1907, 29 June 1907.
[35] *Justice*, 29 July 1893. It was also suggested that women should sell *Justice* dressed in a blue tunic and a red cap (*Justice*, 13 April 1895).
[36] *Justice*, 10 October 1896.

SDFers to take part in all propaganda meetings, not just those of the Women's Circles, and 'to take their share of the organisation, distribution and sale of literature and the general work attendant upon meetings'.[37] In that way they would be seen straightforwardly as SDFers and not just as 'good looking girls' to boost party collections and sales. Nor did branch work have to be an end in itself. Some women did make the transition from this less visible work to becoming public speakers. For example, Enid Stacy recalled in her account of how she became a socialist that she was a background worker for the Bristol Socialist Society from 1890 and only spoke in public in 1892. She resisted such public work for two years because it would jeopardise her livelihood as a teacher.[38] This constraint must have applied to many other working women.

The SDF, like the orthodox political parties, used women for much of the day-to-day jobs of canvassing and election work.[39] Indeed, A. A. Watts argued for a clear sexual division of labour in political work for he felt that women should distribute election addresses and canvass so that men could devote themselves more efficiently to organising and public speaking. But, reflecting the SDF's ambiguous attitude to women activists, he also suggested that there should be more SDF women on public bodies. He complained that 'Although the public bodies open to women are more limited than those open to men, our choice of suitable women as candidates is more limited still.'[40] Certainly the SDF put up very few women candidates for the Boards of Guardians, School Boards and later the municipal councils. This cannot be explained merely by the obvious limits of the local government franchise or by the electorate's supposed bias against women candidates[41] for the SDF did have some long-serving women Guardians, for example Mary Gray, Lena Wilson and Rose Jarvis.[42] In contrast, the ILP had a larger number of women representatives on public bodies. But they were still only a fraction of the male ILP representation and their greater numbers only reflected the fact that the ILP was a larger organisation than the SDF.[43]

---

37   *Justice*, 20 June 1908.

38   *Justice*, 13 October 1894.

39   *Justice*, 1 August 1908.

40   *Justice*, 1 May 1897.

41   It seems that women candidates for the London School Board were popular with the voters and often topped the polls (A. Turnbull, ' "So Extremely like Parliament": The Work of the Women Members of the London School Board, 1870–1904', in London Feminist History Group, *The Sexual Dynamics of History*, Pluto, 1983, p. 123).

42   Mary Gray was a Battersea Guardian from 1894 until she was defeated in 1901, when she stood successfully for the Wandsworth Guardians. Lena Wilson was on the Poplar Board (1895–1907) and Rose Jarvis was elected to the Croydon Board in 1904 and after her move to Northampton was elected as a Guardian there.

43   Taking the ten-year period 1896–1906 the ILP claimed the following amount of female representatives on School Boards and Boards of Guardians. From their figures

In the 1890s women as a whole constituted about 0.004 per cent of the national School Board membership and, after the reforms of the 1894 Local Government Act which abolished all property qualifications for Guardians, about 0.03 per cent of the Boards of Guardians.[44] It is not perhaps surprising that many more SDF women stood for the Guardians than for School Boards as this fitted the national trend and a general feeling that this was an office particularly appropriate to women.[45] But the demands of local government work in terms of time and the isolation of being a minority as a socialist and a woman[46] meant that women SDFers might need particular encouragement and support to put themselves forward for election. That encouragement does not seem to have been forthcoming on an organisational level and the selection of candidates was left to the vagaries of each branch. Unless women were prominent in their branches, were speakers and had the time to do the necessary work if elected, they were unlikely to be chosen as the SDF candidate when their branch felt able to contest a ward. The assumption appears to have been that by encouraging no-one, the party was treating its membership equally. Yet there was little in the SDF's ambivalent attitude to women to encourage female members to promote their own candidature.

As it was, domestic responsibilities which prevented many women from taking an active role in SDF politics, it was deemed appropriate that the work they should be most encouraged to do was bazaar work. For example, after a fulsome report of the work of women members of

the percentage of women holding ILP seats can be calculated (*ILP Conference Report*, 1897–1907):

Year	School Board		Guardians	
	no.	%	no.	%
1896	3	6	6	8
1897	6	8	10	15
1898	4	6	10	14
1899	3	5	9	18
1900	5	8	11	19
1901	3	5	10	18
1902	2	4	6	11
1903			5	8
1904			8	7
1905			11	10
1906			32*	15*

* includes parish councils

[44] D. Rubinstein, *Before the Suffragettes*, pp. 166–7.
[45] For claims for women's particular suitability to being a Guardian, see *Clarion*, 15 December 1894; D. Rubinstein, *Before the Suffragettes*, pp. 166–7. Contrast this with P. Hollis, *Ladies Elect: Women in English Local Government, 1865–1914*, Clarendon Press, Oxford, 1987, pp. 205–31.
[46] See comments of Mrs Evans, Longton Board of Guardians (*Justice*, 6 January 1900).

Plymouth SDF, when several women had taken the chair at outdoor meetings, organised collections and sales of literature, the reporter on *Justice* added: 'Now, then, my Plymouth women comrades, hurry up; there is work to be done in connection with the National Bazaar.'[47] Bazaar work consisted of sewing items for sale to raise funds for the party and to purchase special items for the branch, such as a new banner for Nelson SDF, a tea service for Rochdale SDF and a gas oven for Accrington.[48] Even the more prominent SDF women were involved in these kinds of activities; for example Clara Hendin was a Bazaar Committee member when she was also on the SDF Executive.[49] There was considerable dispute over whether the Women's Socialist Circles should engage in this traditional aspect of SDF women's work. There was certainly a strong assumption on behalf of many male members of the party that woman's primary service to the SDF would be in this domestic area. This took the form of suggesting when the party was short of funds, which it invariably was, that the women fund-raise, for example, by making red ties to sell.[50]

The most common reason for including a woman in a branch report was a social one, for example, for singing at a branch entertainment or for providing the tea.[51] In Emily Warn's obituary these domestic and social aspects of her service to the party were remembered and appreciated. She was the first woman member of Plymouth SDF and one of its founders and when she died, aged 37, she was commemorated thus: 'Our beloved comrade was always to the fore with help and advice regarding socials, sales of work, and branch work in general. She frequently also entertained at her hospitable home our lecturers and other visiting comrades.'[52] Again, prominent women in the party were involved in this work, for example Kathleen Kough was Honorary Secretary of the Women's Tea Committee.[53] What is hard to determine is the extent to which this work was thrust on women or whether they chose to do it willingly.[54] Clearly some women members refused to have anything to do with this aspect of 'women's work'. Dora Montefiore, for example, said, 'I never on principle associate myself with bazaars; I very much deprecate the loss of time, money and energy which they entail.'[55]

[47] *Justice*, 3 July 1909.
[48] *Justice*, 9 May 1896, 16 February 1895, 9 July 1910.
[49] *Justice*, 20 September 1902.
[50] *Justice*, 10 August 1895, 29 September 1906.
[51] *Justice*, 28 April 1900; 6 April 1895; 24 January 1903.
[52] *Justice*, 9 January 1909.
[53] *Justice*, 22 December 1906.
[54] See also Eleanor Marx's experience in the Socialist League (Y. Kapp, *Eleanor Marx*, vol. 2, pp. 72–3).
[55] *Justice*, 11 March 1905.

Her vehemence can best be understood when set beside the kind of comment that male SDFers were wont to make. The Tattler wrote: 'Perhaps I am old fashioned and prejudiced, but a woman always seems in her element at the head of a tea-table, and, for my part, a cup of tea never seems to be really a good cup of tea unless it is received at the fair hands of one of the gentler sex.'[56] Not that this was a complaint specific to the SDF, as Julia Dawson pointed out. She emphasised that there was a price for socialism if it retained such a rigorous sexual division of labour in its political activities:

But still the most important work is left to men. In the ILP this is especially the case. At tea parties and such like women are ever so busy cutting up bread-and-butter and cake, and presiding over tea-urns, while the men are 'organising', discussing wider and better means of propaganda, etc. The bread-and-butter and cake are eaten and forgotten. Propaganda leaves a lasting impression on the people, raising them up out of the depths, and shedding light in dark places.[57]

So, to sum up, what was women's role in the SDF? The Tattler commented: 'we don't look upon women as mere auxiliaries to help the men to victory, but as equals, comrades with us in the fight'.[58] Yet in practice the term 'auxiliary' seems particularly apposite to describe the actual role of rank-and-file women members of the SDF.[59] This does not, of course, mean that women were entirely quiescent within the party. They *were* participating and working hard for socialism, but this took forms which were far more to do with the traditional sexual division of labour than any suggestion of prefigurative practice. This was substantiated by Edith Watson, less than a year after the SDF had become the BSP, when she described women's role in the party: 'women are not voted into many responsible positions unless they force themselves to the front. But they are allowed to hand round and sell cakes and coffee at dances and to wash up afterwards.'[60] Although this fulfilled the social function of keeping women in touch with the branch, it could not develop them as party members. There was therefore an increasing emphasis amongst SDF women on the need for education and organisation to encourage women to become fully active party members.

While SDFers as a whole continued to accept the sexual division of

[56] *Justice*, 11 April 1903.
[57] *Clarion*, 14 October 1904; also 24 July 1897.
[58] *Justice*, 26 March 1904.
[59] For use of the term 'auxiliary' in relation to other socialist organisations, see C. Sowerwine, *Sisters or Citizens?*, p. 3; M. J. Buhle, 'Women and the Socialist Party, 1901–14', in E. H. Altbach (ed.), *From Feminism to Liberation*, Schenkman, Cambridge, Mass., 1971, p. 68.
[60] *Justice*, 19 October 1912.

labour, only exceptional women who had particular determination and particularly favourable circumstances could exercise real choice about the role they undertook within the party. While women continued to be regarded primarily as auxiliaries, their expected, and indeed chosen, role continued to be of a domestic and servicing nature rather than the more public one of propagandist and public speaker. The SDF's understanding of the woman question meant that the ambivalence in their theory provided no spur to male socialists to take practical steps to involve women in the party. There was certainly little interest in challenging the traditional model of the activist which was built upon men's experience. With the woman question as a matter of private conscience, only a recognition of the pragmatic need to increase female participation at all levels of the party could have overridden this ambivalence. As it was, there was no systematic attempt to provide the practical encouragement which many women needed to break with convention and take a more public role in the party.

Dora Montefiore suggested that 'Many intelligent women are kept out of the Socialist movement because of its attitude towards women workers'.[61] But it is difficult to verify this claim because of the very fact that such women were unlikely to join the SDF. Women who had already done so increasingly sought greater control over their activities through women's self-organisation within the party. This is the subject of the next chapter.

[61] *Justice*, 13 September 1902. She did not limit her criticism to the SDF but included socialists in general.

This chapter is concerned with the changing attitudes of SDFers to women's self-organisation. To what degree did the SDF's understanding of the woman question allow for women to organise as a group? This issue brought to the fore the relationship between class and sex as a matter of practice, rather than just one of theory. The discussion about the various functions that women's organisation could perform for the parent party reflected deeply held assumptions about women and their potential. But this was not an issue which split the SDF neatly along gender lines. It brought to the surface all the ambivalence of the party's understanding of the woman question.

The debate was not conducted in the abstract. The various forms that women's organisation took, their stated purpose and relative success, all affected future choices that women made about organisation. They also influenced the parameters later set for women's organisation by the party as a whole. These factors must be borne in mind when weighing the degree of autonomy desired and achieved by the different stages of SDF women's organisation against their access to power and resources within the party as a whole. All women's organisations within the Second International were faced with these same choices: autonomy, but at the price of marginality; access to the resources and power structure of the party, but at the price of absorption. Although these issues were more clear-cut for German and American socialist women, they were also present for SDF women.

Women's right to self-organisation: the debate

The question of women's right to self-organisation was raised when some SDFers decided to form a national women's organisation for the party. Prior to 1904, women had organised in an *ad hoc* manner in some branches, but there had been no attempt to organise systematically across the country. There had therefore been little discussion of the implications of such organisation for the SDF and the woman question.

The central issue which women's organisation raised was whether the identification of a group by sex was compatible with class analysis. In particular, there was a real fear of separatism, with all its associations with bourgeois feminism. In response, socialist women used the Second International's construction of the woman question to assuage their comrades' anxieties whilst ensuring recognition of sex oppression. Nevertheless, the accusation of separatism always haunted the SDF discussions.

The week after Dora Montefiore announced the formation of a 'women's branch of the SDF', Harold Elliot wrote to *Justice* questioning the need for this. He argued, 'As Socialists I take it that we recognise the absolute equality of the sexes in matters religious, social and political. In other words, we do not recognise sex at all in these matters. Then why need we make a sex division in our organisation?'[1] Although Elliot raised this issue speculatively, admitting that there might be arguments for separate organisation, at least on a temporary basis, others were less hesitant. The Tattler did not see any need for a special women's organisation because, he argued, socialists believed in sexual equality and treated women as equal comrades.

The existence of the women's organisation could be used by those outside the party to criticise the SDF. *Justice* reprinted a piece from the *Manchester Weekly Chronicle* which argued that the SDF was playing into the hands of anti-socialists. In forming a women's branch, the party was 'tacitly agreeing with those of our fellow countrymen who say that women cannot be admitted to an absolute equality with men, that their work, their aims and their needs are different, and that they should in such matters as political warfare not mix up in affairs which are more or less purely masculine'.[2] Although women were not equal in number, in power or in their roles within the party, the SDF were not keen that the advent of a women's organisation be used to expose this. It seemed to be quite possible for the Tattler, for example, to believe that his own party was committed to equality and that it practised it, while at the same time stereotyping women within his column as essentially different. His notion of equality, as 'equal in value' rather than absolute equality, allowed him and the others who shared it to believe that their party was a meritocracy. By making no gender distinctions, all were treated equally even if there was no equal outcome. In this thinking there was no need for a separate women's organisation, even in the short term. Indeed, not only was positive action not needed, it was undesirable.

[1]   *Justice*, 19 March 1904.
[2]   *Manchester Weekly Chronicle*, 21 May 1904 quoted in *Justice*, 18 June 1904. See also *Manchester Weekly Chronicle*, 4 June, 11 June, 25 June 1904.

Some women also were opposed to separate women's organisation. Annie Oldacre was particularly vehement in her objections. She felt that the move was 'retrogressive' and that SDF branches would not support it. If women wanted to work for socialism then the SDF was the organisation in which to do that. But if they only wanted to work for women's rights then they should form an entirely different organisation. She did not feel that women's branches would help recruit women to socialism and would only 'pander to this feeling of exclusive sex interests'.[3]

There was great sensitivity about the naming of any SDF women's organisation. In the first announcements, the title used was 'Women's branch of the SDF' followed by 'Women's Social Democratic Party'. The use of these names provoked A. A. Watts, who had been consulted during the formation of the women's organisation, into print. He said that the committee was opposed to the term 'branches' implying approval of the second title, Women's Social Democratic Party. The appeal of the latter was that it presumed a group entirely separate from the SDF, rather than single sex branches within the party which would have split the SDF along sex lines. But Watts was not opposed to women organising and reported positively on the socialist women's organisations in Europe, concluding that 'even if it were desired to commit this crime, you see we in England would be sinning in good company'.[4] Rose Jarvis, a member of the committee, also denied that the proposal was to set up women's branches. She stressed that the desired result was that women, particularly wives of comrades, would eventually join SDF branches.[5] Similarly, Margaretta Hicks emphasised, 'We do not want to separate the interests of men and women, it is not good for either, and as to having separate branches I do not think I should like it'.[6] To forestall further criticisms of separatism, most local SDF women's organisations were called Women's Socialist Circles, while the main committee was originally titled the Women's Committee and later the Women's Education Committee. But the issue remained a sensitive one.[7]

The Circles were designed to address the problem that women 'posed' to the SDF, by educating and preparing them for party membership. In that sense there was never any danger of separatism, for the Circles were conceived as integrally bound to the SDF without being

---

3   *Justice*, 16 April 1904.
4   Ibid.
5   *Justice*, 23 April 1904.
6   Ibid.
7   See, for example, the discussion over the naming of the SW Manchester SDF women's organisation as a 'women's section'(*Justice*, 2 November, 9 November 1907).

part of the party structure itself. But none the less, any organisation by SDF women has to be seen as bounded by the danger of separatism: a danger which was perceived by many of the women concerned as well as by the party as a whole.

The whole question of women's organisation showed how sensitive the SDF was to anything that identified sex as a discrete category. This was a problem which arose from the Second International's construction of the woman question, recognising and then attempting to dissolve 'sex' into 'class'. As I have argued, the SDF recognised women as a problem but were wary of any action to deal with this which might suggest in any way that 'sex' was an equivalent category to 'class'. It followed that the party was unable to recognise organisation around sex oppression as of equal validity to struggle around class oppression. But such a stance became increasingly difficult as women became more vocal in their demands as women, specifically in relation to the vote. The SDF was forced to recognise that the party must have its own women's organisation. The problem then became how to do this on the party's terms, keeping the new organisation restrained within set parameters. Invoking the bogey of separatism was one way to limit the autonomy of any organisation. Another was to introduce conflicting perceptions of the primary function of women's organisation: social or educational. The tensions implicit in these issues were played out over the SDF's lifetime, in terms of conflict between how the party perceived women's organisation and what women themselves desired and were able to achieve through organisation. Therefore the changes in form, purpose and achievement of SDF women's organisation form the substance of the following sections.

SDF women's organisation before 1904

SDF women's organisation before 1904 was sporadic and random. In the 1880s, references to women's organisations in the party press showed that they were centred on London, where the SDF was strongest.[8] Unfortunately, there is little indication of what concerned these groups. We do know that in the earliest days of the party, in 1884, a meeting was advertised in *Justice* for women interested in the Democratic Federation. In one sense it anticipated the later Circles, by aiming beyond the existing female party membership. It also seems that papers were read at its evening meetings, which were held at the

---

[8]   Watmough, 'The Membership of the Social Democratic Federation', p. 38; Thompson, *Socialists, Liberals and Labour*, ch. 6.

Federation's office.[9] Why the group ceased to be advertised after two months is not clear. The other women's groups of the 1880s are even more tantalising. There is no other information about them, other than that Battersea women's meeting was held on Monday afternoons with a discussion class the same evening, and that Chelsea SDF had a Women's League.[10] The dearth of publicity about such groups and their activities indicates the limited impact of women's organisation on the party as a whole in the 1880s. In turn, women's organisation seems to have received little encouragement from the party.

The same pattern prevailed into the next decade, but the centre of activity shifted to Lancashire. The occasional forays into women's organisation depended entirely upon local initiative. It was because of the strength of the Lancashire SDF in the mid-1890s that the most successful of the few women's sections were to be found there. A women's section with twenty-six members was formed at Nelson after the visit of a woman speaker to the branch in 1894. There is little record of its activities. However, it does appear to have promoted an interest amongst women in the local branch. By the end of the next year the branch reported that it had forty female members, although the purpose of the report was to congratulate these women for organising a particularly fine tea party! The long-standing South Salford branch also had a women's committee in 1895 which organised a sale of work in aid of the Parliamentary Fund. But it was in Rochdale that the heartiest women's section thrived, briefly, as 'the life and soul of the branch'.[11] By taking Rochdale women's section as a case study, the nature of an early form of SDF women's organisation can be explored.

Rochdale women's section

Rochdale[12] was a traditionally Liberal town in the 1890s where both the SDF and the ILP were able to organise successfully. Rochdale SDF had been formed in 1887 and was not eclipsed by the formation of a local branch of the ILP in 1892. Indeed, the two bodies worked closely together, running joint slates of candidates for local elections from 1897.[13] Although Henry Pelling stereotypically described Rochdale SDF's socialism as 'uncompromising' and suggested that its existence

---

9   *Justice*, 15 February, 1 March, 8 March, 29 March 1884.
10 *Justice*, 19 May 1888.
11 *Justice*, 14 December 1895; 23 February 1895; 16 February 1895.
12 For Rochdale labour politics, including the SDF, see M. Coneys, 'The Labour Movement and the Liberal Party in Rochdale, 1890–1906', MA dissertation, Huddersfield Polytechnic, nd.
13 Ibid., p. 63.

had distorted the development of labour politics in the area,[14] the branch actually espoused and promoted Socialist Unity in its local practice and through campaigns within the party. In the 1900s it was to oppose the withdrawal of the SDF from the LRC and urge the party's reaffiliation.[15] Rochdale SDF was therefore highly involved in the politics of the town, both in electoral work in tandem with the ILP, and also in the labour politics of trying to win the Lib-Lab Trades Council for socialism. It was not an isolated sect.

In 1895 *Justice* reported the existence of a women's section of Rochdale SDF. By that year the branch had been contesting municipal elections since 1890, as yet unsuccessfully.[16] In April 1895 the branch moved to larger premises to accommodate its membership of over 200. This building consisted of refreshment and conversation rooms with a hall on the ground floor; above this was a spacious lecture room reported to be artistically decorated and used on special occasions for dances.[17] The branch was therefore not only large and well-established but sufficiently secure to contemplate renting such a large property. Nor was this just a working-man's club! One of the first speakers to use the new Socialist Hall was Isabel Tiplady, who spoke there on 20 April with a woman branch member, Mrs Walker, in the chair.[18] Unlike the Pankhurst Hall – built by the ILP in Hightown, Salford – which excluded women, Rochdale SDF's Socialist Hall was open to all and apparently used by both sexes.[19]

In 1895, the SDF also supported the ILP candidate for Rochdale, George Barnes, in the general election. His intervention deeply unsettled the local Liberals as it resulted in the unexpected defeat of their candidate by the Conservative. The general atmosphere of socialist optimism in the Lancashire of the 1890s encouraged this particularly healthy SDF branch to form a women's section. A branch report in *Justice* spoke very positively about the initiative:

They – the women – have, among other things, a sewing class, from which they appear to derive both pleasure and profit. It is quite a treat to drop in on one of their gatherings and see them sewing and singing away all the time as merrily as if the Revolution had arrived. Some of them say they do not know how they

---

[14]   H. Pelling, *Social Geography of British Elections, 1885–1910*, Macmillan, 1967, p. 255.
[15]   For discussion of Socialist Unity as strategy, see K. Hunt, 'Burnley Social Democratic Federation', pp. 83–104; D Howell, 'Was the Labour Party Inevitable?', *Labour's Turning Point in the North West, 1880–1914*, North West Labour History Society, Southport, 1984, pp. 1–18.
[16]   M. Coneys, 'The Labour Movement and the Liberal Party in Rochdale', pp. 22–4.
[17]   *Rochdale Times*, 13 April 1895.
[18]   *Rochdale Observer*, 24 April 1895. See appendix 5 for a brief biography of Isabel Tiplady.
[19]   S. Pankhurst, *The Suffragette Movement*, p. 167.

passed their time, or what pleasure they could have had in their lives, before they joined the branch ... There is no doubt about it, Socialism will buzz along when the women catch onto it, and they seem to have caught on in Rochdale in real earnest.[20]

Such industry raised money for the branch, sufficient to buy a 'handsome tea-service'! Perhaps, more importantly, the women also organised the branch's trading department.[21] Furthermore, in addition to their social function, the section appeared to encourage women's participation in the branch. By June 1895 the branch meetings were reported as having an attendance of about fifty men and a dozen women, a significant female active membership. It was claimed that monthly meetings were even larger. The women's section met on a separate evening to the branch and had a membership of over forty and, it was claimed, this was rapidly growing.[22]

Yet despite this picture of a vigorous women's section, there are no references to it among the three local Rochdale newspapers, although they do contain advertisements and reports of local SDF meetings.[23] Nor are there any further indications in *Justice* of the continued existence of this women's section beyond June 1895, when the group seemed remarkably lively. A year later a local labour newspaper was started, *The Rochdale Labour News*, but although this includes reports of the SDF branch there are no references to a women's section. The paper included a woman's column, but this gave no indication of any specific women's organisation among either the local SDF or the ILP. This does not necessarily mean that the SDF women's section had collapsed. The activities of rank-and-file SDF women were singularly invisible to the press of the time. Even when a visiting woman speaker addressed a meeting on 'Women and Socialism', as Edith Lanchester did in July 1895, this prompted no further comment on local socialist women's activities.[24]

Nevertheless, some general comments can be made. The Rochdale SDF women's section, and the other women's sections of the 1890s, were formed from 1894 to 1895. This was at the height of the boom in socialist politics in Lancashire and was a period of great optimism. In 1894 Lancashire had almost half the membership of the entire party[25] and was at its greatest strength. One would expect such optimism to

[20] *Justice*, 16 February 1895.
[21] Ibid; *Justice*, 1 June 1895.
[22] *Justice*, 1 June 1895.
[23] See *Rochdale Observer*, *Rochdale Star*, and *Rochdale Times* for 1895.
[24] *Rochdale Star*, 5 July 1895.
[25] P. A. Watmough, 'The Membership of the Social Democratic Federation', p. 38; *SDF Conference Report*, 1895, pp. 4, 7.

encourage new initiatives; many new projects were started which drew in the socialist periphery. These included the women's organisations. But even so, there was no attempt to form a national federation of women's sections with a central body to coordinate its efforts. Local activity thus depended almost entirely upon the attitude of male members of the branch and their degree of support. Essentially, these women's sections remained a local phenomenon which incorporated part of the socialist periphery into the party for a short time, primarily to encourage social aspects of branch work. They did not represent a general attempt to propagandise amongst women as a group. Indeed, they can be seen as reinforcing the limited role of women within the party, of bazaar work and social activities.

It seems that any group of women who met within the SDF was seen by male comrades as providing a service of making items for sale in aid of the branch. Clearly, women members would have got much out of these activities when they were undertaken collectively – social contact and mutual support were undoubtedly an attraction. But what we do not know, in this period, was what the women talked about while they sewed and knitted, or prepared the food for a branch social. Although discussions might well have ranged over political topics there was no systematic attempt to use these occasions for educational purposes or for 'making' socialists.

What is clear is the mutual reinforcement of men's assumptions and the women's section's practice. This was to haunt later attempts to organise women in the SDF. There is no evidence which has survived that women desired to use the sections for any other purpose than the social one. Nor did they appear to seek a greater degree of autonomy from the party or of power within it. These women's organisations were simply far too sporadic and isolated to conceive of themselves as having a general relationship with the party as a whole. They depended upon favourable local conditions and never proved to be, or sought to be, a challenge to their local branch. They therefore organised within traditional areas of work for women, reinforcing the sexual division of labour within the party. Even later, when bazaar work within the SDF was organised on a national basis, it is striking that the Bazaar Committee had male officers who urged rank-and-file women to form local women's committees to do the necessary work.[26] Although bazaar work may have been women's sphere, when it was mobilised for the national party it did not remain under women's control.

How did the nature and extent of the SDF women's organisation

[26] *Justice*, 27 December 1902.

compare with that of other socialist women of the 1890s? At first glance
it might seem that ILP women were more ambitious and more
successful in their self-organisation. The impressively titled 'The
Women's National Association of the ILP' was announced in *Clarion* in
February 1894[27] with Katherine Bruce Glasier as its Honorary President. Yet on investigation it appears that this was a national association
in name only and that even the name was only briefly invoked.[28] Rather
like the SDF, women organised in particular localities. Perhaps the most
successful was the Scottish Women's Labour Party based in Glasgow
which lasted from 1894 to 1898.[29]

The nature of the ILP women's branches of this period was broadly
similar to that of the SDF. For example North Manchester Women's
ILP alternated sewing and reading meetings.[30] But in some cases there
were features which went well beyond the tentative women's organisations of the SDF. North Salford women's branch abolished the office
of president and each member took her turn as chairwoman.[31] Some of
the branches were explicitly women-only, as one *Clarion* report made
clear: 'Two visitors appeared who were not qualified for admission by
their sex, and were promptly dismissed, as questions were being raised
in which mothers wanted the field free for themselves.'[32] This contrasts
with the hesitancy of some SDF women to engage in anything which
smacked of separatism. Yet the ILP's male leadership was not
necessarily more liberal. Lily Bell had to defend women's self-
organisation to its male critics within the party. She commented that
'men always fancy our interests are perfectly safe in their hands' and
went on to explain the rationale for women's branches: 'The fact is
women have to learn to think and act for themselves independently of
men for until they can do so they cannot combine with them on a
really equal footing ... I want the women to learn to walk, instead of
being "carried"'.[33] This was not an argument that was voiced
coherently within the SDF at this time.

Despite these arguments, there is little evidence that any systematic
attempt was made to organise or facilitate the self-organisation of
women within the ILP. Although the ILP women's branches were more

[27] *Clarion*, 10 February 1894.
[28] This was a title adopted by the Hightown women's branch and was used predominately in the first half of 1894 although *Clarion*, 13 October 1894 carries an advert for a
Women's National Association of the ILP meeting in Gorton. There is no reference to
a national association in the *Labour Leader*.
[29] *Labour Leader*, 27 April, 25 May 1895.
[30] *Clarion*, 9 May 1896.
[31] *Clarion*, 26 January 1895.
[32] *Clarion*, 10 February 1894.
[33] *Labour Leader*, 21 April 1894.

numerous than those of the SDF and appeared over a longer period, there was no coordination given to their development nor was any official encouragement forthcoming. Their development was as dependent on local circumstances as the women's groups of the SDF. ILP women did, it is true, have the advantage of women's columns in both *Labour Leader* and *Clarion*. These created the possibility of publicity for women's activities, which in turn could stimulate further organisation. But although both columns gave space to reports of women's organisation, this never became their primary function and they therefore never took on any coordinating role. In stark contrast, SDF women did not even have this option – *Justice* did not have a women's column until 1907.

At this stage neither party saw women's organisation as necessary to their practice. Nor, as yet, did questions of the relative autonomy of women's organisation within a socialist party and its access to party resources have to be faced in Britain. Certainly, neither party believed that *ad hoc* women's organisation constituted any real challenge to their authority. These only became issues when the systematic organisation of SDF and ILP women was attempted in the early twentieth century.

The Women's Socialist Circles (1904–1911)

In March 1904 Dora Montefiore announced the formation of a women's branch of the SDF. This inaugurated the SDF's attempt to organise women in Women's Socialist Circles. It is interesting that it should be Dora Montefiore who made this announcement, for despite her long involvement with the SDF she always personified the tension between socialism and feminism within the party. Her commitment to women makes it unsurprising that she should have been part of this move to draw women and socialism closer together. Yet the choice of her to front the initiative showed either that the other women were swept away by her enthusiasm and penchant for organising, or that they were ensuring that they could distance themselves from the proposal, if necessary, by allowing a maverick to be associated with it.

In her case for a women's branch of the SDF, Dora Montefiore emphasised a number of issues which were already part of the SDF's discussion of the woman question and which were to remain controversial for the Women's Socialist Circles. She was critical of socialists for failing to mobilise women despite their commitment to sexual equality. This criticism was underlined by the fact that the orthodox political parties, with no equivalent commitment, had nevertheless successfully organised women's sections.[34] Somewhat optimistically, she ascribed to these organisations the primary purpose of pursuing women's emancipation, specifically the vote, rather than the more usual one of auxiliary to a predominantly male party. She also stressed the importance of education, not just in a general sense but more importantly as political education. In this view she predated the thinking of the Circles by a number of years. But she did share with many early Circle members an identification of motherhood as one of the assets which politically educated women would bring to the socialist movement. Dora Montefiore did not focus her argument on women as a problem for socialism but on women as an untapped resource which, with organisation and education, could prove to be a positive benefit to the SDF.[35]

Although most of the leading woman SDFers were involved in the Circles with Dora Montefiore as their first Treasurer and Clara Hendin as Secretary, they were not the target audience for the new organisation. Although Circles might be organised by established woman SDFers, they were designed to appeal to the 'wives, daughters and sisters' of comrades, with a particular emphasis on working-class women.[36] The purpose of the Circles was 'first to make women Socialists, and later, if possible, get them into the SDF'.[37] This later became more narrowly focused on the recruitment of women to Social Democracy rather than socialism as a whole.

From the beginning, the Circle organisers recognised that they had to move beyond the traditional means of 'making' socialists if they were to reach women. Rose Jarvis suggested at an early stage to Circle members that they should invite women to their own homes in the afternoons.[38] The idea was to make women comfortable and then to show them the advantages of socialism, to influence them to join the branch as well as to bring other women to similar afternoon meetings. The implication was that branch practices and SDF propaganda were not immediately appealing and that other methods might have to be used to win women's trust, particularly those who already had their own perception of the party through their SDF menfolk. As women began to form Circles, they conducted their meetings self-consciously in a friendly and accessible manner with songs, cocoa and cake as well

[34] See, J. H. Robb, *The Primrose League, 1883–1906*, Columbia University Press, New York, 1942; L. Walker, 'Party Political Women: A Comparative Study of Liberal Women and the Primrose League, 1890–1914', in J. Rendall (ed.), *Equal or Different*, pp. 165–91.
[35] *Justice*, 12 March 1904.
[36] *Justice*, 19 March 1904.
[37] *Justice*, 16 April 1904.
[38] *Justice*, 23 April 1904.

as a lecture.[39] It was the convention for political meetings to occur in the evening but a number of Circles chose to meet in the afternoons at members' homes. Although this obviously excluded women in paid work, it was clearly felt that these women might be reached in other ways, such as through trade unionism or traditional political propaganda. In contrast, women at home had far fewer opportunities. It did, of course, mean that such Circles were likely to consist largely of housewives just like the highly successful German socialist women's organisation of the time.[40] Throughout the lifetime of the Circles, women experimented with times and frequency of meetings depending both on their conception of their target audience as well as on their own resources.[41]

Although it had traditionally been assumed within the party that women's function was a social one, Circle women seem to have mobilised this role to their own ends. They recognised that what they had to concentrate on was getting women to come to the meetings in the first place. Making women feel at home, however traditionally defined, was one means to achieve this. But this was a difficult matter to negotiate successfully; the danger was that they would reinforce the pre-existing stereotype of women and their abilities within the party. It would be all too easy for the Circles to be merely organised auxiliaries to the party, attending to social and fund-raising activities for their male comrades. Hence Dora Montefiore's decision to resign from the Women's Committee in 1905 because of the bazaar work undertaken in the Circles.[42]

It was important to the Circles that they had an approach which recognised the realities of women's lives and the pressures upon them, as well as the SDF's lack of previous success in recruiting women. But in addition they needed a structure which enabled the women who came to a meeting to be exposed to socialist ideas; that is an educational programme. Throughout the Circles' lifetime there were tensions between the needs of the party – most of the social activities engaged in by the Circles were in order to raise funds for the party – and the needs of the women, as potential and actual socialists. This was played out in two areas: the changing emphasis between the social and educational function of the Circles; and in the structural relationship between the women's organisation and the party. In order to situate the analysis of these factors, a sketch of the development of the Circles is needed.

[39]   *Justice*, 24 December 1904.
[40]   R. J. Evans, 'Politics and the Family', pp. 264–7.
[41]   For example, *Justice*, 25 January, 23 May 1908.
[42]   *Justice*, 11 March 1905.

The development of the Circles

In the early years there were never many Circles at any one time and there was little central direction and guidance. During 1904, Circles were formed in Croydon and Edmonton and these existed into 1905. Later that year additional Circles were formed in Northampton, Reading, Tunbridge Wells and West Ham, while the earlier groups faded away. These few Circles had a negligible impact on the party as a whole. But they were more successful locally, just like the earlier SDF women's organisations.

Many early Circles were instigated by energetic women who were already in the SDF. For example, Rose Jarvis not only helped to start the Circle at Croydon where she lived but was also instrumental in setting up the Reading Circle.[43] Later, concern was expressed amongst SDF women that individuals could overstretch themselves in their main-tenance of the Circles, become exhausted and that then the Circle would collapse.[44] By the end of the period, SDF women, and the party as a whole, were no nearer understanding and managing the dynamic of groups than their contemporaries. If they were to survive, they had to develop into groups which were strong enough to sustain themselves without relying on the women whose energies had brought the group together. This transition was a difficult one, particularly when, as with the Circles, the group's purpose was to bring together women who had no experience of organisation.

Initially the number of Circles grew slowly. At the beginning of 1906 the Women's Committee was able to report on its wide range of activities and on the four Circles which existed. The Committee, being without funds, devoted its energy to London and to holding outdoor meetings in conjunction with unemployed committees and trades councils as well as SDF branches.[45] They also assisted in the 1906 General Election, much like the women's auxiliary organisations of the major political parties. The main difference was that being few in number the SDF women could only have a limited impact, particularly as their organisation was not structured towards electoral work. Recognising this, the Women's Committee targeted one constituency, West Ham, and worked with the local Circle of over twenty members to help elect Will Thorne.[46]

The Committee also held a series of women's meetings in London

---

[43]   *Justice*, 4 November 1905.
[44]   *Justice*, 10 April 1909.
[45]   *Justice*, 20 January 1906.
[46]   Ibid; see also C. Tsuzuki, *H. M. Hyndman*, p. 160.

during 1906 with such leading speakers as Mary Macarthur, Mrs Despard, Dora Montefiore and Margaretta Hicks.[47] But the Circles still only had a marginal effect on the party as a whole.

Just as 1907 was a year of transition for the SDF in their attitude to the suffrage, so the same year saw the Women's Committee entering a new phase. Although there had been an informal meeting of the Circles in 1906, the 1907 Women's Committee Second Annual Meeting was much more clearly a conference of representatives of all seven Circles. It gave an opportunity for some reassessment of the Circles' role. The resolution on organisation which was carried unanimously suggested a rather different emphasis from earlier practice. Now the object of the Circles was 'to organise and educate women in the principles of Social Democracy with a view to their becoming members of the SDF, and to stand side by side with the men to bring about the abolition of capitalism'. Here was a greater sense that the Circles constituted a national organisation with a clearly-defined purpose. The Circles constituted a federation; they remained autonomous in their rules, the fixing of subscriptions and in the drawing up cf their individual programmes. But it was agreed that they were not to be 'turned into mothers' meetings'.[48]

With a regular annual meeting and the institution of *Justice*'s women's column in January 1907, there existed the means to bring the disparate groups more closely together into a national organisation. The context for women's organisation was also changing for there were now not only the rival women's organisations fighting for the suffrage but also the Labour Party's new women's organisation, the Women's Labour League (WLL). The rivalry of these organisations was never directly acknowledged by the Women's Committee, but it spurred efforts to publicise the Circles within the SDF. The new column in *Justice* now called for all branches to form a Women's Circle at once.

Although individual Circles came and went, their total number began to rise from 1907. By mid 1908, nineteen Circles were claimed by the SDF and the number hovered around twenty until well into 1910. Indeed, from references in *Justice* there seem to have been even more Circles than those officially acknowledged; these peaked at thirty in mid 1909.[49] Despite this significant increase, the numbers of branches which had a Circle were a distinct minority. But there was a greater coherence in the SDF women's organisation in these years which was reinforced by the reformation of the Women's Committee as the Women's Education

[47] *Justice*, 10 March, 17 March 1906.
[48] *Justice*, 27 April 1907.
[49] See appendix 3.

Committee (WEC) in 1909 and the relaunching of the women's column in *Justice* under the title, 'Our Women's Circle'. Once the Circles were of a sufficient number, their function and their relationship to the party as a whole became a more pressing issue for all of the SDF, including its more confident women's organisation.

The function of the Circles

The purpose of the Women's Socialist Circles was to mobilise women in support of socialism and, ultimately, the SDF. What this meant in practice varied greatly in the minds of SDFers. Such groups of women could, in keeping with established tradition, demonstrate their identification with socialism and the party merely by fulfilling an auxiliary function; that is, by doing bazaar work and by providing a supportive social milieu for the predominantly male membership. But Circles could also be the means to bring women into full party membership through a programme of education designed specifically for them. There was a tension between these two functions and the expectations which underlay them. The Circles, as they developed, tried to negotiate a path between a social and an educational function.

There was no forum set aside in *Justice* for the early Circles to exchange information about their work, concerns and preoccupations. It is therefore only in branch reports and through the column 'Bazaar Notes' that these Circles can be glimpsed. For example, the Reading Circle's activities appear to have been successful as they resulted in recruits being made to the branch. Although the main focus of their Circle meetings was 'making clothing and other useful articles for the SDF Christmas Bazaar', they had elected officers and did 'everything possible to make the meetings both educating and attractive'.[50] Even at this stage, it was stressed by the Women's Committee that Circles should conduct their meetings in a business-like fashion, that is with elected officers and minutes being taken. This would not only give women experience of more formal structures whilst still in a supportive environment but was also used as evidence to try to convince male party members that Circle meetings were serious gatherings, not merely bazaar committees. Nevertheless, the social function of the Circles remained predominant. Certainly, it was this feature of the Circles which precipitated Dora Montefiore's resignation from the Women's Committee in 1905. Doing bazaar work was never the exclusive occupation of Circles for they generally also had discussions and

[50] *Justice*, 4 November 1905.

readings, for example Tunbridge Wells Circle read from Blatchford's *Britain for the British*.[51] What Dora Montefiore, and subsequently other Circle women, complained of was the balance between the two functions which, whilst the Circles remained so few and without central direction, tended towards the traditional.

The thirty women who, in 1906, were recruited from the Circles into the branches demonstrated clear advantages for a branch in having a Circle. Circle members helped at meetings, elections, socials; they sold literature; raised money for the branch; started and ran Socialist Sunday Schools; as well as having lectures. Essentially, theirs were the traditional women's activities writ large. But the 1907 Annual Meeting of the Women's Committee passed a resolution which stressed organisation and education as the object of the Circles. Women were beginning to see themselves as potentially more than auxiliaries, and there was now some recognition that women should benefit at least as much as the branch from the existence of a Circle. This implied a partial abandonment of the previous practice of tailoring activities to interest sceptical women, particularly the archetypal 'socialist's wife'. This, combined with the branch's perception of woman's role, could limit the effectiveness of the Circles as educators, as makers of socialist women.

During 1907 there was a much greater emphasis on the Circle as a 'training ground'.[52] Circles adopted and publicised a more educational programme. For example, Central Women's Circle formed an elementary economics class[53] and education meetings were also held by the Women's Committee, with papers read by prominent women and men of the SDF. But the growing emphasis on education also highlighted the involvement of men in the Circles. This could be as lecturers – for example A. A. Watts ran the elementary economics class – or even as members of the audience at Circle events. In the case of speakers, some provincial Circles, in particular, found that the dearth of women lecturers meant that male comrades had to be asked to take classes and give lectures. Although this might make the Circle seem even more of a preparatory school for party membership, with the men leading the women towards socialist adulthood and full party membership, this does not appear to have been the contemporary reaction.

There was certainly an ambivalence about the involvement of men, which had been present from the beginning of the Circles. The problem was that branches might react less favourably to the actions of Circle members if men were barred from their meetings; but if men were able

[51]   *Justice*, 20 January 1906.
[52]   *Justice*, 8 June 1907.
[53]   *Justice*, 6 July 1907.

to attend Circles, what then marked the Circle as different from any other part of the party? The significant difference would be if women could nevertheless organise the Circles on their own terms. Some Circles did meet *in camera*, heartily welcoming, they said, the attendance of all women.[54] Many of the women activists clearly supported this, for example Clara Hendin argued that women 'will be more willing to listen to women than to men'.[55] Although some Circles sought male help and invited men to some of their events and to their socials, this was clearly a women's organisation run by women. In time, as the Circles became more numerous and more confident, there was an increasing need to formalise the relationship between the women's organisation and the party as a whole.

As the Circles became more established, so their emphasis became increasingly and unapologetically educational rather than merely social. At the 1908 SDP Women's Conference, individual Circle reports indicated that the educational approach now predominated.[56] The Committee had already produced leaflets addressed specifically to women and in February 1908 it launched its first pamphlet, *Some Words to Socialist Women*, written by Dora Montefiore.[57] The availability of this material, together with the women's column in *Justice* and the American paper *Socialist Woman*, which Circle members were also advised to read,[58] emphasised the educational purpose of the Circles. But it was not merely that Circles were becoming more didactic; they were also considering how to make their educational work more effective. In regretting that the attendance had not been larger at their series of lectures on economics, Central Circle called a special meeting of its members to discuss the advisability of adopting a more popular form of propaganda.[59] The production of leaflets and pamphlets directed specifically at women was one way in which to reach a wider audience. This of course cost the Committee money. Thus, any attempt to introduce coherence and coordination to the Circles' educational programme was likely to have financial and organisational consequences for the Women's Committee.

The more determined educational focus of these later and more

---

[54] *Justice*, 5 December 1908.
[55] *Justice*, 28 September 1907.
[56] *Justice*, 18 April 1908.
[57] *Some Words to Socialist Women* was reviewed in *Justice*, 22 February 1908.
[58] For details of *Socialist Woman*, see M. J. Buhle, *Women and American Socialism, 1870–1920*, University of Illinois Press, Urbana, 1983, pp. 148, 156–7; M. J. Buhle 'Socialist Woman, Progressive Woman, Coming Nation', in J. R. Conlin (ed.), *The American Radical Press, 1880–1960*, Greenwood Press, Westport, Connecticut, 1974, II, pp. 442–9; *Justice*, 10 August 1907, 25 January, 18 April 1908.
[59] *Justice*, 4 January 1908.

numerous Circles meant both a more considered and structured internal education programme as well as a more self-conscious propagandist approach to non-members. In the latter category was the recommendation to all Circles to affiliate with the Adult Suffrage Society, where it was assumed a wider range of sympathetic women might be found. Greater publicity was sought for the Circles' work externally through reports sent to Julia Dawson at the *Clarion*, and internally by requesting local branches to include Circle meetings in their own advertising.[60] More generally, Circle members were encouraged to participate in the open-air meetings of the party and to take a more active part in branch life, not merely in the auxiliary role still so often expected of them.

Propaganda work was also directed at the parent party. This was particularly evident when a new women's column was started in *Justice* in March 1909 entitled 'Our Women's Circle'. This was much more hard-hitting than its predecessor. The column was headed by a decorated title which stretched across the whole page, drawing attention within the more dour format of *Justice*. It was thought this would enable *Justice* to be sold to more women when paper sellers displayed the paper open at the women's page.[61] Dora Montefiore reported in her first column that the editor of *Justice* had given women this column 'so that we may concentrate on the special side of Socialist propaganda, as it affects women, and interpret everday events from the standpoint of Social Democracy'.[62] 'Our Women's Circle' provided a means to exchange information about socialist women's activities and concerns extending from the parochial to the international scene. This took the form of editorial, reports from the Women's Committee and from the Circles, as well as advertisements directed at female readers.

Despite such efforts to raise the profile of women within the SDF, the old stereotypes refused to disappear. At the 1909 Women's Conference a suggestion was made by Comrade Pegg (a man) that the Circles should be formed into Bazaar Committees. Kathleen Kough replied that it would be better if each branch formed its own Bazaar Committee rather than hand this work over to the Circles. She naturally feared that the educational side of the Circles would be compromised if they were turned into sewing meetings. Nevertheless, some Circle women argued for bazaar work but within a rather different framework. Mrs Cockerton of Deptford envisaged an instructive book being read while some Circle women sewed, while Mrs Murray reported that sewing meetings could be a useful way of drawing women into the movement. At least the

[60]   *Justice*, 18 April 1908.
[61]   *Justice*, 10 April 1909.
[62]   *Justice*, 20 March 1909.

conference remained clear that Circles were 'not formed to run "socials", but to strive for Socialism, and that, while not losing sight of the social side of the movement, the educational side must always be made the most prominent'.[63] The fact that this issue dogged the Circles throughout their lifetime reflected their own, and the party's, difficulty in challenging preconceptions of the sexual division of labour.

The Women's Education Committee took seriously its new title. Improvements to educational work remained premised on the idea that women needed a preparatory education before entering party membership. As one Circle member argued, 'it requires some preliminary mental training to make one capable of assimilating the strong meat of Marxian economics'.[64] The Committee therefore produced a syllabus in 1910 for all the Circles to use during the following year;[65] this covered everyday topics such as rent, food and laundries and more woman-focused topics such as maintenance for mothers. Only more experienced Circle members were encouraged to tackle Bebel's *Woman* and Hyndman's *England for All*. Coherence was provided not only by a national syllabus but also by with essays specially written for Circles by 'experts'. Members were encouraged to look up each subject before the Circle met so that they could contribute something to the discussion.[66]

By 1909 there was an increasing emphasis on educating Circle members for Social Democracy and party membership rather than merely 'making' socialists. It was not that the Circles became more sectarian; but they were more clearly SDF organisations. The example of Coventry Circle, which wanted to delineate itself from the rival WLL, and therefore suggested a debate on the meaning of socialism,[67] was perhaps unusual. Yet the new concern about the organisational relationship of the Circles to the party meant that it was politic for the former to emphasise that their goal was to make female Social Democrats. This raised financial and organisational questions for the Circles and for the party as a whole.

The organisational relationship between the Circles and the party

The initial Circles were the creation of SDF women but they were not an official part of the party. Women graduated from them to party

---

[63] *Justice*, 10 April 1909.
[64] *Justice*, 22 May 1909.
[65] *Justice*, 6 August 1910. See appendix 4.
[66] *Justice*, 2 September 1911.
[67] *Justice*, 17 April 1909.

membership. But existing women members of the SDF also joined the Circles. The mixed nature of the latter's membership made for an ambivalent relationship between the Circles and the party.

A major complaint of the Circles and the Women's Committee was that the party leadership did not call for every branch to form its own Circle and thereby address its own responsibility for recruiting women to the SDF. The service that the Circles gave to the branches could be demonstrated in practical terms as could the numbers of women who were directly recruited to the branches from the Circles. The Circles therefore made much of this aspect of their work. Thus Reading Circle, it was reported, 'will prove a great benefit to their branch in converting the wives to Socialism'.[68] The Women's Committee thought that the Circles had to be seen to be succcessful in this problematic area if they were to win party approval. Otherwise the party's women's organisation would remain marginal.

At the 1907 Women's Conference it was agreed that the Committee should press for a Women's Circle in every SDF branch. It was emphasised that male comrades would not be excluded from the discussion as to how to achieve this goal. Yet two years later, success was no closer to hand. Indeed, as the Circles increased in number and became more ambitious in their work, so the need for a secure financial basis arose and this brought into focus the relationship with the party. Although the Circles wanted to do things for themselves – as Mrs Boyce said, 'They were women capable of managing women without the men's help'[69] – they did increasingly need the party's resources to carry out their work.

The tension between autonomy and dependence came to a head at the SDP's 1909 Conference, where a resolution was put to incorporate the WEC into the party and make its members subject to annual election by the branches.[70] This was the first time that the structure of the women's organisation had been debated at party conference. The divisions were partly along lines of gender. Women active in the Circles put forward a strong case both for the need for Circles and for their status within the party to be 'legalised', as Mrs Boyce put it. Objections from male SDPers centred on the point that Circle members were by definition not socialists and that therefore it would be dangerous to incorporate them into the party. These critics wanted safeguards, such as Circle members being required to sign a declaration of principles. An interim arrangement was agreed, by no means unanimously, that for the

68   *Justice*, 20 January 1906.
69   *Justice*, 10 April 1909. See appendix 5 for a brief biography of Emma Boyce.
70   *SDF Annual Conference Report*, 1909, pp. 18–19.

first year the London branches of the party would elect the WEC; this experiment would be reviewed at the following conference.

This meant that the coordinating body of the Circles would now be elected by all branch members, men and women; recognition within the party had been bought at the price of some devolution of control beyond the Circles. These now became an official part of the SDP. The advent of the new national SDP women's organisation was clearly significant to women remote from London. As one Circle member wrote, 'Formerly, here in a Scottish village we felt remote and detached; now we are not only linked up with the whole body of our comrades in the UK, but we are equally in touch with our sisters the whole world over.'[71]

What difference did these changes make? The introduction of an affiliation fee, 2s 6d for every twenty-five members,[72] at last gave WEC an income. This enabled it, for instance, to print another pamphlet by Dora Montefiore, *The Position of Woman in the Socialist Movement*.[73] Nevertheless, the WEC's finances do not seem to have been particularly secure, and Dora Montefiore suggested that because women of the party contributed such a large amount of work for the SDF Bazaar, they should claim a percentage of the money raised.[74] In 1909 WEC also appointed Emma Boyce as an organiser for the Circles. It is not clear whether this was a salaried position but the inauguration of such a post did mark a greater degree of self-confidence within the WEC. The other development was that the WEC took a much more self-conscious role within the party. It provided a women's voice, for example, in protesting against the pronouncements of Bax. When Bax published his article in the May 1909 *Social Democrat* on 'Why I am an anti-Suffragist', the WEC protested that such an action was 'likely to influence women *against* joining the party'.[75]

Despite these changes, the number of Circles did not grow after 1909; indeed it began to fall at the end of 1910.[76] The healthiest period was the time of the WEC's greatest activity and of the new women's column in *Justice*. Although after 1910 women continued to be recruited to the party via the Circles, the party withheld the wholehearted support that was necessary for further development. Late in 1910 the WEC complained that, despite being asked a month previously, the branches had failed to nominate women for three Committee vacancies. If

[71] *Justice*, 1 May 1909.
[72] *Justice*, 15 May 1909.
[73] D. B. Montefiore, *The Position of Woman in the Socialist Movement* was first advertised in *Justice*, 19 June 1909.
[74] *Justice*, 8 May 1909.
[75] *Justice*, 31 July 1909.
[76] See appendix 3.

nominations were not forthcoming, the WEC threatened to elect Circle members in their place despite this being unconstitutional.[77] The mere existence of the WEC and the Circles did not mean that the woman question moved into the mainstream of SDF politics.

Committed SDF women continued with their work regardless. As Dora Montefiore's influence waned while she travelled abroad, so Margaretta Hicks took her place; elected to the WEC in 1910, she became its Chairman (*sic*) later that year.[78] As a Circle member, she was particularly conscious of the difficulties that Circles continued to face. Margaretta Hicks listed these as lacking a meeting place; no money to pay the rent; the inability of most working women to leave home for long, or to go any distance with a baby to carry; and the difficulty of getting speakers. She looked to branches to help in some of these matters, for example by providing a meeting place.[79] One of her major contributions to women's self-organisation in the SDF was to start a socialist women's monthly paper, *The Link*, which was first published in September 1911. This was designed for 'easy, light reading'[80] and to be accessible to women.

The shape and extent of women's organisation in the SDP was clearly not satisfactory to Margaretta Hicks and the rest of the WEC.[81] In the summer of 1911, negotiations took place between representatives of the WEC and the SDP Executive on the future of the party's women's organisation. In August the Organisation Committee of the party recommended that the WEC be dissolved and that a federation of Women's Socialist Circles be formed. A new Women's Committee would be responsible to the SDP Executive.[82] This was full-scale incorporation into the party structure, but without any promise that all branches would be obliged to form a Circle. But the matter was never resolved, for time was rapidly running out for the SDP. By October 1911 the BSP was being formed and the women's organisation was therefore suspended pending a decision by the new party on this area of work.[83] The Socialist Unity Conference and the foundation of the BSP produced a caesura in Social Democrat women's organisation.

Did the marginality of the SDF women's organisation reveal a

---

[77]   *Justice*, 29 October 1910; *SDP News*, October 1910, p. 8.
[78]   *Justice*, 2 April 1910, 6 August 1910.
[79]   *Justice*, 6 August 1910.
[80]   *Justice*, 2 September 1911.
[81]   For example, at the 1911 Women's Conference the WEC was instructed to produce a scheme for the development of the Women's Circles movement in the party (*Justice*, 1 April 1911).
[82]   *SDP News*, August 1911, pp. 1–2.
[83]   *Justice*, 14 October 1911.

weakness endemic to all socialist parties or was it particular to the SDF? The evidence suggests the former. The Circles' main rival, the WLL, was apparently more successful as an organisation, claiming 100 branches in 1911.[84] Of course, the Labour Party and labour movement to which the WLL appealed were much larger than the SDF. Like the Circles, the League also had its own organiser[85] and during 1911 both groups started their own journals, respectively *The League Leaflet* (later *Labour Woman*), and *The Link*. Yet neither organisation convinced its parent party to make a women's section a mandatory part of branch life.[86]

More broadly, women across the Second International found that assimilation into the party structure might bring some material benefits but it could not of itself change attitudes amongst the male membership. After 1908, German and American socialist women moved from organising separately to doing so through party women's sections, but they found after a time that they had paid a heavy price. In 1908, the American party[87] ended the organisational autonomy of socialist women by forming a Woman's National Committee (WNC) consisting of five women elected by the national convention of the party, with party funding for a national women's organiser. Each branch ('local') of the party was directed to elect its own women's committee, including men if there were insufficient women, and to initiate special agitational work to recruit women into the mixed locals. It seemed as though the woman question, particularly in its organisational aspect, now carried an official endorsement. Yet the locals did not respond particularly well and, although in 1910 the WNC was expanded and given greater resources, its power over the party membership remained limited, particularly in terms of changing attitudes. Meanwhile locals gained a considerable amount of control over socialist women's activities. American socialist women therefore began to demand separate organisation once again, and in 1915 the WNC was abolished.

A similar pattern can be seen in the largest socialist women's organisation of the period, that of Germany. Incorporation, as in America, produced a rapid increase in female party membership but at the price of a considerable loss of autonomy.[88] The party leadership's

84 *The League Leaflet*, June 1911, p. 8.
85 *The League Leaflet*, February 1913, p. 6.
86 See *Labour Woman*, March 1914, p. 179. For an account of the WLL, see C. Collette, *For Labour and for Woman*.
87 See M. J. Buhle, *Women and American Socialism*, pp. 145–75, 304–10 for the rise and fall of the WNC.
88 In Germany the SPD gained about 150,000 women members from 1908 to 1914 (J. H. Quataert, *Reluctant Feminists*, p. 148) while in America in 1912 the Socialist

control over the women's organisation was not matched by the empowering of women SPDers in the party's decision-making processes. For example, the women's conference could not make party policy and was therefore only an advisory body. The new Women's Bureau only had one representative on the national executive. Ironically, this was not Clara Zetkin, who had done so much to promote, develop and sustain the pre-1908 SPD women's organisation. She and her conception of the woman question became increasingly marginalised.

German socialist women also found, like their American and indeed British sisters, that such organisational changes did not bridge the gap between their party's theoretical commitment to the women's cause and the discrimination which existed in practice. But incorporation did mask that gulf for a period. The party hierarchies believed that they had made concessions to their female members; mitigated the external influence of feminism; provided more resources for women's organisation; and that therefore they were beyond reproach on the woman question.

The developments in women's self-organisation within the SDF, although on a different scale, were therefore broadly similar to those of other socialist women within the Second International. All the parties were influenced by the decisions of the International and all the women faced similar problems, particularly the entrenched views of many of their male comrades. Even before the outbreak of the First World War and the shattering of the Second International, socialist women realised that they were going to have to consider alternative strategies which would maintain women's access to resources whilst also empowering women within their own organisation and in the party as a whole.

To sum up, at the time of suspension, the SDF's Circles were declining in number from the highpoint of 1909. Yet with the aid of *The Link* and Margaretta Hicks's leadership, it seemed that the SDF's women's organisation might have considerable potential for development. This was despite the fact that there had been no fundamental shift in attitudes amongst male comrades. This came to be seen as a problem fairly late in the Circles' lifetime. Official recognition, even on a tentative basis, did not give SDF women the means to formulate a strategy to confront the indifference and even opposition of their male comrades. The socialist understanding of the woman question meant that it was all

Party's women's organiser estimated that women now formed 10 to 15 per cent of the party membership (M. J. Buhle, *Women and American Socialism*, p. 160). For the incorporation of the socialist women's organisation into the SPD and the foundation of the Woman's Bureau (1908–12) see J. H. Quataert, *Reluctant Feminists*, pp. 146–53; K. Honeycutt, 'Clara Zetkin', pp. 325–37. For men's attitude to the incorporated women's organisation and the woman question see Honeycutt, 'Clara Zetkin', pp. 337–43.

too easy for theoretical commitment to be given to women without any challenge being made to fundamental assumptions about woman's place in society and her capacities and potential. The SDF's women's organisation was, latterly, more concerned to educate women in Social Democracy and to develop their self-confidence so that they could take their part in the SDF; it did not attempt to change the party from its position on the margin. It is not clear that the Circles even recognised the magnitude of the problem they faced. Nevertheless, the period from 1909 to 1911 was one of self-conscious, co-ordinated women's organisation. It was the most fruitful period for women in that they were able to act together and give one another mutual support, as well as to develop their own and other women's potential. The Circles were thus more than a women's auxiliary to the SDF. They benefited the party in terms of recruitment; and they improved the party's image in the eyes of potential recruits and other parties within the Second International.

Northampton Women's Circle

Finally, in order to anchor this discussion of the effect of the SDF's understanding of the woman question on the organisation and practice of SDF women, I want to look at the example of one Circle. In examining one particular Circle I make no claim for typicality, for the variety of local circumstances produced as many differences of emphasis and of personality in the Circles as it did among the SDF's branches. Nevertheless, such a study can provide insights into the dynamics of the relationship between branch and Circle, and into the influence upon both organisations of the woman question.

Northampton SDF[89] was formed in 1886 as a small branch of no more than ten members. It soon grew, as a result of the struggle to unionise the dominant local industry of boot and shoe making, to become one of the strongest branches of the party. The branch's strength was indicated by the fact that it could sustain its own club, institute and newspaper[90] as well as being confident enough to contest several general elections and participate in municipal politics. The

---

[89] For Northampton SDF, see M. Dickie, 'Liberals, Radicals and Socialists in Northampton before the Great War', *Northamptonshire Past and Present*, 8, no. 1, 1983–4, pp. 51–4; A. Fox, *A History of the National Union of Boot and Shoe Operatives, 1874–1957*, Basil Blackwell, Oxford, 1958; K. Brooker, 'James Gribble and the Raunds Strike of 1905', *Northamptonshire Past and Present*, 6, no.5, 1981–2, pp. 275–90; K. Brooker, 'James Gribble', in J. M. Bellamy and J. Saville (eds.), *Dictionary of Labour Biography*, vol. 7, Macmillan, 1984, pp. 99–103.

[90] Northampton SDF had a series of newspapers, principally the *Northampton Socialist* (1897–99) and the *Northampton Pioneer* (1902–10), as well as the election special, *Red Flag* (1906), and the Northampton BSP's *The Socialist Pioneer* (1913–17).

branch did include women; of two hundred members in 1897, twenty were women,[91] some of whom were clearly activists. The branch gave some support for women's involvement in politics by putting forward one of its female members, Mrs Allen, for the Guardians on two occasions in the 1890s, although, like her male comrades, she was not elected.[92] There is no evidence that women in Northampton SDF organised separately within the branch in the years before the national SDF Women's Committee, unlike, for example, their sisters in Rochdale.

Northampton Women's Circle started to meet in the summer of 1905 and was therefore amongst the earliest of the Circles to be formed. It was also relatively long-lasting as it existed for about five years. The Circle owed a great deal to Rose Jarvis; indeed it is not clear whether it would have been formed but for her arrival in Northampton during 1905. Rose Jarvis was already an experienced SDF activist and was particularly committed to the organisation of women within the party, having been involved in the Women's Committee from the outset. She lectured extensively for the party and spoke a number of times in Northampton immediately before she moved there.[93] One of these meetings anticipated her involvement with the Northampton Circle, for it was promoted as a women-only event. This was unusual locally, and fairly rare for the SDF nationally given the concern about the danger of separatism. Northampton was therefore already showing a more favourable attitude to women's self-organisation than some other parts of the SDF.

Northampton's Circle met initially at Rose Jarvis's home but it soon transferred its weekly meetings to the SDF's hall, the Twentieth Century Club. Socialist and non-socialist women were welcomed to meetings where bazaar work was done as well as reading, singing, and discussion on matters of public interest.[94] The meetings were explicitly women-only although male relatives and friends were welcome at social events organised by the Circle. Soon the meetings were attended by between forty and fifty women, and by the beginning of 1906 the Circle's membership had risen to eighty.[95] The Circle also organised an alternative afternoon gathering for those women who could not attend evening meetings; the latter were curtailed at 9.30 pm, 'so that mothers

[91] *Northampton Socialist*, 17 July 1897.
[92] *Justice*, 24 December 1894; *Northampton Socialist*, 2 April, 21 May 1898.
[93] *Northampton Pioneer*, August 1904, p. 11; October 1904, p. 11; February 1905, p. 3. These meetings were fulsomely reported by the *Pioneer*'s editor C. J. Scott, whom Rose Jarvis married in September 1906.
[94] *Northampton Pioneer*, June 1905, p. 10.
[95] *Northampton Pioneer*, July 1905, p. 9; *Justice*, 20 January 1906.

reach home a little earlier'.[96] These efforts were directed towards reaching women who might be unable or unwilling to attend branch meetings. In order to attract such women, the Circle publicised the fact that 'Our meetings are held in a pleasant comfortable room and are conducted without a trace of formality or stiffness.'[97] This comment was included in one of the regular monthly reports of the Circle's activities which appeared in the branch paper, Northampton Pioneer. The existence of this newspaper, with a circulation of 5,000 at the end of 1905, was a considerable asset to the Circle, particularly as the Pioneer's editor, C. J. Scott, was clearly sympathetic to the group to which his wife, Rose Jarvis, gave so much energy. This put Northampton Circle in a more privileged position than many others as it could expect to reach, through the Pioneer, local women in the party, its periphery and beyond, as well as the womenfolk of male SDFers.

Who, in particular, were the Northampton Circle trying to reach and for what purpose? Was their focus the problematic socialist's wife or the potential woman activist? There is some evidence that it was not the former. Circle members did not publicise their activities in the same terms as Justice had written about the supposed problem of socialists' wives. On the other hand, the Circle did try to ensure that its meetings were accessible to women with domestic responsibilities and those who might find other SDF activities intimidating, and this would probably have included women who were married to male SDFers. But there was explicitly an attempt to galvanise women as activists. Rose Jarvis made it clear in a speech on 'Why women should be socialists' that she wanted to pose a challenge to the sexual division of labour which most SDFers took for granted. She protested that 'Women had, unfortunately, always been taught that politics are for men only, and that it was not for them to bother about what party was in power, but that their place was at home looking after purely domestic concerns.'[98] In her eyes, and indeed in her own experience, women had the potential to be socialist activists. It was not women's capabilities but branch practices and individual attitudes which inhibited women's involvement in the SDF. The Circle therefore attempted to reach a wide range of women, inviting Liberals and Tories as well as Socialists[99] to their meetings. It also staged a debate with Liberal women on 'Is Socialism desirable?'[100] The Circle saw itself in the business of argument and persuasion, rather than following the

---

[96] Northampton Pioneer, September 1905, p. 10; October 1905, p. 13.
[97] Northampton Pioneer, December 1907, p. 2.
[98] Northampton Pioneer, July 1905, p. 4.
[99] Northampton Pioneer, October 1909. p. 10.
[100] Northampton Pioneer, March 1908, p. 6; April 1908, p. 3; Justice, 7 March 1908.

patronising view of sweetening socialism for women's consumption. To this end, education was an important aspect of the Circle's purpose.

Northampton, like other Circles, sought to achieve a balance between a social and educational content within its activities. It organised teas, socials and dances on its own behalf and for the branch. Through these activities, bazaar work and the sale of tea to the membership, the Circle raised money for its piano fund as well as for the local needs of the branch.[101] A further aspect of the social purpose of the Circle, which related to the way in which education was conducted, was that it provided members with much valued mutual support. Women spoke positively of contact with other women through the Circle, and of how much they could learn from one another.[102] As one member explained, 'a few members of the Social Democratic Federation started the Women's Circle with the idea of getting women into closer touch with each other, of teaching them to act and work in harmony and, above all, of enabling them to educate themselves in the principles of Socialism'.[103] This view of the Circle as enabling women was much more positive than the images which *Justice* endorsed.

The early pre-eminence of Northampton's educational programme cut against the grain of the national trend. The Circle had papers on a variety of subjects such as: the effect of alcohol on the brain and nervous system; nationalisation of the railways; child slavery; domestic folklore; motherhood; municipalisation; and electioneering.[104] The male secretary of the branch, W. F. Moss, also gave a paper entitled 'A Message to Women', which was reprinted in the *Pioneer*. He commented favourably on the Circle's activities but called for more women to become involved in the work of the branch.[105] Male SDFers in Northampton were no different from their counterparts in the rest of the country in seeing the Circles as training grounds for full party membership.

The Circle also concerned itself with the suffrage. Admiration for the determination of the suffragettes was expressed, despite doubts about their methods.[106] In 1909, despite national antipathy between the two organisations, the Circle invited a speaker from the WSPU to give a lecture.[107] It also sent a representative to the National Conference on Adult Suffrage and Other Political Reforms in 1908.[108] This interest in

[101] *Justice*, 19 March 1910; *Northampton Pioneer*, February 1909, p. 8.
[102] *Northampton Pioneer*, August 1906, p. 15.
[103] *Northampton Pioneer*, December 1907, p. 2.
[104] *Northampton Pioneer*, January 1908, p. 14; *Justice*, 20 January 1906.
[105] *Northampton Pioneer*, July 1906, pp. 2–3.
[106] *Northampton Pioneer*, August 1906, p. 15.
[107] *Northampton Pioneer*, November 1909, p. 11.
[108] *Justice*, 1 August 1908.

suffrage did not mean that the Circle argued for a separatist position; rather, it took a similar view to the socialist women of the Second International, that is 'every woman has a like duty and right to work for the emancipation not of her own sex only, but of the whole working class'.[109] Such a positive interpretation of the woman question was not always argued, let alone practised, within the SDF.

What did all this imply for the relationship between the Circle and the branch? As we have already seen, the branch gave publicity to the Circle. Clearly, support was also evident in W. F. Moss's speech to the Circle. This was conceived principally in terms of the Circle's 'usefulness' to the branch, of women fitting themselves for office, as well as being informed by the traditional concern that without a Circle women might hinder their husbands' work for socialism. This kind of support did not constrain the Circle's activities; but neither did it mean that there was any understanding of Circle members' perception of their group as a means of enabling women.

Nevertheless, the branch was willing to discuss the woman question, and it even asked the Circle to lead a meeting for the branch on 'The Emancipation of Women'. The opening paper by Miss Sale dealt in a confident and fairly sophisticated manner with many of the salient issues of the woman question.[110] The branch also invited a significant number of women speakers to address its public meetings, again indicating an interest in women's issues while providing positive role models for their own female membership. Women speakers included Mrs Despard, Mabel Hope, Kathleen Kough, Mrs Bridges Adams, Maud Ward and Mrs Boyce, while Zelda Kahan and Margaretta Hicks spoke for nearby Rushden and Higham Ferrers SDF. These were almost all the women available on the SDF lecturing circuit. Many of these speeches were reported at length in the *Northampton Pioneer*, such as Mabel Hope's on 'Socialism, Woman and the Home'.[111] Overall, this evidence suggests that the woman question was viewed less ambivalently at a local level in the SDF than the impression given in *Justice* of the national party.

Finally, given that the purpose of the Circles was ultimately to bring women to socialism and specifically to the SDF, how successful were efforts in Northampton? For about four years the Circle seems to have managed to keep a high profile as an educational group for women within Northampton's socialist and labour movement. At the Annual Conference of the Women's Circles, Northampton always presented a

[109] Ibid.
[110] *Northampton Pioneer*, March 1909, pp. 6–7.
[111] *Northampton Pioneer*, June 1907, p. 7. See appendix 5 for a brief biography of Mabel Hope.

positive picture of its work, and it clearly influenced women in the surrounding areas as Circles were soon established at Wellingborough and at Rushden.[112] Such influence was not just in one direction, for Northampton gained from participating in the SDF's national network of Women's Circles. For example, the Northampton delegate to the 1908 Annual Conference of the Women's Circles told her sister members on her return that the conference was a very positive experience. She reported that 'a feeling of unity and sympathy, was the dominant note of the conference'. Indeed, that, 'To a humble worker in the Socialist cause it is something of an inspiration to come in touch with those stronger spirits, who, in spite of opposition and ridicule, of disappointment and apparent defeat, have yet worked on bravely for so many years'.[113] This is a reminder of the benefits that Circle members drew from their participation in these women's groups; of mutual support and inspiration, as well as education.

It is also a reminder that Northampton was more fortunate than many other, more short-lived, Circles, let alone those areas where women were too few or faced such opposition or indifference that they were unable to organise at all. But not even Northampton's good fortune continued indefinitely, for by 1910 it reported to the Women's Conference that it was finding it increasingly difficult to get women to attend meetings.[114] This may have been because branch effort was going into the first of the two general elections of that year; the Circle was suspended in order for election work to go on.[115] However, it would be unwise to draw too hasty a conclusion regarding the health of the Women's Circle alone, for this period seems to have been one of setbacks for the branch as a whole. The votes for the SDF candidates, Gribble and Quelch, were considerably fewer than the 1906 socialist vote,[116] and the SDF's candidates were defeated in the 1910 elections to the Northampton Board of Guardians. The *Northampton Pioneer* talked of a 'state of disappointment and apathy among the members of the revolutionary party'.[117] These setbacks must have affected the members of the Circle just as much as the branch, and might account for the fact that after 1910 the Northampton Circle was no longer

---

[112] For Wellingborough Women's Circle (1906–11) see E. Corley, 'Wellingborough Social Democratic Federation Women's Section', manuscript, National Museum of Labour History, TM 2066, 1955. Like its sister Circle in Northampton, the activities of Wellingborough were frequently reported in the *Northampton Pioneer*, as were those of the much less secure Rushden Circle.

[113] *Northampton Pioneer*, May 1908, p. 12.

[114] *Justice*, 19 March 1910.

[115] *Northampton Pioneer*, December 1909, p. 7.

[116] F. W. S. Craig, *British Parliamentary Election Results, 1885–1918*, p. 159.

[117] *Northampton Pioneer*, April 1910, p. 3.

listed in *Justice*'s 'Women's Directory'. If this was the case, it shows how closely the fortunes of the branch and Circle were linked, as well as the degree to which such groups depended upon the optimism, enthusiasm, commitment and energy of their members. It was always likely that the Circle would have been the first casualty, as ultimately the priority was to keep the branch going. Certainly, Northampton SDF did continue, later becoming Northampton BSP: but the women's organisation did not revive.

The practical implications of the SDF's understanding of the woman question

As we have seen in part 3, the SDF's understanding of the woman question had direct ramifications for the ways in which women were conceptualised as potential members of the party; for the roles they took in the party; and for the support that the party gave to women's self-organisation. There was therefore a direct relationship between the SDF's theory and practice on these issues, even though the former was particularly ambivalent. Ambivalence and the absence of any clear policy can in their own way set a framework for practice, just as the certainties of party policy do so more obviously. For although there seemed to be no clear criteria for a 'correct' position on the woman question, discussion revealed a hidden agenda. The most persistent and powerful voices within the party were able to create the appearance of an unofficial party position which easily became accepted by others as an official position. Yet when this was questioned, the party could, and did, deny any official line: essentially, the woman question remained for the SDF a matter of individual conscience. This tension between official agnosticism and conservative assumptions severely affected the party's attitude to women. This in turn shaped women's involvement in the SDF.

Although there was a policy vacuum around women, this did have the advantage of enabling women in the SDF to voice their views and their criticisms. They could do this because the woman question was marginal. But marginality also brought a certain level of frustration. A woman might be able to say what she thought, but as the issues were regarded as irresolvable, discussions were often curtailed, either by the editor of *Justice*, or by women themselves, who seem to have felt that extended debate was fruitless. Frustration also existed because the open-ended nature of theoretical debate appeared to offer no means of changing the party's practice. Thus, for example, women's perceptions of the barriers to their participation in the SDF were often aired within the party press, but the party was incapable of agreeing a policy on the woman question which would enable it to take the necessary corrective action. The only possible motor for change was the pragmatic need for women to be part of the socialist project; this might spur the party to overcome its reluctance to take action. Yet despite acknowledging a need to win over at least the 'problematic' socialist's wife and, more broadly, working-class women as a whole, the party was unable to recognise that its model of politicisation was essentially a male one. This created a very ambivalent message for women. On the one hand, they were represented as conservative, trivial and apathetic; yet, on the other, admonished for not taking a more active and positive part in socialist politics. There was certainly little consideration given to the question of what incentive women needed to join the SDF.

The absence of any official policy on the woman question meant that women's roles within the party, with some particular exceptions, tended to be in the background and supportive. Women were rarely activists in their own right. This was hardly surprising given the practical restrictions on women's use of time, which for many could hardly be called their own. This restriction was reinforced by the more widespread contemporary conceptions of what was appropriate for women, from which SDFers were not exempt. It was therefore easier for many women, practically and conventionally, to take on an auxiliary role rather than that of the activist. Those women who did become SDF activists were exceptional in terms of personality and circumstances; they either had a supportive SDF family, an independent income, or few domestic responsibilities. In this sense women's role in the SDF was not significantly different from women's experience in other contemporary socialist parties, or, indeed, in subsequent socialist organisations.

Education, a crucial aspect of the SDF's model of politicisation, was seen as the means to 'prepare' women for party membership. Such preparation could be interpreted narrowly in the interests of the party as creating a socialist's wife who was no longer a brake on her husband's activism. It could also be seen – by women themselves – as a means to building confidence, enabling them to make full use of their party membership. It took time before the need to educate, even in the narrower sense, was recognised by the party.

Early steps to women's self-organisation were not focused on women's education but on women's auxiliary function. Without any central organisation these pre-1900 women's groups had no agreed general function for the party. They merely existed, briefly, in relation to particular branches and therefore did not constitute the women's organisation for the SDF as a whole. It was only in the second stage of women's self-organisation that the issue of its function for the national party was made explicit and the question of education tackled more systematically. The Women's Socialist Circles were initially few in number and took on both social and educational roles. The former was all that was expected by many male SDFers of any group of women associated with the party. Yet with an increase in the number of Circles came a greater self-confidence and coherence as a national organisation of women. The newly formed Women's Education Committee concentrated on the education of female Social Democrats in a much more systematic fashion than hitherto. But the WEC and the Circles were working against the grain of the party, for the assumptions of many of their male comrades were still tied to the existing sexual division of labour and a restricted vision of women's capacities and potential.

For the party, the success of the Circles was measured in terms of their ability to bring forward women for recruitment, rather than the encouragement of more active female participation in the SDF itself. Women, in other words, were to fit in with the party rather than the party accommodate women's needs. In this the SDF was no different from other parties of the Second International. Women organising within them were also forced to weigh the pros and cons of autonomy from or incorporation within the parent party. The former meant marginalisation from the party's power structure and resources, while the latter cost women's self-organisation dearly. Certainly SDF women's eventual recognition within the party structure did give them some access to the organisation's meagre resources. But this was at the price of control over their own organisation, for the WEC was elected by the full (male and female) membership of the party.

Nevertheless, the women who took part in the Circles seem to have viewed them as an opportunity for mutual education and support on their own terms. This gave them the space to build up individual self-confidence as well as confidence as a group. In that sense, the Circles were more important to their members than they were to the party as a whole. But as organisations of Social Democrat women, they were always constrained in their effect on the party. This was not helped by the SDF's unwillingness to insist that all branches addressed their own responsibility for the failure to recruit women in large numbers. For if each branch had had to form a Circle of its own there would have been a symbolic recognition of the neglect of women as well as an opportunity to organise them systematically in relation to the party.

It must remain a matter for speculation whether this of itself would have produced a dynamic organisation of socialist women able to affect the practice of the parent party. Subsequent women's sections within socialist and labour organisations have been expected to fulfill an auxiliary function. Only when the theoretical assumptions which underlie these expectations are challenged can socialist women's self-organisation become anything more than that achieved by SDF women earlier this century. For it seems that organisation for socialist women is still constrained in part by the lack of consensus on the complexity of the theoretical relationship between class and gender.

Conclusion

So who were the 'equivocal feminists'? Not the women of the SDF. Although all were principally socialists, many also held views and organised around issues which we can recognise as feminist. It does not matter that they never identified themselves as such. The polarisation of socialism and feminism, inherent in the socialist construction of the woman question, meant that no Second International socialist could ever adopt such a label. But, I repeat, my argument is that it was not the women who were equivocal feminists: it was the SDF itself, as an organisation, which equivocated. The socialist construction of the woman question is an equivocation over feminism.

I have argued that SDFers' practice on issues which related to women, and the party's practice toward women and their self-organisation, were circumscribed by their understanding of the woman question. The party's theory bore a direct relationship to its practice, and to explore either in isolation would be to produce a partial and therefore misleading picture. The fact that this theory was deeply ambiguous set the framework for the SDF's particular and often ambivalent practice in relation to women. This ambiguity derived from the work of the founding fathers, Engels and Bebel, and in particular from their use of the muddy concept of the sex/class analogy. Its effect was reinforced by the SDF's conception of socialism as essentially economic. Together, these two elements ensured that the woman question joined other 'conscience' issues, on the margins of socialism. But unlike the 'conscience' issues of religion or teetotalism, the marginality of this question affected more than a vocal minority: it concerned a whole sex and their relationship to the allegedly universal emancipatory ideology, socialism.

As we have seen, the SDF's own understanding of the woman question was that there could be no official party policy. This produced considerable ambivalence within the party on a wide range of issues concerning women. Any view could be voiced, however extreme, and without a party policy there was no means to censure those whose views might be detrimental to women's participation in the SDF. Yet an 'unofficial' view did come to dominate on many issues. Despite an open policy toward matters of 'conscience', the distribution of power within the party favoured the patriarchal views of the leadership, and particular men amongst it, at the expense of the rank and file, specifically women. This suited the leadership well. Bax and the Tattler could set the tone of the SDF's discussions on the woman question. But when these appeared too reactionary and caused embarrassment, the official lack of policy was trumpeted. The SDF's understanding of the woman question also meant that there was no basis for a concerted challenge by dissidents to the appearance of a party view.

Nevertheless, the SDF's understanding of the woman question did allow socialist women to explore women's issues and women's self-organisation. But such space was gained at the price of marginality, and some frustration. This problem related directly to the most fundamental aspect of the woman question, namely the relationship between class and sex. The woman question was socialists' answer to feminism; as the SDF recognised, socialism had to gain the support and understanding of women as well as men if it were to succeed.

The irony of SDFers' understanding of the sex/class analogy was that having recognised sex oppression, it was immediately dissolved into class oppression. The consequence was not only that the struggle for socialism could be represented as the fight for women's liberation, but also that participation in the class struggle was all that any socialist need do to address women's needs and interests. This was interpreted in a number of different ways. For example, some concluded that women did not actually have any separate interests from those of the class. On the other hand, it was also argued, drawing on the work of the founding fathers, that women had a special place *within* socialism. In either instance, 'sex' effectively disappeared as a distinctive political category. It was either subsumed within class to the point of invisibility or, when it existed as a category within class, the latter remained pre-eminent. One principle dominated: sex must not be allowed to divide the working class. Feminism was therefore characterised as 'bourgeois' while socialism, it was asserted, would meet the aspirations of proletarian women for emancipation.

Socialist women concurred in this overall analysis, although they gave it their own emphases, in woman-centred politics and practice. But when it came to such issues as the suffrage and women's work, the tensions inherent in the SDF's accommodation between class and sex became apparent. Similarly the practical question of women's self-organisation within the party also exposed the fragile nature of the socialist construction of the woman question and the underlying fear of women's separatism.

Women within the SDF had to formulate for themselves a view on the inter-relationship between sex and class. The party's understanding of the woman question gave them the space to practise a woman-centred socialism, if they so chose. But this could only be an individual solution. At an organisational level, the woman question remained a marginal matter whose resolution would have to wait for a future society.

Although my exemplar has been the SDF, I have suggested throughout that its particular theory and practice regarding the woman question should not be understood in terms of the stereotype of the SDF. The party's apparent ambivalence on the woman question has too often been interpreted in terms of the idiosyncratic views of a few male SDFers, such as Bax. Yet it is the socialist construction of the woman question – which the SDF shared with the rest of the Second International – that framed the party's own understanding of the question. This theory gave 'permission' to Bax and others to be, at worst, misogynists, and, more often, to stereotype women and their potential, whilst remaining indisputably 'socialists'. My argument does not put these SDF men beyond criticism: but, more importantly, it makes a more general and telling point about the nature of socialism as an ideology, particularly in its Second International form. It is a misunderstanding of the SDF and the relationship between its theory and practice to dismiss the party as 'anti-feminist'. The party officially equivocated. It did so *because of* the ambiguous theory of the founding fathers and the Second International's economistic definition of socialism.

Could the SDF's understanding of the woman question have taken another form, making a reality of a socialism committed to taking practical steps to end sexist society? This can only be a matter of speculation. But it is significant that not only were key theorists of the woman question male but so too was much of the SDF. These men reflected the patriarchal assumptions of the dominant culture. So too did those leading socialist women who shared a commitment to the socialist construction of the woman question. If the SDF had had a largely female party membership, this might have made a difference in terms of the experience of the politics of the SDF. But it would not have affected the status of the woman question unless there were a challenge to the whole theory on which it was based. There were clearly significant, individual differences between socialists over how they reacted to feminist issues in their personal and party politics. Yet there seems to have been no attempt to challenge the sexism embedded in the heart of the Second International's theory of socialism. From the beginning there was only space within the SDF, and indeed within socialism, for women who kept their feminism within 'acceptable' bounds. They could develop a woman-centred socialism for themselves: but they were not empowered to challenge the theoretical content of socialism itself. It was all the more ironic that women's marginality was itself an almost inevitable corollary of the socialist construction of the woman question. Feminism remained an optional extra for socialists.

Although this book focuses on a specific socialist party in a particular historical period, it has ramifications for socialism generally, as well as echoes for contemporary socialist women. For many orthodox socialists the ambiguity at the heart of the socialist construction of the woman question remains unscathed by feminist critique. The theoretical inadequacy of socialism in relation to gender remains. Until it is revised, all feminist socialists can achieve will be change at the margins.

For socialist women today, some of the issues of personal practice which SDF women highlighted – such as the use of male language – are gradually being changed. But a few 'chairpersons' and the curbing of sexist language does not of itself open up socialism to the perennial issues which SDFers discussed and evaded a hundred years ago. It remains hard to get 'women's issues' taken seriously by party members, irrespective of their sex or particular socialist commitments. The label 'women's issue' usually implies marginality.[1]

Take one example, the Labour Party. Although it is an organisation whose socialism has long been disputed, it remains a major arena in which individual socialists choose to work. During the 1980s, women who worked in the Labour Party faced many of the same problems as their predecessors in the SDF. If 'free love' was the archetypal 'conscience' issue for SDFers, abortion was the 'conscience' issue of recent years.[2] Labour Party women discovered, as had SDF women before them, that party discipline could not be imposed on an issue

[1]   See Jeff Rodriguez's comments on the labour movement he is part of, in 'Mending the Broken Heart of Socialism: A Roundtable Discussion' in R. Chapman and J. Rutherford (eds.), *Male Order: Unwrapping Masculinity*, Lawrence and Wishart, 1988, pp. 249–71, especially pp. 257, 264.

[2]   See J. Lovenduski, 'Parliament, Pressure Groups, Networks and the Women's Movement: The Politics of Abortion Law Reform in Britain (1967–83)' in J. Lovenduski and J. Outshoorn, *The New Politics of Abortion*, Sage, 1986, particularly pp. 60–3; Phillips, *Divided Loyalties*, pp. 117–19; S. Rowbotham, *The Past Is Before Us: Feminism in action since the 1960s*, Penguin, 1990, ch. 4, especially pp. 66-7; J. Lovenduski and V. Randall, *Contemporary Feminist Politics: Women and Power in Britain*, Oxford University Press, Oxford, 1993, pp. 221–4, 244–51. In the past the Labour Party has had an even wider perception of 'conscience' issues to the chagrin of some of its women members, see Minutes of Manchester Labour Party Women's Advisory Committee, 1 April 1935.

defined as one of 'conscience'. Moreover, just as SDF women were unable to reshape their party's campaign around unemployment to incorporate the issue of women's right to work, so in the early 1980s feminist critiques of Labour's economic policy[3] never really affected the content of the issue. Equally the marginalisation of women's self-organisation from decision-making within the party was still a key issue for many Labour Party women just as it was for SDF women before them. For example, the Women's Action Committee put strenuous efforts into the campaign to empower the women's conference and win 'democracy for women' *within* the Labour Party.[4] Although the language may have changed, there remains a sense that socialist women today hear the same message that SDF women heard from their party; that women were a problem for socialism and that they should fit in with it rather than socialism reform to meet women's needs.

Besides these echoes there are also differences. The most important is the presence today of a developed and wide-ranging women's movement influenced by socialism and, in turn, affecting socialists, directly and indirectly. But socialist-feminists remain caught between two move-ments and have sought a number of ways to resolve the perennial problem of the relationship between sex and class. Individual women have found their own, often tortuous, path through a debate which can never be purely academic. This is apparent in the discussion on the state of socialist-feminism that *Feminist Review* hosted in 1986.[5] Amongst the participants, some had rejected earlier attempts, including their own, to reconcile socialism and feminism as an adequate single theory. Michèle Barrett argued that 'we should recognise the different theoretical objectives of Marxism and feminism. It is far more important for us to understand the ways in which class is, in a profound way, gendered, and to argue for a socialism that is informed by feminism'.[6] Anne Phillips took this further and, as a previously self-defined socialist-feminist, said 'I would describe myself now as influenced by Marxism, or as basically agreeing with the marxist analysis of the capitalist mode of production, but I have reached a point where it just does not help to say I am a Marxist or that I am a Marxist feminist'.[7] Like many other feminists, she

---

[3]   See, for example, A. Phillips, *Hidden Hands: Women and Economic Policies*, Pluto, 1983.
[4]   Sarah Roelofs in 'The Women's Movement and the Labour Party: An Interview with Labour Party Feminists', *Feminist Review*, 16, 1984, p. 78; A. Pettifor, 'Labour's Macho Tendency', *New Socialist*, September 1985, p. 41. See also A .Coote and P. Pattullo, *Power and Prejudice: Women and Politics*, Weidenfeld and Nicolson, 1990, pp. 182–6.
[5]   'Feminism and Class Politics: A Round-Table Discussion', *Feminist Review*, 23, 1986, pp. 13–30.
[6]   Ibid., p. 18.
[7]   Ibid., p. 19.

had found that the complexity of the relationship between class and sex, and indeed between these and race, had made labels such as socialist-feminist inadequate to the reality of practical woman-focused politics.

In contrast, others in this discussion remained committed to making socialism the principal arena of their political work. Some were much more critical than others. Thus Beatrix Campbell felt that 'in the socialist movement we are struggling with a hundred years of history in which there has been constant conflict between the interests of men and women'.[8] Yet like many of the SDF women before her, she did not want to move outside her commitment to class politics; unlike them she was, at this point, much more self-consciously a feminist seeking to 'gender' the politics of her then party, the Communist Party of Great Britain. Nevertheless there are still socialist women who make a spirited defence of the classic socialist construction of the woman question. Elizabeth Wilson, for instance, went onto the offensive against feminist critics of socialism, 'I do not understand why people are socialists if they have nothing good to say about the socialist tradition. One has to look at the relation between feminism and socialism as a two-way street and say that in some ways the socialist tradition has things to teach feminism'.[9] This debate shows socialist-feminism to be a contentious position, contested from within both socialism and feminism.

Yet feminists continue to work within the Labour Party and the Left, trying to negotiate their own accommmodation between sex and class. For them the debate on the relationship between sex and class and the way in which socialism constructs the category of 'woman' is of daily relevance. Yet socialist-feminism, as the site of this confrontation between socialism and feminism, has seemed almost irrelevant in recent academic feminism, particularly as some of its earlier proponents have increasingly come under the influence of post-structuralism. It is striking that in Britain the term socialist-feminist is now often used apologetically, if at all. For example, Lynne Segal has complained: 'I belong to a once healthy but now dying species – the socialist-feminist ... It is now all right to be a socialist and a feminist, in these times of fashionable pluralism. It is not all right to insist upon the hyphen, to seek a more unitary political identity and purpose'.[10] *Feminist Review*, which used to

---

[8]   Ibid,. p. 24.

[9]   Ibid. See also the elaboration of her position in E. Wilson and A. Weir, *Hidden Agendas: Theory, Politics and Experience in the Women's Movement*, Tavistock, 1986, particularly parts I and II.

[10]   L. Segal, 'Slow Change or No Change?: Feminism, Socialism and the Problem of Men', *Feminist Review*, 31, 1989, p. 6; also, from a slightly different perspective, C. Cockburn, 'Masculinity, the Left and Feminism' in R. Chapman and J. Rutherford (eds.), *Male Order*, pp. 303–29.

describe itself as socialist-feminist, has now become a 'feminist journal' still interested in 'rethinking the vocabularies of socialism and class' but recognising a diversity of feminisms.[11] The debate, it appears, has moved elsewhere.

Yet can we really afford to let matters rest as they are? Has the attempt to resolve the sex and class debate been resolved once again into sex or class? Is the Second International's construction of the woman question alive and well in different times, fuelled as much by feminists who have tired of the fight as the socialists who still cling to the excuse that the woman question really is a matter of conscience? Some feminist commentators seem optimistic about the extent to which the labour movement has accommodated feminist principles.[12] But probably more would agree with Sheila Rowbotham's judgement that with feminists joining the Labour Party in the 1980s, 'a separatist politics was grafted on to labourism with some curious results ... this has resulted not in a challenge to interpretations of socialism as a whole ... but in a split between Labour 'politics' and 'women's issues'.[13] Have all women concluded that socialist-feminism is a cul-de-sac? Anne Phillips called her book on the dilemma of sex and class, *Divided Loyalties*, and has written of her own feelings of schizophrenia in relation to socialism and feminism while Cynthia Cockburn writes of 'a tension amounting almost to an impossibility in the lives of feminists within the left'.[14] These tensions seem to have produced a much more fragmented and less self-confident socialist-feminism squeezed between a socialism, where masculinity remains unproblematised, and feminisms, where concern about difference is pre-eminent and the category of 'woman' itself problematic. Each ideology has become more slippery in a time when any form of generalisation has become deeply unfashionable.

With the fall of the Berlin Wall and the particular impact of the issues raised by identity politics, let alone with the shadow cast by 'post-modernism' within the academy, both socialism and feminism are now labels whose meanings are contested to the point where many whose sympathies remain within this broad area feel they cannot now use the name socialist-feminist.[15] Ellen Du Bois is an exception to this trend.

---

[11] 'Editorial', *Feminist Review*, 45, 1993, p. 3; 'Editorial', *Feminist Review*, 40, 1992, pp. 3–4.
[12] Lovenduski and Randall, *Contemporary Feminist Politics*, pp. 353, 356.
[13] Rowbotham, *The Past Is Before Us*, p. 254.
[14] Phillips, *Divided Loyalties*, p. 161; Cockburn, 'Masculinity, the Left and Feminism', p. 304. Also see N. Hart, 'Gender and the Rise and Fall of Class Politics', *New Left Review*, 175, 1989, pp. 19–47.
[15] C. Cockburn, 'The European Forum of Socialist Feminists: Talking on the Volcano', *Women's Studies International Forum*, 15, 1, 1992, pp. 53–6.

She acknowledges the tension between socialism and feminism, but sees it as having a positive outcome. For her, 'contemporary socialist-feminists reside at the point of the hyphen, tolerating the tension between socialism and feminism and making of it a creative and powerful progressive politics'.[16] It is interesting that this is the optimistic, even naive, voice of an American, for it is striking that in Britain the 1990s has seen little engagement in print with the debate on sex and class. This does not, of course, mean that this debate, in its contemporary and in its historical versions, is not relevant to women's politics today. The concerns of the 1980s may have influenced some of the questions we now ask and how we ask them, but if they mean that we no longer consider it relevant to explore the relationship between socialism and feminism, then we abandon many women in their current political battles. We also cease to envision even the possibility of a future society which could be both socialist and feminist. For those women who place themselves, however critically, on the Left, there clearly still is much to do in making the argument for a socialism infused by feminism, as the pragmatic politics of the 1990s continue to marginalise the woman question.

This book emphasises that women have tried before to find a woman-focused socialism. Women in the SDF were remarkably creative in their political work and confronted the patronising and patriarchal assumptions of so many of their male comrades with persistence and courage. They were pioneers, for they were part of the first confrontation of organised socialism and organised feminism. Despite being constrained by the socialist construction of the woman question, SDF women found their own space within the party where they raised many uncomfortable issues for their comrades. But they did not challenge socialist theory itself. They did expose some of the limitations of socialist practice and the ramifications for potential and actual socialist women. Yet, as this book has demonstrated, despite an apparent commitment to sexual equality, socialism as a theory remained deeply flawed. For although it is apparently gender-blind, it is certainly not gender-neutral.

The SDF's theory and practice around the woman question has lessons for socialists, particularly for feminists organising within socialist parties. In this respect there are continuities between Second International socialism and socialism today. Many socialists remain equivocal feminists, and they will remain so until the socialist construction of the woman question is thoroughly reformed and the complex inter-relationship between sex and class recognised at the heart of socialist theory.

[16]   E. C. Du Bois, 'Woman Suffrage and the Left: An International Socialist-Feminist Perspective', *New Left Review*, 186, 1991, p. 22.

| Appendix 1 | | *A comparison between women on the Executives of the SDF and the ILP* | | |

Date	SDF			ILP
1884	Eleanor Marx } Amie Hicks } Matilda Hyndman }	3		
1885	Helen Taylor } Amie Hicks } Edith Bland }	3		
1886		0		
1887		0		
1888		0		
1889		0		
1890		0		
1891		0		
1892		0		
1893		0	1	Katherine S. J. Conway
1894		0	0	
1895	Edith Lanchester	1	1	Enid Stacy
1896	Edith Lanchester[R] } Mary Gray }	2	2	{ Enid Stacy { Caroline Martyn[D]
1897	Mary Gray	1	1	Mrs Bell
1898	Mary Gray	1	1	Emmeline Pankhurst
1899	Mary Gray	1	0	
1900	Mary Gray	1	0	
1901	Mary Gray	1	0	
1902	Mary Gray } Clara Hendin }	2	0	
1903	Dora Montefiore } Clara Hendin }	2	1	Isabella Ford
1904	Dora Montefiore[R]	1	2	{ Emmeline Pankhurst { Isabella Ford
1905	Rose Jarvis	1	1	Isabella Ford
1906	Rose Jarvis	1	2	{ Emmeline Pankhurst { Isabella Ford
1907		0	1	Margaret McMillan
1908	Dora Montefiore	1	1	Margaret McMillan
1909	Dora Montefiore	1	0	
1910		0	0	

[R] resigned during term
[D] died during term

Sources: SDF Conference Reports, ILP Conference Reports.

Appendix 2   *A comparison between women delegates at SDF and ILP Annual Conferences*

Date	SDF				ILP			
	No.	%	with husbs.	women speaker	No.	%	with husbs.	women speaker
1893					3	2.6	1	
1894	2?	4.9	–	2	2?	2.1	–	–
1895					7	8.2	4	5
1896				1	6	5.9	2	3
1897				0	5	5.0	0	3
1898				0	6	6.6	2	4
1899				0	4	4.1	1	1
1900	3	5.1	2	0	1	1.3	1	1
1901	2	3.4	1	0	7	9.5	3	3
1902					5	4.9	1	5
1903	0	0	–	0	6	5.3	1	3
1904	2	2.8		1	7	6.4	3	3
1905	5	9.0	1	0	13	8.5	2	5
1906	4	4.9	-	1	13	8.7	2	8
1907	6	6.5	2	2	15	6.7	4	3
1908	7	5.0	1	3	25	8.9	3	5
1909	12	8.3	5	4	28	8.8	9	5
1910				0	31	9.7	11	6

No.   number of women delegates.
%   women as a percentage of all delegates.
with husbs.   number of women delegates whose husbands also attended as Conference delegates.
women speaker   number of women delegates who spoke at the Conference.

Sources: SDF Conference Reports, ILP Conference Reports.

Appendix 3   *A graph of the number of local Women's Socialist Circles, 1904–11.*

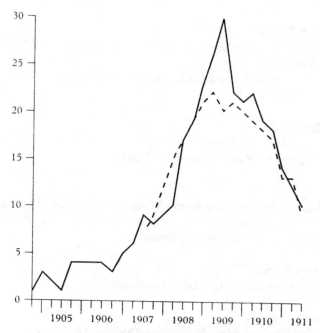

— the number of Circles calculated from references in *Justice*

--- the number of Circles claimed at Women's Conferences and in the Women's Directory in *Justice*.

Source: Justice.

Appendix 4   *SDP Women's Education Committee syllabus of subjects for discussion, 1910–11*

Rent:
Sir F. Pollock, *Land Laws.*
F. Seebohm, *English Village Community: Its Relation to the Manorial and Tribal Systems.*
A. R. Wallace, *Land Nationalisation: Its Necessity and Aim.*

Food:
Public Health Acts
G. How, *To-Day's Work,* 6d.
R. Hutchinson, *Food and Principles of Dietetics.*

Taxes:
F. W. Hayes, *Those Wretched Rates,* Fabian pamphlet, 1d.
G. J. Goschen, *Taxation: Reports and Speeches on Local Taxation.*
B. Anderson, *Local Taxation and Finance.*

Regulations for health:
Lawrence Gomme, *Powers of Local Government.*

Sanitation and baths:
Tenants Sanitary Catechism, Fabian pamphlet 68, 1d.
M. N. Baker, *Municipal Engineering and Sanitation.*

Laundries:
Women Laundry Workers and Legislation, WIC.
Life in the Laundry, Fabian pamphlet, 1d.

Maintenance for mothers:
School for Mothers, 1s.
Miss Murby, *Commonsense of the Woman Question,* 6d.

Care of young children:
Women's Cooperative Guild, *Waste of Infant Life,* 1d.
Mrs Townshend, *The Case for School Nurseries.*
Victor Fisher, *The Modern Moloch.*
Aimée Spencer, *Articles in Women Folk.*

State maintenance of school children:
J. H. Watts, *State Maintenance.*

E. R. Hartley, *Bradford Experiments*.

M. Hicks, *The State and its School Children*, articles in *Social Democrat*, May and June.

J. Richardson, *How it Can be Done*.

S. A. Harris, *School Clinics*.

M. McMillan, *New Life in Our School*.

Training and trades for boys and girls:
The Training of Girls, WIC, 1d.

N. Adler and R. H. Tawney, *Boy and Girl Labour*, 1d.

A. Blair, *Half-time: Present and Future*, 1d.

J. Richardson, *How it Can be Done*.

J. Richardson, *After Care Committees*.

Economy of work:
E. Carpeter, *Desirable Mansions*.

W. Morris, *News from Nowhere*.

School managers and care committees:
LCC Handbooks on School Managers and Care Committees.

Laws affecting women's labour:
Labour Laws for Women and Children for UK, WIC, 1d.

B. L. Hutchins, *Labour Laws for Women, Australia and New Zealand*.

J. O. Goldmark, *Labour Laws for Women, United States*, 1d.

B. L. Hutchins, *Labour Laws for Women, France*, 1d.

Alice Saloman, *Labour Laws for Women, Germany*, 1d.

Mrs Okey, *Labour Laws for Women, Italy*.

Appended is a list of useful books for reading and discussion:
H. Hobart, *Democratic Socialism*.

Z. Kahan, *Social-Democracy*.

H. Quelch, *Economics of Labour*.

E. R. Hartley, *Train Talks*.

L. Gronlund, *Co-operative Commonwealth*.

Higgenson, *Common-sense about Women*.

Crepaz, *Emancipation of Women*.

E. Bellamy, *Equality*.

May Walders, *Socialism and the Home*.

F. Eastwood, *Question Box*.

For advanced circle:
A. Bebel, *Woman.*
Untermann, *Marxian Economics.*
Engels, *Socialism: Utopian and Scientific.*
H. M. Hyndman, *England for All.*
H. Burrows, *Revolutionary Essays in Socialist Faith and Fancy.*
W. Morris and E. B. Bax, *Socialism: Its Growth and Outcome.*

(*Source: Justice,* 6 August 1910)

Appendix 5 *Short biographies of key figures*

ERNEST BELFORT BAX (1854–1926) was born into a non-conformist middle-class family. He joined the SDF's predecessor the Democratic Federation in 1882. Having read *Capital* in 1879, he published an account of Marx's writings in 1881 which was praised by Marx. Bax was part of the group, which also included Morris and the Avelings, that seceded from the SDF in December 1884 to form the Socialist League. He lectured and wrote for the League but returned to the SDF in 1888, before many of his ex-SDF comrades did likewise. From then on he was to be a significant figure in the SDF's leadership, briefly editing *Justice* in 1892. He does not seem to have been particularly concerned to participate in branch life and increasingly spent a proportion of his time abroad. He devoted himself to theoretical writings and studied to become a barrister in the 1890s. Bax lived on inherited income which he supplemented with journalism. Although generally a libertarian, Bax was renowned for his anti-feminism and anti-suffragism. He maintained his particular brand of socialism into the BSP, only leaving in 1916 with what was left of the 'old guard' to form the National Socialist Party. For one account of Bax's life and politics, see his autobiography, *Reminiscences and Reflexions of a Mid and Late Victorian*.

ANNIE BESANT (1847–1933) was involved with a wide range of political, religious and social causes in her long life. The socialist episode in her life was marked by membership of the Fabian Society (from June 1885) and by spirited campaigning for a wide range of socialist and labour causes. She worked very closely with the SDFer Herbert Burrows during these years, including the event for which she remains most famous, the Bryant and May matchgirls' strike of 1888. The practical involvement of the SDF in this campaign meant that this was also the year in which Annie Besant joined the SDF, undoubtedly influenced by Burrows. In 1888 she was also elected as an SDF candidate to the London School Board. Like other socialists she was interested in spiritualism but she took this further than most. As theosophy became increasingly dominant in her life, she broke with socialism, although not before attending with other SDFers the 1889 Possibilist Congress in Paris. Burrows had encouraged Annie to join the Theosophical Society, of which he was already a member, but unlike him she found she could not combine her theosophism with socialism. At the end of 1890 Annie Besant's energetic involvement with the socialist movement ended as she gave her life over to theosophy. The most recent biography of Annie Besant is A. Taylor, *Annie Besant*.

MARGARET BONDFIELD (1873-1953) was a member of the SDF, only later joining the ILP and becoming a stalwart of the Labour Party. The SDF is an aspect of her political career that Bondfield underplayed in her autobiography. Already the assistant secretary of the Shop Assistants Union, she joined the SDF soon after coming to London, in about 1890, under the influence of Amie Hicks and her family. She was very involved in the campaign for adult suffrage, particularly the ASS of which she was President until 1909. Around this time she became very active in the WLL. There is a pen portrait of Margaret Bondfield in *Woman Worker*, October 1907; see also M. Bondfield, *A Life's Work* and her entry in the *Dictionary of Labour Biography*, vol. 2, pp. 39–45.

EMMA BOYCE (1867–1929) first appears in *Justice* in 1907 as a member of Kingsland SDF whose speaking engagements prompt record collections. She was active in the Women's Circles and was a member of the Women's Committee. After topping the poll to the WEC in 1909, she was soon appointed the organiser for the committee. She retired from the WEC in October 1910 but carried on her involvement as a speaker and as a Circle activist into the BSP. Her political activism was sustained despite difficult personal circumstances: she had twelve children of whom only four survived. See K Weller, *'Don't Be A Soldier!' The Radical Anti-War Movement in North London 1914–18*, Journeyman Press, 1985, pp. 74–5, for Emma Boyce's later career in the East London Federation of Suffragettes/Workers' Socialist Federation during the First World War and then as a Hackney Labour councillor (1918–23).

HERBERT BURROWS (1845–1922) was the son of a Chartist and worked as a clerk in the Inland Revenue. He was a founding member of the Democratic Federation and a long time active SDFer. Burrows was the archetypal 'faddist', as he was teetotal, anti-tobacco, a vegetarian and a theosophist as well as being an advocate of women's rights. Despite being an important party speaker, his views placed him at a little distance from the 'old guard' who led the SDF. He was, for example, only a member of the Executive on four occasions. His advocacy of women's suffrage in the early years of the party and his support for women's employment rights, through the Women's Trade Union League and the Women's Industrial Council, placed him in a different strand of the party to Bax. Indeed, he was a leading opponent of Bax. Burrows wrote that Bax 'hates me almost as much as he hates women, and that is saying a great deal' (*Justice*, 26 March 1910). Burrows resigned from the party in 1911 over the issue of disarmament, which the SDF had failed to support. For a pen portrait of Burrows, see *Labour Annual*, 1895, p. 167.

CHARLOTTE DESPARD (1844–1939) only began her journey to socialism after she was widowed in 1890. She moved to Battersea and began to work amongst the local poor. After joining the SDF in 1895, she seems to have remained a party member despite Linklater's claim that she soon became disenchanted. She attended the London Congress of the Second International in 1896 as an SDF delegate. Up to 1906 there are references in *Justice* to her speaking at SDF meetings and demonstrations, at the Women's Committee and even permitting an outing of Westminster SDF to her 'delightful cottage in Oxshott' in September 1906. Mrs Wolstenholme Elmy also noted that in 1906 Mrs Despard was still working with the SDF and in the cause of adult suffrage. She was a member of the ASS until she resigned in 1906 to join (briefly) the WSPU. At this point her political affiliations are listed as ILP and SDF. Neither of her biographers give much space to Charlotte Despard's involvement with the SDF: A. Linklater, *An Unhusbanded Life*; M. Mulvihill, *Charlotte Despard: A Biography*, Pandora, 1989.

MARY GRAY was one of the most prominent woman SDFers in the 1890s and early 1900s. Although her background was lower middle class, from the age of fifteen she had lived the life of the working class. She had been in service and had then married in 1876 a stonemason and staunch trade unionist, Willie Gray. As a consequence of his trade unionism he was unemployed for considerable periods and the Grays, therefore, lived in great hardship until he learnt another trade. She joined the SDF in 1887 and was particularly active in setting up the first Socialist Sunday Schools; she was elected as an SDFer to Battersea Board of Guardians (1895–1901); she was active as an SDF speaker; and she served on the SDF Executive from 1896 to 1903. Mary Gray was concerned with women's politics and campaigned for universal suffrage and later joined the Battersea Women's Socialist Circle. For a pen portrait of Mary Gray, see *Social Democrat*, November 1899, pp. 323-5.

CLARA HENDIN was a long time activist in the SDF based in the Kensal Town branch. She held office at branch level as secretary, was a delegate to the London Congress of the Second International in 1896 and an SDF Executive member from 1902 to 1905. Her involvement in women's politics took a number of forms, including the Women's Cooperative Guild (at least from 1896) as well as the SDF Women's

Circles from their inception. She took part in a wide range of activities from the provision of refreshments and bazaar work to participation in the WEC and providing training for public speaking. In addition, she was also a member of the ASS as well as Honorary Secretary of the Socialist Women's Bureau, the British women's section of the Second International. She continued her activities in the BSP. Clara Hendin was married with at least one daughter.

AMIE HICKS (1839/40?–1917) was the daughter of a Chartist. She joined the Democratic Federation in 1883 with her husband and her daughter, Margaretta. As an active worker for the SDF, she was not only a speaker and stood for the London School Board but she was also a member of the SDF Executive in 1884 and 1885. She was always concerned about women, particularly their working conditions. Her influence and support was acknowledged by other women socialists and trade unionists such as Margaret Bondfield and Margaret MacDonald. Although she became less active in the SDF as her work increased on women's labour issues, she was still attending SDF events in 1907 and speaking at adult suffrage meetings. She had a direct link to the party through her daughter, Margaretta, with whom she lived in the latter part of her life. See her entry in the *Dictionary of Labour Biography*, vol. 4, pp. 89–92.

MARGARETTA HICKS was the daughter of Amie Hicks. Mother and daughter joined the Democratic Federation in 1883. Margaretta maintained her involvement in the party throughout its lifetime. She attended the Annual Conference and spoke there, lectured on public platforms and stood for the Board of Guardians on an SDF ticket in St Pancras in 1904. One of her main concerns was unemployed women and she was the Honorary Superintendent of the St Pancras (Unemployed) Workroom. She seems to have been particularly involved in her local community. Always interested in women's conditions, she became Chairman of WEC in 1910. Later she set up the women's paper, *The Link*, in 1911 and became the prime mover in the women's organisation of the BSP (the successor to the SDF). In 1914 she became the party's first woman organiser.

MABEL B. HOPE (1880–) became a socialist in 1897 and joined the Postal Telegraph Clerks' Association in 1901 and later became a full-time officer for the Women's Trade Union League. A WLL Executive member from 1906 to 1908, she spoke at the 1907 Labour Party Conference, as a representative of her union, on adult suffrage of which she was an assiduous advocate. But she also spoke for SDF branches. It is not clear if she was actually a member of the party although she certainly worked closely with individual SDFers and showed no reluctance to associate herself with the SDF as an organisation. There is a pen portrait of Mabel Hope in *Woman Worker*, May 1908.

ROSE JARVIS (SCOTT) was the daughter of a Baptist minister who educated his daughter himself. As an adult she worked in the temperance movement and did Christian and educational work in Wandsworth and then Tunbridge Wells. She was therefore used to speaking in public and convinced that women could make a contribution in the public sphere. Such a background was one shared by other feminists of her generation. Her conversion to socialism followed the SDF's model of politicisation in as much as her mind was opened to socialist ideas by a concern about the insanitary conditions of many of the houses she visited. She took action by exposing these conditions in a local paper and was threatened with libel action by landlords in Tunbridge Wells, but she refused to retract her statements. This brought her to the attention of progressives in the town including the local Social Democrats. At the same time she was attending a University Extension political economy class. One of her fellow students left a copy of *Justice* behind. She read it and bought socialist books advertised in it. Although she was asked to join the Women's Liberal Association, she decided to join the SDF. Her personal conversion was later reinforced by her marriage to Tom Jarvis, a fellow SDFer. Despite nursing her ailing husband she was active in the SDF cause, for example, standing for the London School Board in Hackney in 1894. She was nominated for the SDF Executive in 1895 and attended the 1896 International as an SDF delegate. Presumably she was also working to support herself and her terminally ill husband. After his death in 1903 she resumed a more prominent role in the movement from her home in Croydon, in particular by becoming a Poor Law Guardian in 1904. It is not clear what prompted her move to Northampton, but given that she had to resign from the Guardians after less than a year it clearly was not a long planned move and may have had something to do with her eventual marriage to the leading Northampton SDFer, Charles Scott. His niece believed that the pair had met when they were both on the Northampton Board of Guardians to which Rose Jarvis was elected in May 1906. It is far more likely that they had met earlier through the SDF and her visits to Northampton prior to her removal there. She was later to become the first woman to be elected to Northampton Town Council in 1920 but her work there was cut short by her death in 1923. For a portrait of Rose

Jarvis see *Northampton Pioneer*, May 1906, pp. 1–2. See also M. S. Robinson, 'A short history of my family who gave much of their lives to helping their fellow men and women, and to the furtherance of the cause of Socialism', manuscript, 1972, National Museum of Labour History, HF 476.

ZELDA KAHAN (1881–1967) was a graduate in chemistry and sister-in-law of the leading SDF theoretician, Theodore Rothstein. She herself was an active SDFer from at least 1906 when she first attended the party conference. As well as speaking for the party she was active in the WEC. She was particularly involved in the party debates on disarmament, taking a firm stand against Hyndman's national chauvinism. Later she became a member of the BSP Executive and of the Communist Party.

KATHLEEN B. KOUGH was an SDFer, at least from 1905 when she first attended the party conference. She was active in the SDF's women's organisation and was on the Women's Committee as well as being an active speaker for the party. She was particularly committed to adult suffrage and spoke and organised for the ASS. She is one of the SDF women pictured on the cover of D. B. Montefiore's, *Some Words to Socialist Women*.

EDITH LANCHESTER (1871–1966) was born into a prosperous middle-class family and attended university. Her teaching career was curtailed because of her politics and instead she learnt shorthand and typing, serving for a time as Eleanor Marx's secretary. After joining the SDF in 1892, she became a speaker at meetings and demonstrations and stood unsuccessfully for the School Board in Lambeth. She was elected to the SDF Executive in 1895. Later the same year the events known as the Lanchester Case made her, briefly, notorious (see chapter 4). She continued to be an active SDFer as an Executive member, resigning only when her first pregnancy was advanced. She also attended the London Congress of the Second International in 1896. After the birth of her two children, she was less in evidence on SDF platforms although there remain occasional references to her in *Justice* up to 1908. Her daughter remembers that she was involved with the WSPU and walked in Emily Davison's funeral march in 1913. Her daughter's memories of her mother are in E. Lanchester, *Elsa Lanchester Herself*.

ELEANOR MARX (AVELING) (1855–98) joined the Democratic Federation in 1883 and was on the SDF Executive from August to December 1894. Then, with, among others, William Morris, E. Belfort

Bax and Edward Aveling (her partner), she seceded from the SDF to
form the Socialist League. She was an energetic lecturer and journalist
for the Cause. Her wide knowledge of the international socialist movement, where she had extensive personal connections, coupled with her
skill at languages meant that she was often called upon to act as an
interpreter or translator. By 1896 Eleanor was reconciled with the SDF,
speaking for local branches and contributing a regular column to *Justice*.
She committed suicide in 1898. The most extensive biography of
Eleanor Marx remains Y. Kapp's two-volume *Eleanor Marx*.

DORA B. MONTEFIORE (1851–1933) was born into a large prosperous family in Surrey and was privately educated. She went to
Australia to be housekeeper to her elder brother and his family and there
met George Barrow Montefiore whom she married in 1879. He died
suddenly ten years later, leaving her with two young children. She
discovered on her husband's death that she had no rights of guardianship
towards her own children unless her husband had willed them to her.
This experience of 'sex disability' led her to meet other women in the
same position and to make the connection with the most obvious sex
disability, the lack of a vote. Dora became a campaigner for women's
suffrage in Australia and then later in England, and progressed through
Fawcett's Suffrage Society, the League of Practical Suffragists and later
the WSPU as she sought an organisation which reflected her evolving
politics. She was also part of a correspondence network of feminists
which centred on Elizabeth Wolstenholme Elmy. Gradually she realised
that the vote was not by itself sufficient and, having tried Liberal politics,
turned increasingly to socialism. She corresponded with Julia Dawson of
the *Clarion* and spent a fortnight doing propaganda work with the
Clarion van in 1898. It is not clear when she joined the SDF but by
1901 she was writing for their papers and by 1903 she was on the party
Executive. At the same time, she was an active suffragist. Her stand of
'no taxation without representation' led in 1906 to a six-week seige by
bailiffs of her Hammersmith home, known in the press as 'Fort
Montefiore'. A member of the WSPU until 1907, she then became
equally active for the ASS, becoming its Honorary Secretary in 1909.
She was also very active as an internationalist: attending international
socialist and suffrage congresses; using her domestic journalism to
publicise international developments in socialist politics and women's
rights; and sustaining her international contacts, particularly with other
socialist women, through travel and correspondence. She remained an
energetic although often dissident worker for the SDF until the end of
1912 and was later to be a founder member of the Communist Party.

One source for Dora Montefiore's life is her autobiography, *From a Victorian to a Modern*.

HARRY QUELCH (1858–1913) came from a poor rural background and started his working life when he was ten years old. He was entirely self-educated; could speak and translate from French and German; was well read and wrote on a wide range of questions as well as short stories on working life which were published in *Justice*. Having joined the Democratic Federation, Quelch was a lifetime member of the SDF and was part of the party's ruling group, 'the old guard'. He first began editing *Justice* in 1886, resigning in 1889 to take a leading role in the Dock Strike. In 1891 he took up the job of editor once again and retained this post until his death. His payment by the party enabled him to give up his work as a warehouseman. Although originally thought to be a dour public speaker, he became one of the most effective of the SDF propagandists and many of his speeches and debates were published. He was active in the London Trades Council (President 1904–6, 1910), stood for public office (local and national) and continued to attend Labour Party Conferences even when the SDF had withdrawn from the LRC. For Quelch's life see his entry in the *Dictionary of Labour Biography*, vol. 8, pp. 198–203; for his writing see those collected and edited by E. B. Bax, *Harry Quelch: Literary Remains*.

ENID STACY (1868–1903) was originally a member of the Bristol Socialist Society, which at the time was closely linked with the SDF, but she left in 1895 becoming a prominent member of the ILP as well as a Fabian. She spoke at SDF branches as well as for many other parts of the socialist and labour movement, and represented both the SDF and the ILP at the 1896 Socialist International in London. In 1894 she agreed to write an occasional column in *Justice* on 'What Women are Doing for Socialism' but only one piece ever appeared. For Enid Stacy see A. Tuckett, 'Enid Stacy', *North West Labour History Society Bulletin*, 7, 1980–81, pp. 41–8; M. B. Reckitt, *P. E. T. Widdrington*, SPCK, 1961; S. Bryher, *An Account of the Labour and Socialist Movement in Bristol*, Bristol, 1929.

JAMES SULLIVAN was second generation Irish, son of a policeman long settled in London. He worked in a black lead factory and was a self-improver. His daughter remembers him sitting by the fire reading encyclopedias and he taught himself shorthand, typing and bookkeeping so that he could eventually transfer to this area of work. Ironically, one of his jobs was as a shorthand typist in a lunatic asylum. He was a member of Battersea SDF, particularly involved in local election campaigns. As an active public speaker, he could be found addressing the crowds at Hyde Park. After the Lanchester Case, he continued to be active in the SDF until the First World War. He died in 1945.

ISABEL TIPLADY's first attempt at public speaking was in December 1893. She was on the innovative Lancashire May Day Women's Platform in 1894 and 1895 as well as speaking around the region and touring with the Clarion Van in the summer of 1896. Increasingly she seems to have spoken for ILP branches and Labour Churches. After the mid-1890s her name disappears from the records.

M. M. A. (MAUD) WARD was brought up in a country rectory. Denied the university education given to her brothers, she trained instead at the National Training School of Cookery and then worked as a cook. She joined the SDF and, in 1904, taught a Marxist economics class to her branch at Tunbridge Wells. As an active supporter of adult suffrage, she served as Secretary of the ASS from 1908–9. Like her close friend Margaret Bondfield she became a prominent member of the WLL before retiring from her public life as a lecturer on socialist and women's issues to become the chief woman inspector under the National Insurance Act. See M. Bondfield's account of her companion in her, *A Life's Work*.

LENA WILSON was a longtime member of the SDF who represented her party on the Poplar Board of Guardians from 1895. She campaigned for workrooms for unemployed women as well as involving herself in the Socialist Women's Circles. Mrs Wilson was secretary of Bow and Bromley Circle and a member of the Women's Committee/WEC. She continued to be active in the BSP.

Bibliography

Note: The place of publication for all published sources is London except where stated otherwise.

MANUSCRIPTS

THE BRITISH LIBRARY

Correspondence of Mrs Wolstenholme Elmy, Additional Mss 47, 449–55.

BRITISH LIBRARY OF POLITICAL AND ECONOMIC SCIENCE

H. M. Hyndman/G. Wilshire Correspondence, MF 78–82 M822–6.
Francis Johnson Papers.

CROYDON PUBLIC LIBRARY

F. G. West, 'The beginnings of Labour in Croydon', typescript, nd.

MANCHESTER CENTRAL REFERENCE LIBRARY

Gertrude Tuckwell Papers, MF 331–4 Tu1.
Minutes of Manchester Labour Party Women's Advisory Committee, 1935.

NATIONAL MUSEUM OF LABOUR HISTORY

M. S. Robinson, 'A short history of my family who gave much of their lives to helping their fellow men and women, and to the furtherance of the cause of Socialism,' Ms HF476.
E. Corley, 'Wellingborough Social Democratic Federation Women's Section', Ms 2066.

NEWSPAPERS AND JOURNALS

British Medical Journal
Burnley Gazette

The Challenge
Clarion
Commonweal
Contemporary Review
Co-operative News
Croydon Times
The Daily Express
The Daily Worker
Fabian News
Justice
Labour Annual
Labour Leader
Labour Woman
The Lancet
The League Leaflet
Manchester Weekly Chronicle
Northampton Pioneer
Northampton Socialist
Our Corner
Red Flag
The Reformers' Year Book
Rochdale Observer
Rochdale Star
Rochdale Times
Social Democrat
SDP News
The Socialist and North East Lancashire Labour News
Socialist Annual
The Socialist Pioneer
The Times
Today
Westminster Review
Wilshire's Magazine
Woman Worker
Workman's Times

OFFICIAL PAPERS

Agenda for International Socialist Workers and Trade Union Congress, 1896.
ILP Conference Reports.
Labour Party Conference Reports.
Manifesto of the Socialist League, 1885.
Programme and Rules of the SDF, Twentieth Century Press, 1888, 1894, 1895, 1904, 1906.
Report to the Socialist International Conference, 1910.
SDF Conference Reports.

OTHER WORKS

Allen, G. *The Woman Who Did*, John Lane, 1895.

Arch, R. *Ernest Belfort Bax, Thinker and Pioneer*, Hyndman Literary Committee, 1927.

Aveling, E. M. and E. 'The Woman Question', in J. Müller and E. Schotte (eds.), *Thoughts on Women and Society*, International Publishers, New York, 1987.

Bax, E. B. *The Ethics of Socialism*, Swan Sonnenschein, 1889.
  The Fraud of Feminism, Grant Richards, 1913.
  Outlooks from the New Standpoint, Swan Sonnenschein, 1891.
  The Religion of Socialism, Swan Sonnenschein, 1891, 3rd edition; first published 1885.
  Reminiscences and Reflexions of a Mid and Late Victorian, Augustus M. Kelley, New York, 1967; first published 1918.

Bax, E. B. (ed.), *Harry Quelch, Literary Remains*, Grant Richards, 1914.

Bax, E. B. and Morris, W., *Socialism: Its Growth and Outcome*, Sonnenschein, 1908, 3rd edition; first published in 1893.

Bebel, A. (trans. H. B. Adams Walther), *Woman in the Past, Present and Future*, Modern Press, 1885.
  (trans. D. De Leon), *Woman Under Socialism*, Schocken Books, New York, 1971.

Bellamy, E. *Looking Backward*, Signet, New York, 1960; first published 1888.

Besant, A. *An Autobiography*, Fisher Unwin, 1893.

Bondfield, M. *The Women's Suffrage Controversy*, Leaflet 1, Adult Suffrage Society, nd, [1905?].

Bryher, S. *An Account of the Labour and Socialist Movement in Bristol*, Bristol, 1929.

Burrows, H. *The Future of Woman*, Twentieth Century Press, 1909.

Carpenter, E. *Woman, and Her Place in a Free Society*, The Labour Press Society, Manchester, 1894.

Clayton, J. *The Rise and Decline of Socialism in Great Britain, 1884–1924*, Faber, 1926.

Connolly, J. *The Connolly–De Leon Controversy*, Cork Workers' Club, Cork, nd.

Deputation of Unemployed to the Rt Hon A.J. Balfour M.P., Twentieth Century Press, 1905.

Drake, B. *Women in Trade Unions*, Virago, 1984; first published 1920.

Engels, F. *The Origin of the Family, Private Property and the State*, Lawrence and Wishart, 1972.

Fisher, V. *The Babies Tribute to the Modern Moloch*, Twentieth Century Press, 1907.

Billington Greig, T. *The Militant Suffrage Movement*, Frank Palmer, 1911.

A Guide to Books for Socialists, Fabian Tract, 132, 1907.

Hamilton, C. *Marriage as a Trade*, The Woman's Press, 1981; first published 1909.

How I Became A Socialist, Twentieth Century Press, 1902.

Hutchins, B. L. *Women in Modern Industry*, E. P. Publishing, East Ardsley, 1978; first published 1915.

Hutchins, B. L. and Harrison, A. *A History of Factory Legislation*, P. S. King and Son, 2nd edition, 1911.

Hyndman, H. M. *England for All*, Harvester, Brighton, 1973; first published 1881.

Further Reminiscences, Macmillan, 1912.

The Historical Basis of Socialism in England, Garland, New York, 1984; first published in 1883.

Kineton Parkes, M. *The Tax Resistance Movement in Great Britain*, Women's Tax Resistance League, nd.

Lee, H. W. and Archbold, E. *Social Democracy in Britain*, SDF, 1935.

Lenin, V. I. *What is to be Done?*, Oxford University Press, 1963; first published in 1902.

Macdonald, J. R. *Margaret Ethel Macdonald*, Hodder and Stoughton, 4th edition, 1913.

Mann, T. *Tom Mann's Memoirs*, MacGibbon and Kee, 1967.

Marx, K. and Engels, F. *The Communist Manifesto*, Penguin, 1967.

Meier, O. (ed.), *The Daughters of Karl Marx: Family Correspondence, 1866–98*, Penguin, 1984.

Montefiore, D. B. *From a Victorian to a Modern*, E. Archer, 1927.

The Position of Women in the Socialist Movement, Twentieth Century Press, 1909.

Some Words to Socialist Women, Twentieth Century Press, 1908.

Women Uitlanders, Leaflet 14, Union of Practical Suffragists, October 1899.

Pankhurst, S. *The Suffragette Movement*, Virago, 1977; first published 1931.

Pease, E. R. *The History of the Fabian Society*, A. C. Fifield, 1916.

Perkins Gilman, C. *Women and Economics*, Harper and Row, New York, 1966; first published 1898.

Quelch, H. *The SDF: Its Objects, Its Principles and Its Work*, Twentieth Century Press, 1907.

Salt, H. S. *Company I Have Kept*, Allen and Unwin, 1930.

Sanders, W. S. *Early Socialist Days*, Hogarth, 1927.

Schreiner, O. *Women and Labour*, Virago, 1978; first published 1911.

Sharp, E. *Unfinished Adventure*, Bodley Head, 1933.

Shaw, G. B. *The Fabian Society: Its Early History*, Fabian Tract, 41, 1892.

Snell, H. *Men, Movements and Myself*, J. M. Dent and Sons, 1936.

Strachey, R. *The Cause*, Virago, 1979; first published 1928.

Toole, J. *Fighting Through Life*, Rich and Cowan, 1935.

Wells, H. G. *Experiment in Autobiography*, vol. 2, Faber and Faber, 1984; first published 1934.

Wolstenholme Elmy, E. *Woman – The Communist*, ILP, 1904.

Zetkin, C. *Social Democracy and Woman Suffrage*, Twentieth Century Press, 1906.

Woman Suffrage, Twentieth Century Press, 1907.

BOOKS

Balabanoff, A. *My Life as a Rebel*, Indiana University Press, Bloomington, 1973.

Banks, O. *Becoming a Feminist: The Social Origins of 'First Wave' Feminism*, Wheatsheaf, Brighton, 1986.

Faces of Feminism, Robertson, Oxford, 1981.

Barrett, M. and Phillips, A. (eds.), *Destabilizing Theory: Contemporary Feminist Debates*, Polity, Cambridge, 1992.

Bealey, F. and Pelling, H. *Labour and Politics, 1900–06*, Oxford University Press, 1958.

Bell, G. *Troublesome Business: The Labour Party and the Irish Question*, Pluto, 1982.

Bellamy, J. M. and Saville, J. (eds.), *Dictionary of Labour Biography*, vols. 4, 5, 7, 8, Macmillan, 1977, 1979, 1984, 1987.

Bolt, C. *Victorian Attitudes to Race*, Routledge and Kegan Paul, 1971.

Bondfield, M. *My Life's Work*, Hutchinson, 1948.

Boston, S. *Women Workers and the Trade Union Movement*, Davis Poynter, 1980.

Boxer, M. J. and Quataert, J. H. (eds.), *Socialist Women: European Socialist Feminism in the Nineteenth and Twentieth Centuries*, Elsevier, New York, 1978.

Brandon, R. *The New Women and the Old Men*, Secker and Warburg, 1990.

Bristow, E. J. *Vice and Vigilance: Purity Movements in Britain Since 1700*, Gill and Macmillan, Dublin, 1977.

Brockway, F. *Towards Tomorrow*, Hart-Davis, 1977.

Brome, V. *Havelock Ellis*, Routledge and Kegan Paul, 1979.

Brown, K. D. *Labour and Unemployment 1900–14*, David and Charles, Newton Abbott, 1971.

The English Labour Movement, 1750–1951, Gill and Macmillan, Dublin, 1982.

Buhle, M. J. *Women and American Socialism, 1870–1920*, University of Illinois Press, Urbana, 1983.

Burgess, K. *The Challenge of Labour*, Croom Helm, 1980.

Caine, B. *Victorian Feminists*, Oxford University Press, 1992.

Calder-Marshall, A. *Lewd, Blasphemous and Obscene*, Hutchinson, 1972.

Campbell, B. *Wigan Pier Revisited*, Virago, 1984.

Challinor, R. *The Origins of British Bolshevism*, Croom Helm, 1978.

Chapman, R. and Rutherford, J. (eds.), *Male Order: Unwrapping Masculinity*, Lawrence and Wishart, 1988.

Cliff, T. *Class Struggle and Women's Liberation*, Bookmarks, 1984.

Cohen, S. *That's Funny, You Don't Look Anti-Semitic: An Anti-Racist Analysis of Left Anti-Semitism*, Beyond the Pale Collective, Leeds, 1984.

Cole, G. D. H. *History of Socialist Thought*, vol 2: *Marxism and Anarchism, 1850–1890*, Macmillan, 1954.

History of Socialist Thought, vol 3: *The Second International, 1889–1914*, Macmillan, 1956.

Cole, M. *The Story of Fabian Socialism*, Heinemann, 1961.

Collette, C. *For Labour and for Woman: The Women's Labour League, 1906–18*, Manchester University Press, 1989.

Coote, A. and Pattullo, P. *Power and Prejudice: Women and Politics*, Weidenfeld and Nicolson, 1990.

Cowley, J. *The Victorian Encounter with Marx: A Study of Ernest Belfort Bax*, British Academic Press, 1992.

Craig, F. W. S. *British Parliamentary Election Results, 1885–1918*, Macmillan, 1974.

Craik, W. W. *The Central Labour College, 1909–1929*, Lawrence and Wishart, 1976.

Delphy, C. *Close to Home: A Materialist Analysis of Women's Oppression*, ed. D. Leonard, Hutchinson, 1984.

Dwork, D. *War is Good for Babies and Other Young Children*, Tavistock, 1987.

Eisenstein, Z. R. *Capitalist Patriarchy and the Case for Socialist Feminism*, Monthly Review Press, New York, 1979.

Elshtain, J. B. *Public Man, Private Woman*, Martin Robertson, Oxford, 1981.

Ensor, R. C. K. *England, 1870–1914*, Clarendon Press, Oxford, 1936.

Ettinger, E. *Rosa Luxemburg*, Harrap, 1987.

Evans, R. J. *The Feminists*, Croom Helm, 1977.

Foote, G. *The Labour Party's Political Thought: A History*, Croom Helm, 1985.

Fox, A. *A National History of the National Union of Boot and Shoe Operatives, 1874–1957*, Basil Blackwell, Oxford, 1958.

German, L. *Sex, Class and Socialism*, Bookmarks, 1994.

Gilbert, B. B. *The Evolution of National Insurance in Great Britain: The Origins of the Welfare State*, Michael Joseph, 1966.

Gillis, J. R. *For Better, For Worse: British Marriages, 1600 to the Present*, Oxford University Press, 1985.

Goot, M. and Reid, E. *Women and Voting Studies: Mindless Matrons or Sexist Scientism*, Sage, Beverly Hills, 1975.

Gordon, E. *Women and the Labour Movement in Scotland 1850–1914*, Clarendon, Oxford, 1991.

Graves, P. *Labour Women: Women in British Working Class Politics*, Cambridge University Press, 1994.

Greaves, C. D. *The Life and Times of James Connolly*, Lawrence and Wishart, 1976.

Grosskurth, P. *Havelock Ellis*, Allen Lane, 1980.

Guttsmann, W. L. *The German Social Democratic Party, 1875–1933: From Ghetto to Government*, Allen and Unwin, 1981.

Halévy, E. *History of the English People*: vol.5, *Imperialism and the Rise of Labour, 1895–1905*, Ernest Benn, 1961.

Hannam, J. *Isabella Ford*, Blackwell, Oxford, 1989.

Harris, J. *Unemployment and Politics: A Study in English Social Policy 1886–1914*, Oxford University Press, 1972.

Harrison, B. *Separate Spheres: The Opposition to Women's Suffrage in Britain*, Croom Helm, 1978.

Hayden, D. *The Grand Domestic Revolution*, MIT Press, Cambridge, Mass., 1981.

Hinton, J. *Labour and Socialism: A History of the British Labour Movement, 1867–1974*, Wheatsheaf, Brighton, 1983.

Holcombe, L. *Victorian Ladies at Work*, David and Charles, Newton Abbott, 1973.

Hollis, P. *Ladies Elect: Women in English Local Government, 1865–1914*, Clarendon Press, Oxford, 1987.

Holton, B. *British Syndicalism, 1900–14*, Pluto, 1976.

Holton, S. S. *Feminism and Democracy: Women's Suffrage and Reform Politics in Britain, 1900–1918*, Cambridge University Press, New York, 1986.

Howell, D. *British Workers and the Independent Labour Party, 1888–1906,* Manchester University Press, 1983.

Humphries, S. *A Secret World of Sex,* Sidgwick and Jackson, 1988.

Hynes, S. *The Edwardian Turn of Mind,* Princeton University Press, New Jersey, 1968.

Jackson, T. A. *Solo Trumpet,* Lawrence and Wishart, 1953.

Jeffreys, S. *The Spinster and Her Enemies,* Pandora, 1985.

Joll, J. *The Second International,* Routledge, 1974.

John, A. V. *By the Sweat of their Brow: Women Workers at Victorian Coal Mines,* Croom Helm, 1980.

John A. V. (ed.), *Unequal Opportunities: Women's Employment in England, 1880–1914,* Basil Blackwell, Oxford, 1986.

Jones, G. *Social Darwinism and English Thought: the Interaction between Biological and Social Theory,* Harvester, Brighton, 1980.

Joyce, P. *Visions of the People: Industrial England and the Question of Class, 1848–1914,* Cambridge University Press, 1991.

Kahan Coates, Z. *The Life and Teachings of Friedrich Engels,* Lawrence and Wishart, 1945.

Kapp, Y. *Eleanor Marx:* vol. 2: *The Crowded Years, 1884–1898,* Lawrence and Wishart, 1976.

Kendall, W. *The Revolutionary Movement in Britain, 1900–1921: The Origins of British Communism,* Weidenfeld and Nicolson, 1969.

Kent, S. K. *Sex and Suffrage in Britain, 1860–1914,* Routledge, 1990.

Kent, W. *John Burns: Labour's Lost Leader,* Williams and Norgate, 1950.

Koven, S. and Michel, S. (eds.), *Mothers of a New World: Maternalist Politics and the Origins of Welfare States,* Routledge, 1993.

Lanchester, E. *Elsa Lanchester Herself,* Michael Joseph, 1983.

Levine, P. *Victorian Feminism, 1850–1900,* Hutchinson, 1987.

   Feminist Lives in Victorian England: Private Roles and Public Commitment, Blackwell, Oxford, 1990.

Lewenhak, S. *Women and Trade Unions,* Ernest Benn, 1977.

Lewis, J. *The Politics of Motherhood,* Croom Helm, 1980.

Lewis, J. (ed.), *Labour and Love: Women's Experience of Home and Family, 1880–1914,* Basil Blackwell, Oxford, 1986.

Liddington, J. *The Life and Times of a Respectable Rebel: Selina Cooper,* Virago, 1984.

Liddington, J. and Norris, J. *One Hand Tied Behind Us,* Virago, 1977.

Linklater, A. *An Unhusbanded Life,* Hutchinson, 1980.

Lovenduski, J. and Randall, V. *Contemporary Feminist Politics: Women and Power in Britain,* Oxford University Press, 1993.

McCarthy, M. *Generation in Revolt,* Heinemann, 1953.

Macintyre, S. *A Proletarian Science: Marxism in Britain 1917–1933,* Cambridge University Press, 1980.

McLaren, A. *Birth Control in Nineteenth Century England,* Croom Helm, 1978.

McShane, H. and Smith, J. *Harry McShane: No Mean Fighter,* Pluto, 1978.

Mappen, E. *Helping Women at Work: The Women's Industrial Council, 1889–1914,* Hutchinson, 1985.

Marcus, J. (ed.), *Suffrage and the Pankhursts*, Routledge and Kegan Paul, 1987.

Marsh, M. S. *Anarchist Women, 1870–1920*, Temple University Press, Philadelphia, 1981.

Meehan, E. M. *Women's Rights at Work: Campaigns and Policy in Britain and the United States*, Macmillan, 1985.

Meier, P. *William Morris: The Marxist Dreamer*, vol.1, Harvester, Brighton, 1978.

Mitchell, D. *Queen Christabel*, McDonald and Janes, 1977.

Mitchell, H. *The Hard Way Up*, Virago, 1977.

Moore, R. *The Emergence of the Labour Party, 1880–1924*, Hodder and Stoughton, 1978.

Morgan, D. *Suffragists and Liberals*, Blackwell, Oxford, 1975.

Morgan, K. O. *Keir Hardie, Radical and Socialist*, Weidenfeld and Nicolson, 1975.

Morris, J. *Women Workers and the Sweated Trades: The Origins of Minimum Wage Legislation*, Gower, Aldershot, 1986.

Morris, M. *William Morris, Artist, Writer, Socialist*, vol. 2, Blackwell, Oxford, 1936.

Morton, V. and Macintyre, S. *T. A. Jackson*, Our History, 73, 1979.

Mulvihill, M. *Charlotte Despard: A Biography*, Pandora, 1989.

Nethercot, A. H. *The First Five Lives of Annie Besant*, Hart-Davis, 1961.

Newton, J. L., Ryan, M. P. and Walkowitz, J. R. (eds.), *Sex and Class in Women's History*, Routledge and Kegan Paul, 1983.

Oldfield, A. *Woman Suffrage in Australia*, Cambridge University Press, 1992.

Owen, A. *The Darkened Room: Women, Power and Spiritualism in Late Victorian England*, Virago, 1989.

Pankhurst, C. *Unshackled*, Hutchinson, 1959.

Pelling, H. *The Origins of the Labour Party*, Oxford University Press, 1965.
Social Geography of British Elections, 1885–1910, Macmillan, 1967.

Phillips, A. *Hidden Hands: Women and Economic Policies*, Pluto, 1983.
Divided Loyalties: Dilemmas of Sex and Class, Virago, 1987.
Engendering Democracy, Polity, Cambridge, 1991.

Pierson, S. *British Socialists, The Journey from Fantasy to Politics*, Harvard University Press, Cambridge, Mass., 1979.
Marxism and the Origins of British Socialism: The Struggle for a New Consciousness, Cornell University Press, Ithaca, NY, 1973.

Porter, C. *Alexandra Kollontai*, Virago, 1980.

Pugh, M. *Electoral Reform in War and Peace, 1906–18*, Routledge and Kegan Paul, 1978.

Pugh, P. *Educate, Agitate, Organise: 100 Years of Fabian Socialism*, Methuen, 1984.

Quataert, J. H. *Reluctant Feminists: In German Social Democracy 1885–1917*, Princeton University Press, New Jersey, 1979.

Ramelson, M. *The Petticoat Rebellion*, Lawrence and Wishart, 1972.

Randall, V. *Women and Politics*, Macmillan, 1982.

Reckitt, M. B. *P. E. T. Widdrington*, SPCK, 1961.

Reid, F. *Keir Hardie: The Making of a Socialist*, Croom Helm, 1978.

Reid, J. H. S. *The Origins of the British Labour Party*, University of Minnesota Press, Minneapolis, 1955.

Rendall, J. (ed.), *Equal or Different: Women's Politics 1800–1914*, Blackwell, Oxford, 1987.

Rendall, J. *The Origins of Modern Feminism: Women in Britain, France and the United States, 1780–1860*, Macmillan, 1985.

Reverby, S. M. and Helly, D. O. (eds.), *Gendered Domains: Rethinking Public and Private in Women's History*, Cornell University Press, Ithaca, NY, 1992.

Rich, P. B. *Race and Empire in British Politics*, Cambridge University Press, 1986.

Robb, J. H. *The Primrose League, 1883–1906*, Columbia University Press, New York, 1942.

Roberts, R. *The Classic Slum*, Pelican, 1973.

Rosen, A. *Rise Up Women*, Routledge and Kegan Paul, 1975.

Roth, G. *The Social Democrats in Imperial Germany*, Bedminster Press, Totowa, New Jersey, 1963.

Rover, C. *Women's Suffrage and Party Politics in Britain, 1866–1914*, Routledge and Kegan Paul, 1967.

Rowbotham, S. *Hidden From History*, Pluto, 1974.

Women, Resistance and Revolution, Pelican, 1974.

The Past is Before Us: Feminism in Action Since the 1960s, Penguin, 1990.

Rowbotham, S., Segal, L. and Wainwright, H. *Beyond the Fragments: Feminism and the Making of Socialism*, Islington Community Press, 1979.

Rowbotham, S. and Weeks, J. *Socialism and the New Life: The Personal and Sexual Politics of Edward Carpenter and Havelock Ellis*, Pluto, 1977.

Rubinstein, D. *Before the Suffragettes: Women's Emancipation in the 1890s*, Harvester, Brighton, 1986.

A Different World for Women. The Life of Millicent Garrett Fawcett, Harvester Wheatsheaf, Hemel Hempstead, 1991.

Sears, H. D. *The Sex Radicals*, Regents Press of Kansas, 1977.

Sargent, L. (ed.), *Women and Revolution: A Discussion of the Unhappy Marriage of Marxism and Feminism*, Pluto, 1981.

Scott, J. W. *Gender and the Politics of History*, Columbia University Press, NY, 1988.

Showalter, E. *The Female Malady: Women, Madness and English Culture 1830–1980*, Virago, 1987.

Soldon, N. C. *Women in British Trade Unions, 1874–1976*, Gill and Macmillan, Dublin, 1978.

Sowerwine, C. *Sisters or Citizens?: Women and Socialism in France since 1876*, Cambridge University Press, 1982.

Steedman, C. *Childhood, Culture and Class in Britain: Margaret McMillan 1860–1931*, Virago, 1990.

Tanner, D. *Political Change and the Labour Party 1900–18*, Cambridge University Press, 1990.

Tax, M. *The Rising of the Women: Feminist Solidarity and Class Conflict, 1880–1917*, Monthly Review Press, New York, 1980.

Taylor, A. *Annie Besant*, Oxford University Press, 1992.

Taylor, B. *Eve and the New Jerusalem: Socialism and Feminism in the Nineteenth Century*, Virago, 1983.

Thompson, E. P. *William Morris: Romantic to Revolutionary*, Merlin, 1977.

Thompson, L. *The Enthusiasts*, Gollancz, 1971.

Thompson, P. *Socialists, Liberals and Labour: The Struggle for London, 1885–1914*, Routledge and Kegan Paul, 1967.

Thönnessen, W. *The Emancipation of Women: The Rise and Decline of the Women's Movement in German Social Democracy, 1863–1933*, Pluto, 1973.

Tilly, L. A. and Scott, J. W. *Women, Work and Family*, Holt, Rinehart and Winston, New York, 1978.

Torr, D. *Tom Mann and his Times* vol. 1, Lawrence and Wishart, 1956.

Trudgill, E. *Madonnas and Magdalens*, Heinemann, 1976.

Tsuzuki, C. *Edward Carpenter: Prophet of Human Fellowship*, Cambridge University Press, 1980.

H. M. Hyndman and British Socialism, Oxford University Press, 1961.

Usher, J. *Women's Madness: Misogyny or Mental Illness*, Harvester Wheatsheaf, Hemel Hempstead, 1991.

Vicinus, M. *Independent Women: Work and Community for Women, 1850–1920*, Virago, 1985.

Vogel, L. *Marxism and the Oppression of Women*, Pluto, 1983.

Walkowitz, J. R. *Prostitution and Victorian Society* Cambridge University Press, 1980.

Weeks, J. *Sex, Politics and Society: The Regulation of Sexuality since 1800*, Longman, 1981.

Weintraub, R. (ed.), *Fabian Feminist: Bernard Shaw and Woman*, Pennsylvania State University Press, University Park, 1977.

Weller, K. *'Don't Be A Soldier!' The Radical Anti-War Movement in North London 1914–18*, Journeyman Press, 1985.

Wilson, E. and Weir, A. *Hidden Agendas: Theory, Politics and Experience in the Women's Movement*, Tavistock, 1986.

Wiltsher, A. *Most Dangerous Women: Feminist Peace Campaigners of the Great War*, Pandora, 1985.

Wolfe, W. *From Radicalism to Socialism*, Yale University Press, New Haven, Conn., 1975.

Yeo, S. *Religion and Voluntary Organisations in Crisis*, Croom Helm, 1976.

ARTICLES AND ESSAYS

Aaby, P. 'Engels and Women', *Critique of Anthropology*, 3, 9 & 10, 1977.

Ainsworth, A. J. 'Aspects of Socialism at Branch Level 1890–1900; Some Notes Towards Analysis', *North West Group for the Study of Labour History Bulletin*, 4.

Alexander, S. 'Introduction', to M. Pember Reeves, *Round About a Pound a Week*, Virago, 1979.

Baron, A. 'Gender and Labor History: Learning from the Past, Looking to the Future', in A. Baron (ed.), *Work Engendered: Toward a New History of American Labor*, Cornell University Press, Ithaca, NY, 1991.

'On Looking at Men: Masculinity and the Making of a Gendered Working Class History', in A. L. Shapiro (ed.), *Feminists Revision History*, Rutgers University Press, New Brunswick, NJ, 1994.

Barrett, M. 'Marxist-Feminism and the work of Karl Marx', in A. Phillips (ed.), *Feminism and Equality*, Blackwell, Oxford, 1987.

Barrett, M. and McIntosh, M. 'The "Family Wage": Some Problems for Socialists and Feminists', *Capital and Class*, 11, 1980.

Belchem, J. 'A Language of Classlessness', *Labour History Review*, 57, 2, 1992.

Bevir, M. 'The British Social Democratic Federation: From O'Brienism to Marxism', *International Review of Social History*, 37, 1992.

Bhavnani, K. K. and Coulson, M. 'Transforming Socialist-Feminism: The Challenge of Racism', *Feminist Review*, 23, 1986.

Bland, L. 'Marriage Laid Bare: Middle-Class Women and Marital Sex, 1880s–1914', in J. Lewis (ed.), *Labour and Love*.

Bornat, J. 'Lost Leaders: Women, Trade Unionism and the Case of the General Union of Textile Workers, 1875–1914', in A. V. John (ed.), *Unequal Opportunities*.

Brooker, K. 'James Gribble and the Raunds Strike of 1905', *Northamptonshire Past and Present*, 6, 5, 1981–2.

Brown, K. D. 'Anti-Socialist Union', in K. D. Brown (ed.), *Essays in Anti-Labour History: Responses to the Rise of Labour in Britain*, Macmillan, 1974.

Buhle, M. J. 'Socialist Woman, Progressive Woman, Coming Nation', in J. R. Conlin (ed.), *The American Radical Press, 1880–1960*, vol. 2, Greenwood Press, Westport, Conn., 1974.

 'Women and the Socialist Party, 1901–14', in E. H. Altbach (ed.), *From Feminism to Liberation*, Schenkman, Cambridge, Mass., 1971.

Canning, K. 'Gender and the Politics of Class Formation: Rethinking German Labor History', *American Historical Review*, 97, 3, 1992.

Clark , A. 'The Rhetoric of Chartist Domesticity: Gender, Language and Class in the 1830s and 1840s', *Journal of British Studies*, 31, 1992.

Collins, H. 'The Marxism of the Social Democratic Federation', in A. Briggs and J. Saville (eds.), *Essays in Labour History, 1886–1923*, Macmillan, 1971.

Cockburn, C. 'Masculinity, the Left and Feminism', in R. Chapman and J. Rutherford (eds.), *Male Order*.

 'The European Forum of Socialist Feminists: Talking on the Volcano', *Women's Studies International Forum*, 15, 1, 1992.

Coser, L. A. 'Introduction' to A. Bebel (trans. D. De Leon), *Woman Under Socialism*.

Dancis, B. 'Socialism and Women in the United States, 1900–17', *Socialist Revolution*, 27, 1976.

Davin, A. 'Imperialism and Motherhood', *History Workshop Journal*, 5, 1978.

Delmar, R. 'Looking again at Engels's "Origin of the Family, Private Property and the State" ', in J. Mitchell and A. Oakley (eds.), *The Rights and Wrongs of Women*, Penguin, 1976.

Dickie, M. 'Liberals, Radicals and Socialists in Northampton before the Great War', *Northamptonshire Past and Present*, 8, 1, 1983–4.

Draper, H. and Lipow, A. G. 'Marxist Women versus Bourgeois Feminism', *Socialist Register*, Merlin Press, 1976.

Du Bois, E. C. 'Woman Suffrage and the Left: An International Socialist-Feminist Perspective', *New Left Review*, 186, 1991.

Evans, R. J. 'Introduction: the Sociological Interpretation of German Labour History', in R. J. Evans (ed.), *The German Working Class, 1883–1933*, Croom Helm, 1982.

'Politics and the Family; Social Democracy and the Working Class Family in Theory and in Practice before 1914', in R. J. Evans and W. R. Lee (eds.), *The German Family*, Croom Helm, 1981.

'Theory and Practice in German Social Democracy, 1880–1914: Clara Zetkin and the Socialist Theory of Women's Emancipation', *History of Political Thought*, 3, 2, 1982.

Feurer, R. 'The Meaning of 'Sisterhood': The British Women's Movement and Protective Labor Legislation, 1870–1900', *Victorian Studies*, 31, 2, 1988.

Feminist Review, 'Feminism and Class Politics: A Round-Table Discussion', *Feminist Review*, 23, 1986.

'The Women's Movement and the Labour Party: An Interview with Labour Party Feminists', *Feminist Review*, 16, 1984.

Fleming, S. 'Introduction,' to E. Rathbone, *The Disinherited Family*, Falling Wall Press, 1986.

Hall, C. 'Rethinking Imperial Histories: The Reform Act of 1867', *New Left Review*, 208, 1994.

Hannam, J. ' "In the Comradeship of the Sexes Lies the Hope of Progress and Social Regeneration": Women in the West Riding ILP, c. 1890–1914', in J. Rendall (ed.), *Equal or Different*.

'Women and the ILP, 1890–1914' in D. James, T. Jowitt and K. Laybourn (eds.), *The Centennial History of the Independent Labour Party*, Ryburn, Halifax, 1992.

Harrison, B. 'The Act of Militancy: Violence and the Suffragettes 1904–14' *Peacable Kingdom*, Clarendon, Oxford, 1982.

Harriss, K. 'New Alliances: Socialist Feminism in the Eighties', *Feminist Review*, 31, 1989.

Hart, N. 'Gender and the Rise and Fall of Class Politics', *New Left Review*, 175, 1989.

Hartmann, H. 'Capitalism, Patriarchy and Job Segregation by Sex', in Z. R. Eisenstein (ed.), *Capitalist Patriarchy*.

Hobsbawm, E. J. 'Hyndman and the SDF', in *Labouring Men*, Weidenfeld and Nicolson, 1964.

Holton, S. S. 'In Sorrowful Wrath: Suffrage Militancy and the Romantic Feminism of Emmeline Pankhurst', in H. L. Smith (ed.), *British Feminism in the Twentieth Century*, Edward Elgar, Aldershot, 1990.

Howell, D. 'Was the Labour Party Inevitable?', *Labour's Turning Point in the North West, 1880–1914*, North West Labour History Society, Southport, 1984.

Humphries, J. 'Class Struggle and the Persistence of the Working-Class Family', *Cambridge Journal of Economics*, 1, 3, 1977.

'Protective Legislation, the Capitalist State and Working Class Men: The Case of the 1842 Mines Regulation Act', *Feminist Review*, 7, 1981.

'The Working Class Family, Women's Liberation and Class Struggle: The Case of Nineteenth Century British History', *The Review of Radical Political Economics*, 9, 3, 1977.

Hunt, K. 'Making Socialist Woman: Politicicisation, Gender and the Social Democratic Federation, 1884–1911', paper given to Ninth Berkshire Conference on the History of Women, Vassar College, 1993.

Jeffreys, S. ' "Free from All Uninvited Touch of Man': Women's Campaigns around Sexuality, 1880–1914', *Women's Studies International Forum*, 5, 6, 1982.

John, A. V. 'Comment' on J. Humphries, 'Protective Legislation', *Feminist Review*, 9, 1981.

Johnson, L. C. 'Socialist Feminisms', in S. Gunew (ed.), *Feminist Knowledge: Critique and Construct*, Routledge, 1990.

Kidd, A. J. 'The Social Democratic Federation and Popular Agitation amongst the Unemployed in Edwardian Manchester', *International Review of Social History*, 29, 1984.

Land, H. 'Eleanor Rathbone and the Economy of the Family' in H. L. Smith (ed.), *British Feminism in the Twentieth Century*.

Lane, A. J. 'Charlotte Perkins Gilman: "The Personal is Political" ', in D. Spender (ed.), *Feminist Theorists*, The Women's Press, 1983.

Langan, M. 'Reorganizing the Labour Market: Unemployment, the State and the Labour Market, 1880–1914', in M. Langan and B. Schwartz (eds.), *Crises in the British State 1880–1930*, Hutchinson, 1985.

Lewis, J. 'Beyond Suffrage: English Feminism in the 1920s', *The Maryland Historian*, 1975.

'In Search of a Real Equality: Women between the Wars', in F. Gloversmith (ed.), *Class, Culture and Social Change*, Harvester, Brighton, 1980.

Lovenduski, J. 'Parliament, Pressure Groups, Networks and the Women's Movement: The Politics of Abortion Law Reform in Britain (1967–83)' in J. Lovenduski and J. Outshoorn, *The New Politics of Abortion*, Sage, 1986.

Lunn, K. 'Race Relations or Industrial Relations?: Race and Labour in Britain, 1880–1950' in K. Lunn (ed.), *Race and Labour in Twentieth Century Britain*, Frank Cass, 1985.

Maconachie, M. 'Engels, Sexual Divisions and the Family', *University of Kent Women's Studies Occasional Papers*, 1, 1983.

Mappen, E. F. 'Strategies for Change: Social Feminists' Approaches to the Problems of Women's Work', in A. V. John (ed.), *Unequal Opportunities:*.

Mark-Lawson, J. and Witz, A. 'From 'Family Labour' to 'Family Wage'? The Case of Women's Labour in Nineteenth-Century Coalmining', *Social History*, 13, 2, 1988.

McCandless, P. 'Dangerous to Themselves and Others: The Victorian Debate over the Prevention of Wrongful Confinement', *The Journal of British Studies*, 23, 1, 1983.

McKibbin, R. 'Why was there no Marxism in Great Britain ?', *English Historical Review*, 1984.

Minor, I. 'Working Class Women and Matrimonial Law Reform, 1890–1914', in D. E. Martin and D. Rubinstein (eds.), *Ideology and the Labour Movement*, Croom Helm, 1979.

Mort, F. 'Purity, Feminism and the State: Sexuality and Moral Politics, 1880–1914', in M. Langan and B. Schwartz (eds.), *Crises in the British State 1880–1930*.

Nettl, P. 'The German Social Democratic Party, 1890–1914, as a political model', *Past and Present*, 30, 1965.

Paul, D. ' "In the Interests of Civilization": Marxist Views of Race and Culture in the Nineteenth Century' in M. C. Horowitz (ed.), *Race, Class and Gender in Nineteenth Century Culture*, University of Rochester Press, Rochester, NY, 1991.

Pedersen, S. 'The Failure of Feminism in the Making of the British Welfare State', *Radical History Review*, 43, 1989.

Pettifor, A. 'Labour's Macho Tendency', *New Socialist*, September 1985.

Pierson, S. 'Ernest Belfort Bax (1854–1926): The Encounter of Marxism and Late Victorian Culture', *Journal of British Studies*, 7, 1, 1972.

Quataert, J. H. 'Unequal Partners in an Uneasy Alliance: Women and the Working Class in Imperial Germany', in M. J. Boxer and J. H. Quataert (eds.), *Socialist Women*.

Reid, F. 'Socialist Sunday Schools in Britain, 1892–1939', *International Review of Social History*, 11, 1966.

Rose, S. O. 'Gender Antagonism and Class Conflict: Exclusionary Strategies of Male Trade Unionists in Nineteenth Century Britain', *Social History*, 13, 2, 1988.

Rowan, C. ' "Mothers Vote Labour!" The State, the Labour Movement and Working-Class Mothers, 1900–18', in R. Brunt and C. Rowan (eds.), *Feminism, Culture and Politics*, Lawrence and Wishart, 1982.

Rubinstein, D. 'Annie Besant', in D. Rubinstein (ed.), *People for the People*, Ithaca Press, 1973.

Saville, J. 'Robert Owen on the Family and the Marriage System of the Old Immoral World', in M. Cornforth (ed.), *Rebels and their Causes*, Lawrence and Wishart, 1978.

Seccombe, W. 'Patriarchy Stabilized: The Construction of the Male Breadwinner Wage Norm in Nineteenth Century Britain', *Social History*, 11, 1, 1986.

Segal, L. 'Slow Change or No Change?: Feminism, Socialism and the Problem of Men', *Feminist Review*, 31, 1989.

Snell, M. 'The Equal Pay and Sex Discrimination Acts: Their Impact in the Workplace', *Feminist Review*, 1, 1979.

Stanley, L. 'Feminism and Friendship in England from 1825 to 1938: The Case of Olive Schreiner', *Studies in Sexual Politics*, 8, 1985.

Steinberg, H. J. 'Workers' Libraries in Germany before 1914', *History Workshop Journal*, 1, 1976.

Thane, P. 'Women and the Poor Law in Victorian and Edwardian England', *History Workshop Journal*, 6, 1978.

'The Women of the British Labour Party and Feminism, 1906–45' in H. L. Smith (ed.) ,*British Feminism in the Twentieth Century*.

'Visions of Gender in the Making of the British Welfare State: The Case of Women in the British Labour Party and Social Policy, 1906–45' in G. Bock and P. Thane (eds.), *Maternity and Gender Politics: Women and the Rise of European Welfare States 1880s–1950s*, Routledge, 1991.

'Women and the British Labour Party and the Construction of State Welfare, 1906–39' in S. Koven and S. Michel (eds.), *Mothers of a New World*.

Thom, D. 'The Bundle of Sticks: Women, Trade Unionists and Collective Organisation before 1918', in A. V. John (ed.), *Unequal Opportunities*.

Thompson, D. 'Women and Nineteenth Century Radical Politics: A Lost

Dimension', in J. Mitchell and A. Oakley (eds.), *The Rights and Wrongs of Women*.

Tsuzuki, C. 'The "Impossibilist Revolt" in Britain', *International Review of Social History*, 1, 1956.

Tuckett, A. 'Enid Stacy', *North West Labour History Society Bulletin*, 7, 1980–1.

Turnbull, A. ' "So Extremely Like Parliament": The Work of the Women Members of the London School Board, 1870–1904', in London Feminist History Group, *The Sexual Dynamics of History*, Pluto, 1983.

Vickery, A. 'Golden Age to Separate Spheres? A Review of the Categories and Chronology of English Women's History', *The Historical Journal*, 36, 2, 1993.

Walker, L. 'Party Political Women: A Comparative Study of Liberal Women and the Primrose League, 1890–1914', in J. Rendall (ed.), *Equal or Different*.

Walkowitz, J. R. 'Science, Feminism and Romance: The Men and Women's Club, 1885–1889', *History Workshop Journal*, 21, 1986.

Watmough, P. A. 'The Membership of the Social Democratic Federation, 1885–1902', *Society for the Study of Labour History Bulletin*, 34, 1977.

Yeo, S. 'A New Life: The Religion of Socialism in Britain, 1883–1896', *History Workshop Journal*, 4, 1977.

THESES

Blunden, M. 'The Educational and Political Work of the Countess of Warwick, 1861–1938', MA, Exeter University, 1966.

Brady, N. '*Shafts* and the Quest for a New Morality', MA, Warwick University, 1978.

Colbenson, P. D. 'British Socialism and Anti-Semitism, 1884–1914', PhD, Georgia State University, 1977.

Coneys, M. 'The Labour Movement and the Liberal Party in Rochdale, 1890–1906', MA, Huddersfield Polytechnic, nd.

Cowley, J. C. 'The Life and Writings of Ernest Belfort Bax', PhD, London University, 1965.

Honeycutt, K. 'Clara Zetkin: A Left-Wing Socialist and Feminist in Wilhelmian Germany', PhD, Columbia University, 1975.

Hunt, K. 'An Examination of the Burnley Social Democratic Federation, 1891–1914', MA, Manchester University, 1979.

'Equivocal Feminists: The Social Democratic Federation and the Woman Question, 1884–1911', PhD, Manchester University, 1988.

Lohman, J. S. 'Sex or Class? English Socialists and the Woman Question, 1884–1914', PhD, Syracuse University, 1979.

Tichelar, M. 'Labour Politics in Croydon, 1880–1914', BA, Thames Polytechnic, 1975.

Index

Adams Walther, Harriet, 31, 32
Adler, Victor, 171
Adult, The, 107
Adult Suffrage Society, 159, 167, 171, 173
  attitudes to, 176, 177
  local branches of, 178
  SDF and, 177–180
Allen, Grant, *Woman Who Did, The*, 89, 90
  n.26
Anderson, W. C., 93, 177
Arch, Robert, 62
Askew, J. B., 44, 72, 73
Asquith, H. H., 98
Aveling, Edward, 33, 89, 93, 94

Baader, Ottilie, 30
Bain, Agnes, 146
Baker, H. Jennie, 177
Balfour, Arthur, 144, 146
Banks, Olive, 15
Barrett, Michèle, 2, 255
Batten, Ellen, 188, 194
Bax, Ernest Belfort, 40–41, 57–63, 91–92,
  141, 265
  access to press of, 61
  attitude to anti-semitism of, 74
  attitude to 'conscience' issues of, 58, 63
  attitude to feminism of, 41, 45, 47, 52,
    53, 59, 60
  attitude to marriage of, 101–102,
    110–111
  attitude to racial equality of, 70–71
  attitude to sex/class analogy of, 34, 45
  attitude to sexual equality of, 49, 50
  attitude to woman's oppression of, 46,
    47
  attitude to women's suffrage of, 16, 47,
    71, 153, 155, 180, 237
  ethical theory of, 58
  finances of, 61 n.24
  language of, 42, 59, 61, 111
  Legal Subjection of Men, The, 62, 181

membership of Men's Anti-Suffrage
  League of, 180
misogynism of, 15, 37, 41, 59–61, 62, 63
review of *Woman* by, 34–35, 36
bazaar work, 213–215, 224, 228, 231
Bebel, August, 23–29, 34, 35, 42, 63, 72 *see*
  also founding fathers; *Woman*
Bebel House, 33
Bedborough Case, The, 106–109 *see also*
  Legitimation League
Bell, Lily, 103, 225
  identity of, 103 n.82
Bernstein, Eduard, 9
Besant, Annie, 14, 32, 112, 133, 265
Billington Greig, Teresa, 166, 167, 170
birth control, 193
Blandford, Dr George Fielding, 95–96, 98,
  99
Blatchford, Robert, 91
Bloodworth, Nellie, 194
Boer War, 72
Bondfield, Margaret, 147, 148, 170, 173,
  176, 266
Boston, Sarah, 130
Boyce, Emma, 236, 237, 245, 266
Boyd, Mary, 195
Bridges Adams, Mrs, 33, 245
Bristol Socialist Society, 212
Brooke, John, 121
Brown, K. D., 13
Browning, Beatrice, 52, 127–128
Burgess, Keith, 9
Burns, John, 97, 147
Burrows, Herbert, 40, 75, 133, 266–267
  attitude to sexual division of labour of, 49
  attitude to domestic labour of, 119
  attitude to women's suffrage of, 156,
    158, 161, 162, 167, 171, 173–174,
    177, 181
  attitude to women's work of, 129
  criticism of Bax by, 41, 51, 59, 62, 181
  criticism of Dora Montefiore by, 168